IDEAS for a New Century

Also edited by BERNIE LUCHT

Ideas: Brilliant Thinkers Speak Their Minds

IDEAS

for a
New
Century

Edited by
BERNIE LUCHT

Copy editing by Barry Norris.
Cover photo © Steven Puetzer, Getty Images.
Cover and interior design by Julie Scriver.
Printed in Canada.
10 9 8 7 6 5 4 3 2 1

Library and Archives Canada Cataloguing in Publication

Ideas for a new century / Bernie Lucht, editor.

ISBN 978-0-86492-514-5

1. Civilization — 21st century. 2. Ideas (Radio program).
I. Lucht, Bernie, 1944-
CB428.I34 2008   909.83   C2008-904944-6

Goose Lane Editions acknowledges the financial support of the Canada Council
for the Arts, the Government of Canada through the Book Publishing Industry
Development Program (BPIDP), and the New Brunswick Department of
Wellness, Culture, and Sport for its publishing activities.

Goose Lane Editions
Suite 330, 500 Beaverbrook Court
Fredericton, New Brunswick
CANADA E3B 5X4
www.gooselane.com

Contents

IDEAS for a New Century

The "Idea"
of the Interview

There's never been a form of human communication more overhyped and less understood than "the interview."

Interviews are generally considered to be a crucial activity for anybody involved in the profession of journalism. In fact, they're widely believed to be the basic tool of our trade. Reporters are supposed to get to the truth about a story by interviewing participants and questioning eyewitnesses. But different types of stories require different approaches. What, for example, does a cub reporter standing on a front porch in the suburbs say to the parents of a very recent teenaged fatality, all the while knowing that the basic aim is to get a photograph from the family album for the next day's front page? Does that extremely painful process have anything in common with the task of asking prominent thinkers and intellectuals abstract questions about the meaning of life?

As a broadcaster, I've frankly never considered interviewing to rank among my strengths. I've often said, "I'm not good at interviews." In my work as a documentary maker, I've always viewed the interviewing process as something not unlike what Winston Churchill once said about democracy: it's a flawed system, but it's the best we have. Ultimately, it's the only way to gather raw material. That doesn't mean that it's perfect. Interviews can sometimes be surprisingly stimulating. They can also be mind-numbingly boring. Major consolation comes from the hope that most of the dross will ultimately end up on the editing room floor. So, when I'm interviewing anybody for a documentary, I usually let them finish their sentences. As a basic rule, I try not to interrupt. I'll challenge people, for sure, but my fundamental aim is to get them to say what *they* want to say. I encourage them to tell *their* story, howsoever *they* want to tell it.

In the end, my documentary background makes me believe that an interview should be no more complicated than a simple conversation with another human being. Conversation involves talking. Talking implies listening. It's all pretty fundamental, really, although often overhyped and frequently misunderstood. Interviews may be a far from perfect, but they are one of the best tools that we have for understanding each other...

PAUL KENNEDY
Toronto, August 2008

Introduction

The CBC Radio program *Ideas* went on the air in October 1965. In October 2005, we marked the program's fortieth anniversary by publishing *Ideas: Brilliant Thinkers Speak Their Minds*, a compilation of thoughts of some of the great minds who appeared on the program during its first four decades. In this second volume, *Ideas for a New Century*, we present a selection of interviews broadcast on *Ideas* during the not-quite-finished first decade of the new millennium.

For the first months of its life, the program we now know as *Ideas* was called *The Best Ideas You'll Hear Tonight*. It was founded by two CBC program organizers: Phyllis Webb, a West Coast poet who had come east to Montreal to work at McGill University and then moved on to the CBC in Toronto; and Bill Young, an American who had come to Canada as a graduate student and studied with Marshall McLuhan. Phyllis had been in charge of a lecture series called *University of the Air*. Bill produced a series called *The Learning Stage*. The CBC, looking for ways to save money, encouraged the producers of programs with similar mandates to consider amalgamating their efforts. Phyllis and Bill proposed combining their programs to create *The Best Ideas You'll Hear Tonight*, and the new program was born.

Since its very beginning, *Ideas* has been firmly rooted in the trad-

Since its very beginning, *Ideas* has been firmly rooted in the traditions of adult education. On the night the program was launched, it was described as "the new look in CBC educational broadcasting" and "radio for the mind." Over its long life, the show has continued to nurture its relationship with academia and scholarship, but it has shifted its approach to an emphasis on feature documentary journalism.

Ideas underlie every aspect of our lives. They shape how we think and speak about the world, how we behave, how we see ourselves, individually and in society. Ideas drive the imagination; they frame the ways in which we conceive the past, the present, and the future; they inform our political and social arrangements, our arts and culture, science, technology, and religion, our personal relationships and beliefs.

Ideas, the program, is an unending work-in-progress. As a production team, we continually struggle with who we are and what we are trying to achieve, working in a world of exponential change. I use four adjectives to describe the ideal *Ideas* program. The first is "insightful": I hope that listeners will learn something they didn't know before, or think differently about something they did know. The second adjective is "eclectic": this is our goal in our choice of subjects, variety of contributors, and genres of presentation.

The third adjective I use to describe *Ideas* is my favourite: "resonant." As CBC programmers, we have talked for years about the importance of being relevant: you have to be relevant or people won't pay attention, and you'll fade away into irrelevance. It is hard to argue with that. But, in thinking about this in connection with *Ideas*, I began to feel that "relevant" was overused and at risk of losing its meaning along the way. "Resonant," however, seemed to me to extend and deepen the idea of relevance. The *Canadian Oxford Dictionary* defines resonance as "the reinforcement or prolongation of sound by reflection or synchronous vibration." Synchronous vibration — that's what I hope the best *Ideas* programs create in our listeners. Great works of art help us discover truths that reside deep within us, truths that are felt but not articulated; the words of the poet, the notes of the composer, the brushstrokes of the painter reach out and give voice to a truth within us, with an effect that can be electrifying. In its own way, *Ideas* aspires to do no less.

The fourth adjective I use is "delightful": I want *Ideas* shows to be a pleasure to listen to — to be both informative and entertaining.

Most *Ideas* programs are documentaries: journalistic compositions that draw on a variety of sources — interviews, sounds, actuality — and mix and match them to tell a story and explore an idea. Over the course of a season, however, we also produce a number of hour-long feature interviews. Unlike a documentary, an interview allows you to spend time ranging over the life, thought, and work of a single individual. This collection of interviews broadcast on *Ideas* is organized into four broad themes: "The Culture of Society," "Canada and the World," "The Eye, the Word, and the Ear," and "Futures." Apart from these thematic divisions are two interviews about the nature of ideas that serve as bookends for the rest of the collection.

The book begins, appropriately, with the words of the brilliant and erudite Lister Sinclair, who was the host of *Ideas* from 1983 until 1999. His ideas, gathered in a series of extended interviews conducted over a number of months during the final years of his career by *Ideas* producer Sara Wolch, are a meditation on thought, creativity, and imagination. He draws on some of intellectual and cultural figures that most influenced him: Darwin, Einstein, Goethe, Molière, Mozart, Newton, Shakespeare, among others. "I've been influenced," he says, "to try and see what everybody has seen and then think what nobody has thought."

The British political philosopher John Gray, author of *Black Mass: Apocalyptic Religion and the Death of Utopia*, opens "The Culture of Society." Although many people in the Western world like to think of themselves as secular, Gray argues that secularism itself has been shaped by ideas that have come from religion: history can be seen as a story of moral redemption, a struggle between good and evil that good actually can win. But, he cautions, human beings are imperfectible. Science and technology may be inherently progressive, but ethics and politics are not. We are still dealing with age-old human impulses, needs, and flaws. Perhaps the best we can do is work out reasonable ways of living with each other.

"The Culture of Society" also includes interviews with Mark Lilla, the New York-based historian of ideas; Theodore Dalrymple, retired British psychiatrist, social critic, and self-described "vulgarity correspondent"; Jerome Kagan, the Harvard developmental psychologist; Elliot Aronson, the eminent US researcher on cognitive dissonance; and Leonore Tiefer, educator, therapist, and specialist on male and female sexuality.

"Canada and the World" begins with Donald Savoie holder of the Clément-Cormier Chair in Economic Development at the Université de Moncton and one of Canada's most distinguished experts on public administration. Savoie addresses what he sees as a breakdown in the way the federal government functions. More than a hundred years ago, a bargain — an unwritten agreement, rather than part of the Constitution — was struck outlining the roles of Parliament, the prime minister and cabinet, and public servants. Savoie says that "MPs knew their role. It was to hold government accountable. It was not to govern... [T]hat bargain's come unglued."

In February 2007, the Conference Board of Canada released a massive report, *Mission Possible: Sustainable Prosperity for Canada*, which warned that Canada's economic performance was slipping compared with that of other industrialized countries and recommended steps we needed to take to achieve sustainable prosperity. Shortly after the report was released, *Ideas* interviewed the president of the Conference Board of Canada, Anne Golden, who discusses its main findings and argues that Canada must excel in the global economy, in the intelligent use of our resources, and in the way our cities function.

"Canada and the World" concludes with an interview with Louise Arbour, who retired in 2008 as the United Nations High Commissioner for Human Rights. She had come to the role after serving on the Supreme Court of Canada and, before that, as chief prosecutor of the International Criminal Tribunals for the Former Yugoslavia and Rwanda. In 2005, she delivered the annual Lafontaine-Baldwin Lecture in Quebec City on the theme of Canada and human rights. In her interview, which is based on that lecture, she laments that

Canada, a democratic and wealthy country that is respected internationally for its support of traditional freedoms, civil liberties, and human rights still wrestles with persistent domestic poverty. Arbour argues that Canada has been reluctant to embrace social and economic rights and wonders when we will move "from charity to entitlement."

"The Eye, the Word, and the Ear" begins with Mary Pratt, the eminent painter and printmaker and resident of Newfoundland and Labrador. *Ideas* interviewed her in early 2007, the year Canada Post issued a stamp in her honour. She has been described as "a visual poet of femaleness." Her interview is full of self-revelation. She recalls her first visual memory and talks about how her childhood experiences of light and colour have influenced her work.

Quite different is the Salish artist Lawrence Paul Yuxweluptun. His work illustrates the political, cultural, and environmental concerns facing Aboriginal peoples today. He is driven by rage. His imagery is striking and disturbing. Yuxweluptun documents, in his own words, "contemporary indigenous history in large-scale paintings."

"Futures" consists of interviews with Stewart Brand and Ray Kurzweil, prominent futurists who have helped to shape the world we live in and how we see it. Both continue to amaze and inspire.

Stewart Brand believes that human progress is best served through decentralized technologies, which allow people the freedom to shape a world that is socially and environmentally sustainable. In 1966, he campaigned to have NASA release a satellite photograph of Earth as seen from space. The photo, he said, "gave the sense that the Earth's an island, surrounded by a lot of inhospitable space." But Brand is probably best known for having created the *Whole Earth Catalogue* in 1968, which he hoped would "catalyze the emergence of a realm of personal power." Today, he is president of The Long Now Foundation, which he established with musician, composer, and record producer Brian Eno in "01996" to "creatively foster long-term thinking and responsibility in the framework of the next 10,000 years." "What do I actually do?" Brand writes, "I find things and I found things."

Ray Kurzweil is a genius. An engineer, inventor, and futurist, he invented the first omni-font character recognition system, the first print-to-speech reading machine for the blind, the first CCD flat-bed scanner, and the first music synthesizer that could faithfully reproduce the sounds of many orchestral instruments. In his 2005 book, *The Singularity Is Near: When Humans Transcend Biology,* Kurzweil suggests that through what he calls "the law of accelerating returns," we are moving toward a "singularity" — a future period, within the lifetimes of most of us today — when the pace of technological development will utterly and irreversibly transform human life.

The book closes with an interview with Peter Watson, a British journalist, researcher, and author of *Ideas: A History from Fire to Freud.* Watson talks about three great ideas and one bad one. I'll leave it to him to tell you what they are.

I want to end with a few words of thanks: to Susanne Alexander, publisher of Goose Lane Editions, for her enthusiastic support for this project; Barry Norris, for his meticulous copy-editing; and Julie Scriver, for the book's beautiful design. The CBC's Ian Godfrey, Mike Housego, and Nancy Millar transcribed the broadcast audio; without their front-line work, the radio interviews would never have made it to the page. Finally, I owe a special debt of gratitude to my colleagues at *Ideas,* whose work is featured in this book. Each day they bring their brilliance, their insights, and a ferocious commitment to the task of imagining and creating the *Ideas* program: our host Paul Kennedy, and producers Richard Handler, Mary O'Connell, Sean Prpick, Dave Redel, and Sara Wolch. I hope you enjoy the result.

BERNIE LUCHT
Toronto, August 2008

ONE

What Is an Idea?

LISTER SINCLAIR

On January 9, 2002, Lister Sinclair, who hosted Ideas *for sixteen years, turned eighty-one. Mathematician, dramatist, musicologist, actor, director, producer, critic, birder, teacher, author, and sports nut, Lister was no dabbler but a master in every one of those fields. He was also in broadcasting for almost sixty years. Some of the best radio plays and documentaries ever put on radio and television were written and produced by Lister. He had more honourary degrees and awards than one person has a right to, and he was one of the most polite, touchingly vulnerable, and genuinely gracious guys one could ever meet, with one of the most beguiling voices ever heard on the radio. Lister's long-time colleague and friend,* Ideas *producer Sara Wolch talked with him about his ideas and his influences. A longer version of this interview with Lister Sinclair was broadcast on 10, 23, and 30 January 2002.*

SARA WOLCH

As I sit here looking at you, a man I've worked with and admired for twenty years, I'm thinking, where on earth do we begin?

LISTER SINCLAIR

I think that it doesn't really matter too much where you start, because sooner or later you'll get to all the other pieces. One nice little parlour trick that mathematicians like to do is to get a strip of paper, glue the two ends together and give it a half-turn as you do it, and that makes what's called a Möbius strip. Möbius was a mathematician who spotted this, and the point about a Möbius strip is that it looks very much as if it's got two sides, the front and back, but it doesn't. If you run your finger along it, you discover that you keep changing from one side to another as you go along. So a Möbius strip is an interesting thing: start anywhere and you always wind up on the other side. And I think my life has been a Möbius strip. I start somewhere and wind up in the exact opposite.

Very often, when people think about something being creative, they look forward to having their eyes opened onto a completely new world. Well, that's very nice when it happens. It's not happened very often to me. What has happened to me very often, however, is that somebody has opened my eyes onto the same old world, and I've realized there was nothing "same old" about it. In other words, I've been influenced to try and see what everybody has seen and then think what nobody has thought. Somebody actually said that specifically, a guy whom I greatly admire: Albert Szent-Györgyi — St. George in Hungarian. He won the Nobel Prize in 1937 for medicine. He's the guy who first identified that there were such things as vitamins and that Vitamin C actually existed. He was finally able to isolate and get a specimen of Vitamin C, and that's pretty big news. And what he had done was he'd tried to see what everyone had seen and then think what nobody had thought.

SW: So, to see the same old thing with fresh eyes.

LS: Yes. Then it's no longer the same old thing. Out the window goes the "same old" right away. The whole world is then endlessly fresh and new. I can give you a musical example — it's getting on for two hundred years ago. Paganini, the great violinist — he was such a strange, dramatic figure — devised a whole series of little tunes, one of which he thought he could make variations on. And everybody else thought they could make variations on it, too. Incidentally, I once put together a tape, just for my own entertainment, of variations on that theme, and there were something like two hundred variations. Schumann had a go, Liszt had a go, Brahms had a go — they all spotted that theme, and they all did all the standard things you do to it. And one of the things you can do to it, by the way, is turn it upside down: instead of the notes going up, they go down. Does that get us anywhere? Sometimes it does. Evidently, mostly it doesn't, because everyone passed that up until, all of a sudden, Rachmaninoff comes along, about the time of the Second World War, and writes a piece for piano and orchestra called *Rhapsody on a Theme of Paganini* — same old thing. Rachmaninoff, like everybody else, had seen that theme, but he had thought something that nobody had thought — namely, that embedded in that theme was the result of turning the theme upside down. For example, you just look at any two notes, and where the original two notes go "bom, bee," you'd put it upside down, so they go "bom, ball" and so on.

One of the great non-musical examples, I think, is Charles Darwin. Charles Darwin spotted something that was right under our noses all the time. He just chose examples, one after another — a lot of hard work went into that — and he laid them all out on the table. His book, *On the Origin of Species*, has been not superseded but enormously expanded on since Darwin's day. And Darwin's great friend Thomas Huxley finished reading the book and said, and I think it's the most flattering and wonderful book review that anyone could hope for: "How stupid of us not to have thought of that."

SW: What exactly did Darwin help us think about?

LS: What he helped us to do, I think, was to ask what used to be called "silly questions" and expect them to be real questions with a real answer. It's answering the "why" about things. Some gulls have a red spot on the beak. Why? "Oh, that's a silly question. Gulls have a red spot on the beak — that's why." And some perhaps said that God put the red spot on the beak, and that's all very nice. But Darwin expected a reasonable answer — asking why is a reasonable question, and maybe there's a reasonable answer. Does the gull use the red spot on the beak to survive? And, it turns out, it does. What happens is that a gull will load up with food and return to the nest. There's the chick sitting there, and the gull is perfectly prepared to regurgitate food so that the young can eat, but she doesn't really know how to. She just sits there sort of gazing into space. What has to happen is that the young bird has to tap the red spot. That's a trigger. The red spot is a trigger for the young bird. The young bird taps, and the adult regurgitates. So that red spot is very important.

SW: The idea of asking the right question seems very important here.

LS: Asking the right question is absolutely essential. Seeing what everybody has seen and thinking what nobody has thought — perhaps another way of putting it is to say that you see what everybody has seen, and then you ask the right question. And it's true of all these people. Somebody else who did that just as much, perhaps even more so, was Isaac Newton.

SW: What's your favourite question that Newton asked?

LS: That's a nice one, I think. I've always been fond of the night sky, even when I was a kid. In Arizona, where the skies are so clear and bright, you can see artificial satellites tracking across the sky. And people say to me, "Isn't that amazing! What's holding it up?" Well, that's not a good question. You could look at the moon, and say, "What's holding that up?" But Newton looked at the moon, and he thought something quite different. He asked the right question: "What's holding it down? What doesn't it fly off into space?" It's like tying a rope to a bucket of water and swinging it round and round your head. We know what's holding the bucket in place — it's the rope. Now, there's the moon going round and round in this sort of way — no rope, no apparent rope. And that's the right question. The moment you've asked that question, immediately answers begin to suggest themselves. Perhaps what's holding it down is the same force that is pulling the apple in Newton's own orchard towards the centre of the Earth.

SW: What do you admire about Sir Isaac Newton?

LS: I admire the way his mind worked universally. You can't get interested in science, you can't work in science, without being endlessly confronted with Newton.

SW: What have you taken from Newton and integrated into your being?

LS: I guess the firm belief that, indeed, the universe lies under an order of a kind, of several kinds, and we ought to be able to get at it. And that's kind of difficult to do sometimes because it's very hard to let something hang in your mind as unsettled. It hasn't been decided, but I'm convinced nonetheless that it can be decided in principle. [The Nobel prize-winning physicist] Richard Feynman, whom I also admire very much, was very good at that. If you can't get an answer, you don't really have to invoke little green men and angels and things of that ken. What you can say is, "I'm sure there's an answer, and I don't know what it is, and I don't think anybody knows what it is, but I'm sure there is one." Feynman's very much the opposite of Newton. Feynman was a cut-up and very funny and lively and cheerful and amazing. Newton was the exact opposite. He was a stern and rockbound coast — no question of it whatever. But he did say this: "I don't know how I may appear to the world, but to myself, I seem to have been only like a boy, playing on the seashore and diverting myself and now and then finding a smoother pebble or a prettier shell than ordinary while the great ocean of truth lay all undiscovered before me." That's a marvellous remark, isn't it?
    When Einstein was cremated, they sprinkled his ashes on a little stream and went and drank hot buttered rum and talked about him, and somebody said, "So nobody knows what became of him." And a colleague of Einstein's, another physicist, replied, "On the contrary, we all know what became of him. He went to join the ocean on whose shores Newton played." That's a metaphor. I think it's the kind of spirituality that I would feel very strongly, and so would

Einstein — and Newton would not, incidentally. But me and Einstein — that's not too bad.

SW: Lister, what is it that enables some people, like Newton or Darwin, to ask the right question?

LS: One of the things that's a great problem with people who are trying to learn foreign languages is that they don't like to make fools of themselves, and they don't like to ask stupid questions — seemingly stupid questions. And some of those questions are really extremely, blindingly, stupid. I remember, when I was a very, very little kid, I was always asking questions, as kids always do, and my relatives liked to tease me, as relatives always do. And I remember watching a steam engine — here's this great big steam engine moving slowly along and puffing. And the way they used to move was, a puff of steam would appear every so often moving slowly along the platform. And I said, "Why is the engine puffing like that?" And I got the answer, "Well, it's puffing like that because there is a little old gentleman in a green coat who is inside the cylinder and inside this thing here and he is smoking a pipe, and every so often he puffs on the pipe and it puffs like that." And I was amused by that. I thought something like, well, that's a very amusing, nice story. Now, why is it really puffing? And what I got was, "Well, that's what's really puffing. There's a little, old man..." No, there isn't — why is it really puffing? Well, they didn't know. But they didn't say or dream of saying, "I don't know but maybe we can find out. Why don't we ask the engine driver?" But no, I just got a little old man with a pipe until I was screaming and yelling and carrying on in frustration. I never got a straight answer on that one.

SW: So, daring to ask seemingly silly questions is important?

LS: Yes. Language, of course, is daring to make silly noises.

SW: What about your perspective, your point of view? If you think that human beings are the centre of the universe, you'd ask a particular constellation of questions, wouldn't you?

LS: Oh, absolutely, yes, indeed. I'm going to dig a little further on this one. I believe as a matter of evidence and much more that the Earth is rotating and that this covers up the Sun and, therefore, causes the illusion of sunset. I've spent a lot of time gazing steadfastly at sunsets and seeing the Sun go down and trying to perceive it firmly and saying, "No, it's not really going down. The Earth is coming up and covering it," and try as I will, I can't do it, I cannot make it work that way. Perhaps it's because we always see it in the same way all the time, and that's curious and remarkable, I think. The Earth certainly seems to be at the centre of everything. The stars are all going around us. The planets, strange wandering things — because that's what the word "planet" means: "wanderer." But along came Copernicus and Kepler and Galileo, and they were working on something very serious. What they were doing was carefully pointing out that we are not special — the Earth is not special. The Earth is not even special in the solar system. The Sun is special, but not the Earth. Then Darwin came along and did it again to us and said that not only is the planet not important; the star is not important, even the galaxy is not important — that's just one of billions of galaxies — and human beings are not important — that's just one of many millions of species of living things. They're all special. We happen to be special in special sorts of ways, but they're all especially special.

SW: This idea that we should be skeptical about our specialness seems very close to your heart. Why is that?

LS: I think we should be skeptical about everything. I think everything needs testing. There's a famous old saying, "The exception proves the rule" — in other words, if there's an exception, that shows that the rule is true. Of course, that's rubbish. That's the little man puffing a pipe inside the steam engine. The word "prove" in that

sense means the exception tests the rule. It proves the rule in that
sense. We've got an exception. Whoops! Now really, we have to
check out the rule to see why it's not working in this case, and there
may be many more cases.

Modern scientists are up to something which I always think fascinating: you try not to verify anything because you can't. Hume, the
great Scottish philosopher, was very good on that one. And that's a
little troublesome. Crows are black, swans are white. And the paradox, the end of the line in something that's impossible, is a black
swan. Now, are there such things as black swans? We could keep
looking at swans, and every time we see one it would be white. You
could verify it, but you'd never get anywhere. What you can do,
however, is falsify it. If you find one example where it isn't that way,
then we're in business. And, in fact, there are black swans, but they
come from Australia.

SW: You're making everything sound so clinical, Lister.

LS: When we're talking about this sort of clinical analysis, it sounds
clinical. But how is it done really? It's done, I think, by having very
strong feelings about these things. And somewhere along the line,
you have to think about your feelings, about your thoughts. I think
it's extremely important to look at the universe, to pick out what's
going on in more than one way. And there are at least four ways of
doing it. One way is by being coldly rational — "clinical," as you put
it. Intuitional is another, and that's having a gut feeling about it, and
it may be that the gut feeling is in fact the accumulation of a large
number of little things that you have noticed, but you didn't notice
you were noticing them. The third way is sensual — directly through
the senses. People who have that quality are able to walk into a room
and walk straight out again and tell you how many people were in
the room and what each one of them was wearing, which means a
direct pickup of the whole room just like that. That's the sensual
personality. And finally, there's the judgmental one, which asks, "Is
it right? Is it wrong?" And that's very common, too. We all go in for
all four of those things, and we have a little problem with that, too,

simply because, for most of us, we have developed one particular way of reacting to everything.

SW: You've been talking about the nature of questions, the "why" questions that Darwin taught us to ask, the ability to ask seemingly silly questions, the story from when you were a little boy, the idea of asking questions that yield simple answers. What do all these questions have in common?

LS: What all these questions have in common is a way of undoing locks. The university was full of locks, some big and important ones, some very small ones, and some that are so small you barely notice them. And we can usually get a handle on answering them, because our heads, fortunately, are loaded with thoughts and ideas and dreaming, and dreaming certainly consists of reshuffling all these things and checking them out and throwing some of them away and rearranging them, and all the rest of it. And the result is that, very often, if you think hard about a problem and then sleep on it, the next morning it seems suddenly clear, and we all feel that. And sometimes you may have to sleep on it, so to speak, for years, as Einstein did and as Bertrand Russell did. And what you first have to do is to press home as hard as you can, to think as hard as you can and then forget it. You can't do impossibilities, so forget it, back off, lighten up. The boys in the backroom or the girls in the backroom will do it for you.

SW: I'd like you to read something. It's something that Einstein wrote at one point.

LS: "The most beautiful experience we can have is the mysterious. It is the fundamental emotion which stands at the cradle of true art and true science. Whoever does not know it and can no longer wonder, no longer marvel, is as good as dead, and his eyes are dimmed. It was the experience of mystery — even if mixed with fear — that engendered religion. A knowledge of the existence of something we cannot penetrate, our perceptions of the profoundest reason and the most radiant beauty, which only in their most primitive forms are accessible to our minds — it is this knowledge and this emotion that constitute true religiosity; in this sense, and in this alone, I am a deeply religious man."

I agree with it. I think it's absolutely true — no question about it.

SW: Are you a religious man?

LS: Yes, in exactly the sense that Einstein is. I am filled, I would say, with delighted spiritual amazement all the time, but I certainly do not believe in any of those peculiar trappings that people seem to go for — old gentlemen in long white nightshirts being very angry and throwing thunderbolts at people and a general sense of rage and the jealous god and all these sort of things.

SW: Do you believe in God?

LS: No. First of all, we could go round the mulberry bush and say, "What do you mean by 'God'?" Do I believe that the universe was put together by some all-powerful creator? No, I don't, particularly. Or, if so, I would probably agree with Spinoza, who was a very great philosopher, indeed, and much beloved by anyone who knew him at all — wonderful man. I suppose Spinoza thought that you could possibly say that God laid down the laws of nature and then left town and hasn't been seen since. You might say that, but there's no particular point in saying that. What we can do, I think, is talk about the watchmaker. That was the famous example of argument by design. If you see a watch, you infer a watchmaker, and the people who thought they saw a watch didn't realize how immensely complicated the carefully evolved design in nature is.

SW: What are you amazed by? You said "spiritual amazement."

LS: I'm amazed by the truth. Every time things suddenly work out, I think that's absolutely amazing and totally wonderful. I'm amazed, of course, by mathematics, which I think is delightful, and there's a wonder and beauty and wit in it. I am amazed by beauty. I'm amazed by pretty well anything, as a matter of fact. Also, I'm very naive — I can be amazed again and again by the same things. I'm always amazed by the first robin and the last robin and all those things. It's wonderful to see something new in nature, of course, but also what's wonderful is to go around for a little walk and see that all the birds and all the trees have all read the book. They're doing it exactly. There they are. There should be a hermit thrush there, and there he is. It's that sort of thing. I think that's truly wonderful.

SW: Are you amazed by human beings?

LS: Yes, I would think so. I'm amazed by people like Einstein. I think his power of insight was absolutely stunning. And all these people have this extraordinary trick of seeing below the surface of things all the time and enjoy the looking. They enjoy the search. I'm very impressed by what Darwin wrote to an agonized clergyman — a man who was deeply upset because he felt that Darwin had displaced God from the universe. The clergyman wrote to Darwin and said, "Why on earth did you do this? Why did you dismantle religion? Why did you take away from people the sense of hope in looking for an afterlife and things of that kind? If you had been present at as many deathbeds as I have, you would never dream of doing such a thing." And Darwin replied very sincerely, as he always did, saying, "I'm sorry, I don't have any training in philosophy. I'm not learned like you are. I don't know these things at all. I don't know theology. I don't know philosophy. All I can do is to give you an answer which I thought was true." Darwin said things because he thought they were true, and he believed that, in the end, the truth shall make you free, but the truth was certainly a weapon of some sort.

SW: Darwin, Einstein, Copernicus, Kepler, Galileo — all men of science and of a particular kind of science. Why have you been focusing on them, Lister?

LS: We just happen to have been talking about those. There are other people that I would focus on as well, and those are some of the great artists. The two, I think, are just aspects of creativity, aspects of that sense of seeing what everyone has seen and thinking what no one has thought. Science — yes, and the great artists do exactly the same thing. They're putting things together that you didn't really notice — that's the trick — and as soon as you put them next to each other, suddenly the sense of dramatic irony comes up. We really are forced to see the connection and the bitter ambivalence.

SW: You used the word "connection." What does that mean?

LS: Connection, I think, means seeing underlying patterns, to suddenly realize that what you're seeing is actually another instance of something that was around all the time, maybe right under your nose, and you didn't notice it. It's nice to feel, I think, that the stuff of the world, which is ideas and thoughts and feelings and all those things, actually hang together, isn't just lying there as separate little lumps. They do hang together, and it's that sense of them hanging together that's very important, I think. Facts are interesting and very important, but I don't think a shower of facts is the same as wisdom. It's not even the same as mulch.

SW: And what's the difference?

LS: They're not standing in any perceived relationship. They haven't been arranged in a significant pattern. What's the difference between a pattern that's significant and one that isn't? I think all patterns can be made significant. It's up to the artist to make it significant.
      The guy whom I admire a lot in this is Johann Wolfgang von Goethe, the great German poet and scientist. Goethe was both a scientist and an artist, and he knew it.

SW: How has he influenced you in your own work?

LS: I think he influenced me so much because he was prepared to look anywhere and at anything and to ask questions about it and not to take things for granted at all. And he was absolutely prepared to throw out all his preconceptions on anything and start again, and his starting again nearly always turned out to be not replacing all the preconceptions with new ones, but adding new ones to the old ones. He made a celebrated journey to Italy. In the middle of the night, he suddenly decided to get up and go to Italy. And he seems to have experienced sexual passion for the first time in Italy. Goethe has a wonderful description, and he is behaving exactly like a poet. That's this wonderful sense of the truth. She's asleep, and he is dozing beside her and tapping out on her back pentameters with his finger. She's an object of poetry, and he learns from her how to appreciate the ancient statute in the works of art, and he learns from the works of art how to appreciate her. He learns, as he says, to "see with a feeling hand and feel with a seeing eye" — the touch, the feeling of the hand is contributing to what you're seeing. You have to combine that with seeing with the feeling eye. Your eye touches it. So it's two aspects of the same thing.

SW: So we've moved from seeing what everyone has seen to thinking what no one has thought, and we're now bringing in feeling.

LS: That's right, yes, exactly. And I think "see" in a broad sense — it's not just looking but seeing.

SW: Hovering in the background all the time is this idea of the two cultures: the arts and the sciences.

LS: Yes, I guess so. Jacob Bronowski used to say over and over again, and he was dead right, too, I think, that it's not that there are two cultures. There's really only one culture, only most of us are not even half-cultured. That's the catch.

SW: Jacob Bronowski — most of us, I think, know him from a television series that he hosted a number of years ago, *The Ascent of*

Man, and he was popping up in all kinds of exotic locations, like the Alhambra, and telling us the meaning of it all. But you knew him.

LS: Yes, I knew him very well. *The Ascent of Man* — by the way, notice not the "descent" but the "ascent." He's going up.

SW: Up Jacob's ladder.

LS: That's right, yes. Bronowski was a mathematician, and he was always urging people to press the limits. For example, the age of the universe — what is it since the Big Bang? We've got ideas about what it might be. Now I think they're saying it may be somewhere between ten billion years and eighteen billion years. That's huge — eight billion years. Nonetheless, it's not two thousand years, nor is it a billion billion years. In other words, it's a rough sort of feeling about it. And the way Bronowski used to say it always delighted me, and it delights my students. He used to say, "If a thing's worth doing, it's worth doing badly." In other words, if you're going to wait until it's going to be perfect, it's never going to get done. And Bronowski considered science as the greatest of the humanities. It's humane because it requires understanding and judgment and feelings, and if you can do that, you've got the whole thing going for you at once, and he felt that and showed it in his life. I feel that, too, very much indeed. I believe whatever the individual is doing, it's worth doing badly. It's worth having a go at it. It's worth trying all the time and never resting. And if things don't go quite right necessarily, that's all right, too.

W.H. Auden used to say that Shakespeare, our national muse, is "forever tottering on the brink of chaos," because he puts in so many things. He puts comedy in the middle of tragedies, and tragedy in the middle of comedies, and little colourful bits and plays within plays and all kinds of things — anything he can think of, he sticks it in, in the hope that it will not be boring.

SW: I take it that it's not by accident that we're talking about Shakespeare all of a sudden.

LS: No. Shakespeare is the greatest dramatist, and if you want to be a dramatist, you'd better do exactly what he did, which is to steal as many things as possible from the best possible sources and stick them in wherever it's convenient to you. That's what he did. That's what I do. That's what everybody with any sense does.

SW: So, he's on your list of influences?

LS: Absolutely. He is the greatest dramatic influence. He's by far the biggest influence on anyone whose craft and trade is in drama, because he had everything.

SW: We could probably spend thousands of hours discussing how and why Shakespeare has influenced you. Is there a way, though, that you can pull together some of these ideas, since you specialize in arranging ideas?

LS: Yes, I think so. It seems to me that what an artist should be doing and, in particular at the moment, a playwright, is a little group of things: to see, to know, to shape, to show — those are the four things you have to do, in that order. To shape, to show — no more extra words. I think that's vital. That's how you do it. What you have to do, I think, is to look at human beings, see what they do, see what they don't do, see how people behave, see what they feel, see the way they express their feelings, and see very carefully what they're really doing and not what they think they're doing. And to see, for example, when people don't quite play fair, and sometimes we dislike that and sometimes we admire it.

Portia, the brilliant lady lawyer in *The Merchant of Venice*, has in some way been required to marry whoever correctly guesses the right casket. There are three caskets: gold, silver, and lead. And every so often there's a scene: somebody comes in and chooses wrong casket. Somebody chooses the gold casket — that was a mistake. Somebody else comes in and chooses the silver casket, and that's a mistake too. And then the guy that she's in love with shows up. His name is Bassanio, and he's a sturdy, decent sort of fellow, the kind of chap

Shakespearian heroines ought to be in love with and the kind of person she is going to take charge of, because Shakespeare's heroines are always very strong. And she calls for music — Shakespeare loves music, so he's forever sticking in bits of music. The jester's looking around her caskets. He looks at the gold one, the silver one, the lead one, and a voice says, "Tell me where is fancy bred, Or in the heart, or in the head? How begot, how nourished?" What rhymes with "head"? Gold? "Where begot, where nourished?" Silver? Lead.

SW: How is that an example of seeing?

LS: What Shakespeare is seeing is that Portia is cheating. She is running the jester. She is supposed to stand there and allow the stooges to choose whatever they want. She is not supposed to be giving hints to the one that she wants. The jester is watching her all the time, and when Bassanio turns up, she gives the signal to the jester, and away we go, and she is innocently giving hints — a song that rhymes with "lead" all the time. And Shakespeare thinks, and so do we, that it's delightful that people don't behave necessarily all that straightforwardly. And that's seeing, and Shakespeare is full of that. He's very good at seeing these little discrepancies between behaviour and feelings and attitudes all the time.

What you have to do is digest the things that you've seen and put them together and realize that very often things that look really rather different aren't necessarily all that different. What you have to do, on the one hand, is to learn how to look for distinctions and differences where everything seems the same; and, on the other hand, look for similarities where everything seems different. The two together immediately enrich what you're doing, and that's the question of knowing, of seeing things, and splitting things up, and joining them together, and Shakespeare is very, very good at that.

It's very interesting that people often quote Shakespeare as if these are his views: "Neither a borrower nor a lender be" — that kind of stuff. He produces these mottos that belong on a calendar, and somebody thinks, how come Shakespeare sounds like your grandmother? Well, Shakespeare doesn't sound like your grandmother.

One of his characters, Polonius, sounds like your grandmother, and Polonius, in fact, is very smart and successful. He has successfully advised King Claudius, the king of Denmark, who has murdered his way to the throne, and Polonius is certainly pompous and quite a few other things, but he's not stupid. And the advice that he gives to his son is pretty good advice, if what you want to do is to make the right impression and be careful. They're politically correct impressions all the time: "Neither a borrower nor a lender be." Why? For moral reasons? No, no, no, no, no: "for loan oft loses both itself and friend." You lend somebody money, you may lose the money, and you may lose the friend, too, so don't do it. The idea that you should be carried away by generosity, that compassion should cause you to do it, won't work, says Polonius — not Shakespeare, but one of his characters.

SW: If you're Shakespeare and you're shaping, what are you doing?

LS: What you're doing now is putting together the many diverse tricks that make the thing dramatic, and he's very good at it and very fond of it. And the main thing, I would say, is this thing called "dramatic irony." Kids always understand it — little tiny children understand it perfectly. And that's a situation in which we in the audience know something about what's going on that someone on the stage doesn't know. It's so important, because it drags the audience in, and it makes them participate, and it's no longer a matter of sitting there passively while wisdom is heaped on you from a great height. You actually take part.

There was an actor who was a great friend of mine, Eric Christmas — he died a few years ago at a great age — and he was wonderful at pantomimes. He knew exactly how to operate. He would walk to the front of the stage, address the audience directly, and say to the kids, "Now the demon king is going to appear any moment, and I want to get away from him. Will you help me, please?" And they would say "Yes." And then he would ask them to say, "There he is" and to practise that. And they would all practise, "There he is," and they would get it. And the demon king would appear in the back and everyone would shout, "There he is." And he would say, "Yes, it's OK. You've got it right. We don't need to do it anymore." They would say, "No, there…" And he would look round and, of course, there he isn't — he's gone. And you could keep that up all night. It's irresistible, isn't it? And the kids have to be taken away and put into intensive care, with all this screaming and yelling and worrying about it. That's dramatic irony.

SW: What's your favourite example from Shakespeare?

LS: I think probably in *Twelfth Night*, where Malvolio is the pompous and conceited steward, and they drop a letter to make him think that the lady of the house has fallen madly in love with him. And there he is, pompously walking up and down and thinking, my Lady is in love with me. Isn't this marvellous! Isn't this wonderful! I recognize this. He thinks that the letter has come from Olivia, and we know it hasn't. And hiding behind a hedge are the people who wrote the letter, and they're watching Malvolio to see what kind of an idiot he makes of himself. And we, of course, are on their side, and we are watching him too. And he says, "By my life, this is my lady's hand" — the handwriting of the thing — "these be her very Cs, her Us and her Ts." Did you get the gag? Perhaps not. Someone at the back of the stage pops up and says, "Her Cs, her Us and her Ts — why that?" You, in the third row, get it? Oh, yes, oh, my. And the next line is, "And thus makes she her great Ps." See what I mean? That's very much sharing it with the audience. It's very much dramatic irony.

SW: Every example you've given so far — Malvolio walking up and down, Portia — people are doing something all the time.

LS: People *are* doing something. That's all drama consists of. All drama is doing. It's not speech-making. And sometimes we say of a certain play, "This is very wordy," meaning that people are talking but not doing anything. If they are doing something in the speech, then it doesn't seem talky at all, because the words are doing something.

SW: What's the difference between doing and saying?

LS: Shakespeare has a great scene in *Julius Caesar* in which the noble conspirator Brutus, who is a pompous ass in some ways, makes a speech to the crowd which is excruciatingly boring. And it's wonderfully symmetrical — on the one hand, this; on the other hand, that — and nothing is happening. It's boring on purpose. And Brutus ends up by saying, you've listened to me very politely, and I'm a very fair, decent sort of fellow, so I would like you please to listen respectfully to Mark Antony, who is a friend of Caesar's. Thank you very much. And off he goes. And Mark Antony says flatly he can't make a speech, "I come to bury Caesar, not to praise him." That's all I do. He was my friend. And so I can't make speeches about Caesar. I can't even tell you about his will. Oh, I shouldn't have mentioned it, should I? And Mark Antony's speech consists, as we all well know, not of words, but of doing things. It's an endless little series of actions: "But Brutus is an honourable man." That's a little dig at Brutus, and we don't find that one boring. The one in which he's talking, that's boring — words only. The one which is action is very, very exciting, and, in fact, it's one of the great pieces of rhetoric in the language or in any language.

SW: Rhetoric — that brings to mind the idea that Shakespeare is consciously and deliberately designing things.

LS: He's persuading us all the time. That's what the art of rhetoric is. It's the art of persuasion.

SW: Persuading or manipulating, Lister?

LS: All the same thing. If he's one of the bad guys, you say, "Oh, he's manipulating us." If he's one of the good guys, you say, "Isn't it wonderful how much he enthralls us and enchants us and catches all these rare and delicious meanings." And all the great artists do it, and they would think you were crazy if you thought differently. Beethoven, noble and wonderful as he is, is he manipulating our feelings? Damn right he is! Does he expect you to walk out of the symphony concert after you've heard the Fifth Symphony feeling exactly the same as you did when you walked in? He would be very upset indeed if that's what happened. He wants to change your feelings. He wants to change them in the direction that he is interested in. And if you think that Beethoven's is a good direction — he is always on the side of freedom, of liberty, of courage, and things of that kind — you say that it's a wonderful inspiration. Is Beethoven manipulating? Sure, he is, absolutely, and does it very well indeed.

And so does Shakespeare. You look at something like *King Lear*. The old man is pompous and arrogant, and he does something silly, and that's the famous tragic flaw. In other words, it doesn't happen quite by accident. It happens because the character has done something in character, which is a bad mistake. And we can sit in the audience shouting to King Lear, "Don't give the stuff away. Don't trust your dau..." Oh, dear, he's done it again. Every time you go and see that play, he does it. He never pays any attention. It's that kind of thing. King Lear does it and, sure enough, terrible things happen. And Macbeth is ambitious. Up to a point, that's fine. But he's got this terrible wife, and she is — I was going to say ambition incarnate, but she's not quite ambition incarnate; in *The Pilgrim's Progress*, she might be, but not in *Macbeth*. And she says surprising things. For one thing, she has a nervous breakdown. She forces her husband to commit the murder; she doesn't do it herself. Here, take the dagger. You do it. I would have done it myself had he not looked like my father as he slept. And then when they've done the murder, she gives her husband, Macbeth, the knife and says, "Gild the faces of the grooms" — the two guys who are sleeping in the bedchamber with the king — "Gild them withal," put blood on them, "for it must seem their guilt." He can't resist a pun, and there it is. And then she says, "Who would have thought the old man to have had so much blood in him?" — literally, words of one syllable, very plain and very direct. And that's not Mrs. Ambition in a personification. That's a real person.

SW: "Who would have thought the old man to have had so much blood in him?" — not a wasted word there.

LS: No, absolutely not. And many of Shakespeare's greatest lines have no wasted words whatsoever. At the end of *Julius Caesar*, Brutus commits suicide, and the guy who turns out later to be Augustus Caesar comes along and makes one of these wonderful statements to round it off nicely, something very nice and straightforward: "This was the noblest Roman of them all." Try and paraphrase that. Try and make it more concise. You can't do it. And he's very, very good at that when it's called for. Washing the blood off the hand in the ocean: "Will all great Neptune's ocean," and suddenly, we've got into mythology — "wash this blood clean from my hand? No, this my hand will rather the multitudinous seas incarnadine" — here, we go, "Wow! Great big long words. And that's splendid. We're really getting our money's worth this afternoon, aren't we? But he continues, "making the green one red." That's what it means: "making the green one red," all red. One red is heraldry. It means everything red. Making the green sea — all you can say is "making the green one red."

SW: Why all the double meanings?

LS: I think that was very much the way his mind worked. He loved ambiguities. It's not quite double meanings. It's deliberate ambiguity, because ambiguity leads to richness.

SW: What do you think makes a play well done?

LS: I think it should leave us feeling enriched, feeling that our emotions had been extended, feeling that our emotions indeed had been amplified. We don't walk out of *Hamlet* feeling glum. Usually, people actually leave quite exhilarated if it's well done, and you've

been exhilarated by a play in which all the principal people are dead
— often at the very end all at once, the stage is littered with dead
bodies, and there's a lot of murders and killing going on. There is
a very gruesome murder attached to the ghost. It's full of incest,
because that was perceived as incest, marrying your husband's
brother. And the hero, such as he is, seems to be very depressed
and very good at expressing depression, and yet at the same time,
when he dies, what does his friend say? "Thus cracks a noble heart.
Good night, sweet prince; And flights of angels sing thee to thy
rest." "Good night, sweet prince" are four great words, very hard to
translate into another language because each of them has a special
flavour in English. "Prince" is something noble in English. When we
call Satan the Prince of Darkness, that's elevating him. If you call
him Baron Samedi, it makes him wicked. Barons are wicked. Earls
are wicked. Princes are noble.

SW: Why don't we leave *Hamlet* feeling glum?

LS: Because what we've perceived is the power of the imagination,
the power of creativity, and that's always exhilarating, even to people
who are not themselves playwrights. Nonetheless, you can't help
feeling it. We feel, as Bertrand Russell said, "so well that tragedy is
the queen of the arts." Rightly so. Why? Because if we're surrounded
with despair and destruction and no future and forlornness and
tyranny and betrayal and all those things, tragedy raises her citadel
in the heart of the enemy country, and tragedy turns all that into
beauty and delight, without being soppy about it, either. It's not a
matter of saying, "No, no, let's deny it." On the contrary, it's exactly
"See life steadily and see it whole."

There's a spectacular example of that in Beethoven. He was dying
and he had a rough time of it. He had suffered from lupus. He
had congestive heart failure. It was an unpleasant, rough time. And
people were saying, "Can we bring you something?" And he said,
"Yes, there's a mass by, I think, Bach, and the *Crucifixis*, the part
of the mass in which it says He was crucified under Pontius Pilate,
is the most serious part of the mass. The *Crucifixis* goes something

like this…" And he scribbled it out and, sure enough, it's the *Crucifixis* of the B minor Mass by Bach, and they brought that to him. A little while later, somebody found him sitting up in bed chuckling. He's chuckling and shaking his head in admiration and looking at the *Crucifixis*, and he's chuckling, not at the fate of Jesus, but with admiration for the power of the artist, the power of Bach. That creativity is overwhelming, and it reached his heart immediately.

One of the things that I personally think is very important is that plays, in particular, are supposed to please the audience, not the playwright. And one thing that's always in there, in my opinion, is impression. They make an impression. They sometimes are an expression at the same time, but if the work is done solely as an expression, you're dead in the water. Expression is just from me, and that's not enough. Impression — that's from me to you and reaching you in a certain way, and if it also expresses something that I feel, that's fine, that's a bonus. And the great artists are all hung around with bonuses.

SW: What's the most important thing you've learned from Shakespeare?

LS: If you know what you're doing, anything goes. Molière, a French playwright whom I greatly admire, had a wonderful remark when people complained that his plays were not properly put together: "Anything that goes on the stage for which people will pay money is a play, as far as I'm concerned." That's the only rule. And it's the same rule that the great opera composer Verdi had. Verdi is very down-to-earth too. An opera can be anything you like, except for one thing: not boring. Shakespeare may be tiresome at times, he quibbles sometimes, he goes into these silly word games, which was very much an Elizabethan trick that they loved to do — it's like, "Knock, knock. Who's there?" It's that sort of stuff. They loved that stuff — at the same time, it's not boring.

When I was quite young, there were influences that I didn't realize I was getting, and now I'm quite old, I realize that, all my life, I've been influenced by two of my uncles. Now, I look back on things that are the passions of my life — music and birds are certainly two of the main ones — and I can't help thinking that it keeps going back to my Uncle Parker and to another uncle, my Uncle Harry.

My Uncle Parker was a fat man, very shortsighted, and with a short fat man's nose, and he insisted on wearing pince-nez glasses, and it really wasn't very helpful. But there was something very special about Uncle Parker. He had two things that he was absolutely dedicated to. One was music. He was a singer himself. He sang alto, a countertenor sort of voice, and he was a good singer. And the thing that he loved most of all was the Proms — the Promenade concerts conducted by Sir Henry Wood. And my uncle was very fond of Beethoven — that was one of his great loves. Uncle Harry was a musician. He conducted a theatre orchestra in the days when the pit orchestra was quite important. He was the man in the pit waving the baton and always referred to by the performers as "the professor." The pit orchestra would play things in between acts of a play, and they would play incidental music and things of this kind, so you had to be fairly versatile. My Uncle Harry was also extremely fond of Beethoven.

SW: How did he influence you?

LS: He influenced me by frightening me to death. I didn't see my parents for a long time, but when they finally returned from India — I didn't remember them from before, and I was then seven-and-a-half — we went up to the north of England and Scotland to see various relatives. We wound up in a place in the north of England where my mother was born, a little coal-mining town called Spennymoor, and there was my Uncle Harry. It was a Sunday. There was an upright piano, and Harry was playing it, and it struck me as being very nice. It wasn't something that I ever heard from my Uncle Parker because it was a piano piece. It was fascinating, and you couldn't get away from it. And I said, "What's it called? Does it have a name?" And he said, "Yes, this is 'The Moonlight Sonata,'" to which I said — and I hope we're in a building which is proof against lightning and things of that kind — "What? That old thing?" A large mushroom cloud appeared over Spennymoor, and that was my uncle really telling me off: "You never must say 'that old thing' to Beethoven, and you don't say 'that old thing' because you mustn't feel 'that old thing.'" In other words, every time you hear it, it should sound fresh as the spring, and of course it does.

SW: What was your childhood like, Lister?

LS: Very lonely, very lonely indeed. I didn't play with other kids much. My aunt was very worried about play. She thought it was dangerous — he's going to get hurt, and it's my responsibility. I read a lot. I would say I taught myself to read very early on. It opened your eyes to all kinds of interesting things. It took you somewhere else. I was also very fond of the radio, and that meant the children's hour on the BBC, which was very popular and very successful.

SW: When you said that reading took you somewhere else, where did you want to be?

LS: Anywhere, but not here. My Uncle Parker died when I was twelve and from then on, things got really bad. Now, my aunt, she was alone. They didn't have any children. And her troubles and worries, her real, terrible anxieties all the time, were loaded full strength onto me.

SW: What kind of a student were you?

LS: Appalling. I was a very bad student, and I now realize I was a very bad student on purpose. It was an extremely loud cry for help, I would say. But I was in a very curious educational situation. It was a classical school, which meant that you did the classics: Latin composition, Greek composition, Latin translation, Greek translation, Latin grammar, Roman history, and Greek history — all that stuff. And that occupied, I should think, three-quarters of the time. The rest of it was miscellaneous subjects, which were not taken seriously by the school structure. French was one, German was another — and mathematics. My favourite subject was science, but there was very little of that.

SW: And this was a prestigious boarding school.

LS: Oh, very prestigious, indeed. St Paul's was then regarded as the top academic school, and I'm told it still is. There was one truly interesting thing about it, I think. It was founded by a guy called Dean Colet, who was a close friend of the great philosopher Erasmus. It was, in fact, intended to bring the Renaissance to England, and the interesting founder's stipulation was that there should be no test of religion. In other words, unlike nearly all the public schools, which are religious schools — Church of England schools and all the rest of it — you were admitted without regard to what country you came from or what your religion was. To begin with, it was this Protestant-Catholic thing, then the Lutheran thing for a while, and then it kind of fell into abeyance. It sure wasn't in abeyance in the '30s. St. Paul's was the public school, which could and did take in a large number of Jewish refugees.

SW: What did you miss the most in your childhood?

LS: Nurturing, the sense that, somewhere, there was someone who was on my side — that's all. My parents, who were certainly on my side, didn't really register, because, by airmail, it took two weeks to get an answer. That's far, far away and very remote.

SW: What influence do you think your childhood had on you when you became an adult?

LS: I'm not very good at personal relations. I recognize myself a little in Doris Lessing, who wasn't very good at personal relations — so she said. I've certainly tried, and I've been married three times. It's hard to get a sense of family, hard to get a sense of home — not impossible. It was done, but I notice, with most people, it comes very naturally and very strongly. I've done a lot of travelling as part of my work, and I've certainly always enjoyed it very much. What I did notice was that other people usually are very keen to get home. I wasn't.

SW: Have you ever truly felt at home anywhere, Lister?

LS: Oh, yes. I was at university in Vancouver, and I knew when I arrived in Vancouver that I had come home. For the first time in my life, I really felt at home, and that was among the mists and the beautiful scent of the woods and Emily Carr country, essentially, and it was certainly like that then.

I was very keen on learning stuff. I was anxious to find out about everything. One of the things I thought I should find out about was music, and it seemed to me that one of the ways to find out about music was to put on the radio. I would listen to it or let it go on in the room, anyway. Sometimes, things would seem more or less nice, then suddenly a little tune walked right out of the radio and followed me home. It clung to my heart, and it has never let go. It was Mozart. I didn't know it was Mozart. I went to some trouble to find out what on earth it was, this incredible tune, which has childlike simplicity about it, but it is the simplicity of great wisdom. It's childlike but not childish, and so, it's the kind of wisdom in which you've been through all that and come out the other side. It's a little phrase in the slow movement of the Haffner Symphony. I've heard that and loved it for sixty years, and it has never got stale. It's always fresh, because…Mozart put it very neatly himself — he tried to write music for *amateurs*, meaning people who love it, and *connoisseurs*, meaning people who know about it. And if you know what you're doing, you can manage to do it for both, and that's very important. It's very important because it means that what the music is doing is amplifying whatever emotions and perceptions you bring to it.

SW: What do you mean by "amplify"?

LS: That, whatever emotions or perceptions or feelings or thoughts you bring to it, the music will intensify for you. As you get older, as you get perhaps wiser, or sometimes as you've suffered more or even enjoyed more, you always keep bringing something different to the party. That's why time goes on and these pieces of music sound forever fresh, forever different. But that sense of amplification — amplifying ideas and emotions — all the arts do that, but music does it the most, and that, I think, is because music, of all the arts, is the only one that is truly moving. I mean physically moving. It's picking up the natural rhythms of the body, whether you intend it to or not.

I say I'm serious about these things, and I'm serious because I take them personally. I was encouraged to take them personally by Bernard Shaw, whom I never met, unfortunately, but close friends of mine met him and knew him very well indeed. He is far and away the greatest critic in both music and drama, and his criticisms, now well over a hundred years old, still read fresh and evergreen and totally unbitter. And that's important because Shaw had a very tough time of it. He was a failure for the first thirty-five, forty years of his life. His mother supported him while he was trying to write novels. He says very amusing things about all this, but at his own expense, not at other people's. He says, for example, "My first novel was named with shattering irony *Immaturity*, and when I dug out the manuscript, I found it was half-eaten by mice. Even the mice couldn't finish it."

SW: You said that Shaw taught you to take these things personally. What do you mean, "personally"?

LS: Sometimes, when Shaw wrote reviews, people would say, "That's just your personal opinion. I don't want to hear your personal opinion. I want to hear what it was really like." Well, come on — it's the guy's personal opinion. And Shaw used to reply, saying, "Do I take it personally? I certainly do take it personally. If it's a bad performance, I take it personally, and the only way I will let the guy off the hook is if I hear a good performance, then I'll relent." Taking it personally is something you have to do, and without being malicious or malevolent or jealous or envious, and Shaw managed to do all those things. He was always very generous and open-hearted.

SW: Why do you have to take it personally?

LS: Because if you're not taking it personally, you're not allowing it to reach the inside of your being. You're not allowing it to reach that centre of thoughts, emotions, perceptions, all those things that Goethe had: the rational, intuitive, sensual, judgmental. If you can allow art — life, in fact — to reach all four of those things, you're going to take things personally. And if you're taking care not to take them personally, you're shutting something out.

SW: What did you learn from Shaw?

LS: I think I learned two things. Shaw wrote plays with a very powerful sense of craft. They're very well written. They're very easy to deliver. If they're done right, it's not hard. He is on your side. He is always on the side of the actor. He talks about plays sometimes as being a little like operas. An opera, among other things, should be an exhibition of singing, and a play, among other things, should be an exhibition of acting, and that's very nice. There should be opportunities for the actors to act, and, of course, good actors are acting all the time, but they are looking for these opportunities, and one of the things that Shaw does is offer theatrical flourishes.

SW: It would seem to me that really good actors act as if they're not acting.

LS: That's certainly true. That's a certain kind of acting and very important and very telling. Dr. Johnson tells a story about his great friend David Garrick, who was the greatest actor of his day in both comedy and tragedy. Someone persuaded a countryman — a country squire who had never been to the theatre and was a kind of Colonel Blimpish person, evidently — to go to the theatre and see Garrick performing Hamlet. So the poor, old chap was hauled in and sat in front of *Hamlet*. And when it was all over, his friend said, "What did you think of it?" And he said, "Oh, it's very exciting. It's very, very good." "What do you think of the acting?" "Oh, the acting was marvellous. The king, what a wonderful actor he was. It was so impressive. And the queen, she was so powerful. And that old chap who's the advisor, what a wonderful actor..." And he went on through the whole cast, but leaving out Hamlet. Finally, someone said, "Yeah, but what about Hamlet, which Garrick was playing?" And the old chap said, "Oh, Hamlet, yes, I felt so sorry for him. He was so unhappy and depressed and so brave, and you couldn't help feeling very sorry for him in this terrible situation." There's no acting. And, in fact, Garrick was famous for this. One of Garrick's friends wrote a series of little poems. They'd all been drinking at a party, and they all fell asleep at the table drunk on port, and this guy wrote little epitaphs on them, and one of them was on Garrick, and it said, "On the stage, he was natural and quite unaffecting. 'Twas only when he was off that he was acting."

SW: So Shaw gives actors the opportunity to act.

LS: Yes. And Shaw is also always on the side of the victim. He does not speak for the rich and the powerful. Shaw is always speaking truth to power, which is so hard to do and so important to do.

I'm a bit weary of Filosophy, with a capital F, if that's how you spell it, because it tends to be somewhat pompous and unreal and often in an ivory tower, or sometimes when we're deliberately trying to be down to earth, you feel you're in an ivory gutter. Bertrand Russell was a man I had a lot to do with — his work, I should say; I never met him. He was an ancient philosopher when I was young. He died in 1970 as a very, very old man. And Russell, as a philosopher, didn't sound at all like a professor of philosophy. He wrote a big fat book called *A History of Western Philosophy*, and the example he starts with right off the top — I'm remembering this, and it may be a little bit of creative quotation, but it's not very far from it — is about Thales, the father of philosophy. Russell says that students of philosophy often find it difficult to give the subject the respect they think it deserves when they discover that Thales, the father of philosophy, thought that everything was made of water. This is especially difficult for modern students, who know for sure that everything is made of electricity. As distinct from Thales' "thought it," our guys know for sure — so he's taking no prisoners. At one time, electricity was a great puzzle, and there are many stories that catch exactly that flavour and particular sense of fascinated puzzlement.

There's a story that Lord Kelvin, a very great scientist, was busy lecturing away, and he noticed that one of the students had fallen asleep. Kelvin says, "Mr. Smith," and the poor guy wakes up. "Yes, sir?" And Kelvin says, "Mr. Smith, what is electricity?" And poor Smith says, "I'm sorry, sir. I've forgotten." And Kelvin says, "The one man in the universe who knows what electricity is, and he's forgotten." So there's a lot of that stuff going around, and it's nice because some of these guys are really quite pleasant cut-ups — Russell certainly was. Russell was interested in everything. He was a very political person. He was an atheist and got into a lot of trouble over it. Someone once denounced him for being an atheist, saying, "What are you going to say, Russell, when you die and God says to you, 'Now then, Russell, you didn't believe in Me. What do you have to say?'" And Russell said, "I should reply, 'Well, sir, You know even better than I do that the evidence was not sufficient.'" That's taking no prisoners, and Russell is like that all the time. He had a very clear, bright way of talking, of writing. To me, it's very important that Russell won the Nobel Prize for literature. He won the Nobel Prize because he wrote so well, and his style is so firm and deliberate and powerful. He said that all writing should be as simple as possible, and by "simple," Russell meant, not that everything should be immediately intelligible to a twelve-year-old, but that the difficulties, if any, should arise from the subject and not from the author. You only have to read any sort of solemn book, solemn rather than serious, and find it loaded with puzzling footnotes. And then, in academia, you get this sense that the guys are exchanging footnotes, that a sort of footnote duel is going on: footnotes at dawn, coffee for one — that kind of thing. And Russell didn't like that.

SW: What did you learn from Russell?

LS: I learned from Russell what the "good life" should be, and once again he weighed every word very carefully. Russell thought that the good life should be what we try to do. That's very important, because you're not going to succeed. You should try and you should be ready to keep on trying. You pick yourself up and try again. You don't say, "Well, I tried. Off the path is off the path. Let's forget it." No. What you should try to do is to live a life that is motivated by love and guided by reason. Reason doesn't motivate you. It's the emotions that motivate you. And by "love," Russell means the positive emotions, the emotions that speak of compassion and tenderness and closeness and sharing. Things of that kind are motivated by love and guided by reason. And by "reason," he meant you should think about it a little bit as well. You should think about your feelings, just as we were saying, and you should get feelings about your thoughts.

SW: Why does that speak to you so deeply?

LS: Because I think it's true, and I think it works. And when I succeed in doing it, it works, and when I see other people doing it, it works for them. We can't get away from the fact that we're animals. That's very important. Darwin certainly showed us that. You can't repudiate it. We bear the indelible marks of our lowly origin. And one of the things that animals go in for very powerfully, as they must for survival, is self-interest. You cannot avoid self-interest. But what you can do, perhaps, is get hold of enlightened self-interest, the self-interest that will be helpful both to you and to the rest of humanity and to the rest of the world, for that matter, and that's very important. That's guided by reason.

SW: Why do you not think that the good life should be guided by love?

LS: Because the emotions don't guide you, as a rule. The emotions motivate you. The emotions tell you where to go. How to get there in a way which is not clumsy and, above all, does not inflict unnecessary pain — one of the things about the emotions is that they do inflict pain on others and on oneself also, of course. Russell was involved in many passionate personal relationships, as he called them, and something which I would value very highly also, and they're very often painful. It's very difficult not to be painful. As Shakespeare so wonderfully said, "Ruin has taught me thus to ruminate that time will come and take my love away." All love ends unhappily. Either the love itself disappears or one or the other of the lovers disappears. Love is the motivation, but how do you manage to love your children in such a way as to give them roots and wings, but without smothering them? It's very hard to love your children so that you can teach them to leave, to do without you, and yet so that they can perhaps pick up some of the values, motivations, and guidelines that you want so that the kids are themselves motivated by love and guided by reason in their way? Because it has to be done in your own way. You can know things with other people's knowledge; you can't be wise with other people's wisdom. You have to form your own wisdom, and you have to just keep living as hard as possible. I'm certainly living full blast, as hard as possible, and I don't know what I'll be when I grow up.

SW: You said that Russell taught you about the nature of the good life. Have you had a good life?

LS: That's not the same question. Have I had a good life? Have I been fortunate in all kinds of things? And the answer is, yes, I've been very lucky. Lots of nice things have happened. Have I led a good life? That's not quite the same thing. I've tried to lead a good life. I've tried to lead a life which is motivated by love and guided by reason, and sometimes I've succeeded and sometimes I've disastrously failed. At the same time, I've always picked myself up and tried again.

SW: What's given you the most pleasure?

LS: I would say it's a combination of things. It's a little structure. It's a little pattern, and it's the pattern of passionate personal relationships framed in nature and in the arts and of the arts, especially music framed in nature and passionate personal relationships. By "nature," I mean everything that's out there: the world of nature, the world of the birds... It's not all things bright and beautiful; it's also all the nasty things — they're in there, too. And that's the importance of the dance of the Hopi, the rattlesnake dance, which, in a sense, is showing the value of the rattlesnake. Any fool can see that a deer is worthwhile. Can you really feel that a rattlesnake is? That's the importance of feeling empathy with nature.

SW: What's the most important thing that you've learned, Lister?

LS: Connect and don't despair. That's very hard sometimes. If you get depressed... I've been very depressed, but I've never despaired. I've had a serious depression, but not the kind that completely loses touch. There are depressions that are much worse than mine, and you do in fact lose touch completely. It's a terrible illness, there's no question about that. Fortunately, I've not had that illness. It was bad enough for me. I could handle it. Just.

SW: "Connect and don't despair." Connect with what?

LS: Connect with everything that you perceive as worthwhile. Perceive, which means that you feel it, and you think about it, and you judge it. All those things have to be put into the mix. By looking for them, you are, in fact, connecting. It is really not proper, not appropriate, to say, "I now perceive that this is very important, and I think about that, and intuition tells me that, but I'm going to leave it alone." That you can't do and you mustn't do. You can do it easily enough, but what you've now done is deliberately cut away a big chunk of yourself and thrown it in the garbage. You have to connect with it. You have to see that it's all part of you, all part of us.

SW: Are you still learning?

LS: Yes, all the time — no question about that. I'm still learning and I still spend my time with my eyes open in amazement and astonishment, and I'm pedalling as hard as I can all the time. Stop pedalling, and you fall off. I don't wish to fall off. I don't wish to rust out. I don't mind wearing out. Wear out, yes. Rust out, no.

The Culture of Society

TWO

Radical Imperfection

JOHN GRAY

Modern politics is a chapter in the history of religion. So says British author, John Gray. No, John Gray isn't talking about the so-called War on Terror or the fight against religious fundamentalism. He's talking about much of what we think of as political activity. In his opinion, modern politics operates with the same fervour and the same impulse that feeds religious experience. John Gray is Emeritus Professor of European thought at the London School of Economics. He also writes sharp and trenchant journalistic pieces for the New Statesman, The Guardian, *and other publications. Among his books are* Straw Dogs, Heresies, *and his most recent,* Black Mass: Apocalyptic Religion and the Death of Utopia. *One profile of him in* The Guardian *was titled "The Contrarian." This interview with John Gray was broadcast on* Ideas *on 7 January 2008*

PAUL KENNEDY

Do you like the term "contrarian"?

JOHN GRAY

Well, it captures a feature of the way I've thought throughout the years, which has typically been critical of the prevailing consensus. But, in fact, I rather prefer to think of myself as a realist, as one who attempts to think as clearly as I can about the actual condition of the world at any particular time. And that means that I've normally been in opposition to the prevailing consensus of the time.

PK: Let me read from the first paragraph of *Black Mass*. I think this is going to give us a chance to talk about what you think about politics, and religion, and, I guess, history. You say the greatest of the revolutionary upheavals that have shaped so much of the history of the past two centuries were episodes in the history of faith. Can you tell us a little bit about what you meant when you said that?

JG: Well, of course, a common view of the last two centuries is that it's been dominated by the long, sometimes slow, sometimes rapid retreat of religion. A common view is that the world as a whole, or at least large part of it — parts of Europe, for example — have been dominated by new movements of ideas and new political movements which were secular, which rejected religion, put it behind them. And, of course, there were large intellectual movements in Europe going back to the eighteenth century, often called Enlightenment movements, the most radical of which saw themselves as rejecting the religious inheritance of the West entirely.

But my view is that, in fact, what happened was not that the central beliefs of Christianity disappeared altogether. The formal beliefs did. That's to say, French Jacobins or Russian Bolsheviks didn't accept any of the tenets of Christianity or Judaism, say. They were, in that sense, anti-religious. But, although they rejected the explicit beliefs of Western religion, I think they continued to have their thinking shaped by myths, which they'd inherited from Western religion. And among those myths was a view of history as a kind of a single, continuous narrative. But not only a narrative, which might even have an end — it's also a story of redemption and consummation at the end. That's to say, history is seen as not just a pattern of events, partly random, partly fated, as perhaps it was by the ancient Greeks, but as a narrative, a story of moral redemption, of a conflict between good and evil in which, in the end, evil can be defeated and good can prevail.

And that's a distinctively religious view. It comes from Christianity, above all, but it goes back even before Christianity — I think ultimately probably to Zoroastrianism. Zoroaster seems to have been the first religious prophet who saw a struggle of good and evil in the world which good could actually finally win. Other cultures had seen conflict between light and dark, good and bad, as being central in the world, but they thought that these conflicts were recurrent and cyclical, that they simply went on. And neither side actually ultimately prevailed.

From Zoroaster onwards, there were a whole series of apocalyptic myths, myths of final conflict, final redemption, often myths of titanic war and violence, followed by an end of the world or an end of history and a new world in which all of the old evils had been abolished. Those types of myths gained hold in Western religion. And what happened in the eighteenth century, and in the nineteenth century, and the twentieth century, I think, was not what many social scientists and most political theorists and perhaps even now most people think, which is that these myths were ditched, abandoned, given up. Rather, these myths were recycled, they reappeared as the central idea in modern radical secular thought. So, you constantly find in Marx, for example, in the nineteenth century that he talks about the end of history. That's an idea that was actually unknown among the ancient Greeks, the ancient Romans, the ancient Chinese, or the ancient Indians. It's an idea which comes straight from Western religion. It's a religious idea.

And the communist movements of the twentieth century were a reaction to particular local situations. The Bolsheviks would never have come to power in Russia when they did if it hadn't been for the First World War, for example, and for a number of other factors. But they were nevertheless animated by secular versions of these myths. In other words, they said humanity can bring about an end to history. There'll be no more states, there'll be no more war, there'll be no more poverty, there'll be no more power structures. Sometimes, they said there'd be no more family life, there'd be no more of any of the central institutions and practices that featured in human life up to that point. There'd be a wholly new condition of human affairs. Now, of course, that didn't happen.

What happened was what always happens when one of these radically utopian movements gains power: history went on as before, but with much more blood, with much more human sorrow, needless death, conflict, famine, and terror. That's what happened in the former Soviet Union. This, of course, is another major part of my new book. When I wrote during the Cold War period, I'd been a rather uncompromising anti-communist. I don't regret that. I opposed communism then as an immensely humanly costly and destructive utopian project. But when communism collapsed, that was a great gain for human freedom. Unfortunately, it was immediately replaced in the West by another utopian project: not world communism but a global free market. In Russia and everywhere else, we were told by Francis Fukuyama and by many Western politicians, the same type of market economy, the same type of what they call democratic capitalism was coming about all over the world. I think I published one of the very first critical attacks on Francis Fukuyama's article, which appeared in August of 1989. I published it in October. I argued that history hadn't ended. History doesn't end. It just goes on. What had happened instead was that a large totalitarian system had collapsed. And when that happened, what one would expect would not be a new world dominated by a new, single, utopian system — global capitalism. You would expect the traditional conflicts of history to be resumed — that's to say, ethnic and national conflicts, conflicts between religions and conflicts between states over the control of natural resources. That's what I argued in late 1989.

And that was considered terribly pessimistic, as is often the case with what I write. But I didn't see it as being terribly pessimistic. I saw it as being the normal, predictable result of the collapse of a great totalitarian structure, the normal and predictable course of history. And broadly speaking, that's what happened.

PK: You said at the very beginning that you would characterize yourself as a realist rather than a contrarian. I mean, you're just looking at the world and seeing the facts as they are, not as people would like them to be.

JG: That's right. I think the oddity of the late twentieth century and the start of the twenty-first century is that unrealistic and utopian patterns of thinking spread into the democracies, spread into liberal societies, and even gained power in the form of neo-conservative policies for what they called global democratic revolution, which have been in power in the Bush Administration for some time in the United States. In the past, in the nineteenth century and the twentieth century, these kinds of utopian patterns would have led to the idea that a huge revolution in many parts of the world could bring about an entirely different world from one that had ever existed in the past — one in which the traditional conflicts I mentioned earlier, ethnic and national conflicts, conflicts within religions, and conflicts over natural resources would all be swept away. That idea had really been confined to the extremes of politics. It was mainly found on the far Left, among communists and anarchists, and it was mainly embodied in dictatorial and totalitarian regimes.

And many people thought that when communism collapsed, that would be the end of that kind of utopianism. But it wasn't. In fact, what happened was that very similar types of ideas began to animate foreign policy in the United States and in Britain. Thatcher, whom I had supported throughout most of the eighties when she was pursuing a necessary set of policies to deal with Britain's long economic decline, towards the end of the eighties began to see herself as the leader of a kind of global movement of market capitalism, which could prevail everywhere. And, of course, that view is also very strong in the United States and was theorized by Fukuyama, although Thatcher herself never subscribed to simple ideas of the end of history.

In its strongest form, a kind of utopian project of the Right was most clearly embodied in the war in Iraq, which, of course, had many other causes. It was in part a geopolitical strategy and still is. It was in part an oil war. There's no doubt about that. But even as an oil war, even as an exercise in geopolitics, the Iraq war, it seems to me, was utopian because there wasn't any way of securing control over Iraqi natural resources by regime change and installing some new type of democracy. Because the predictable result of doing what was done when the invasion occurred was that the Iraqi state was broken up. The Kurds have seceded. There is no state of Iraq anymore. The state that the British founded in the 1920s, which survived for almost eighty years, even throughout Saddam's dictatorship, is no more. It has ceased to exist. And within what remains of Iraq, there is an intractable conflict between different sectarian groupings, and also over control of the country's oil reserves, as a consequence of which oil production is dramatically down. And far from being the case, as Paul Wolfowitz predicted before the war, that the war would be self-financing because the price of oil would collapse to $20 or less, it's now around $100 and still rising. And part of the reason for that — only a part, but still an important part — is the colossal but predictable failure of that utopian project in Iraq.

So, a large part of the book's subject matter about the late twentieth century is the way in which utopian projects in politics, whose roots were ultimately religious but which had been expressed in secular forms in the nineteenth and twentieth centuries, mostly on the far Left, moved to the Right. Not the fascist or the anti-democratic Right but the neo-conservative and so-to-speak liberal Right. And they weren't recognized as utopian projects.

In fact, one of the striking features of utopianism today is that it never thinks of itself as utopian, and it's hard to recognize as being utopian until you start to pay the price, until [we see] the actual consequences of launching projects which are unrealizable. I mean, a utopian project is one that's either inherently impossible, like communism, or one that is known to be unrealizable in any circumstances which we can reasonable foresee. And that was true, for example, of the Western project of installing an American-style market economy in post-communist Russia. It was impossible — could be known to be impossible, and yet it went ahead and then failed. And now we have a completely different type of regime in Russia, wholly different from anything that anyone in the West anticipated or wanted.

Similarly, what's emerged in post-Saddam Iraq is not a secular, liberal democracy on an American model, but a mixture of popular theocracy, more or less on the Iranian model, and a kind of elective, theocratic regime and anarchy, and the break-up of the state. In other words, pretty much the opposite of what those who launched these projects intended. But then, again, that's always what happens in utopian experiments. If the experiment is persisted in, what happens is not only a lot of human suffering, but also a lot of violence and bloodshed, sometimes on a vast scale as was the case in communist Russia or in Maoist China, and now the scale is rising pretty high in Iraq, too — perhaps six or seven hundred thousand war-related casualties and millions of refugees. They're terrible human costs, of course. Hence my strong opposition to utopianism in politics in all of its forms. But also, normally, the results of the utopian project are the opposite, not just different, but in many respects the opposite of what those who launch it intend. And that's happened again.

So the virus of utopianism hasn't yet been exorcised. It may be that Iraq will set it back for some time.

PK: Have you ever been attracted by a utopia?

JG: That's a very good question. I don't think I ever have been. I mean, some people have looked at what they see as my changes of viewpoint over the years, and they've said, "Well, he used to believe in Thatcherism and then he stopped believing in it." But I never believed in Thatcherism in the way that Thatcherite ideologues did. I first started to support the main policies that Thatcher was then associated with immediately after she became the leader of the Conservative Party in 1975. In other words, right at the beginning, before she even came to power in 1979. And even in 1979, it's worth remembering that privatization, which subsequently became part of her Thatcherite ideology, wasn't even mentioned in the election manifesto that Thatcher put before the British voters in 1979. Policies at that time were mainly about dealing with excessive trade union power, a serious issue, a major issue, which Labour had proved unable to deal with. And for me, Thatcherism in its earlier form was what politics always is — that's to say, it was a modest expedient for dealing with the evils of the time.

It should be mentioned, however, that Thatcher was a strong anti-communist, as I was then, and that was also part of Thatcherism, a central feature of it, and that I supported right through really to the end of the Cold War. To my mind, politics is the art of the possible. At its best, politics is shabby. At its best, it's dealing with compromises and partial solutions to insoluble human problems. Compromise isn't always possible. The Second World War is a good example. The evil of Nazism couldn't be compromised with. It had to be eradicated. So compromise isn't always possible. But one should embark on large wars, which are great human evils, only when confronted with major evil that can be dealt with in no other way. One should not use war, or systematic violence, or terror, as a means of improving the human lot, as a means of perfecting human beings or promoting social progress.

PK: It almost sounds as though you're characterizing politics as the opposite of religion, as something that stands completely on the other side of the spectrum, something that is not absolute, something that is not complete, and does not provide all the safe and easy answers.

JG: I think that's a very perceptive way of summarizing my view. How does politics differ from religion, in my view? Well, first of all, politics is not about human salvation. Human salvation is pursued by religious believers in their prayers, in their congregations, in their churches, and synagogues, and mosques, and temples, and elsewhere. They pursue some kind of resolution of the underlying dilemmas of human life. They pursue salvation. And what happened really with the French Jacobins in the late eighteenth century and onwards was that a project of salvation entered into politics and to my mind corrupted and damaged politics. Politics shouldn't be about salvation.

What politics is about is responding skilfully to the challenges of events, responding to the flux of historical change, and, I would say, preserving and sometimes extending the essential elements of civilization, if you like. I don't mean in a missionary way. I mean hanging on to and, as I say, sometimes extending the main practices and elements of a civilized form of life.

And, of course, according to the way in which that's done, even the patterns of civilization will differ to some extent in different places and different times. There are universal human values — I'm not an out-and-out relativist. There are certain goods that are good for all human beings. Even more, there are certain evils that are bad for all human beings. No one wants to be tortured, separated from their family, suffer persecution or humiliation, be the victims of pogroms and other types of persecution and violence. But that doesn't mean to say that there's going to be a universal civilization, or universal system, or even a universal morality, because those universal values, universal goods, universal evils, which all human beings experience, conflict with each other. Sometimes we can only have peace as a result of war.

PK: Are there no universal values? I mean, what about the drive towards the end of slavery, for example. Is this not something that everybody can jump on the bandwagon for and say, yes, this is good?

JG: Well, yes. But, of course, what typically happens, and did happen in the twentieth century, is that, after the abolition of slavery in most of the world in the nineteenth century, the twentieth century was a time of unparalleled slavery. Of course, it wasn't called slavery. In the Soviet Union, it was called socialist construction. In Maoist China, it was called something similar. In both cases, there was a vast Gulag of slave workers. And, of course, Hitler had his policy of *Lebensraum*, which involved the extermination of Jews and others, but also the enslavement of large parts of the peoples of Eastern Europe. Many of them simply became slaves in all but name. So, while, of course, slavery is a universal evil, we can agree that it should be abolished.

In fact, what very often happens with evils of that magnitude is that they're not abolished. They're abolished in parts of the world, and that is a change for the better, but they recur under different names. This has happened quite recently, in my view, with torture. I had always supported and still support the prohibition of torture. I think torture is a degrading practise. It's not only hideous for the victims, but it corrupts those who practise it and the societies that sanction it. So I've always supported the prohibition on torture. However, what's now apparent is that the definition of torture has been fudged and shifted so that a practice which, for example, in the Second World War was categorically regarded as torture, like water boarding — which resulted in the Japanese who practised it being given fifteen years hard labour — is now regarded as not necessarily torture. It's simply a rather assertive form of interrogation, although it often ends in death. So that's an example of a torture that has come back, if you like. It's even being to some extent legally and morally renormalized, but under a different name.

That's one of the differences between ethics and politics on the one hand and science and technology on the other hand. In science and technology, you have cumulative and nowadays certainly irreversible advance or, if you like, progress. We're not going to go back to alchemy. Whatever the creationists say, Darwin's Theory of Natural Selection isn't going to be dumped and replaced by ideas about divine creation. Science and technology are inherently progressive enterprises in that the gains which are made are real gains. Ethics and politics aren't like that. As I've said, there are universal human values. Genocide's always a great evil. I think torture and slavery are always great evils. So they're always to be struggled against. But typically, what is gained in one generation or one part of the world is lost in another, and what's gained is normally lost. And certainly, the advances that are made are often reversible, as with torture — the relaxation of the prohibition of torture has happened almost in the blink of an eye.

That leads me to one of the features of my views that is hardest for many people to accept: my rejection of conventional ideas of progress. Conventional ideas of progress don't just say what we all think, which is that some societies are better than others, some practices are worse than others. There are genuine improvements. Ideas of progress say that these kinds of improvements can be cumulative, that the whole human species is somehow advancing and getting to a better condition than it had been in before — maybe better than any part of it ever had before. I think that's just a myth that comes from religion. It comes from the idea of human history as a single, continuous narrative of redemption for the species as a whole — in other words, a kind of narrative of salvation. And I am more than skeptical about such ideas. I think when wrenched out of their context of religious faith, they're... harmful.

PK: You really do not believe in progress.

JG: No.

PK: You believe that the world is, if anything, no further ahead than it ever was.

JG: Well, if you don't believe in progress, it doesn't mean you can't believe that there are any situations better than any others. After all, the ancient Greeks didn't believe in progress, the ancient Romans didn't, the ancient Jews didn't, the ancient Indians and Chinese didn't. But they all knew and understood that anarchy, warring states, was much worse than a reasonable government. And they all understood that it's better to live a long, peaceful life than have your life end in violence.

PK: There's a strange irony that we are entering a new dark age, almost, because we are living with a kind of world view that is more medieval than was the medieval world. I mean, we have a system of beliefs that is so successful we don't understand that it's belief anymore. We think of it as knowledge.

JG: I think that's it. We think we have fact when what we have is myth. We talk about the myths of other cultures or about the myths of past societies, but we never consider the possibility that our beliefs are also mythical. And I'm not speaking as a relativist here, because I do think there's a truth of the matter. I actually think that some of the pre-modern systems of thought, such as elements of traditional religion — not that we should go back to them — are closer to the truth about human beings than modern thinking. I mean, the idea that humans are imperfectible is closer to the truth, even if it's expressed in mythical form. If my way of thinking remains very controversial, it's because many of those who are very critical of it don't accept, can't accept, and won't even entertain the possibility that their fundamental beliefs about the world — for example, ideas of progress — are myths and, if I'm right, rather shallow myths.

I don't think it's ever possible, actually, or even desirable, conceivably, for human thought to proceed without myths. But some myths are truer than others. Not in the sense of being better scientific theories — myths aren't scientific theories, they're stories or images which represent the world and our place in it to ourselves. And they can be deep myths, like the Genesis myth in the Bible. I think it is a deep myth. Or they can be shallow myths, by which I mean ones which really don't capture enduring features of the human situation, such as the idea of progress. Even shallow myths can be useful. Maybe, in the past, the shallow myth of progress was useful. It motivated the activists who first got engaged in the movement to prohibit torture. But I think its utility has diminished, because the costs and the dangers of large-scale interventions by powerful states are imbued by those myths.

The world is smaller, there are more human beings in it, and the military and technical might available to large states in promoting their goals is just so much greater. So these myths of progress, shallow as they are, might once have been useful but are now harmful. And that's one of the reasons I'm as relentlessly skeptical and critical of them as I am. I'm a skeptic in matters of religion; I don't belong to any religion. I simply try and see the world as clearly as I can. But in doing that, I find that my view of human beings in many ways reflects some of the features of the way human beings are seen in the great religions. It's a feature of pretty well all the great religions of humanity, to see humans as being in some deep sense a flawed species. That's to say, they see humans as eternally conflicted and as being imperfectible — as having certain defects and contradictions within themselves which can't really be resolved. And we find that in the myths the Hebrew Bible as well as in Christianity. We also find it in ancient Greek myth — the myths of Prometheus and Icarus, for example — and, of course, in non-Western religion, such as Buddhism, which has an idea of fundamental human ignorance, that there is some sort of deep distortion in the way humans think of themselves and think of the world.

So, one of the ways in which I view the world is that humans are like this. Humans are radically imperfect, humans are a flawed species. This is seen nowadays as pessimistic or even misanthropic, but it was the orthodox view up to about 1800. Everyone thought like this in one way or another. Christianity did, Buddhism did, most the world's great religions did. Pretty well all of the great myths of human civilization had within them some idea of the inherently flawed character of human beings.

PK: Why did people suddenly start thinking that they could be perfected? Why did people come to believe in utopia?

JG: It's a very interesting question, but obviously a very complicated one to answer. Part of the answer is that a part of the religious myth of Western civilization — whereby God or His son, God or His agent, could transform the world and history and create an entirely new and almost unimaginably better world — was secularized. That's to say, part of it was wrenched out of its religious context, and it came to be believed that humanity could do what God had done in the past — to my mind, a belief or, if you like, a myth more absurd, more unbelievable, more incredible, more fantastical than anything in traditional religion. We humans know about our history. We know all the follies and disasters which history contains. The idea that humanity could act as a single agent, as a conscious agent with purposes, when what in fact exists is not humanity but simply millions upon millions of different human beings with desperate and changing needs, illusions, and frailties — that humans could bring about such a radically better world — that's impossible.

Humans really began to feel rather god-like, or had the illusion of being rather god-like. That's to say, they acquired powers over nature and even over each other through the growth of scientific knowledge that they'd never had before. They multiplied in numbers. They live longer now and are, at least for the time being, richer than they've ever been. So the last two hundred years has been a period of an enormous expansion of human power rooted in the expansion of human knowledge. So that's partly it.

Of course, feeling god-like is an illusion, because the growth of knowledge confers ever greater power on humans, but it doesn't make humans any more reasonable, or less savage or destructive. I mean, humans use the expanded power given to them by their expanding knowledge to pursue whatever objectives seem important to them. And they may be objectives of genocide as well as of alleviating hunger or disease. They may be objectives of war and oppression as well as objectives of enhancing freedom or making human life more comfortable. Humans simply use their growing power and their growing knowledge to do whatever it is that they want to do.

Then again, the conflicts among human needs, among human impulses, have been noted by all the great world religions and also perceived by great secular thinkers like Sigmund Freud, perhaps the greatest secular thinker of the twentieth century, who argued that humans not only have an impulse for Eros, for love or creation, but also an impulse for Thanatos, for death and destruction. He thought of that as a scientific theory. It obviously isn't this sort of secular myth, but a rather illuminating one, because what it captures is the inwardly torn, conflicted character of human beings. It was once human orthodoxy to think like that about ourselves, but now it's tremendously unpopular. It's seen as a form of pessimism or even of misanthropy when, for most of the human species until very recently, it was just common sense. And I think the reason that it was common sense is that it's evidently true.

PK: Is there any way, though, that one can look at utopian projects
or idealistic political goals as things that are worthwhile? You talked
earlier about slavery and about torture, but what about Iraq or
Yugoslavia, for example? What about, right now, Darfur? What do
we do about the places in the world where humans intervene, perhaps
idealistically or even motivated by utopian thoughts of making the
world a better place for all people to live in? Are those projects that
must be abandoned because they're just foolhardy and don't understand human nature?

JG: Well, these projects of intervention are more dangerous than
they were before because the collateral damage they inflict is greater
than before. The weapons that are now available, the conventional
weaponries which were used in shock-and-awe tactics, for example
— the scale and magnitude of the machinery we have at our disposal
for intervention are greater than before. So the costs, as it were, are
potentially larger. The costs are, in the case of Iraq, the destruction
of a large, modern state. Now, it was a tyrannical state, of course.
It was a despotic state which had done terrible things, but I think if
you were a woman in Iraq now, if you were a Christian, if you were
gay, if you belonged to one of the religious minorities such as the
Mandaeans or the Yezidi, you'd be far more at risk in terms of your
well-being and your life than you were under Saddam. And once
you've destroyed a state that way — since the human skills involved
in ruling such a society no longer exist and its colonialism has been
rightly, no doubt, discredited — what you simply have in Iraq is
a state of anarchy which will persist probably for decades, maybe
even for generations. So that's a terribly high cost of well-meaning
intervention, just as a terribly high cost was inflicted on Russia by
the Bolshevik Revolution, in China, and in other parts of the world
where utopian movements gained power.

PK: But what about places like Darfur, for example, where there
is a genocide going on, and the world is watching, and nobody is
stepping in to prevent it or to stop it?

JG: Well, is the world ready to enhance the troops that are already there to the point at which it can be prevented and to keep them there indefinitely? Of course, that involves taking sides in complicated, often multi-sided civil wars. It may involve changing the existing regime in that country and perhaps in neighbouring countries. Is the world ready to do that? And what does "the world" mean anymore? I think at the back of this idea of liberal intervention there is a neo-colonial understanding of the world in the following sense. What should we do, we say, about this? Well, "we" means America and possibly Europe, Canada, and so on. But the world now is very rapidly changing. For example, the main donor in Africa isn't the World Bank or any Western country or probably not even all the Western countries put together, but China. China is an enormously important factor in international relations and world politics. The Chinese are not going to intervene for that purpose. They may not even support intervention for the purposes that have been given. So, this idea that "we" — meaning America, meaning Canada, meaning Europe — should go around intervening in the world to alleviate these circumstances reflects a picture of the balance of world power that is really out of date. It's a sort of faded neo-colonial conception of Western responsibility.

But the other point is, humanitarian aid is important. Where it can be given it certainly should be, and it should be open handed. But the idea of humanitarian intervention which is now being pro-moted by some people in North America and Europe and Canada, is not a matter of going in — as is perfectly legitimate and, indeed, I would even say humanly obligatory — to alleviate suffering where it exists. It's a type of humanitarian intervention which transforms the entire society, transforms the state in which these human evils exist, changes it into something better. That's extremely difficult to do, and there are very few examples — I don't say none — but very few examples where it's been successful. And it always carries great risk.

Think of a different example, motivated to begin with by the War on Terror, the invasion of Afghanistan. Now, I supported that inva-sion at the time, and I think it had achievable goals at the time. The goals were, to begin with, related to the War on Terror. There were goals about closing down the terrorist training camps and getting rid of the Taliban regime, which was not an indigenous Afghan regime. It persecuted many aspects of the traditional life and indigenous cultures of Afghanistan. It was a regime really imported from elsewhere, funded in other countries, so I think getting rid of it was good. I'm not adamantly opposed to all forms of military intervention.

But, then, after the Afghan invasion, we had Iraq. And Iraq has sucked away resources and it's also reinforced Islamist movements in many parts of the world, and it's made it much harder to do anything successfully in Afghanistan. What does it mean in, say, the context of Afghanistan to have a systematic humanitarian intervention? The Taliban are back in control of probably more than half the country now. If you're going to get rid of them, how are you going to do that? You're going to wage an unending war? How is that going to be done? Now, the Taliban, of course, are an appalling regime, but there is a view emerging in Britain that the war can't be won, but also that it's important that it not be lost. So, in the end, what will have to be done is some kind of bargaining with the large parts of Afghanistan which remain outside of control of the Afghan government or even of any government.

PK: So you're basically pushing an argument that we should be more modest in our ambitions. If we are to intervene, regime change is certainly something we should not be interested in. But we should be interested in mediated humanitarian improvements.

JG: Yes. But we should try to detach them from world-transforming schemes, try to detach them from the idea that, by the use of military or other types of power, some states in the world, the West, whatever that now is, or the international community, whatever that once was, can go in and radically transform a society or a region. Societies and regions are terribly complicated. They have long histories. They have masses of internal conflicts. And normally it's not possible to transform them in any short period of time or often at all. They can only be improved in various ways for a time by the people who live there, by the people who know local conditions, by the people who understand the culture and society and the histories that have produced them. It's hardly ever possible for intervention to work for very long anywhere, and it's hardly ever possible to achieve more than very limited gains. So I think there should be a presumption against it. There should be a presumption against resorting to it. It should only be seen as a resort to limited goals to achieve ends that can't be achieved in other ways.

PK: So we come back again to realism and to relativism, which seems...

JG: Not relativism. I don't see why relativism comes in. I mean neo-conservative thinkers always say that, but let me give you an example. I wouldn't have thought that Thomas Aquinas was a relativist, or that traditional Catholic thought was relativistic. But one of the features of the Theory of the Just War is that no war can be justified unless its goals are attainable, unless there's a reasonable chance of success. You shouldn't fight a war, or you shouldn't engage in a type of intervention, where you don't have good reasons for thinking you can actually be successful. Nor should you do so when there's some reason or good reason to think that the cost, the collateral damage, the human havoc created by the intervention will resemble or perhaps even be larger than that which you're trying to prevent. I mean, that's a traditional Western view, which has nothing to do with relativism.

Relativism is just a kind of meaningless bogeyman in this context. The view that I put forward is, I think, a relatively traditional one. The form in which it's perhaps best expressed in recent centuries is in the political thought of Hobbes. Now, Hobbes wasn't a relativist. He thought that all human beings dreaded violent death, and I think that, although human beings often enjoy inflicting violence, very few enjoy being subjected to it. I think that's a fairly deeply rooted feature of human beings. And one can go beyond Hobbes and say that there are certain other evils which are evil for all human beings — like persecution, like humiliation.

So, there are universal human values in that sense. But where the difficulty comes in — and this is what modern liberal interventionists and theorists of universal human rights, for example, are very unwilling to accept — is that these goods and evils chronically conflict with each other. If you topple a tyranny which has great evils, you quite commonly get anarchy, which also has very great evils attached to it. If you institute democracy in a dictatorial state which has a number of distinct communities which have been historically at odds with one another, you very commonly — in fact, nearly always — get ethnic cleansing and sectarian civil wars. If you protect one set of rights — for example, you may find yourself protecting rights to freedom of religion in many parts of the world — the exercise of those rights can end up with religious conflicts, riots, and persecutions.

Now, if you're lucky, you might live in a highly developed democracy where these conflicts can be moderated, but they still break out. Let me give you an example. In Britain, it's taken over thirty years of very consistent — not always right, but basically very consistent — policy by a succession of governments to contain and reduce the sectarian and terrorist violence in Northern Ireland. It's taken decades and decades of consistent political, economic, and security measures, which have succeeded to a considerable extent. But in even in that context there were conflicts of rights. For example, one of the issues that British governments had to deal with was the demand by different religious communities to exercise their freedom of expression and their freedom of religion by marching through each other's neighbourhoods, which would have immediately provoked violence. So the exercise of those rights had to be curbed, often with discussions with the various groups. And it was tremendously difficult to do so, because if it had been allowed, there would have been violations of lots of other rights, including unnecessary violence and mayhem.

PK: When it comes down to it, I can't help but observe that what you really are is a historian. That what you're doing is looking at everything that's gone before us and saying, look at it hard, and try to find out what's really going on. You come back to realism again. Is it true that you're looking for a return to studying history?

JG: Well, it's very important not to forget the past. I think it was George Santayana who originally penned the thought that those who've forgotten the past repeat its mistakes. That's certainly true. And I think that's a particularly great danger now for all kinds of reasons. Large numbers of people don't really want to study the past. They think it's irrelevant. They think it's redundant. We've moved beyond it. We're in an entirely new period. But we're not. We are the same human beings basically unaltered, but with more power based on more knowledge than we ever had before. The conflicts of human needs, the flaws of human nature, are exactly what they were in the past. All that's changed are the conditions in which they work themselves out. So we should be even more cautious than we were in the past because the power we have to make big mistakes is greater than it was in the past.

I suppose the basic difference between the way I look at things and the way most people who write about world affairs now do is that I don't base my analysis on the assumption that the future will be radically better than the past, or even that it can be. I base my analysis on the assumption, which I think is well founded and realistic, that, in ethical and political aspects, it will be much the same. And that means we must guard against familiar evils rather than attempting to scale unprecedented heights. Being a missionary in politics, being a proselytizer in politics, seeing politics as a surrogate for religious salvation, seeing the goal of politics as a world transformation, universal emancipation, vast programs of human liberation — that's what I'm against. What I want instead is for the religious impulse to remain where it should be, which is in religious life in the human heart, in temples, and synagogues, and churches, and mosques, and so on, and for politics to be seen as very important but as an essentially unheroic activity which is at its best when it's engaged in the grubby business of seeking a reasonable *modus vivendi* among human beings who will always be imperfectible and often at odds.

Political Theology

MARK LILLA

At one time, in the West at least, history seemed to be headed towards secularism. Politics and religion were to be placed in different domains. Politics was for the public sphere, and religion was to be placed in a more private sphere. Church and state were to be separate. After centuries of bloody war, religious faith was supposed to be sidelined. Tolerance was to be the order of the day. Yet, religious passions have resurfaced in many parts of the world. They are behind many of today's conflicts and make people who are schooled in Western secular thinking uneasy. Mark Lilla, professor of humanities at Columbia University, noted intellectual, and frequent contributor to the New York Review of Books, *writes about a world filled with the drama of rekindled religion and politics. Paul Kennedy's interview with Mark Lilla was broadcast on* Ideas *on 11 March 2008.*

PAUL KENNEDY

I want to begin with an article you wrote in the Sunday *New York Times* summarizing your recent book, *The Stillborn God: Religion, Politics, and the Modern West.* In May 2006, President Mahmoud Ahmadinejad of Iran sent an open letter to President George W. Bush. It was translated and published all around the world in newspapers. The letter began, "If Prophet Abraham, Isaac, Jacob, Ishmael,

Joseph, or Jesus Christ, peace be upon him, were with us today, how would they have judged such behaviour?" What struck you about this letter, about the way it was written? What can we read into the letter?

MARK LILLA

Well, I think two things. The first thing that struck me, I have to say, was his utter confidence. It's the same confidence he showed when he spoke at Columbia University a couple months ago. You know, he strikes one as someone who not only holds certain theological beliefs, but holds them without a shadow of a doubt. And his letter to President Bush is written like he's extending a helping hand to a wayward brother hoping that he will return. And return to what? Well, a return to what I call in the book political theology. That is, an understanding that all legitimate authority on Earth is given directly by God, and that the only way to understand our condition here on Earth is to begin with that presupposition. And, according to President Ahmadinejad, the source of the problems with the West, what he sees as problems with the West, with modern democracy, all stem from the fact that we've departed from this revealed truth.

PK: What's curious, though, couldn't you turn the thing completely over and say that a similar letter could have been written by George W. Bush back to the president of Iran, just with different names or with a different direction in thought, but not really different in tone or style?

ML: No, I don't think so. And I think it's important to insist on that — that, whatever private beliefs President Bush has, not only about God himself, but, let's say, about public policy and how they connect up with religion, President Bush believes in the rules of the liberal democratic game, that legitimacy ultimately derives from the consent of the governed and that our constitutional system is based on that consent. And we rule through public laws. And that, while it's permissible for people to vote as they like and to encourage other people to vote in a certain way based on their theological beliefs, at the end of the day we count the votes and whoever has them wins that election or is able to decide on that policy. He might have sympathies with one group or another, and those are pretty obvious, but he does not think that the rules of the liberal democratic game are based on a revelation, and President Ahmadinejad does.

PK: So, when George W. Bush says "God Bless America" or invokes the godhead, this is quite different from what the president of Iran was saying, not just in tone, but in content?

ML: Yes. If you look at the rest of the letter or even the bit that I quote in the *New York Times*, he essentially says that the game of liberal democracy is over. We can see that. God wants something else. God is bringing the nations together. And essentially he treats the idea of public consent and legitimacy through the consent of the governed as fundamentally improper, as a kind of sinful rebellion against God himself.

PK: So, the gist of what you're saying in the book and in that article is that, in the West, we are now facing something that is not really new at all. It's something that's quite old, and it's something that we've actually faced before, and this is political theology. I think that's the term you use. Can you tell us what you mean by that?

ML: Well, I mean a doctrine that establishes the legitimate exercise of authority based on a divine revelation. That seems perhaps like a technical definition, but it's actually crucial to understand the distinction between the kinds of political arrangements or societies that are based on that assumption and those that are not based on that assumption. I thought it was important when I wrote this book not to talk about contemporary Islam, about which I know only as much as the last book I've read, I'm afraid. But to talk about our history in the West, and to make clear that the struggle with political theology is not a military struggle, it's a struggle within ourselves over how we think we ought to be governed. And it's a struggle that took place in the history of the West. It did not end with the modern Enlightenment but continued on through the early twentieth century. It remains a live possibility all the time for people who think that human political arrangements need to be put under the direct authority of God.

And even though we can have debates in the West about where the line between church and state ought to be drawn, there's great variety among Western countries concerning how they do that. In the United States, it's unthinkable that we would have direct public funding of religious schools. You have it in Canada. But that doesn't mean that political theology is alive in Canada. It just means that, though we share the same principles of legitimacy, we decide to draw the line a little differently. There's a huge difference. There's a fundamental difference between societies like our own, where they are at this moment, and where they were a few centuries ago and where the Islamic world is today.

PK: You are an intellectual historian, and what you're saying, in a sense, is that we are forgetting. I think at one point you say we live in a state of forgetfulness because we don't remember that once we were different, that we are something new and distinct right now. What exactly are we forgetting?

ML: Well, we're forgetting at first blush the existence of our tradition of political theology, which was Christian for fifteen hundred years. It was simply taken as axiomatic that political authority legitimately derived only from God. And there were long debates throughout that period over how to conceive of that authority, a search for metaphors to understand how we divide up secular authority within that general picture. So, in the Middle Ages, writers tried to develop images of the king having two bodies or two swords, one is the church and one is the parliament. Or the legs of the kingdom belong to secular authorities but the head belongs to the church. There were many attempts to make sense of the Christian version of political theology, but that was the way we thought for fifteen hundred years because alternatives just did not present themselves.

Perhaps more importantly, we have substituted for this political

theology certain fantasies about secularization, a process of secularization that tells us that, to the degree to which we remember this
past, we think of it as entirely past — that, somehow, since the rise
of the modern Enlightenment, political theology has beat a slow and
steady retreat and no longer presents a challenge. And that leads us
into another fantasy, which is that other nations, other civilizations,
once they're put on these same train tracks, will end up at the same
station. That's another, to my mind, more insidious kind of forgetfulness, because we forget why political theology is attractive — the
things that it explains and the comfort that it gives.

PK: Are there no other examples in all of history of this kind of
secular movement to take politics out of the religious realm?

ML: Oh, there are lots of examples. I think our path in the modern
West is rather unique because, prior to the rise of Christianity, there
were political theologies around the globe. They were not based on
a certain monotheistic, Abrahamic faith that raised the stakes very
high. Essentially every little kingdom had its own little gods, and
when they were defeated those gods died out. Or you had cults of
the emperor in China and Japan, and he was sort of a quasi-divine
human figure. But it's really with the rise of the Abrahamic faiths
that the possibility of a fully comprehensive divine law becomes
articulated, so that Jewish law and, later on, Islamic Sharia become
fully comprehensive guidebooks to life that cover everything and give
a theological explanation for why things should be laid out in this
way. In Christianity, it's more complicated still, because you don't get
a law; instead you get certain principles having to do with the heart
and moral principles that are pretty inward looking. And translating
that into political theology turned out to be very difficult.
    But otherwise, yes, there were tribes and even nations and civil-
izations that didn't make these sorts of appeals for certain points in
their history — for example, in ancient Greece. But the gods were
always lurking there in one way or another. And what did not exist
was a full philosophical alternative to a strong political theology. So,
really modern political thought in the West is a reaction to a certain

form of, and perhaps the most potent form, of political theology that human beings have ever seen. And that's the one that grew out of these Abrahamic faiths. That set us off on another path, so that we developed a way of thinking about politics without this appeal to God's authority, and built up certain barriers against the rise of political theology that I think are unique historically.

PK: If I was to look at the book as a novel rather than as a piece of intellectual history, if there was a hero or a main protagonist in the book, the person who was responsible for the kinds of changes you're talking about at a very specific period in Western history would be Thomas Hobbes. According to what you say in the book, he did something completely different: he changed the subject. He literally took us onto a completely different track. Can you talk about Hobbes and what he did?

ML: Yes, my beloved Hobbes. What Hobbes did was the most important thing anyone can ever do, and that is he changed the subject. For fifteen hundred years, the subject of Western political thinking, the active subject, the most important subject was God. And the intellectual game was to figure out exactly what God wanted on Earth, and then to try to understand human beings and why they aren't doing what God wants, and then try to put these two things together. So, you draw from the Biblical sources. You have sources for thinking about God's authority over us, on the one hand. And on the other, you have resources for thinking about why we are fallen creatures, to speak Christian language. And then the task is to try to find a way to get fallen creatures to live together in ways that God wants them to, not only individually but collectively.

Well, Hobbes comes along in the wake of the English Civil War and the wars of religion before that and says, essentially, why are we talking about that? Let's talk about something else first. Why is it that human beings have beliefs about God and what he wants for politics? Let's settle this question first. So Hobbes begins talking about this and never gets back to what God wants. Instead, the question of why human beings are built the way they are and why they come up with certain ideas about God absorbs him from then on, and he gets us thinking about that. And he develops a way of thinking about the human mind, about its limits, its ignorance, and why our limits make us fearful of the afterlife, and what happens to us in the afterlife make us fearful of other people.

Hobbes begins explaining why it is that religious wars happen, and what he sees is there's a subtle and complex cycle of violence that's both theological and political, and it goes something like this. The human mind is a limited thing. It doesn't know everything it needs to know. And because of that, because we don't know how nature works, and we don't know what lies over the horizon, we become fearful. And because we're fearful, we invent ideas of the gods that satisfy our fear. These may be right ideas or wrong ideas, but this is how our ideas get generated. Not from God himself, but by us and because we're fearful. So we invent ideas of the god or gods to relieve our fear. But then it turns out that leads to more fear because, on the one hand, we start fearing God and, on the other, we discover that there are other people out there who have different views about God. And since these views are not things we find easy to check at the door because they concern the most important thing, which is eternal life, people are apt to start arguing about God and how he should be worshipped. And when that happens, they start squabbling. So then we start fearing religious war. So, once those wars start taking place, we become more fearful, which makes us believe in God even more, which makes us more dogmatic. Which makes us argue more, and on, and on, and on.

So we develop this really fantastic account, just working from the single principle of the mind that we're ignorant. We can see how all of these things happen. Then Hobbes says, look, if that's why political life is, as he says, nasty, brutish, and short, how can we get out of this cycle? And what he does, essentially, is he develops certain principles for politics that relieve us of this original fear of our fellow man, and his hope is that, once that happens, people will become less aggressive and probably they'll be less dogmatic religiously and maybe not believe at all any more. Because the source of their fears is also the source of their beliefs, and if they cease being fearful, they'll cease being believers. And that offers a way of thinking about how we ought to set up our political institutions without any reference to what God wants, but simply by asking how we can set up a political order in which human beings aren't slashing each other's throats.

PK: It's interesting, because it is the sort of dime-store version of Hobbes, the cliché that he's the guy who said life is nasty, brutish, and short. And you put it directly in the same line — I mean, you connect it to the fact that he liberated us from political theology. Those two things are actually connected.

ML: Right. What happens afterwards, though, is that just about everyone who reads Hobbes was horrified because his clever idea for getting out of this cycle of fear is to establish a single sovereign and authoritarian figure who would essentially control everything within the state. And that's the only way to relieve people of their fears. Once that happens, then people go about their business.

Well, no one liked that solution. But Hobbes got a lot of seventeenth- and eighteenth-century thinkers to go down this path of looking at some fundamental principles of human psychology and trying to build a better political system based on his psychological assumptions and without appealing to God. So, someone like John Locke comes along and says, Hobbes has this half right. We're ignorant and we're fearful, but, in fact, if we allow people liberty to make money, to govern themselves, to believe what they want at home, and allow a thousand flowers to bloom in a thousand different churches, you don't have to control religion as Hobbes thought you did. Rather, you'll discover that people who are in churches will realize that, as believers, they have a stake in a limited government that's governed by the rule of law, public laws that everyone can see, and based on public consent — that once people see that, they won't try to impose their religious views on other people, but instead will just want to ensure that they can worship privately. And rather than turning politics into a theological capture-the-flag game, you'll see lots of different churches with people with different practices. Individuals move in and out of them. They'll go to work in the morning, come back at night, go to church in the evenings or weekends. And you'll get the kind of peace that Hobbes was searching for without creating a more dangerous authority figure like Hobbes's sovereign.

So people went off in lots of different directions after Hobbes, and no one was particularly interested in his solution to the problem. But they were talking about Hobbes's problem. They were no longer opening up their Bibles in a serious way and asking, what kind of laws does God want us to have? How can we understand the king as exercising authority given directly by God to him, and to his ancestors, and to his progeny? And that was the sea change.

PK: Obviously, it was a very complex and long tradition, but how are we sure, when we look at all the people who are in that tradition, that we're not just repressing the fundamental human need to have religion, that we're putting it aside and confining it, and thereby taking care of it but not getting rid of it.

ML: I think that's the right worry to have, actually, for two reasons. One is that I think that it's there. I think that, at some level, my assumption is that we're phototropic creatures, like plants that turn towards the sun; there's something in us that wants to understand what connects life here to life beyond here. So there's a natural human tendency to seek out answers to those sorts of questions and to connect those answers to how we govern ourselves politically. And it's only through a certain kind of training and acculturation that this natural tendency to question begins to atrophy, so to speak.

And it's important for another reason: it makes us vigilant when there are threats to the kind of compact that we've established here. And I don't mean external threats at the moment, I mean internal. For instance, ever since the French Revolution, a lot of people have worried about the fact that we've let this vitalistic urge to seek out God wither and because of that we've become deracinated. We're no longer fully human. Even in human terms, we're no longer what we were, because we no longer seek out God's advice. And people like that — who want to reinvigorate our politics with concern about God, not even so much because they believe in God, but because they feel that we've lost some vital essence — those people we ought to pay attention to and worry a bit about. Those people didn't disappear with a wave of a wand after Hobbes happened to write his book, but were quite active in European intellectual life right through World War Two.

PK: If there's another protagonist in the novel called *The Stillborn God*, that would probably be Jean-Jacques Rousseau. I'm really interested in the response he had to the kind of issues Hobbes was raising.

ML: Well, Rousseau really is the first in the line of worriers about our loss of religion that I just mentioned. Like Hobbes, Rousseau thought that religious war was the worst thing that could happen in political life. Not only because of the bad things that people would do to each other, but because of what it did to the religious impulse, which he saw as fundamentally moral. Rousseau thought that it was the corruption of religion and the outbreak of religious wars that distorted this originally good instinct and then delegitimized the exercise of religion.

So, his great concern was that human beings who do not have faith in God begin despairing about their moral lives. What they need is a faith that's been stripped down to its moral essence and is not irrational, and on the basis of that we not only can defend religion, but we can understand what role it plays in our human lives. Rousseau was not terribly interested in talking about God and about what God wanted. He was more interested in talking about what religion does for us, psychologically and socially. So, in a sense, he's a child of Hobbes, because he's talking about us and why we believe what we believe rather than asking directly what God wants. But he comes up with a different answer, and that is that it's only through a properly reformed religion that human beings can become fully what they ought to be, not because it's been revealed by God, but because it just so happens that's the way we are. And out of that tradition you get a very different kind of approach to the political problem in the century-and-a-half that follows.

PK: Now, you call the tradition that began with Hobbes — and obviously had a number of offshoots — the great separation. It is the separation of church and state, or of theology and politics.

ML: Well, it's more the latter. And that's the thing to insist upon, because it's separating out appeals to God from the kind of reasoning we do about our institutions. That is the crucial divide. That is the river that you cross. Once you're on the other side and simply talking about us and our institutions, then you can divide up powers between church and state in all sorts of ways. Everyone focuses today on the separation of church and state without focusing on this first separation, which is far more important.

For example, in Islamic societies today, there is a separation in certain areas of life between church and state, because Sharia law does not establish a precise understanding of what the functions of government are and how it should be structured exactly. So, what that means is that you have all sorts of functions that are handled by secular authorities. But the basic understanding of the society, where authority derives from, is a political theology. So, even in the past in the West — in the Middle Ages, for example — you had emperors and kings and princes who exercised authority apart from the Pope, but they all shared an idea that authority derives from God. So that's the distinction that I want to insist upon and that helps us understand where we've been. And I hope that it helps us to understand where other societies are today.

PK: Well, in fact, the book, although a piece of intellectual history, is set in the context of what we're looking at today in the world, and that is that we in the West are confronting another kind of political theology in Islam. What do you say about where we are right now?

ML: Well, I should say to begin with that the book was begun a decade ago, before all of this... I mean, we understood what happened in Iran, and Afghanistan was already moving in the direction of the Taliban, but, essentially, the continuing force of political theology to light up the hearts and minds of people to get them to do extraordinary things just wasn't obvious to us. So I began the book really to talk about how this political theology was revived in the Weimar years by Jewish and Christian thinkers. And sure enough, along come these Muslim thinkers and political actors who seem to be acting out a chapter in my book.

What I hoped for is that the book would induce modesty and sobriety — modesty when it comes to thinking about the universality of our own way of doing politics. Essentially, what the story the book tells is of a certain lucky break we got in the West because of the fact that the wars of religion happened. There was a big intellectual reaction against that. Someone like Hobbes comes along, and out of that pops an alternative. We really have been on a special path. It's not a providential path. It's a unique path, not in a value sense, but in the sense that no one has quite gone through the wringer the way we have with Christianity and then the reaction against it. So, the idea of our institutions and our understanding of political life and of religion being exported anywhere out in the world, I think, takes a serious blow once one goes through the history that I recount in the book.

On the other hand, I also hope the book makes clear that it's important that we recognize the fundamental difference between ourselves and any civilization or society that's based on a political theology. We might be able to find political common ground, but we're not going to find intellectual common ground, and that is what shows up in the letter of President Ahmadinejad of Iran to President Bush — that there's really no way to translate his language into our own. I don't think people should draw belligerent conclusions from that but, rather, prudent ones.

It also gets us to think about how traditions of political theology change from within. Everyone and his brother wants to come up with a way of liberalizing and modernizing Islam, but the people who write about that often don't understand how tenacious traditions of political theology are, what kinds of questions they answer, and how they change really from within, that renewals and transformations from within can be lasting, as opposed to simple liberalizations on the surface, which tend not to last over time.

PK: Now, there are people looking specifically again at Islam now. There are people who call for a kind of reformation within the Muslim world, the kind of reformation that happened with Martin Luther in the Christian West, I suppose. And they say that, because Islam never had any kind of a reformation like that, it is fundamentally different. What do you make of that argument?

ML: Well, it's an interesting argument to me because of the assumption that it expresses, that somehow a reformation is one more station on the train tracks, and it's a necessary one, it's an obvious one. And why are the Muslims lagging behind so much if it's destined historically that religions eventually go through a process like this, which I don't think is the case — there's no reason to think that.

PK: Is it the same kind of thinking that we're guilty of, a kind of hubristic thinking that what you call a complete exception, a historical exception that never happened anywhere else, we extrapolate from that. We're doing the same thing when we look at the Muslim religion and say that they should have a reformation because we did.

ML: Yes, and not only because we did, but because it's somehow in the DNA of history that these things happen, that the reason it happened in our history is because it was destined to happen, therefore it's destined to happen elsewhere. History simply doesn't work that way. It's not just a question of us; it's that there's nothing necessary about these changes and movements.

Also, I think it's important to remember what Luther was about. I prefer using the term "renovator" rather than "reformer" for Luther because a weak idea of reform is that, well, your religion really isn't up to date and, like getting a new PC or new software, you need to get version 2.0 or one that's more in tune with the way we live now. But that kind of trimming and adjusting to the spirit of the times almost always backfires. Part of the book recounts the story of how, in the early twentieth century, the attempt to reform Protestantism and Judaism in Germany led, in the wake of World War One, to a reaction so that some of the crassest messianism and apocalypticism in these faiths was restored and then applied to political life. Luther was not about bringing Catholicism more in tune with the present. On the contrary, he thought that the problem with Catholicism was that it was too much in the present. He wanted to renew Christianity by taking it back to its original sources, to its fundamental revelation. To go back to the roots and to strip away everything that had developed historically, to get back to the original faith of the Apostles.

When you look at the people who write about potential changes in Islamic thought and practice today, they fall into these two groups. There are those who say, well, it's kind of embarrassing, some of the things said in the Koran about women, about punishments, about jihad, and so on. Why don't we just ignore those or de-emphasize them and add a few contemporary things about human rights and hope that that will satisfy the demands of the present. Then there are those — and I'm thinking here of writers like Khaled Abou el Fadl, who was a professor of Islamic law at UCLA, or the more controversial figure, Tariq Ramadan, the Swiss Muslim thinker — who say, no, the problem is that Islam has been hijacked by a certain kind of puritan in Saudi Arabia, by conniving rulers and princes, and that the only way to restore the dignity of Islam is to go back to the sources, cut away everything that's been added that is not essential. And once we do that, we will discover a more dignified, sane, pure Islam that actually will make it easier for Muslim believers to live in the present, not harder, because they will be sure of their faith, and they'll know how to negotiate the present in a way that they're unable to right now. And that call to renewal by these renovators is a much more powerful call, because it speaks from within the tradition of the faith in a way that Luther did. He was speaking much more in the tradition of the New Testament than the Catholic Church at that time was, which is why his message was so popular. So, I think those are the people to pay attention to in contemporary Muslim thinking.

PK: I want to spend some time talking about the implications of the argument you're making for things that are happening right now. When we look at societies in which these two traditions are blending, through immigration — in France, for example, throughout Europe, and also in Canada and the United States, where people are brought in who don't necessarily agree on the ground rules. There are people who are secular in the political world, and there are people who are theological in the political world. Is there any way that we can get these people talking to each other?

ML: Oh, well, they're talking to each other.

PK: They're yelling at each other.

ML: Yes. The question is, are they understanding each other? That's why someone like Ramadan interests me. I can understand why many people distrust him and wonder what he's up to, but Ramadan has written books essentially saying that the problem Muslim thinking has gotten itself into is that it's taken one idea that one finds in the Koran, which is that Muslims should live in Muslim countries and that, if they're living anywhere else, they have to treat that as an alien place. In fact, there's a much more productive way of thinking about what it's like to live in a Muslim country and what it's like to live with dignity outside of a Muslim nation and still be an active citizen, one who follows the law and sees the legal system around him as legitimate.

That's a very difficult trick pull off, theologically, but it's a fight worth fighting, it seems to me. Because Islam is not very easily adaptable in that way, because of the priority it gives to nations themselves, recognizing nations as a whole, not just private individuals [who] recognize Islam and think about what it's like to live elsewhere. [That] is just not as developed. It's certainly not developed in the more puritanical, fundamentalist traditions of the Wahhabis, for example, who come out of Saudi Arabia. So, there really isn't an intellectually compelling alternative out there for believing Muslims who, on the one hand, want to hold on to their faith in dignity because of what it gives to them and, on the other hand, live in the West and want to live peacefully and enjoy it and want to feel that they're good citizens as well. They need a manual for that, and there's no manual for that at the moment.

So, that's what so often leads to misunderstanding, because people feel pulled in two directions. And when they're criticized, they experience a quite understandable desire to defend what they are and what they believe in their traditions. It's just not a good situation to be in for anybody on both sides of this issue right now. The kind of massive immigration that Western Europe has experienced, the people who've come as workers tend to come from backward areas, villages, and they've really not seen the world outside of their villages until they arrive in the West. So they experience these multiple shocks, and then their children feel betwixt and between. They don't quite know the Islamic tradition, but they feel shut out of these societies. So they're easy pickings for someone who comes along and is funded by the Saudi Wahhabist who says, I can show you how to live a dignified life as a Muslim, I know how to unlock the keys of the Koran. They don't know who else to turn to. There aren't other thinkers around. These people tend to be self-educated themselves. It's just a bad situation we've gotten ourselves into, and the most one can hope for, I feel, is that some kind of accommodation on both sides can be found until, over time, an intellectual alternative develops or Muslim faith becomes weaker, in the sense that people become what we call more secular. I don't have a dog in that fight. I don't care which of them happens. But the present situation is really an uncomfortable one, especially for those who are believers.

PK: I can't ask you as a historian to change your stripes and predict the future by looking into a crystal ball or anything, but are we entering a new age of messianic politics? I mean, the world does seem to be dividing again, and it's your hero, Thomas Hobbes, who said that messianic theology eventually breeds messianic politics.

ML: Yes, and crisis politics also tends to flame messianic fires. That's the story I tell in the book. When I get up to World War One, when you have a liberal theology that develops at the end of the nineteenth century in Germany, where Protestant and Jewish thinkers think they've found a way to reform their religions and make them acceptable to other people, to make religious education part of the life of the state. And they feel that they've solved the problems that Hobbes saw, not by taking religion out of politics, but by somehow developing a theology that would justify the way we live politically.

Well, in the wake of World War One, young Protestant and Jewish thinkers who saw what their elders had justified — and I'm talking about theologians and Jewish thinkers who supported German war aims in World War One — were so disgusted by what they saw that they turned, because of this political event, to these older messianic strains in Christianity and Judaism. Some of those figures were OK politically, but some of them, especially among the messianic Jews, supported Lenin and Stalin and the Soviet state, and some of the Protestants supported Hitler.

So, these things play off each other in a kind of frightening way, really, and in ways that Hobbes himself understood. I don't see a threat at the moment of a revived Christian political theology. There are Jewish political theologies that are causing people headaches in Israel right now, especially in the settlers' movement. But the problem at the moment just happens to be in the Islamic world. And it's touching not only those who are the wretched of the earth, but it's affecting doctors who are building bombs and driving them into airports in Scotland. So, at a point, these ideas take on a life of their own and inspire people who you would think don't have a problem with the way we live now. That's where I see the danger and the challenge.

One reads a bit, too, about what's going on in Hindu nationalism. It's hard for someone who's on the outside, like me, to know, but, in terms of writing, certainly there are works that look like political theology among some Hindu thinkers who want to drive Muslims out of India and establish a new kind of state there.

PK: I've seen you quoted somewhere saying, literally, coping is the order of the day, which sounds like a sort of mediated suggestion. Can you explain that? What do you mean by that? Coping is the order of the day.

ML: Well, I've been criticized for this, notably by Paul Berman in this country, who argued that I was saying that we should abandon principle. I don't think our principles are under threat right now. I think, rather, that we don't know how to adapt our principles to the peculiarities of Muslim theology, which makes it difficult for Muslims to live in the West right now and recognize the source of authority that we have here.

I think there are ways of coping. You know, we've had to figure out what to do about religious dress. We have to figure out what to do about certain kinds of speech that are interpreted as hate speech. And it turns out we are coping in different ways in different countries. You're not allowed to wear a headscarf in school in France. You are allowed in the United States, at least in most states. We have different ways of coping with these things, and I think it's important just to turn down the heat when it comes to these things that pop up — everything from Danish cartoons to other things. I mean, when people are threatened, they have to be defended. Period. End of story. But a lot of these other matters really can be handled just with a little bit of good sense.

PK: What do you say, though, to people who say that coping isn't enough — that, in order to be a society or a nation or whatever you want to talk about, you actually need something more? You need — I wanted to say belief, but, no, you need coherence. You need some kind of shared values.

ML: Yes. Well, it's interesting that you almost said belief because that's the path people can go down.

PK: But it could be belief in democracy, you're saying, or belief in a civil society.

ML: All we ask people to do is to recognize the fundamental principles of legitimate authority. That's really all we ask — that they
recognize that the cop on the block is allowed to do what he does
because he's under certain laws that we come up with together, not
because we search them out in a holy book. And beyond that, we
pretty much let people be. Now, whether you need some other kind
of cultural coherence in order for people to recognize those rules of
the game, well, I'm sympathetic to that. But I've also seen historically
that we in the West in different countries have found different ways
to do that, for better or worse. We don't do that in the United States
or in Canada because we all look the same, and cook the same kind
of food, and remember the same sorts of stories about our ancestors
fifteen hundred years ago. We do it because we recognize certain
institutions. We do it through popular culture. We do it through a
kind of civic education. We do it through all kinds of ways at once.

There are other nations that find it harder to have immigrants
and difference within simply because of their own coherence. It's
hard in Switzerland, because you've managed to put together three
different peoples there who speak different languages, but somehow
they managed to share a kind of Swiss-ness, and they work it out by
making it very difficult to be a citizen and by making people into
participant citizens in their local communities, and that requires a
lot of trust and a lot of saneness within the communities. It's very
hard to imagine Switzerland becoming a happy, healthy immigrant
society.

So, it depends on where we're looking. But it's interesting to see
that all of the dire predictions that Europeans made in the eighteenth
and nineteenth centuries about their former colonies like the United
States and Canada holding it together, it turns out we've been able
to do that.

PK: So, you're hopeful?

ML: Oh, I'm hopeful about us, sure. We still require vigilance. I mean,
unlike a lot of people who write and talk about religion and politics,
I'm not worked up about the evangelicals in politics now — though

I disagree with them. I think they just need to be voted out of office, that's all. But I am worried about things like home schooling. I don't know how this works in Canada, but there's a very large home-schooling movement in this country, which takes kids not only out of public schools but even out of private schools, so they're educated really in their living rooms by their parents. And I'm not sure, given the religious tinge to this education, that the kids who are there are learning the rules of the game politically. That for me is a very tiny, little bomb that's ticking.

Novelty and Coherence

JEROME KAGAN

Jerome Kagan, Professor Emeritus of Psychology at Harvard University, has helped to reshape contemporary psychology: he is one of the handful of psychologists who reintroduced the old notion that temperament is a key to a child's development. Today, this might not be such a revelation — many parents see their child's temperament etched from early on. But when Jerome Kagan started in 1950 as a graduate student at Yale, the idea that biology or the character traits you were born with had anything to do with how children grew up was pretty revolutionary. His numerous publications, for both the scientific community and the general public, include The Nature of the Child, The Long Shadow of Temperament, *and his most recent,* An Argument for Mind, *which might be called his intellectual memoir. Paul Kennedy's interview with Professor Kagan was broadcast on* Ideas *on 8 February 2007.*

PAUL KENNEDY

I was really intrigued, shocked almost, by something you said: that, when you were a student, specifically a graduate student at Yale studying psychology, almost everything you learned at that time was wrong. What do you mean by that?

JEROME KAGAN

I mean two things. In the middle of the last century, 1950, in the social sciences, there were two overpowering views of how people developed and why people are different. One was what we called in those days "learning theory" — today, you'd call it "conditioning theory" — and the other was Freudian psychoanalysis. And both of those views said that, although there might be differences in biology among humans, it was irrelevant, and that the language we learned, the values, our consciences, and any differences among us were almost completely due to the different experiences we had. That was a very dogmatic, extreme, and incorrect position, and yet most in my generation believed it to be the gospel.

PK: Now, this argument or this dichotomy has been simplified, I suppose, into what's been called the "nature-versus-nurture debate." Is that right?

JK: That's right. You said it the way the newspapers describe it and, of course, that's not the right way. Here's the way to phrase it: that each of us is born with a biology. The biology is not determining — it's a bias. And then our environments — we live in different environments — grab us and shape that biology. If you want a crude analogy, some people are pine wood, some cherry wood, some oak, some maple, and you can't make maple into cherry, but you can make desks out of both, but there's a limit. Biology doesn't determine what you will be so much as it says, "I'm sorry, you can't be that." I play tennis moderately well for my age, but I can't be Roger Federer because my biology prevents it. I played the trumpet when I was an adolescent, but I never could be Wynton Marsalis because my biology prevents it. In that sense, biology excludes. It determines what you can't be rather than what you will be, and I think that's the best way to view the relationship between nature and nurture, not nature versus nature, but rather how they're related to each other.

PK: The two are engaged in a very interesting dance where the balance between the two is what's constantly in play.

JK: Exactly. It's a ballet between the two.

PK: Now, why was it that people were so wrong back in the middle part of the twentieth century? Why did they think that conditioning was pre-eminent and biology was nothing?

JK: That's easy to explain. First, for very good reasons, scientists are loathe, they're very reluctant, to speculate about explanations for which there is no evidence. I remind our listeners that in 1950 one couldn't measure the brain, so you could spin many fairy tales about how the brain might be producing this or that, but there was no way to produce any evidence, and scientists don't like that. That's one reason. The second reason is that, in the laboratory, people were demonstrating, primarily with animals, that you could condition rats and dogs and cats to do things they don't ordinarily do. So, here was science showing you that, through experience, you can shape, sculpt, alter an animal's behaviour, so that looked like good science.
  The third reason is political. In a new science, in new fields, the politics and the ethics of a society are always important. So we must remember that America was an immigrant country, and in the early part of the twentieth century, there were thousands and thousands of immigrants from all parts of Europe who were settling in our large cities, and a lot of them were illiterate. Their children were poor, not well clothed, they weren't doing well in school. But America, in its egalitarian ethos, insisted that, with the right training and education, everyone could attain dignity and financial security and happiness. Therefore, there was political pressure to say it's all experience and education, and these children are not in trouble because they're "biologically tainted" or "compromised" in some way. Now, that's very important.
  So, you put those three factors together: no way to study the brain; good demonstrations that learning and experience are important; and a strong political motive to believe that everything you are at age thirty is due to your experience.

PK: Now, at the beginning of that answer, you also mentioned another part of the problem, and that was Sigmund Freud, who definitely was ruling the roost in the world of psychology at the time. Talk about that for a bit as well. Why was that a problem?

JK: Well, it wasn't a problem. The puzzle I raise in the book — and I haven't solved it, and no one has, to my knowledge — is that Freud made some very strong statements. For example, all children pass through three phases — an oral phase in infancy, an anal phase during the second year, a phallic phase, a general phase — that all are neuroses, all are neurotic symptoms: insomnia, depression, fearfulness, the repression of our conflicted urges, primarily sexual. Now, none of that's true, so here's the puzzle: why did so many — leave me out of it — brilliant, erudite, educated people, not just in the sciences, but in the humanities, believe that? And the only approach to an answer I can come to is that Freud spoke to the intuitions of Americans. I should point out that, in the early part of the twentieth century, Europe was not very friendly to Freud; it was America and England, Protestant countries with a much more prudish attitude toward sexuality. So here is my attempt at some sort of an explanation. The availability of cheap contraceptives toward the end of the nineteenth century meant that young men and women could begin to think about sexual activity outside of marriage; otherwise, you couldn't, especially if you were middle class. So now you're allowing these thoughts to bubble up, but still there is a lot of tension and shame and uncertainty about it. It's sitting right on the cusp of consciousness and creating a sort of tension. And what I think happened was that the tensions that are due to a sick child, losing your job, your parent having cancer, frustration with your boss — all those tensions, which have nothing to do with sexuality — were interpreted as due to this conflict over sexuality. That's the only way I can understand this idea... Incidentally, when I was twenty-one years old, I thought that Freud was absolutely dead right.

PK: It would be hard to believe anything else because that was the orthodoxy, as you say.

JK: Yes. But there was a minority of scholars who rejected it. Not everyone thought it was a good idea. But many people did. And I'm sure the explanation I just gave can't be all of it. There have to be other factors, and someone smarter than I will have to come up with it. But at least the explanation I just offered, I think, makes some small contribution. But it is amazing.

PK: I would like to try to get some deep background not only to this book, *An Argument for Mind*, but also to your entire career. And without risking going to Freudian limits here, I'd like to look at your childhood first and ask if you could describe it and how you think it may have affected your decision ultimately to do the work you do.

JK: When I was in high school and went off to college at Rutgers University, I was toying with three possible careers. First, I was toying with medicine. Then I had a strong motive to be a lawyer because I grew up in a small town in New Jersey where my uncle was a successful lawyer, and he kept on saying to me, "Look, why don't you go to law school and then, when you graduate, you can come into my firm." So, from a practical point of view, that seemed appealing. But for an irrational reason — and, of course, irrational elements usually determine careers — I was attracted to being a university professor. When I was an adolescent, I saw the black-and-white film *Goodbye, Mr. Chips*, with Robert Donat, and I remember leaving the theatre thinking, my God, what a wonderful life! You can read. You can nurture the young. It's gentle. It's pure. And it had very strong appeal. So I'm thinking about those three things, and I should add one element: although I never met my mother's father, my grandfather, I recall my mother saying to me hundreds of times what a wise man he was and how she discovered her father one night dead with a heart attack, with a book on human nature on his chest, and how admiring she was. I had strong affection for my mother, who I believe had strong affection for me. So you can see a desire to be that admired person in my mother's eyes — namely, her own father.

PK: There's an incident you describe that's even earlier that may have pushed you more towards biochemistry than psychology, but certainly took you towards the social sciences or towards a scientific way of looking at the world. This is the story which I'd love you to tell, about finding a dead squirrel and dissecting it.

JK: There are two incidents. One was when I was about twelve or thirteen and I had an interest in living things. For some reason, although I found the stars beautiful, the moon and the stars did not give me a high the way they do to young sixteen-year-olds who want to be cosmologists or astrophysicists, but living things did. I remember coming home one afternoon from school and seeing a dead squirrel, recently killed, and then realizing, gee, I could see what was inside this squirrel. I wrapped it in newspaper and took it home and hid myself — apparently, I thought this must have been illicit activity — and then slicing open the squirrel to look at its intestines and stomach and so on. And I remember being very excited about this, and I interpret that as meaning that I had a fundamental interest in life, in living things, not chemical molecules, and I do believe that that experience rested there, and it's not surprising I chose psychology.

The second event I thought you might be referring to was that I did take many chemistry courses, and there is a course called Quantitative Analysis, in which you have to estimate the number of milligrams of a substance, and the determination this time was barium sulphate. You're given a little solution, and you've got to figure out how many milligrams of barium sulphate [there are]. It took about six hours then — maybe today it takes twenty minutes — but in those days, six hours. And at the end of six hours, I had finished it. I had my little bit of white powder. I took it over to the balance to weight it and turned in my answer. My seatmate, he carried his, and on his way, he tripped and the powder spilled on the floor. He was not about to do it again. So he called the eight of us who were there and said, "Would each of you estimate how many milligrams of barium sulphate you have." He took the average, and I was chagrined when he got a better grade than I did, and I remember deciding, I'm afraid God's giving me a message that chemistry is not for me.

PK: Probably a good message from the way things have developed since then. You describe yourself as an anxious child.

JK: Yes, I was an anxious child, I think, not temperamentally, even though I study temperament, but probably because of experience. I had a very protective mother, very protective of my independence. I had a father who was bitter over the fact that he contracted arthritis as a thirty-year-old and he was always in pain, and that, I think, inhibited his empathy — a bitterness about not making as much money as his five brothers, who lived in the same town. I think that combination of a rather aloof father and an overprotective, restrictive mother made me an anxious child. I stuttered for two years between five and seven, and if my mother had taken me to a child psychiatrist, he would have said, "Yes, I'm afraid your son has anxiety disorder."

PK: It sounds as though you were making young observations of your own family, observing your mother and father from close hand. Did you have any inkling then that you would end up where you did end up, as a research psychologist?

JK: Oh, no, no, that was too young. I would say the first time I consciously entertained psychology was when I got to college, seventeen or eighteen. Now, the forces I described to you earlier — my mother's father, the interest in mind and life — they were now coming together like a perfect storm. That was the time I began to entertain becoming a professor of psychology, studying the mind, with the goal of trying to understand myself, trying to understand why I was an anxious child, trying to understand, since I'm Jewish, why I was a target of prejudice, since I didn't do anything wrong. I was not a bully. I remember saying, "How is it that people can have prejudices against others? It doesn't make any sense. What's tumbling around in their crazy minds?" All of these things came together to focus an interest on human minds and why they behave and why they are the way they are and why they have such irrational thoughts.

PK: Now, psychology is a huge field. You specifically narrowed in, ultimately, on the study of children. Why is that? What got you interested in children?

JK: The answer goes back to your first question about why psychology was dominated by learning theory and Freud. I know that listeners will find this hard to believe, but you must trust me. In 1950, the majority view among most social scientists, not just psychologists, was that criminals, alcoholics, schizophrenics are the way they are because of what happened to them as children. I know that's crazy, but that's what we believed. Therefore, if you had a benevolent motive in you, which I did, then what would be a more reverential way to run a life than to study young children and determine what it is that makes adults criminals, alcoholics, schizophrenics? My generation thought we were doing God's work, because if we found out what makes an alcoholic or a criminal, then we would tell people what to do, and there would be no more alcoholics and no more criminals. That may sound to you ingenuous to the extreme, but you must believe me that I was not alone in that belief. All my peers believed that.

It took three experiences over a period of ten to fifteen years to finally persuade me that I should study temperament. So here was the first experience: my very first important research post was at the Fels Research Institute, which doesn't exist today, on the campus of Antioch College, in a tiny town in Ohio called Yellow Springs, between Dayton and Cincinnati. Now, this institute was founded on the notion that they would enrol a large number of typical middle- and working-class infants who lived in the southwestern Ohio region and follow them, and then one day someone would look at all this information and see if they could understand why each adult was the way they were. So, when I got out of the army in 1957, that job was offered to me. There was a large group of adults in their twenties on whom very rich information was available from birth. Each child had four or five very thick three-ring notebooks of information. I took the job and worked four or five years on that. And, relevant to this question, here was the important finding: that there was a small group of children who were extremely timid, anxious, and fearful in the first two or three years of life, and they never lost it, regardless of what happened to them. And I thought about that. Now, actually, that was temperamental, and in the book we wrote called *Birth to Maturity*, which was published in 1962, my co-author, Howard Moss, and I actually suggested that, and the word we used was "constitutional." We said, "Well, maybe these children have a constitutional tendency." Today, we'd say "temperamental," but I was still so heavily imbued with environmental determination that I didn't pursue it. I should have pursued this in 1962.

The second important experience happened when I took a sabbatical in 1972 and studied an isolated Mayan Indian village in northwest Guatemala. I wanted to see what that environment was like. And I saw the importance of biology, because the belief held by the Indians is that the infant is vulnerable to the evil eye for the first year of life, and therefore infants are put in the back of the hut. No one talks to them, no one plays with them, and, of course, they're retarded at one year. But after one year, they're now protected against the evil eye, so now they come out, and in a few years they look just like normal children. I remember writing in the notebook that I kept that, oh, my God, the biology is powerful, it overcomes the early experience. And I should have been pursuing temperament then.

The third event occurred in the late 1970s, when two of my colleagues, Richard Kearsley and Philip Zalazo, ... we were studying the effect of daycare on young infants because, in the late seventies, the US Congress — this wouldn't be true today — was considering a bill to establish national daycare centres so that mothers who were going to work would have places for their young infants. Now, my colleagues and I believed that daycare for infants might be dangerous. I don't believe that anymore, but in those years I did. So we established a daycare centre in Boston where we had some children who attended the centre and some children who didn't, and they were [from] the same social class and ethnic group. But because we were in the area near Boston's Chinatown, half of our children were Chinese-American and half were European Caucasian. And what we found was dramatic temperamental differences in infancy between the Chinese-American infants and the Caucasian infants, even though they were in the same daycare centre. And then I realized I should be studying temperament — this is pretty strong. But, of course, I should add that, by now, two psychiatrists, Alexander Thomas and Stella Chess, had published their work on temperament, so temperament was just beginning to enter the consciousness of social scientists. But had I been less timid, I would have begun this work earlier.

PK: We talked about the two things that might dance, I suppose, and I think there are a lot of such things within your work. Obviously, there's biology and environment. And then one of the things you talk about in *An Argument for Mind* is the dichotomy in all human beings, not just children, between novelty and coherence. Can you talk about that and about the dance that goes on between those two factors?

JK: Right. I'm not the first to say this. Other people, including Benjamin Franklin, have said it. But each generation puts a good idea into different words. The human brain — the animal brain, too — the brain of living things is, first and foremost, sensitive to change: a change in sound, a change in smell, a change in motion. And, of course, it would be very adaptive for nature to have made brains that way because a change could mean danger, and therefore you better stop what you're doing and get out of there, and so that's adaptive. It's as if it is the first signal to the brain. Now, if you assimilate, if you understand the change and everything's fine, of course, a sensitivity to change is adaptive, because that's how you learn new things. That's why we go on vacations. We want to see Venice if we haven't seen Venice. We want to read a new book if we haven't read that book. We watch *Nova* and nature programs because novelty that we can understand is pleasurable. On the other hand, new things that are not understandable terrify us. Part of the malaise and low-level tension in the modern world is that it looks absurd. We're poisoning old KGB retirees in London. We're massacring people for no reason, not just in Iraq, but Hutus and Tutsis, too. There are things that many, many millions of people find hard to understand. If you can't understand new things, then you get nervous and anxious, so human beings walk in a very narrow corridor each day between attraction to the new that can be understood and comprehended and a terrifying avoidance of the new that cannot be understood, and it's that dance.

Now, it so happens that, in our work on temperament, children vary in how much newness they can tolerate, and I've spent twenty-five years studying that. There are some infants who are born with a chemistry — and I wish I understood that chemistry; I don't — that renders their brain unusually vulnerable or susceptible to reacting to the slightest change, and they get tense and clam up and become cautious. Other children have a much higher threshold, and you have to turn up the game far more — you have to present extreme novelty before you provoke cautiousness in them. And it turns out that that's one of hundreds of temperamental traits, but it's the profound differences among humans. If you want the caricature of it, it would be Jack Lemmon and Walter Matthau in *The Odd Couple*. And what's interesting is that Hippocrates, the great Greek physician from 400 BC, talked about melancholic and sanguine people, and if you read his description of melancholic and sanguine people, it is this difference that he is describing. Of course, we have the classic terms "introvert" and "extrovert," which are related to these tendencies, though not synonymous with them. And so those are the two temperaments that I have been studying. Now, they're only two, because there will be hundreds and hundreds of temperaments, but they're prevalent and they're easy to study and they have interesting ramifications over the course of development.

PK: Can you talk specifically about the experiment — it's a very famous experiment — where you took infants and held brightly coloured objects in front of them and literally watched their reactions, and then you historically traced it as they developed and grew up?

JK: Sure. For reasons that are too technical to go into, when we started this work about twenty years ago, many other scientists, working with animals primarily, had demonstrated that a structure in the brain called the amygdala, which sits right under the convoluted cortex at the level of your ear, reacts to unexpected, ambiguous, or unfamiliar events, sends its projections, its axons to many places that we associate with fear — like a rise in heart rate, a rise in blood pressure, tension in your muscles, freezing in place.

So we presented unfamiliar events to five hundred four-month-old infants. Here's what I mean by an unfamiliar event: we would take mobiles of coloured dolls and move them in front of the infant's face. Sometimes it would be one doll, sometimes four dolls, sometimes seven dolls. They had never seen these dolls, so that was new. Notice that none of these unfamiliar events was threatening or dangerous; they were just new. Or we would turn on a tape recorder, and suddenly the sixteen-week-old infant would hear sentences coming from the speaker, like, "Hello, baby, how are you today? Thank you very much for coming. Would you like some warm milk?" That's a very strange situation because the baby is hearing voices but isn't seeing anybody speaking. Or we would dip a cotton swab in some very dilute alcohol and present it to the infant's nostrils. Now, those are all unfamiliar events, but none of them is dangerous. And what we saw was that twenty per cent of the infants were qualitatively different from all other infants. They would thrash their arms and legs, their bodies would become stiff, and they would begin to cry, as if they were telling us, "You have passed my threshold. That's too much for me." Remember, look at the innocent events we're showing to them. Forty per cent were just the opposite. They lay there, very relaxed, never cried, occasionally babbled. We called the first group "high reactive," and we expect them to grow up to be the more fearful, cautious, timid children. And forty per cent we call "low reactive." They're the infants who didn't move very much and didn't cry. And we're assuming they have a higher threshold in the amygdala, and we expect them to be the Walter Matthaus: more sociable, more exuberant, less fearful.

Now, we followed these children, and the last time we saw them was when they were fifteen. We've seen them five or six times. And even though they've had external persona changes, they have preserved their style, their personality. Let me give you an example of each. Here's a typical high-reactive infant. Now, at one and two years of age, this is a fearful child — that is, the mother recognizes the child is fearful. The child is shy. This child flees when something very novel occurs. But by the time you're four years of age, your brain is more mature. You're able to handle novelty, and so now the behaviour is more subtle. You're less obviously fearful. And by the time you're fifteen, it's all gone underground, so now fifteen-year-olds who were high reactive are not necessarily shy anymore, but they will say things like, "I have to keep lists. I must know what's happening tomorrow." This is the Jack Lemmon personality. "I don't like the future. I don't like taking the subway into Boston," which is only three miles. One fifteen-year-old who's not shy at all said, "My class is taking the bus to Washington next week, and I'm very nervous about that. I've never gone to Washington on a bus before." Or one girl would say, "I don't like being touched." So the temperamental quality that expressed itself as public fearfulness when you're two years old is now all inside, and it's a low threshold to become nervous when you can't predict what's going to happen in the immediate future.

The low reactives, on the other hand, were fearless when they were one and two, and now, when they're fifteen, they're very sociable. They like high-risk things. They are relatively fearless. One anecdote persuaded me a lot. When they were fifteen, we had a long interview with them at home, so now we're in a very familiar setting. They're wearing blue jeans. They're sitting in their room, relaxed as can be. And after the interview, which is two-and-half hours and videotaped, the interviewer says, "Thank you very much. You've been very cooperative. We appreciate it. I just have one more question, and that is: what would you like to be when you're an adult?" They're fifteen. Now, the vast majority said exactly what you'd predict. Remember, these are middle-class children from good homes. They said they wanted to be a doctor, lawyer, journalist, businessman, engineer, teacher. Two boys — two only — and they were serious, said, "I want to be president of the United States," and they meant it. Both boys had been low-reactive infants when they were sixteen weeks old. Now, I say to you, if you're fifteen years old and you really think you can do that, that requires an inner consciousness, an inner temperament that has told you you don't get nervous very often, so why not?

PK: Did all of the cases stay on track? In other words, did low-reactive people remain low reactive, and the high-reactive people remain high reactive?

JK: About half of each group retained very important traits that you'd predict from their temperament. But here's the important point: less than five per cent became the other type. Remember what I said earlier — what does their biology do? By that, I mean their temperament. Being a high reactive doesn't guarantee that you're going to be a tense, anxious adolescent, but it does guarantee that you're not going to be a fearless, sociable, high-risk adolescent. You see what I mean? Being high reactive prevents you from saying, "I'm going to be president of the United States."

"Novelty" is the word we use when we're talking about events in the world — so, novel sounds, novel sights, novel people, novel places. But, of course, humans, unlike animals, have a very rich and elaborated symbolic system made up primarily of language. The mind likes consistency among the beliefs that it holds. That is, we don't want to believe that peas are both vegetables and animals — that would be a semantic inconsistency. We use the word "coherence" for that. Humans demand that the simple systems they hold — the vast store of knowledge they have acquired — have coherence. That comes naturally. It doesn't require an education. It's built deep into the biology of being human. People become disturbed when they feel that their beliefs are incoherent, and societies begin to show malaise and disintegration when there is too much incoherence. And I do believe that, at the moment, in the modern Western world, the absurd events that we watch on television each evening are beginning to compromise the coherence that humans demand, and that is a serious problem. For example, humans, and this is in the Tree of Knowledge allegory in Genesis, have to believe that some things are correct, right — not arbitrarily right, but right — and it is therefore very important that you believe that your value system, whatever it is that you learned as a child, is the correct one. You'd like to believe it's the most correct one because that gives you confidence that the decisions you're about to make, the life choices you're about to enter into, are the right ones.

Now, because history has created such diversity, because of migrations and the ability of people to pick up and go from one country to another, we have enormous diversity in Europe and North America, unlike Indonesia or the jungles of New Guinea. And because it's necessary for civil harmony that we be tolerant of all ethical beliefs, we put a strain on the coherence of each person's ethical system because they've got to deal with the following: the value system I was taught is the correct one — it might even be the most correct one — but I am told and urged by my society that I must be tolerant of this other group that obeys the law and takes care of their children, that has totally different values than mine. Look at the furor in the United States over gay marriage. Enormous! When you get that kind of incoherence — incoherence about whether abortions are OK, are morally right or not, whether gay marriage is morally right or not, whether Ethiopian mothers have a right to do the ritual of genital mutilation of their thirteen-year-old girls, which some Americans find horrific, and yet the culture does that and says that's what we wish to do — now you're beginning to tear the fabric of coherence, and this is a problem that Western society is going to have to deal with. Indeed, I do believe that one reason for the confidence of the Islamic world is they sense great coherence, and they take a great deal of moral authority from it — that's why coherence is so important — and the West is going to have to find a way to deal with this.

I don't have the answer. This is one of the most profound dilemmas, I think, that faces the world, which is, of course, totally interconnected at the moment.

PK: As you say, it's a dance of the dichotomies that's something that must be constantly played out and certainly constantly watched.

You mention another factor that I'd like you to talk about for a while as well, and that is goodness. Where does goodness fit into all of this?

JK: Goodness — OK. There has always been a debate in the West about whether a conscience, whether a sense of right and wrong, good and bad, is innate, given to us as profoundly as speech and the ability to climb a tree are given to us. Now, the ancient philosophers said, of course, it's given. You remember that in the Tree of Knowledge allegory in Genesis, God says, after Adam and Eve eat the apple, OK, I'm going to make you different from all the animals, you're going to know right from wrong — that is, good from bad. That was a curse for disobeying God. So I think it is innate, even though, during the twentieth century, because of the emphasis on environment, a lot of people actually wrote that you have to teach a child right from wrong; otherwise, it will never have a conscience, which, in my opinion, is wrong. But, of course, infants don't have a sense yet, and, in research, we have demonstrated — and other people have supported our demonstration — that, somewhere in the second year, somewhere between twenty and twenty-four months of age in all healthy children, no matter where they live — suddenly realize there are good and bad things. They are sensitive to the fact that they are being frowned at or punished for certain acts, and they immediately make these categories, "good," "bad." There is no three-year-old in the world, no matter where you and I, on a magic carpet, drop ourselves, no matter how isolated, who wouldn't know the difference, given the language of that community, between good things and bad things. So that is fundamental, as the ancient philosophers said.

Now, if there are always good and bad things, and good things are those you want to possess and bad things are those you want to·

avoid, then by the time you're three, when you realize that you, too, are an object, like an apple or a pear, because you have a solidity and a place and a location, then you want to be a good thing. You want to be the "goodest," and you want to avoid having features, traits, beliefs, feelings that are bad. So, in my view, it's that pair of motives that is the gyroscope, the central command that guides our lives. Why are we different? Because we regard different things as good or bad as a function of our culture. For some, being attractive is good. For others, it's being smart. For others, being wealthy. For others, being strong. For others, being athletic. And so on. So, because, given our experience, we adopt different definitions, we go off in different ways. But that's exactly like language — that is, every brain in a healthy child is ready to learn a language, and if you're in Kenya you learn Swahili, and if you're in Paris you learn French. I'm saying that is exactly the model you want for the human conscience — that every child will know there are good and bad things, and then the culture in which it raised will tell it which actions to find good and which actions to find bad.

PK: You say in the book that your favourite word is "maybe." This is an interesting thing to hear you say because you're certainly known as a person who's not afraid of controversy and somebody who's held strong opinions from time to time. Why do you choose "maybe" as your favourite word?

JK: I choose "maybe" because, first, in the social sciences — that is, psychology, sociology, anthropology — there is no determinism, zero. That is, there is no way you could say, "These are the conditions, and therefore everyone in those conditions will think or do the following thing." Never. There is no "maybe." If I have a glass in front of me and I have a hammer, and I strike the glass with the hammer, a hundred per cent of the time the glass will shatter. Now, that was the model in physics for so long. As a matter of fact, Einstein was very bothered by the introduction of quantum mechanics in the 1920s because quantum mechanics, which is the accepted theory in physics today, says there is no determinism. You can never know anything exactly. It's always probability, always "maybe." And now, quantum mechanics is regarded by every scientist as the best answer we have for how relations are in nature, and therefore there is no determinism. You can't look at a person's brain state and determine what they're thinking or feeling or even what they might do. So that's why "maybe." And, as I say in the book, I think that social scientists have to stop imitating the physics of the nineteenth century, hoping for determinism, and appreciate that the answer will always be a probabilistic one, always "maybe." I think I use in the book the wonderful fable of the king who asks his wisest scholars to take all the books in his palace library and reduce them to one word, and they say, "That's impossible." He says, "That's what I command you to do." And they come back twenty years later and give the king a piece of paper on which is printed the single word, "maybe."

PK: You are a social scientist of long standing. You have been at the peak of your profession for decades, and you are, I hope, not at the end of your career, but you are certainly at a point where you can look back and look ahead. And I would like you to do just that: look ahead more than backwards. What are the kinds of questions, the kinds of issues, that you would be addressing if you were just beginning your career now?

JK: That's a good question. Every scientist has two motives: to be of use to the society and, like an artist, to produce something of beauty, which may not be useful. As I get older, I realize that, if you want to help society, get elected to the Senate or Parliament, it's much more difficult to do it through science. So the need for beauty, the need for an elegant result, begins to take precedence. And history determines how sciences go. It could have been another way, but the point is that machines were invented that made study of chemistry of the brain and the physiology of the brain possible, and therefore more elegant, more beautiful science. I guess if I were twenty years old now, I would do what most twenty-year-olds are doing at McGill and UBC and Harvard and Yale — that is, they're going into the study of the nervous system, the chemistry of the brain, the physiology of the brain, and seeing if they can predict simple aspects of behaviour. And some of the results are elegant. They're aesthetic. And I guess that's probably what I would do if I were twenty years old today.

As for the future, I'm afraid — and I say this with great sadness — that disciplines, like nation-states, split. And therefore I fear — only because I'm being sentimental about the past... you don't like to see the breakup of what was once a unitary field — that it will happen in the future. It's happening at some universities. Already, you're seeing divisions in which the people who study biology are breaking away and forming their own departments, separate from those who study just behaviour.

The "Vulgarity"
Correspondent

THEODORE DALRYMPLE

In that terrifying and prophetic book and movie A Clockwork Orange, *thugs rule the streets of British cities, entertaining themselves by indulging in wanton and indiscriminate acts of violence. Ordinary people are forced to hide behind closed doors. That's fiction, but it's not too far from the world that Theodore Dalrymple portrays in his writings. A British doctor, psychiatrist, and prolific essayist, Theodore Dalrymple is not his real name — it's a* nom de plume, *which he assumed early on to protect the confidentiality of his patients and perhaps himself. For years, he's worked in "slum" — that's his word — hospitals and prisons, but his reach and his interests are far wider: from slums to travelogues to Shakespeare to intellectuals and their effect on the social mores of our time. Underneath his demure English accent is a fierce, plainspoken man who's alarmed by the direction in which Britain, and no doubt the rest of the Western world, is going. Theodore Dalrymple is the author of* Life at the Bottom *and* Our Culture, What's Left of It: The Mandarins and the Masses. *His interview with Paul Kennedy was broadcast on 1 May 2006.*

PAUL KENNEDY

Let's go directly into your work now, and I'm looking at the cover of your latest book, *Our Culture, What's Left of It: The Mandarins and the Masses*. There's a picture of a Caucasian male with dyed orange dreadlocks tied with sort of purple endings. There's lot of piercing and rather strange cat-like eyes. Who is this person? Is this somebody you know?

THEODORE DALRYMPLE

No. It isn't me. It was not chosen by me, the cover, although I think it is a quite startling cover, but it does say something about the antinomian nature of our culture.

PK: What does "antinomian" mean?

TD: Going against laid-down regulations, laws, for the sake of doing so.

PK: Sort of rebelliousness just for being a rebel.

TD: Yes. Rebelliousness is a good in itself, irrespective of what is being rebelled against, which is, of course, a deeply conventional attitude.

PK: And one that you take on full force in a great deal of your work. The other book that I've read of yours, *Life at the Bottom*, describes your work with your patients in what I would have to call an underclass in the British Midlands, and your work there both as a psychiatrist in a hospital, but also in a prison.

TD: Yes. I'm not very keen on the idea or on the concept of the underclass, because that rather tends to conjure up an image of a group of people who have no connection with the rest of society, who are perhaps three or five per cent of the population, and it's hard luck for them, but it doesn't affect the rest of the population very much. My point is, however, that many of the social pathologies and ideas that permeate the underclass first came from the intellectual elites and now are spreading — and, in my view, with very bad effect — up the social scale.

PK: So the Bloomsbury Group or the British intelligentsia could play with these ideas, but they're not so happy when they're worked out in real life by people other than themselves.

TD: Yes. Circumstances alter cases. That isn't a very original idea, and it's an obvious idea, but, unfortunately, it's not one that, even now, has permeated at least the British intelligentsia.

PK: Let's go back to the man on the cover of the book. Is he your patient? Are these the kind of people that you meet when you're dealing with them as a psychiatrist?

TD: No. The man on the cover actually looks rather different. I deal with people who are too often drunk, malnourished through taking drugs, beaten up, so actually he looks pretty clean and spruce by comparison.

PK: What prompted you to get involved in that kind of work? What took you to those kinds of people? Why did you need to go there?

TD: First of all, I was offered a job — I'd come back from abroad. But, secondly, in any case, I've always worked in poorer areas, and I actually find the problems more compelling and more interesting than those of the richer areas.

PK: How so?

TD: I suppose, in an odd kind of way — and this might come as a surprise to people who read my books — I have more sympathy for those people, and I think they tell us more about the wider society in which we live. I don't like what I see, but I think it's very important that people should see what is in front of their faces, actually, and one of the problems in Britain — I don't know whether it's the same in Canada — is that people don't want to see what's in front of their nose.

PK: That means the problems that they might be facing are drug users, drug abusers.

TD: I'm talking about people who don't have those problems. One of the things that I think I mention in one of my books is that I had lunch one day with a very distinguished BBC correspondent, a very nice, cultivated, decent man, and he asked me whether I made all my stories up, as if I might have been writing fiction. And in a way I was quite flattered that he thought I could make it up, but I thought it was very alarming that a man could be so blinkered about his own society that he couldn't see what is to be seen, in fact, on British trains, for example, at ten o'clock at night, wherever you go. All you have to do is go on a British train at ten o'clock at night or go into a town centre on Friday or Saturday night and you can see what I'm talking about. You don't even have to go to the bad areas of towns and cities.

PK: What you're talking about — and I don't want to put words into your mouth or characterize what your analysis is — is the complete collapse of what people used to think of as British civilization in some ways. In the last forty years, you think that the bottom has fallen completely out and that society has crumbled and collapsed.

TD: Yes. I think it's not just that it's crumbled and collapsed, it's been destroyed, and, if you like, there's been a gestalt switch, so that what people once thought was good, they now think of as bad, and what was once thought of as bad is now considered good, and I could give you examples of that.

The British not long ago were thought of as being rather re-strained, perhaps absurdly so, and, I dare say, in some cases, that was so. They were absurdly restrained or, if you like, self-controlled. And now the idea of self-control is anathema to most British people.

They feel, they've got some kind of sub-Freudian idea, that emotion is a bit like poison: it just accumulates, and if you don't let it out by expressing it, then it will poison you. I suppose the ultimate example of that was a patient who said to me — he'd killed his girlfriend — "I had to kill her, or I don't know what I would have done," and he felt that obviously his emotion had to be expressed. In Britain, actually, there's something, a very strange phenomenon, which one might call "ideological drunkenness" — that is to say, people get drunk, extremely drunk, and behave in a pretty disgusting and uninhibited way in public. And if you ask them why they do it, they actually believe that they are acting both virtuously and healthily. It's good for them to, as they call it, "let their hair down." And this is not a problem of the bottom two or three per cent of the population. It goes right throughout the population now.

I can give you another example. For a time, I was virtually the vulgarity correspondent of one of our newspapers.

PK: The "vulgarity correspondent"?

TD: They used to send me anywhere where the British were abroad, or sometimes in Britain, where British people were behaving en masse in a bad and disgusting way.

PK: Soccer hooliganism.

TD: That kind of thing, yes, and the way people behaved on holidays. Clearly, there's quite a lot of work to do. They sent me to a friendly football match, a so-called friendly international match, to Rome, and there were ten thousand British people there. I don't think the Romans had seen anything like that since Alaric the Goth. And I was the only one who was not shouting obscenities at the Italians for hours on end. They shouted disgusting things for hours and hours on end, and I, of course, refused to do so, and at half-time, when things calmed down a tiny, little bit, I turned to the chap next to me. And, certainly, these people were not poor. Anyway, the chap next to me was a computer programmer. So I said, "Excuse me. I hope you don't mind me asking, but why have you come all this way to shout abuse at the Italians?" And he said, "Well, you've got to let your hair down." And I said, "Why do you have to? I personally think you should keep it up." And he was completely unable to give any explanation as to why he had to let his hair down, but he clearly thought that it was necessary and that behaving in that fashion was a good thing to do.

PK: And you trace this now fairly widespread social phenomenon to ideas that emerged from the British intelligentsia twenty, thirty, forty years ago, things that, in your opinion, they were toying with and playing with, not understanding the ultimate potential social implications.

TD: Yes. I don't think it's just the British intelligentsia, nor are the phenomena I describe solely British ones. If you go to Belgium or Holland, you can see the same thing. It's quite as widespread as in Britain. And also, what is perhaps more alarming in Britain is that it's spread up the social scale to quite an astonishing extent. But I do think it is connected with the ideas that were expressed rather playfully, if you like, by intellectuals, who, of course, would claim that they were trying to bring about improvement. And, of course, improvement is always possible. I'm not a dyed-in-the-wool conservative who thinks that nothing can be improved. In fact, no doctor could possibly be a conservative in that sense, and certainly not culturally, either. But, of course, if improvement is possible and has to start somewhere, then deterioration is always possible and has to start somewhere. And I don't think that the people that I'm talking about in my book, many of them, gave much thought to that possibility.

PK: I'd like to know how you deal with these people as patients, not when you're talking to them in a Roman football stadium, but when they're actually sitting in your office, dealing with you and their problems. What do they tell you? What do you tell them?

TD: As usual, of course, I take their history, and I try to do it in a reasonably detailed way. And, of course, it's rather focused on their problems and the development of their problems. In most cases where I don't think the problem is fundamentally a medical one — sometimes it is a medical one, but in the majority of cases it wasn't medical, it was a problem of how to live and perhaps not knowing how to live — I would say the kind of things that I say in my book. If I can give you some examples, I saw thousands of women who had been badly abused by men — not husbands usually, because there aren't any husbands.

PK: Just a sequence of monogamous relationships? Not necessarily monogamous.

TD: Not necessarily monogamous, yes, but often monogamous. And the sequence actually usually results in jealousy all round, and jealousy is a great promoter of violence. Of course, I made it quite clear to the women that I thought that the way they had been abused was terrible and completely unjustifiable. However, I thought it was very important that they should understand their own complicity in it, so that, for example, they understood that the way they chose men and their refusal to see signs, which they were capable of seeing, resulted in their misery.

To give you a complete example, I would say to them, "This man of yours, who's very nasty to you and drags you across the floor and puts your head through the window and sometimes even hangs you out of the window by your ankles, how long do you think it would take me to realize he was no good as he came through the door? Would it take me a second or a half a second or an eighth of a second, or would I not notice that there was anything wrong with him at all?" And they would say, "Oh, it would take an eighth of a second. You'd know immediately." And I would say to them, "If you know that I would know immediately, then you knew immediately as well" — so, a logical consequence really, and they would accept that. "And yet you chose to associate with him knowing full well that he was no good, and I tell you this because it's very necessary you should understand your own part in the predicament you now find yourself in, because if you don't understand it or don't think about it, you're just going to repeat it," which, of course, is a very, very common pattern.

PK: Have they ever given you an answer that was satisfactory that allowed them to perhaps change the pattern in the future?

TD: I think it does change them eventually, but the point about it is that I was the first person, in most cases, I think, to talk to them straight.

PK: As a psychiatrist?

TD: As any kind of person.

PK: So they were not getting any kind of help or counselling anywhere else?

TD: They often did, but, of course, their own responsibility in the situation was skated over.

PK: And it was blamed on society at large or...

TD: Or the man was a terrible man, which, of course, he was — there's no denying it. I think the fundamental error is that we live in a very sentimental age, and we sympathize with people, but we feel that, in order to sympathize with people, they must be victims and nothing but victims, and therefore we turn people who are self-destructive into victims. But it's important that they should understand the destruction comes, to a large extent, from within. And in fact, even where they are victims of circumstances — and, of course, in many cases they are — knowing that you're a victim of circumstances isn't going to help you very much. All it can do is allow you to fester in your own resentment. Resentment is one of the few emotions that never lets you down, really, but it's useless. In fact, it's worse than useless; it's harmful. And we all suffer from it at some time in our lives.

PK: What do your colleagues say to you? Since you're the only person telling these people these hard, almost tough-love, truths, you must be alone in a profession that largely goes along with the underlying assumption that it's not my fault, it's somebody else's.

TD: I think the underlying thing to do is to prescribe medicine and medicalize it, so that most of the people I'm talking about are on medicine, cocktails of medicine or single medicine, and there's a kind of absurd pas de deux between the doctor and the patient, where the patient pretends to be ill and the doctor pretends to treat him. And what happens is that the patient comes with his or her unhappiness, which is the result of the way he or she is living, the doctor gives some medicine, it doesn't work, but you have to give it time to work, so the patient comes back a little while later, and they double the dose, and you have to try that for a length of time, and then that one doesn't work, so the doctor says, "If that one doesn't work, don't take that one anymore. Take this one," and so on and so forth, and this can go on actually for years.

PK: It sounds like a downward spiral. How could you even get out of it?

TD: You have to get out of it by trying to establish the truth of the situation. And incidentally, you may say, "What happens? Do the women get very angry?" I used to use the same technique in prisons as well. Of course, there were a few people... one has to choose people. There are people who are quite beyond it, of course. In prison, for example, there would be cold-hearted psychopaths. There wouldn't be any point in using that technique with them. But most of the people in prison were not cold-hearted psychopaths.

PK: Tell me about your work there. You worked in prisons as a psychiatrist?

TD: As a psychiatrist, but also as a general doctor, so I used to treat the physical illnesses as well. The main difference between working in an NHS [National Health Service] hospital in Britain and a prison is that prison is much safer.

PK: Explain that for a moment. Things are going roly-poly over here, but that does seem like quite the inversion of what one would expect.

TD: The thing is that the doctor is protected by very large men who are just outside the door if anything begins to go wrong, which isn't necessarily the case in the hospital.

PK: But it's the same people in both places.

TD: They're not identical people, but people drawn from very similar backgrounds and areas and so forth, and one of the things that's very noticeable to me is how much British public housing resembles prison, but it's a prison without warders, and a prison without warders is the worst kind of prison because, of course, the most psychopathic person rules, and those who just want to obey some kind of rules and get on with their life are at the mercy of the worst people. That's what living on a British housing estate is like. And, in fact, one of the things that's very striking is how similar the argot of prison and the argot of the housing estates is, and that's because, for those people, freedom is a prison.

PK: It's Dickensian with a nasty twist.

TD: Yes. Of course, it can be very funny, but the peculiar thing is that one wants to laugh and commit suicide at the same time, which is a rather peculiar sensation. One doesn't know whether to throw oneself off the roof or fall on the floor in laughter, and that's the absurdity of it. But a lot of it comes from, first of all, intellectual dishonesty and also a kind of emotional and political dishonesty that I see as being very prevalent in Britain. I'm not optimistic about anyone changing the situation.

PK: Obviously, your work must have tremendous emotional cost to you. This is not something that would be easy to do every morning — wake up, have a cup of coffee, and go into the office and deal with a collection of people who are plainly frightening in many ways.

TD: That's not actually true, because, from a very early age as a doctor, you are both involved with your patients but also detached from them, so it didn't exert any emotional cost on me really at all.

PK: I know you've written that your mother was worried about your working under these kinds of conditions.

TD: Yes, she thought that it warped my sense of reality, if you like, because it's like policemen who tend to think that everyone is a criminal until proven otherwise because he's dealing largely with criminals. And intellectuals think that everyone is an intellectual because he meets only intellectuals. But I would say to her, "If you think my view is so warped, why is it that you can't walk out at night?"

PK: And she can't now, whereas she could maybe forty years ago in Britain?

TD: Oh, absolutely.

PK: So it's no longer safe to be in the streets in a...

TD: Perhaps this is a slight exaggeration, but the fact is that elderly people in Britain are effectively under curfew, which has been decreed by young men.

PK: So that, when it gets dark, they can't leave their homes.

TD: Exactly. It's like those old Dracula films, and after dark Dracula comes out, and you had better be indoors.

PK: But can you prescribe a solution to this problem? How can we make it safe for elderly people in Britain to walk out the front door after eight o'clock at night?

TD: I don't think it's an easy thing. If you're saying, "Give us the answer," I don't think there's a single answer. I think the law can do quite a lot, but it can't do everything, and in any case, one doesn't want a population that behaves in a reasonable and civilized way only because it fears that, if it doesn't, there'll be a tap on the shoulder and they'll be taken off to prison. First of all, I don't think that's possible, but secondly it would be very unpleasant, even if it were possible.

So, I think the first thing — and this is what I've been trying to do — is to draw attention to the phenomenon, because if you don't accept that the phenomenon exists, you can't even begin to think about what you should do, and we're still at the stage, if you like, where we have to think about whether the phenomenon exists. And, in fact, an enormous amount of intellectual energy has gone into trying to deny that the phenomenon exists. The first stage is to say, "It doesn't exist." The second stage is to say, "It exists, but it doesn't matter." The third stage is to say, "Oh, well, it exists, and perhaps it matters, but it's always existed, and it's always been exactly the same." If you take the question of public drunkenness, for example, if you came to Britain and asked ten intellectuals about the public drunkenness you saw in the street, I can guarantee that nine, and probably ten, would immediately say "Gin Lane." They would immediately say, "Hey, Hogarth."

PK: It happened a long time ago and it's still happening.

TD: Exactly. But I can guarantee that, if you raise the question, "Gin Lane" will be the first thing that they...

PK: But why? What is in it for the intellectuals to deny something that is plainly in front of their face?

TD: The fundamental reason is that, if they accepted the reality of it, they would have to rethink their presupposition. Now, you might think the job of intellectuals is actually to think, but I don't think that is the case in a sense. What they want to do is to feel virtuous and generous spirited and so on, and it's very easy, if you apply moral judgments to these phenomena, to sound censorious and Pecksniffian.

PK: Dalrymplian.

TD: I hope they're not entirely in the same category.

PK: Can we go back to prison, and go back to the work that you've done in prisons? I'm really interested in the way you've characterized the changes that have happened among the population within British prisons in the last little while. You say that things have been changing. There's a particular, striking essay called "When Islam Breaks Down." Tell us about what's happening inside British prisons.

TD: When I started in the prison, which is not that long ago historically, there were very few prisoners of Indian subcontinental origin, and now they're full of prisoners of Indian subcontinental origin, but the interesting thing is that they're practically all Muslims. There are no Sikhs, no Hindus, even where there are large numbers of Sikhs and Hindus living, so there is this difference.

PK: So that the Muslim population is grossly overrepresented inside British prisons.

TD: It's becoming so, yes.

PK: Why?

TD: I haven't got the full explanation. I've been thinking about it, but I can't say that I've actually put my finger on what it is. I suppose that when you have a very rigid system that is beginning to break down, then it breaks down completely. It's strong, but rigid. It's not supple. Some people might say, "They came from different social classes in the first place," and it is to me a very remarkable and astonishing, but not very pleasant, change. Incidentally, one of the interesting things is how secularized the young male Muslims are. The idea that they're all religious fanatics is absurd. They're not religious in any way whatever.

PK: So these are not terrorist crimes, for sure.

TD: Oh, no, no, no, no, no, no.

PK: Not in any way committed with a religious motivation.

TD: No, no, no, no, no. They're just common crimes. And they're not religious. They're not interested in halal food. They never pray five times a day. The only thing about Ramadan that interests them is that, occasionally, it gives them an excuse not to go to court, but they're not otherwise interested in religion, although they will claim to be believers and so on, but they don't manifest it in any way. And one of the interesting things you can do is to go into the entertainment areas of cities, where there are large numbers of Muslims and where people are behaving in this rather disgusting and uninhibited way that I described, and you will find that the young Muslim men are exactly the same as the whites. They're not integrated, because they go around in their own groups, but they're behaving in the same way. However, you don't see young Muslim women in the same areas, because one of the things that [the men] are interested in is preserving their domination over women — that's a great interest of theirs — and that's why, in the name of honour, for example, they will go out and be violent to somebody of whom they don't approve seeing their sister, because they want the system to remain as it is, because it's very convenient for them.

PK: And a dangerous one.

TD: Yes. I think the danger comes, of course, because it is such an unsatisfactory existence. The way of life that they see around them is so wretched, they search for an answer to it, and, of course, one is ready to hand. The supposed answer to it is ready to hand for those who are more intelligent and more reflective.

PK: Which is?

TD: Which is a kind of fundamentalist Islam.

PK: You've travelled a great deal more, I would say, than the average psychiatrist. You've been around the world. How have some of the experiences you've had — and some of them have been fairly graphic experiences as well — coloured your work within Britain with the kind of people that we've been talking about?

TD: I think it's quite important, because, of course, I've travelled and lived in countries that are very, very much poorer than Britain, dramatically poorer than Britain, and yet I can see, or I saw, in poor populations much less of the social pathology that I see in Britain. And, of course, that was one of the things that made me start thinking about whether poverty was the explanation of the social pathology that I was seeing in Britain.

PK: Can you talk specifically? What places in the world did you see?

TD: I lived in Africa for a few years, I worked in the Central Pacific, and I also lived in Central America for a time. And incidentally, I travelled pretty extensively as well. For example, once I crossed Africa by public transport from Zanzibar all the way to Timbuktu.

PK: There's about an hour's worth of conversation in that, I think. Give us the Cook's Tour version.

TD: I went by public transport, and I saw life from the bottom up in Africa. I saw, for example, real oppression one time in Mali. The entire busload of people was arrested three times in a hundred yards, with a view to extracting bribes from them to get on, and, in fact, some of them were imprisoned three times in a hundred yards.

PK: Then, you were also assumed, I assume.

TD: No, no, oh, no, no, no, because, as they used to say, "The death of one white man will give you more trouble than the deaths of a thousand black men." They were always very polite to me. They would say, "Stand aside, *monsieur*. This has nothing to do with you." And, of course, I would wait there while the various officials would then set about extorting money from the other passengers, and if I made any protest, they would say, "But, *monsieur*, we haven't been paid for three months," and it was true. It was a form of taxation, but it was going directly into the pockets of the state's employees rather than through the president, who never disgorged any of it. It was only what the people expected, but one can't say it's a good thing. The fact is that people bore it with the most astonishing dignity, and these were people who had really very, very little indeed, and the behaviour of people to me who had absolutely nothing was extremely dignified and very generous.

PK: And in stark contrast to what you notice among the people you work with in Britain.

TD: Exactly. And, therefore, it set me thinking that raw poverty, as it were, couldn't be the explanation of what I was seeing.

PK: In Africa, you also confronted a rather horrendous setting where mass murder had taken place. Can you describe that?

TD: It was in Liberia. I went during the civil war, and I went to a church where a — I was going to say famous, but I suppose I should say an infamous — massacre took place. Six hundred people were shot to death. I didn't see it myself and, in fact, the bodies had been removed, but the dry blood was still on the church floor, and you could see the mounds where there was a mass grave. And I met, for example, one of the leaders of the civil war, the brigadier general Prince Y. Johnson. I had to go and see him in the morning because, in the afternoon, he was drunk and high on cannabis and used to take his AK-47 and go and kill people. I interviewed him. I remember I said, "After the war is over, what are you going to do?" He said, "I want to be a pastor," and I believe he is a pastor, actually. I think he went to Nigeria and is now a pastor.

PK: Those kinds of incidents, meeting those kinds of people, has to colour one's world view, and I would think the colour is more dark than light.

TD: It is, and it makes you always aware of what people are capable of. I never thought, oh, well, this applies just to Africans in Liberia. How could one think that after all that's gone on in Europe and everywhere else, really? And that again is one of the themes of one of my books: civilization may be a veneer, but it is the veneer that protects us from brutality and barbarism. You may say, "That's a very banal thought." I think it is a very banal thought and a very obvious one, but it doesn't seem to have occurred to many people who have set about undermining things, I think, for fundamentally egotistical reasons.

PK: There's another incident I'd like you to recall in that context, and I think it paints that picture very vividly in palette-knife kind of strokes. You were in Pyongyang, and you were at a large socialist rally for the Great Leader, Kim Il-Sung, and somebody came up to you. Could you tell us that story?

TD: It wasn't at a socialist rally. You could say that North Korea is a sixty-year-long socialist rally, really. But it was in the square in front of the Great People's Study House, which is like the cross between a railway station and a fascist mausoleum and a pagoda. It was completely deserted, as Pyongyang mostly is, and I was walking in this deserted square. Incidentally, nobody in North Korea talks to you.

PK: It's illegal, of course, to talk to a foreigner.

TD: Yes. And even if it were legal, it would be very foolish. And this man came past me and said, "Do you speak English?" He was Korean. "Do you speak English?" And I said, "Well, yes." And he said, "I am a student of the Foreign Languages Institute." One thing that the communists did was to teach foreign languages extremely well. And he said, "Reading Dickens and Shakespeare is the greatest, the only joy of my life," and, of course, what he meant by that was that reading Dickens and Shakespeare gave him an intimation that language could be used for something other than the dissemination of lies and oppression of people's minds, so it freed him really for the first time in his life and the only time in his life from that most terrible of oppressions. I was at a very large gathering called the International Festival of Youth and Students, which used to be held every four years in communist countries. I was neither a youth nor a student. Anyway, I managed to get into this. Incidentally, the entire production of food of the country was devoted to making sure that these people from abroad were fed and so on. He said, "Would it be correct English to say that this festival is as welcome as the snowstorm before the harvest?" So I said, "It's correct English, but you know better than I whether it's true," and then we parted, because obviously he couldn't communicate any more than that. But it seemed to me amazing that a man could communicate so much in two or three sentences in a completely foreign language and with a seriousness of intent which, I'm afraid, puts a lot of our intellectual life completely to shame.

PK: I asked the question initially in the context of what you'd said about the veneer of civilization, and I was touched by this man's courage, but also, I guess, by the breadth of his understanding that he would choose, of all the English writers in the canon, Shakespeare and Dickens as the two that give him the sense of what life should be about.

TD: Yes. Because in Shakespeare or Dickens, the character speaks in his own voice and, in that sense, is free in a way that no one in North Korea was free. And if you imagine what it's like to live in a country where the dullest and most mendacious political speeches are literally inescapable — they're on the buses, they're in the trains, they're relayed by public address systems in the street, and you can never say, "No, this is not true" — you can imagine what the experience of reading about, shall we say, Falstaff and even Mrs. Gamp is in those circumstances, and that's the kind of liberating power of culture, I think, and that's why the trivialization of culture is a very bad thing.

PK: Shakespeare is somebody you come back to fairly frequently. What is the lure for you in William Shakespeare?

TD: I suppose it's because I think that, really, human understanding has never gone beyond Shakespeare. Of course, we understand many things that Shakespeare didn't understand in the scientific sense, but the understanding of life is as deep in Shakespeare as I think man is ever going to achieve. I know that people think they understand how the brain works, or claim that they do, and there are claims that we understand consciousness and so on. I think it's all hogwash, myself. I don't think we do understand it. I suspect we're never going to understand it. And I suppose, in my heart of hearts, I hope we never understand it, because, if we do, I'm sure we're going to abuse it. But I actually don't think that we understand ourselves or understand life better than Shakespeare understood it.

PK: One of your favourite plays is *Macbeth*.

TD: Partly because, of course, I've been to countries where there have been such dictatorships and people have behaved like Macbeth.

PK: Don't you actually describe, I think, a performance in Zulu?

TD: Yes, that's right. And the interesting thing, of course, is that it's instantly understandable to Zulus. In fact, it's a play that is understandable to the entire world.

PK: Why?

TD: Because they understand that this desire, for example, for power and the unscrupulousness that it can unleash is a perpetual and universal human possibility.

PK: Would your patients in the British Midlands understand *Macbeth*?

TD: Yes, absolutely.

PK: How would they understand it?

TD: In fact, they would understand it better than most, because, of course, one of the things that has happened is that power relations have become absolutely more important in their daily lives. In fact, power is the only relation that now exists in large areas of the country, and you can see this. I'm digressing slightly. If you see the way the mothers now discipline their children — and I've observed it myself — what you get is a child that's behaving badly, shall we say, in a supermarket or a shop. The mother screams abuse at it. The child continues to behave badly, and the mother threatens it and screams and so on, and the child continues. Then the mother gives up and gives it a chocolate bar. So, what the child learns then is that everything is a matter of struggle, and if you take the struggle far enough, you can sometimes win. Also, the grossly inconsistent way of disciplining children means that there's no underlying principle involved. What's important is how the person that you're annoying feels at the time and whether that person is more powerful than you, and that is the basis of all social relations, because they never experience any reliable or stable principles.

And, incidentally, that explains why so many prisoners in Britain actually like being in prison. I got on very well with them because I spoke to them very directly, as I'm speaking to you now, and I think on the whole they respected that, and it meant that, fundamentally, I was treating them as an equal. Anyway, I would ask them confidentially, "Do you actually like being in prison?" Because you'd look at their record, and they'd gone to prison many times, often. And they said, yes, actually they do like it. They prefer to be in prison. Life is better for them in prison than outside. I'm glad to say that quite a lot of the brutality associated with British prisons isn't there so much now, anyway. And this is a terrible thing, that people should prefer imprisonment to liberty, but many do, and one of the reasons is that life in prison has a set of rules, it's fairly predictable, and if you obey the rules, you can more or less tell what's going to happen to you, and you'll probably be left more or less alone.

And, of course, they're also — this is interesting to me, anyway — pleased to be free of women, and this isn't, of course, because they're homosexual — they're not homosexual. The reason they're pleased to be free of women is that their relations with women are so chaotic and lead to so much distress and violence and chaos that they're pleased to be free of those complications.

PK: You're quite happy to take on all kinds of what I would call shibboleths, the truisms that are accepted and generally adhered to or acknowledged by society at large. You can take all those things on and say things that are sometimes, I think, quite unpopular. For example, you say we need repression. That's not something that would be generally a bandwagon that a lot of social scientists or anybody would jump onto these days, but you are quite content to go out there and say it.

TD: I say it because I think it's true.

PK: You're not afraid, then, of being guilty by association? Some of the people who would give some of the same sorts of arguments...

TD: Would be very nasty.

PK: Very nasty. One could say fascist almost.

TD: Yes, you could say that. But I'm sufficiently sure of myself that I'm not a fascist that I can say those things.

PK: What gives you that kind of confidence? Why can you be so confident that you are not going to move in that direction?

TD: Because I'm not proposing that there should be arbitrary power, that we should remove protections from people who are accused, that there shouldn't be due process, that there shouldn't be freedom of expression, and so on and so forth. I'm not proposing any of those things. What I am saying is that I think people should think very carefully about the ideas that they propose. In particular, I now realize that, if I hadn't done the work that I've done, I would have come to this conclusion myself, but they have to think of the effects of their ideas on people who are in many ways different from themselves or differently placed from themselves, so that I can't just say that a proposal is OK for me, therefore it's OK for society. And I think that's very much the level of understanding of a lot of intellectuals. That's their process of thinking.

PK: You actually also use words that a lot of intellectuals would be very embarrassed or ashamed to use, and I think specifically about "evil." "Evil" is a word that comes up in — I didn't count it — but it might be one of the most frequently used words in your work. "And," "but," "the," and "evil" are probably the first four words you use. It's not a popular word. It's not a word that people can use comfortably these days, but you have no trouble using it.

TD: Let me give you an example. There was a young boy who'd just been found guilty of murder, who was on probation, having previously strung up by his ankles a mentally subnormal boy, whom he then beat unconscious and injured very severely. That's a pretty evil act, and I don't think many people would say, "That's not evil." Your first instinct is to say, "That's evil." I don't think that's the end of the matter, but it is evil. If evil exists, if evil means anything, it means that kind of thing, and, unfortunately, we do see quite a lot of that kind of behaviour in Britain. And it seems to me that we're doing violence to our own reaction to our own humanity if we don't characterize something like that as evil. As I said, I don't think you just say, "That's evil. That's the end of the matter. That's that." You don't inquire where it comes from or what it means and so on and so forth. But I have no real difficulty calling that evil. I don't know. Perhaps you would.

PK: No, no, no, not at all. What I'm saying, though, is that it's a word that people are not comfortable using. It's a word that does come value laden.

TD: It is an evaluation. Actually, I think it's a jolly foul thing for someone to take a mentally subnormal and helpless person, suspend by his ankles, and then beat him just for the pleasure of doing it. If you're not going to say, "I think that's really rather a bad thing," what are you going to say is a bad thing? And if you're not going to say, "That's very bad," how are you ever going to think about stopping it?

Cognitive Dissonance

ELLIOT ARONSON

Elliot Aronson, one of social psychology's elder statesmen, has been studying cognitive dissonance for almost half a century. In his recent book, Mistakes Were Made (But Not By Me): Why We Justify Foolish Beliefs, Bad Decisions, and Hurtful Acts, *co-authored with Carol Tavris, he presents an engaging account of all the ways in which cognitive dissonance displays itself. As a student, Elliot Aronson worked with two great psychologists. One was Abraham Maslow, a founder of the Human Potential Movement, which was highly influential in the field of therapy and helped fuel the popular self-help movement. His mentor and greatest influence, however, was a more hard-headed scientist, Leon Festinger. Paul Kennedy's interview with Elliot Aronson was broadcast on 21 April 2008.*

ELLIOT ARONSON

Leon Festinger was a genius — he invented the notion of cognitive dissonance — and I started working with him in 1956 at Stanford, when I was a first-year graduate student. We actually both arrived at Stanford at the same time, Festinger as a distinguished young professor in his late thirties, and me as a very insecure first-year graduate student. Festinger had a reputation for being a very difficult, rather harsh person, which he deserved, and my first impulse was to keep away from him because of my own insecurity. But I ended up taking a seminar with him where he first articulated the ideas for the theory of cognitive dissonance, and I realized that, although he was difficult and sometimes harsh, the rose was worth the thorns. He was a terrifically smart and also a warm human being.

The theory of cognitive dissonance, which he first published as a book in 1957, simply states — it's a very simple theory, with huge ramifications — that, if a person holds two ideas or cognitions or attitudes that conflict with each other, the experience is cognitive dissonance, which is a negative drive state, like intense hunger, except it takes place in the brain, and that person, he or she, is motivated to reduce that dissonance. So, for example, if a person knows that cigarette smoking causes cancer and he also knows that he smokes three packs a day, those two ideas are dissonant with each other, and he needs to reduce that dissonance, so the best way, the easiest way, would be to stop smoking. Then his cognitions would be consonant with each other. But that's not so easy to do. So, if a person has tried to quit smoking and failed, then he or she will try to reduce dissonance by working on the other cognition, by trying to convince himself or herself that smoking isn't that bad: if I didn't smoke, I would gain a lot of weight, and gaining weight is bad for your heart, so it sort of evens out, and actually the research showing that smoking causes cancer has flaws in it, et cetera, et cetera, et cetera — in that way, making it easier to continue to smoke in spite of the fact that, deep down, you suspect that it might kill you.

The very first experiment I ever did testing the theory of cognitive dissonance was based on the notion that, if you work hard for something, then you will like that thing better than if you get it without working hard. We invited people to join a very high-level discussion group, and we made some of those people go through a rather harsh initiation in order to get into the group, while the others got in by going through a very mild initiation procedure. Then, they listened to a rather dull and boring tape recording we made of that group in action. What happened was that the people who got into the group while going through a mild initiation talked about how dull and boring our group was, and many of them wanted to resign from it.

But the people who went through the severe initiation convinced themselves that the group was really very interesting, and they loved it, the idea being that the two cognitions — I went through hell and high water in order to get into a lousy group — are dissonant with each other. So what people do is they ignore or downplay or make themselves oblivious to all the negative aspects of the group and emphasize in their own minds the positives and good aspects, so that they end up really liking the group a lot more than they should.

Now, that is a fascinating phenomenon because, in the past, psychologists always believed that things associated with pain or difficulty would be liked less — and, indeed, in most situations, they are. But if you go through pain or difficulty in order to achieve something, that particular something becomes more attractive, and that was one of the great breakthroughs that dissonance theory led to.

PAUL KENNEDY
Couldn't it mean that you're just lying to yourself?

EA: Indeed, you are. But you are lying on a level that's beneath awareness, so that you're not trying to pull the wool over anybody else's eyes, but you've succeeded in pulling the wool over your own eyes. Cognitive dissonance operates just beneath the level of awareness. We know that because, for example, after this experiment I did was over, when I debriefed the participants and told them what the theory was and what the hypothesis was, almost all of them said, "Wow! That's really very interesting." But most of the people in the severe initiation condition said, "Oh, that's a very interesting theory, and I'm sure it works for some people, but it didn't work on me. I really liked the group because it was a good group, not because I went through that initiation." But, of course, the data were very clear: there was no overlap between the mild initiation group and the severe initiation group, so whatever was happening was happening below the level of awareness.

PK: And that level can be moved by people when they discover that they are perhaps being dissonant. They can change it for their own convenience...

EA: They change it in order to reduce the stress caused by the dissonance. We can look at all kinds of real-world examples, and the one that immediately comes to mind, of course, is the political. If you take a guy like George W. Bush, who started this horrendous war in Iraq because he maintained that Saddam Hussein had weapons of mass destruction, most people in this country, most liberals, will assume that Bush was lying from the outset because he wanted to invade Iraq. I may be one of the few liberals left in this country who don't think he was lying to us. I think he was fooling himself. I think he had convinced himself that Saddam did have weapons of mass destruction. The CIA reports and the reports from other agencies were mixed. Some of them suggested that he might have had these weapons at the time. Others suggested that he probably didn't have these weapons. I suspect very strongly that the Bush administration was reading those reports in a biased way in order to justify their notion of attacking Iraq. In other words, they were convincing themselves, not necessarily just us, they were convincing themselves that he had weapons of mass destruction.

Why do I believe this? A few weeks after we defeated Saddam, when Bush really believed that the mission was accomplished, when we were occupying Baghdad, people were saying, "Where are the weapons of mass destruction?" And Bush and Cheney were saying, "They will turn up. Iraq is a large country. They're hidden some-place." And they kept saying things like that five, six, seven, eight months later, until finally they had to admit that there were no weapons of mass destruction. Well, if you're lying to other people, you probably want to lie in a way that you can't get caught at the end. So that's why I believe that Bush and Cheney, who are canny politicians, would not have invented an excuse for entering Iraq belligerently if they didn't themselves believe it. The fact that they believed it on the basis of flimsy evidence is what I'm talking about. It's the self-justification that results from dissonance, the notion that they wanted to invade Iraq, they were looking for a reason, and, therefore, they tended to accept the aspects of the reports that indicated that [Saddam] might have weapons of mass destruction and to ignore or downplay those other aspects, very much like the people in my initiation experiment, who, on an unconscious level, downplayed the negative aspects of the group they had joined.

PK: I like the initiation example because it also reflects you and Professor Festinger at the same time. He made you understand that you were joining a group, and you had to go through something of a rite of passage. Can you talk about that, the first paper you handed in?

EA: I don't think Leon did that on purpose. I think that was his character. He did not suffer fools gladly. Leon could not abide sloppy thinking. In my first experience with him, I thought my career as a graduate student was over. I was in a seminar — it was a terrific seminar — and about three weeks into it, he assigned a term paper, and I wrote the term paper the way I usually write things. And a couple of days later, I was walking past his office on my way to the teaching assistant room, where I had a desk, and he called me in. He said "Aronson" and waved me into his office. He took my paper off a stack on his desk, and he put it between his thumb and forefinger, held it at arm's length with his head turned away, as if he were handing me a piece of particularly smelly garbage, and he said to me, "I believe this is yours." So I tried to exercise a little false bravado there. I said, "Oh, Leon, I guess you didn't like it very much," and he gave me this look, which anyone who ever worked with him will recognize immediately. It was a mixture of contempt and pity — contempt for someone who was wasting his time, and pity for me because, obviously, I had been born brain damaged. And he said, "Yes, that's right. I didn't like it very much."

So I took the paper and walked back to my desk in a room that was about thirty yards away, but it seemed like it was a couple of miles away. I left it on my desk for a few minutes — I didn't have the courage to even open it because I was expecting to see all kinds of angry marginalia, angry statements of criticism written in the margin. Finally, I opened it up, and there wasn't a mark on it — nothing — so I said, "What is this?" I walked back into Leon's office, gathered all my courage, and I said, "Leon, there must be something wrong. You didn't tell me what I did wrong. How am I supposed to know what I did wrong?" And he again gave me that look of pity of contempt, and he said, "What?! You don't have enough respect for your own ideas to follow them to their logical conclusions? Your thinking is up in the air without really being grounded, and you expect me to tell you what you did wrong? This is graduate school, not kindergarten. You're supposed to tell me what you did wrong." So I walked back to my office, and I re-read the paper, and I tried to re-read it through his eyes, and I realized that it was a sloppy paper, that it wasn't well reasoned or well thought out.

Now, I was at a choice point there, and it was one of the most important choice points of my entire life. I could have quit the seminar and said, in effect, "To hell with that guy. I don't need him. I'll work with someone else." But again, he was brilliant, so the choice was, do I work with this brilliant, harsh, difficult person, or do I quit? And I decided that I really wanted to work with him, so I went back and I rewrote the paper — it took me three solid days — and I made it as tight as I possibly could. I brought it into his office, put it on his desk, and said to him, "Maybe you'll like this one better," and I then I walked back to my own desk. And to his great credit, he must have dropped whatever he was doing and read it immediately because, twenty minutes later, he came into my office, put the paper in front of me, sat down on the corner of my desk, put his hand on my shoulder, and said, "Now, this is worth criticizing." At the time, it seemed like a very hard statement, but over the next fifty years as an academician, I've come to realize that it was a brilliant statement. I've said the same thing to many of my graduate students: if you want someone with a really good mind and a lot of experience to work with you, to criticize your work seriously, then you have to meet him or her halfway, you have to do the initial work and show that you are there. And then Festinger, in this case, and I, when I finally got my spurs, will do anything for you, including criticize your work, which is a great gift, as it turns out.

PK: It is amazing that, in your career, you've had these choice points, or critical moments. Are they fortuitous? I guess cognitive dissonance could tell something about this, too. You also, as a young academic, confronted one of the other giants in twentieth-century psychology, Abraham Maslow. And Festinger and Maslow weren't necessarily compatible, but they both had major effects on your career.

EA: They hated each other. It's not that they weren't compatible — they couldn't abide each other. I didn't know that at the time.

I've been very lucky. I stumbled into Maslow's first class at Brandeis University when I was nineteen years old quite by accident. I was majoring in economics. People often ask me when I first realized I was a social psychologist, and I often answer that question a little bit cutely. I say I first realized I was a social psychologist when I was nine years old, before I even knew there was a field called social psychology. My family was Orthodox Jewish, and they sent me to Hebrew school, and we lived in the middle of a virulently anti-Semitic neighbourhood in a blue-collar town in Massachusetts near Boston. And in order to get back and forth to Hebrew school, which I went to in the evening every day, five days a week, I had to run a gauntlet through gangs of teenagers who were shouting anti-Semitic epithets at me and telling me that Hitler had the right idea and all that sort of thing. And every once in a while, they pushed me around, and once in a great while, they actually beat me up, and I remember very distinctly, after one of these beatings, sitting on a curbstone nursing a bloody nose and a split lip and asking myself, why do these kids hate me so much when they don't even know me? Were they born hating Jews, or did something teach them to hate Jews? And I thought, gee, if they got to know me and realized what a sweet and charming little boy I was, would they like me more? And if they liked me more, would that mean that they would hate other Jews less? Of course, I didn't realize it at the time, but these were profound social, psychological questions.

Now, I went to Brandeis University on a scholarship, and the only reason I went there was because it was the only school that offered me a scholarship, otherwise I couldn't have afforded to go — we didn't have any money in our family. So, at Brandeis, I was majoring in economics, and I was having a cup of coffee one afternoon with a young woman I was courting, a very gorgeous young woman, but then she looked at her watch and she realized she had to go to class, so I followed her to class. I wasn't stalking her or anything, but I walked along with her to class, and it turned out she was in a class in introductory psychology taught by some guy named Abraham Maslow. Now, at that time, I thought he was just some guy named Abraham Maslow — I didn't realize that he was the father of the Human Potential Movement. He was quite a guy. So, I was sitting in the back of the room with this young woman, hoping that maybe we could hold hands or something — those were innocent times — and I began listening to Maslow's lecture. It turned out that he was lecturing about prejudice, and he was raising some of the same questions that I had raised ten years earlier, sitting on that curbstone in Revere, Massachusetts. I was absolutely enthralled to discover that there was an entire field of psychology that dealt with the very questions that I thought were terribly important. I quickly lost interest in the young woman sitting next to me and began to pay close attention to Maslow. I lost the girl, but I gained a profession, in a sense, and the next day I changed my major from economics to psychology, and I became a protegé of Maslow's, and it was a very exciting time for me. Maslow taught me a great deal. He was a visionary who had wonderful ideas, but he wasn't a very good scientist.

Then, when I went to Stanford, to graduate school, and started to work with Leon Festinger, I realized for the first time what scientific psychology could be. Now, when Festinger found out that it was Maslow who had inspired me to go into psychology, he looked at me with his very strange look, as he was wont to do, and he said, "Maslow! Maslow! That guy's ideas are so bad, they're not even wrong," which is a very interesting statement, and what he meant was, this is a guy who has ideas, but you can't test them. There's no way to test them because they're so amorphous.

Then, that summer, when I came back to New England, I visited with Maslow, and he invited me out to lunch, and he said, "So who are you working with at Stanford?" And I said, "I'm working with this guy, Leon Festinger." He says, "Festinger! That bastard! How can you stand him?" So there I was, my two mentors, and they hated each other. And, although I don't think I did this on purpose, a lot of my work has been described as a marriage between Maslow and Festinger, the kind of humanistic psychology that was trying to deal with improving the human condition that Maslow represented and the hard-nosed science that Festinger represented. Now, Festinger didn't give a fig about the application of his ideas to real-world problems. He invented several theories, but the most prominent is the theory of cognitive dissonance, and he did a lot of experiments to test that theory, but, for Festinger, it was like a chess game. He didn't think of psychology as being applicable. He didn't care. His idea was to figure out how the human mind works, and that for him was like theoretical physics as opposed to engineering. He didn't care about the engineering part.

But my inspiration to get into psychology was to do something about such things as prejudice and aggression and hostility and war and stuff like that, to try to make things better. And what Festinger gave me were the scientific tools to do that, so in a sense my entire professional career has been, to some extent, a combination of Maslow's humanism and Festinger's "take no prisoners" science.

Casablanca's a great movie — all of the critics say it's one of the three greatest movies of all time. There's a wonderful scene, which everybody who has seen the movie will remember. Let me set the stage: Victor Laszlo, as played by Paul Henreid, is an underground, anti-Nazi worker, and he's a very important man. Ingrid Bergman is married to Paul Henreid, but Humphrey Bogart is her real love. She is crazily in love with Humphrey Bogart. The scene takes place at the Casablanca Airport. There are two visas that will get them out of the country and into the free world, and it's a foggy night at the airport. Ingrid Bergman thinks that they're going to put Paul Henreid on the plane and she's going to stay behind with Humphrey Bogart, but at the last minute, Humphrey Bogart tells her that she has to go with

Paul Henreid because it's the best thing for the world, and so he says this very romantic thing. She's standing there with tears in her eyes, wanting to stay with him, and he says to her, "If that plane leaves the ground and you're not on it, you'll regret it, maybe not today, maybe not tomorrow, but soon and for the rest of your life." It is a beautiful statement. It's a very romantic statement, and it's dead wrong.

PK: No — say it ain't so. No. It's gotta be true.

EA: Let me tell you, if the plane left the ground, and she was there with Humphrey Bogart, she might regret it today, she might regret it tomorrow, but soon and for the rest of her life, she would have reduced the dissonance and convinced herself that the best thing she could have done was to stay with Humphrey Bogart. If she had left with Paul Henreid, which she did, my guess is that she might have regretted it today, she might have regretted it tomorrow, but soon and for the rest of her life, she would have convinced herself that going off with Paul Henreid was the right thing to do.

What cognitive dissonance teaches us is how to deal with our regrets and how to convince ourselves that the important decisions we make were the right decisions, by and large. Now, that doesn't mean that we never have regrets, but when you think about all of the thousands of decisions we make every month, some big, some small, the ones we actually regret are amazingly few. When we buy a new car, a new house, when we make a decision about whom to go out with or whom to marry — all of these important decisions — ninety per cent of the time we don't regret them. Now, that's partly due to the fact that we make good decisions, but it's also partly due to the fact that we make our decisions good after the fact by downplaying the negative aspects and playing up the positive aspects. As Benjamin Franklin, that wise old man of American politics, once said, "A person should keep his eyes wide open before marriage and half closed after marriage." Part of what that means, of course, is that we convince ourselves that we made the right decision.

Now, marriage is an interesting situation because we find over and over again in these books written by marriage counsellors and people who really have studied marriage counselling from the inside out, while they are not dissonance theorists, that people do a very good job of making the best of a marriage until it reaches a tipping point — and it does in about half the marriages in this country — when a person decides there's too much crap to be putting up with here. And once that tipping point is reached, then the eyes suddenly snap wide open, and you begin to dredge up every single negative thing you know about your partner, again as a way of reducing the anticipated dissonance that might come from a divorce. Once you reach the tipping point and start moving toward the idea of a divorce, you begin to shore that up. It's an amazing phenomenon, and I'd like to talk about that tipping point in some detail.

PK: Absolutely. You spend quite a bit of time in the book talking about marriage, for example.

EA: We do. But I want to leave marriage for a second because I want your listeners to have in their mind a pyramid. This is the example I want to give on this one, and again it relates to marriage or to anything else. Suppose a bunch of students are taking an exam in, say, biology, and they need to get a good grade so they can go to medical school. Now, let's say that they feel reasonably well prepared as they enter the exam, but then, when they look at the questions, they draw a complete blank and they break into a cold sweat, and one of these guys is saying, "Oh, my god, I'm going to fail this exam. There goes medical school. There goes my entire future. I don't know what I'm going to do," and his blood runs cold. Then, he happens to look up, and he's sitting behind a young woman who is the smartest person in the course, who also has the largest, most legible handwriting in the course, and all he needs to do is look over her shoulder, and there are all the answers ready for him to copy. What does he do? He knows that cheating is not a good thing to do, yet he really wants to pass this course, and he wrestles with his conscience.

Now, let's suppose there are two people in exactly that same situation, and imagine they're sitting on top of a pyramid and that they have exactly the same attitude toward cheating. They think it's not a good thing to do, it's a bad thing to do, but it's not the worst thing in the world. And let's say that, after wrestling with their conscience, one person decides to cheat and the other one decides not to cheat. Now, both of them will experience a great deal of dissonance. The person who cheats in order to get into medical school will experience dissonance when he says to himself, "I've always considered myself a good, honest, moral person, and now I've committed this immoral act." How does he reduce dissonance? He tries to convince himself that cheating isn't such a bad thing. It's really not immoral. It's a victimless crime. Anybody in the same situation would have cheated, so I would be foolish indeed not to cheat. And with each one of these things, he's sliding down the pyramid toward the base — his attitude about cheating is becoming softer and more and more forgiving, and he's convincing himself more and more that it's not a bad thing to do.

The other person, who decided not to cheat, is experiencing dissonance, too. He says, "My god, all I had to do was cheat and I would have gotten a good grade and I would have gotten into medical school. But I didn't cheat." Now, how does he feel about cheating? He's sliding down the pyramid in the other direction. He's convincing himself that cheating is a terrible crime. Of course, it's not a victimless crime: "If I get a good grade, since we're being graded on the curve, then somebody else is being knocked off the curve. If I get into medical school on the basis of this performance, that means somebody more deserving is not getting into medical school. Cheating is a terrible thing to do. Boy, am I glad I didn't cheat. Anyone who is caught cheating should be immediately expelled from school. As a matter of fact, we should put him in a stock and throw vegetables at him." By the time a few weeks pass and they've reduced dissonance — at the beginning they were standing next to each other at the top of the pyramid, with almost identical attitudes toward cheating — they're each at the other side of the base of the pyramid, with very different attitudes toward cheating. That's exactly how it works in this situation.

PK: But what does it tell us? If it explains both behaviours, it can't predict which one would make either decision, can it?

EA: You can't predict which one will make the decision. Once they make the decision, though, you can predict exactly what will happen. Just to take a non-random example, the people who began by defending waterboarding — this horrendous thing that we're doing — Bush and his colleagues say it's not torture. Americans don't torture. Therefore, it's not torture. So waterboarding becomes an OK thing to do. Sleep deprivation becomes an OK thing to do. Now, once you start sliding down that pyramid, that slippery slope, you can begin to justify anything, and that's exactly what's happening. Once you start defending a particular practice, it goes deeper and broader, and it's very difficult to reverse course, just as it's very difficult for people in the present administration to get us out of Iraq because staying the course becomes an example of reducing dissonance by convincing yourself, on the basis on flimsy evidence, that the Iraqis are beginning to self-govern in a very reasonable way.

PK: Since we're back in the world of politics — and I think it's someplace we're obviously going to end up — the title of your book comes from an almost direct quotation from an American political figure, Henry Kissinger, who said at one point, "Mistakes quite possibly were made in the administrations in which I served." Now, that's a slightly different kind of example in that he's admitting his own guilt, isn't he? Quite possibly, he's backing off a little bit.

EA: Not quite. Kissinger was a great example. Almost every president that I can think of, certainly from the time of Ronald Reagan, has used the phrase, "Mistakes were made," which is the passive voice, and I call that the "passive self-exonerative."

PK: Somebody else made those mistakes.

EA: Because mistakes were made, but not necessarily by me. Now, Kissinger is a wonderful example because, in the Nixon administration, when we were in the Vietnam War, the last disastrous war we were in before this one, Kissinger served Nixon as both the National Security Adviser and the Secretary of State simultaneously, so, as far as foreign policy was concerned, Henry Kissinger was the administration. So, for him to say, "Mistakes were quite possibly made by administrations in which I served," is a little disingenuous. But again, I don't know whether Kissinger was lying to us or maybe lying to himself, reducing dissonance, but it certainly allowed Kissinger to live with himself, to sleep at night, and to accept the Nobel Peace Prize with a clear conscience and a straight face. Imagine giving the Nobel Peace Prize to Henry Kissinger. As my friend Tom Lehrer once put it, "That was the death of satire." How can you satirize that one? That's self-satire if I ever saw it. I think, in evolutionary terms, the advantage of cognitive dissonance, of dissonance reduction, and the reason why it's hard-wired — and it's been going on probably from the time of the caveman to the present — is that it makes evolutionary sense to be able to reduce dissonance because it helps you sleep at night. George Bush gets a good night's sleep. He does not look any the worse for wear. His sleep is fine. But, of course, when important decisions are involved that are wrong and that involve a lot of other people, one shouldn't sleep well at night. In minor situations, if I make a pass at the dean's wife at a cocktail party because I've had a few drinks too many — and if you knew the dean's wife, you'd realize what a ridiculous thing that would be to do — when I get home at night and my wife says to me, "What were you thinking?" I would love to believe that nobody noticed or that people realized I was just being affectionate, and then I could sleep well at night. But when it comes to important decisions, we really shouldn't sleep well at night. We should really examine those decisions and not leap so quickly and so easily into dissonance reduction.

One area that is of momentous importance is the legal system, where, as I speak, there are hundreds of people languishing in prison for major crimes who are innocent, where DNA evidence has turned up showing that they're innocent. For example, in one case that I can think of, a guy was sentenced to life imprisonment for a rape and murder, and before the woman died she said that he was the only assailant. He's been in prison for twenty years, and suddenly DNA evidence turns up that demonstrates that the semen inside her body was not his. It was not his DNA. So you would think that the prosecuting attorney would release the person or at least reopen the case and give him a new trial, but it turns out more often than not, when the prosecuting attorney who's currently in office is the same person who put the guy away for life imprisonment, that they're very reluctant, they even refuse, to reopen the case. Now, why? The simple answer, which I think is wrong, is that the prosecuting attorney is an evil person. The more complex answer is that he believes himself to be a good and competent person, and he cannot accept the fact that this guy has been languishing in prison for twenty years and is innocent due to the prosecuting attorney's own error. So, in order to convince himself that he is a good and decent and moral and competent person, he keeps him in prison for another twenty years. That's the tragic irony of this kind of situation, where dissonance theory, in essence, is the theory of the self-concept. We want to believe that we are moral. We want to believe that we're competent. We want to believe that we're smart. Therefore, if we do something stupid or immoral or incompetent, we try to cover it over in our own minds and compound the error.

PK: But there are exceptions as well. There are people who are actually crippled by actions they've taken and the guilt they feel because of those actions. They maintain the state of dissonance and can't reconcile the two opposites in their minds in any way. Talk about those people.

EA: They do exist, and it's a small percentage of the population that does really focus on their errors, that experience buyer's remorse all the time, and they can't reduce the dissonance. They buy a new car and immediately say, "Oh, my god, I made a terrible mistake," or they buy a new house, and they begin to notice a lot of horrible things wrong with it. They do exist. Now, for unimportant decisions, the people who really fret about the mistakes they've made by focusing on the dissonance are what we would call neurotic. They sweat and strain over trivial things, they haven't really adapted or adopted the evolutionarily successful strategy of convincing themselves that nobody noticed or that it isn't so bad as they think. For minor decisions, that kind of dissonance reduction is a very useful strategy, but I think a small proportion of the population can't do it, and we call them neurotic. They go to therapists, who try to convince them not to sweat the small things. There's even a self-help book out called *Don't Sweat the Small Stuff,* and most things are small. Yes, those people do exist, but they are in the minority.

PK: There's another minor corrective or amendment that I'd like you to talk about as well, and that is, in the book, you say that cognitive dissonance doesn't only apply to spirals that seem to be going downward or to negative things, violent things, or criminal things. Sometimes there is a virtuous dimension or direction that can be taken. Can you talk about that?

EA: Yes. I'm glad you got to that one. When we commit an aggressive act, we try to convince ourselves that the person deserved it so that we can live with ourselves for harming that person. Then dissonance theory comes into play. But it also comes into play in exactly the same way if we commit an act of virtue. So, for example, if you're driving along a lonely country road in the rain at night and you see a person parked by the side of the road, obviously with a flat tire, and you stop and help that person because you're a good guy, and you get all wet and you jack the person's tire up and change it for them, you will try hard to convince yourself that this is a good human being. You will try hard to convince yourself that this person is worthy of the help you gave him, that this person is worth all the effort and energy you put out on his or her behalf. So, it's a kind of a virtuous circle, where working hard for another person will help you like that person.

When the schools in Austin, Texas, where I lived, were desegregated in 1971, all hell broke loose. Black kids, white kids, Mexican-American kids were at each other's throats. They were really angry at each other. There had been residential segregation up until that time, so these kids didn't know each other at all. They never had contact with each other. And fist fights and riots broke out in the schools. When I was called in to consult, what I developed was a way of getting kids to work together. Most classrooms are highly competitive, where kids are pulling against each other, and that results in a lot of negative things. If you're pulling against someone, you want to find things about that person that you don't like, because that person is your opponent. But if you're pulling with him, if you're working together, working hard to help each other solve problems, whether it's mathematical problems or writing problems or whatever it is, that kind of cooperative support leads you to find the good in the other person, because you're putting yourself out for that person. And we developed a very successful program for reducing prejudice and for helping people learn to find the good things in each other. It reduces bullying. It reduces prejudice. It reduces interracial violence in schools. If you put yourself out for another person, you want to convince yourself that he is or she is a decent, generous, nice person, and that's exactly why the cooperative jigsaw technique that I developed works. It's because the virtuous circle, the desire to see the best things in the other person that are brought about by behaving in a supportive way.

PK: In preparing for this interview, I learned that you recently became legally blind. There was a macular degeneration that meant that you could see less and less, and now you can't read or do many of the things that sighted people can do. Do you think that the training you've had as a social psychologist, specifically, I suppose, in dissonance theory, has in any way helped you to deal with the situation you're facing now?

EA: No.

PK: A short answer.

EA: It's a very difficult situation. The training I've had — I think I'm a critical thinker. I think like a scientist, and I end like a humanist.

I've been doing a lot of thinking about it, of course. I first contracted macular degeneration eight years ago, in the year 2000, and it's been a rough go. Losing one's eyesight — it's not an easy thing to reduce dissonance about. But one of the things that I've learned to do over the years is to play the hand that you're dealt, and to play it as well as you can, with as little whining as possible. And that general notion — I don't think it has much to do with dissonance reduction — has helped me a lot.

One of the difficult things about macular degeneration is that you lose your eyesight in spurts. When I first developed the symptoms and went to the best expert in the Bay Area, he told me, "Chances are you will lose most of your eyesight, but if you're lucky, it'll stop before you lose almost all of it." And what happened is that I would lose some, and at that point I would get dizzy, the world would look more blurry, and I would be bumping into things. Then, gradually, within four or five or six weeks, I would learn to adjust to that, and I'd say to myself, "This isn't bad. I can deal with this. If it doesn't get any worse than this, I'll be OK." Then, a couple of months later, it would get worse than that, and I would go through the same cycle again, where I'd be bumping into things, and I'd get dizzy, blurry, and then I would adjust to it. Finally, it hit rock bottom about three years ago, where I've now lost about ninety-five per cent of my vision. It's not going to get any worse than that. And it's almost like I'm breathing a sigh of relief. At least, I don't have to deal with another decrement in vision, and maybe that is dissonance reduction. I haven't really thought of it that way. I've adjusted to what I needed to adjust to, and I get along pretty well. I can't read now. For a scholar, not to be able to read is a tough one, but it's doable.

I just wrote this new book, *Mistakes Were Made*, with my friend Carol Tavris, and one of the things that was good about it was that I got to collaborate with a good friend. We would talk about it, and she would be typing, and I would be talking, and then she'd be talking, and then she would read it back to me, and I would make some changes. And we both realized that listening to a book is a lot better than reading a book, in a lot of ways, in the sense that we noticed things that were missing — it's almost like reading poetry. We noticed bad construction, we noticed sloppy, clunky sentences much better than if we were reading it visually. Again, I may be reducing dissonance by making that point. You've put an idea in my head! I'm a dissonance reducer! In any case, it was a great joy to write that book with Carol. In a sense, it brought me full circle because — I talked earlier about having combined Maslow with Festinger — what the jigsaw classroom did was allow me to take the science that Leon Festinger taught me and bring it into a situation where I finally began to work on the problems that brought me into social psychology to begin with — the ones I first discovered when I was sitting on a curbstone in Revere, Massachusetts, wondering why people hated each other — and find a way to reverse that process. Writing *Mistakes Were Made*, which came out in 2007, the fiftieth anniversary of the development of the theory of cognitive dissonance, was a gift to Leon Festinger, who died twenty years ago. It was saying, OK, Leon, you didn't care about the application of your theories; you only cared about finding out how the human mind works. Now, as a gift to you, I'm going to write this book, which takes the theory of cognitive dissonance and applies it to the areas of politics, marriage, law, and all of those things that you didn't care about, but now here it is being applied, just as you would have done it.

Phallocentrism

LEONORE TIEFER

Pioneering sexologist Leonore Tiefer, clinical psychologist and associate clinical professor of psychiatry at the New York University School of Medicine, has declared war on pharmasex. She thinks the pharmaceutical industry is reshaping the way we think about our bodies and how we practise sex. She believes that if men learned how to dance and diaper babies — not at the same time, of course — maybe we wouldn't need Viagra. Leonore Tiefer is smart, funny, controversial, a feminist who calls herself a revolutionary on behalf of sex. In her landmark book, Sex Is Not a Natural Act and Other Essays, *she describes the consequences of living in a hypersexualized culture. Constant images of sex bombard and numb us. Plastic surgery creates the improved or "perfect" body. Drugs can help us perform. And this is killing sexual creativity. Leonore Tiefer reminds us that we're diverse creatures, shaped by cultural, historical, social, and individual forces. She believes that, as a culture, we're losing sight of this richness and diversity, and an increasing homogeneity is creating an epidemic of insecurity around sex and our bodies. She was interviewed by* Ideas *producer Mary O'Connell for a documentary series called "Phallus in Wonderland." This interview was broadcast on* Ideas *on 27 September 2007.*

LEONORE TIEFER

A kiss is not a kiss in this perspective. Your orgasm is not the same as George Washington's. Premarital sex in Peru is not premarital sex in Peoria. Abortion in Rome at the time of Caesar is not abortion in Rome at the time of John Paul II. All of these actions remain to be defined by individual experience within one's period and place.

MARY O'CONNELL

Now, in your book, *Sex Is Not a Natural Act and Other Essays*, you talk about expectations. You talk about a lot of anxiety that's created by the importance of sex. But first of all, I want to ask you about the title.

LT: Well, it really sums up my most profound insight and the message that I want to get across. Obviously, it's sort of funny and provocative, but the point is that people rely on the assumed naturalness of sexuality like dying people hanging onto the side of a sinking ship. I mean, it's kind of a desperate conviction rather than anything that they've arrived at as the result of observation or reflection. My belief is that, if you keep your eyes open and if you reflect about things, you'll realize that sex isn't natural at all, that it has a whole lot to do with culture, and media, and previous experience, and expectations, and so on. So I thought that *Sex Is Not a Natural Act* summarizes this counterintuitive notion that is at the heart of my philosophy, and my therapy, and my research.

MO: Do we think that everyone else is having more sex than we are? I mean, what is our idea about ourselves and our sexuality and others?

LT: I feel quite certain that two or three hundred years ago, much less five hundred or a thousand years ago, nobody could care less about how much sex other people were having. It was not a priority. But in the last fifty years or so, maybe even escalating over the last ten or fifteen or twenty years, sex has become so much a measure of one's worth in a relationship and in society that adequacy, and frequency, and all of these things have taken on great meaning. I think that's becoming truer for men. I see a lot of men in my practice who are feeling pressured to have sex to prove that they're OK.

MO: Feeling pressure from?

LT: Peers. Peer pressure and internalized. You internalize these norms. Think of the case that I saw last night: a twenty-four-year-old guy and he's only had three partners, and he's absolutely convinced that he's so far behind his peers. It's tragic.

MO: And he's deeply troubled by this?

LT: He's deeply troubled. Now, all of these things fall on fertile ground. You know, it's the anxious person, the obsessional person, the perfectionistic person, and so on. People don't think that these things affect them. Nowadays, it's important that people feel that they have a sense of whether they're normal, whether they're in the ballpark. On the cover of every magazine is how to have sex twenty-five ways, how to keep your guy, how to look good, liposuction — and you can't go two steps without some sexual image crossing your path.

MO: Well, do you think we live in a hypersexual culture in terms of the imagery?

LT: Is there a stronger word than hypersexual?

MO: I don't know.

LT: Yes, out of control, over the top, ridiculously so. So that people are being taught to be highly desirous. And whatever desire people used to have, which was an on-again off-again thing and dependent a lot on the novelty of a relationship or personality or previous experience, there was a huge amount of variation. That variation is being eliminated as a kind of standardized image is promoted that says, do it a lot, want it a lot, enjoy it a lot, flaunt it a lot, brag about it a lot, and there's this inexhaustibility thing.

MO: Now, you've written that the word impotent was rarely mentioned in the psychological literature for decades, like it didn't even exist, but that this started to change by the 1980s with the emergence of what some call phallocentrism. What does this mean?

LT: I think the phallocentrism of our time is symbolized perhaps best by the explosion around Viagra. I think that the advertising campaigns promoted by Pfizer and the other companies — now that there are other drugs out there on the market and Viagra's not all by its lonesome anymore — have promoted the idea that a successful erection is the centrepiece and *sine qua non* of a successful sexual experience and sexual life, and everything else just kind of comes along automatically. There's never any talk about tenderness, or romance, or knowing what you're doing, or not all women like a hard penis... I mean, all of that is completely invisible.

MO: And what does this do to the partner and, we're talking heterosexually here, to the woman? I'm just wondering, on a psychological level.

LT: Well, I'll tell you, I really would like to see a lot of research on this. Of course, companies that fund their research on Viagra and the other drugs are not very interested in finding out any bad news. So there there's very little research. But what limited research there is — there are maybe four or five studies I know from New Zealand and Australia, in particular, two or three from the US, a couple from England — is consistent in saying that women's experiences are diverse. Some women are thrilled to bits. Some women are horrified, disgusted, and turned off. And some women are tolerant, and some women are angry, and some women are just patient.

If those relationships were humdrum, or uncommunicative, or boring, or painful, or conflicted, or whatever, they're probably going to be the same way with a drug as without the drug. If, on the other hand, relationships were more mutual, and inventive, and creative, and had some energy and effort in them, then they'll incorporate drugs in the same way they might incorporate a vibrator, or incorporate memories, or incorporate a glass of wine, or incorporate whatever. Of course, those are the relationships that probably don't even need the drugs.

MO: Is there something implicit with the use of Viagra that it will improve other areas of the relationship as well?

LT: I think it's implied in the ads. I remember the first set of ads that came out in 1998. They showed a couple dancing, and she was wearing high heels, and she had a nice little dress on, and she had a big smile on her face. And they were dancing. How many women have desperately tried to get their husband to go dancing? And the impression was, you give him this pill and he'll want to go dancing. So, the implication was not only that the drug would restore the choreography of their sex life but it would make him a more romantic person also. Well, show me the evidence for that.

The point is, we all change our physiology month to month, year to year. You know, things ache, they break, you have a cold, the kid is sick, you get poor, you get rich. I mean, life happens — you change, and so your sexual experience changes along with it. And if you go through a period of time where you can't perform intercourse in the usual way, you do something else and enjoy that. I mean, it's about pleasure. But maybe now it's just about performance.

To get back to phallocentrism, I do think that this is a critical issue and that Viagra is clearly linked to vaginal intercourse. Again, there is very limited research on this, but it suggests that there are changes in foreplay as a result of taking these drugs. "That cost me ten bucks, you know, I want to get my money's worth here. Let us not fool around. Let's get right to it." So Viagra is likely to change the choreography of sex, the "sexual script" as we call it.

Here's another way to look at it. We are nothing but physicality. I mean, I'm sitting here in a chair. It's the physical me. I don't exist as some kind of floating spiritual essence. But that may not be the only way to think about the effects of Viagra — emphasizing the physical. I think men take Viagra as insurance against failure. And I have spilled so much ink trying to explore how it is that people are more willing to adopt a physical explanation for things than a psychological, or social, or cultural, or interpersonal one. It's amazing. People would rather have something broken, they'd rather have low hormones or a vascular blockage, than be thought of as anxious. People want to have sexual security a way that I find astonishing, to be kind of robotic.

But I know that treating something that's psychological is not that difficult. It's even fun. It's about learning. It's about talking. It's about thinking about things in a new way. It's not insoluble. Somehow, a lot of the people who are behind the engine of Viagra have come out and said the psychologists, the psychotherapists, haven't been able to solve this for hundreds and thousands and millions of years. They say, "Thank God we've got pills now." That isn't true. I have been treating people with all kinds of sexual problems for decades, and I know lots, and lots, and lots of other people who have also been treating couples and individuals in a psychological way with success. But the rap, the rhetoric, the myth is that a psychological problem is demeaning.

MO: It's weak.

LT: It's weak. My feeling is exactly the opposite. Pills? Pills have side effects. Pills are dangerous. Pills interact with other pills. Pills cost money. You have to remember to take them. Whereas your attitudes you have with you all the time. But you know, we've been talking about biology versus psychology, and I would like us just to make sure that we add to that picture social factors, because I really believe that social factors cause more sexual problems than either psychological or biological ones.

MO: Social factors like what?

LT: Social factors like changing expectations, for example. I think expectations are changing and escalating to the point where it's very easy to "fail." If you have to have an orgasm every single time you have sexual relations, it's going to be hard to accomplish that. But we're all supposed to be robots and it's all supposed to be biological and automatic. These expectations are part of the culture now. So I feel that social factors — let's put in there the lack of sex education, the lack of comfort in talking about sex, the fact that it's still embarrassing for a lot of people to talk about it, that they lack a diverse vocabulary for expressing how they feel, what they want. That's a lot of what we do in sex therapy. You know, people come in, they're practically tongue tied. I saw a guy the other night, he must have said, "I never thought of that," a hundred and fifty times. I would say, "How did you feel about that? Why did you want that? Why did you say that to her? How often do you want to have sex?" "Well, I'd like to have sex every day." "Why?" Long pause. "What do you mean, why? I never thought of it." It would be that kind of thing. "Well, think about it now." "Why? Well, everybody wants to, don't they?" "Well, maybe everybody does, but tell me why you do." Long pause. "I never thought about it." So, there are so many ways in which people lack comfort in the topic and lack vocabulary for dealing with the topic. And I see that as a social problem.

MO: Right. Now, you're an associate clinical professor of psychiatry at the New York University School of Medicine. You lecture widely about sexuality all over the world. You have a private psychotherapy practice. But when you went off to Berkeley in the 1960s, you studied a very different aspect of reproduction.

LT: That's for sure. Well, I went to Berkeley as a junior in college. I spent my first two college years here in New York and then I went to Berkeley. And I started working with rodent sexuality because I was under the impression, as were we all in the field, that there was some kind of big mammalian thing about sexuality. Mammals — we were all variations on a theme, and if you could see how the mechanisms worked in the rat, how the hormones affected the learning environment, affected the testing environment, the psychobiology of the rat would tell you something about the psychobiology of the dog, of the monkey, of the camel, and of the human being. We were all just one big happy, mammalian family. So I thought, well, that's interesting. And watching animals mate, that was mildly interesting. A little bit goes a long way, but still, there are things to learn. So I did that at Berkeley and did my dissertation and went off to have a career.

MO: Now you got a Ph.D. in the hormones and mating habits of the golden hamster.

LT: Right. *Mesocricetus auratus*, the golden hamster.

MO: Is this something now, when you look back, you understand why you went this route, or is it something you think, well, I wouldn't have done that now?

LT: I wouldn't have done that now. Underscore. Underscore. To me the world changed in the 1970s with the women's movement. My head completely changed. This happened to so many of us, but each story is the story of profound reconsideration of your whole life and of everything that you used to think and believe. So, you know, I was just cooking along, studying rodents and teaching psychology in 1970, '71, and then another woman joined the psychology department where I was working, and where I was the only woman with twenty-seven male colleagues! This is the event I look back on. Pamela Pearson came from Chicago and she was a lesbian, and I didn't know any lesbians at that time. She was a lesbian, so she had a girlfriend. So that was really interesting. She said, "Do you know about the movement?" I said, "The movement? What movement?" And she said, "You know, the women's movement. There's speeches, there's marches, there's pamphlets, there's a revolution going on. It's the Women's Liberation Movement, WLM." And I thought, oh my God, gimme, gimme, gimme. So I started reading, and reading, and reading, and reading, and as I read I thought, oh my God, that's me. Sexuality was a big topic back then. You are in charge of your body.

You should know about your body. Get a speculum. Look at your cervix. I got involved in a consciousness-raising group, and we got some of these plastic speculums and we looked at our cervixes.

Then there were these papers, like [the one by] Anne Koedt. You remember her? "The Myth of the Vaginal Orgasm"? That was a stunning paper. It was very energizing. There was a lot of work to do, and there was a lot being written about sex.

MO: Now, Betty Dodson, she was a big name then.

LT: She's here in New York. She's in her late seventies and still absolutely a ball of fire. She had been a graphic artist, and in 1974 she published a pamphlet of her genital drawings. She became a kind of erotic artist, drew a lot of nudes. And then she got this idea to draw women's genitalia, partly for artistic purposes, because she thought women's genitalia were beautiful, like flowers — you know, an infinite variety, no two the same. Then she wrote this book called *Liberating Masturbation,* and it was full of these drawings and it was the story of how she learned to call masturbation a meditation on self love. The book described how women could learn about their bodies and their capacities for pleasure through masturbation. That was totally, totally revolutionary.

MO: It doesn't seem like that would happen today, or just seems almost improbable.

LT: Yes, well, you know, there was a brief thing in the middle nineties. No, AIDS was discovered in 1981 or '82 or so, and people started really getting acquainted with the methods of transmission and so on in the late eighties, there were so many interesting things that happened in sexuality. And one of the programs that came out of the AIDS time was called "Sexual Healing." There was a trend of sexual healing workshops that were about outercourse, a term you have probably never heard of. This term never took off. But the idea was that, since AIDS was transmitted by bodily fluids and penetration, if we could find activities that were safe but highly erotic, intensely pleasurable, we could teach people these things and shift the focus of sexual activity from penetration to outercourse and it would be much safer. Outercourse, of course, involved a lot of manual stimulation and group learning. So the sexual healing workshops did in fact involve group masturbation, but that came and went.

MO: Describe how that has happened, how outercourse took off, so to speak.

LT: Well, I guess it's the same reason that I think Viagra took off. The culture, despite the tremendous commercial explosions of sexuality, is not really a sensual-pleasure-oriented sexual culture. And outercourse was ahead of its time. That whole rhetoric of penetrative sex being real sex was still completely dominant, and there simply wasn't enough time to make a change and there wasn't the educational infrastructure. I mean, you never saw an article in *The New York Times* about outercourse. But you see endless articles in *The New York Times* about erectile dysfunction and fixing you with this, that, or the other drug. Now why is that? Is outercourse somehow seen as just a little bit dirty? You know, it's a little bit prurient, it's a little bit too lubricious, whereas medicalized sex, and functions of the body, this all seems so basic and bedrock, as if the functions of sex were built in. They're not built in. Sex is anything you want it to be. It could be outercourse. It could be intercourse. It could be dancing.

MO: Perhaps something is needed — do you think that a penetration-free week should be declared each year where it is suggested strongly that people indulge in outercourse?

LT: You'll have to have an extremely macho male politician to promote an outercourse week.

MO: Well, we have a lot of those.

LT: That'll be good, because otherwise it'll be seen as anti-male, man hating. That's how a lot of things get delegitimized from the feminist point of view. We had all these great ideas — let's have much more foreplay, let's have less intercourse, let's have more tenderness and touching and manual stimulation and not so much intercourse. You know, it's all the same story. It's about the weird way that sex is dealt with in this culture. I mean, I'm an intellectual. That's why you've invited me to talk on *Ideas*, right? I ought to be in academia. But there are no departments of sexology or sexuality studies in academia. The academic study of sexuality is embryonic. So, after I decided that I couldn't do animal research any more because I just didn't believe in the model, I still thought of myself as a sexologist. And I looked around. What were my options? Well, it seemed like the main options were that I could be a high-school sex educator — not too many jobs there, but at least there are some — or maybe I could go into clinical work. And that appealed to me — you know, listening to people's stories and trying to be helpful. That seemed like a good idea. So I respecialized as a clinician. I got another degree. But then where was I going to get a job? Well, I got an opportunity by word of mouth to work in a urology department.

MO: You worked in the Center for Male Sexual Dysfunction and the Department of Urology at Beth Israel Medical Center in New York City?

LT: Actually, yes. I worked in two urology departments, Beth Israel and Montefiore Medical Center. So, combined, thirteen years.

MO: Now, we'd never witnessed on the social landscape these kinds of male sexual dysfunction clinics before run by urologists. Why?

LT: There were a few urologists who began to see that this might be a legitimate sub-specialty, and they began opening these centres for male sexuality. And they began having urological meetings. Years later, I went back and thought to myself, why? Why did they start then? And I discovered that two of the main ways that urologists had been making money had disappeared because of technological progress. One of them was kidney stone surgery. There was the invention of this lithotripsy machine that used shockwaves to break up kidney stones, so you didn't need to do surgery anymore, and almost overnight kidney stone surgery became much, much less prevalent. And the other thing was surgery of the non-cancerous prostate. They used to do surgery for benign prostatic disease. My father had that surgery in 1977. I remember that very well. But drugs were invented in the 1980s to shrink the prostate so you didn't need to have surgery for a benign condition anymore. So urologists had the rug pulled out from under them. This is how I understood it then in retrospect. And they began looking around. What else could they do?

MO: This is very interesting. You're saying [there was] this confluence of events. Did the feminist movement itself have anything to do with these centres for male sexual dysfunction popping up, so to speak?

LT: I don't think so.

MO: Because that's part of the rap, in a sense. People say, well, men started feeling much more insecure and women were saying, "I can make rules or demands of my own body. I don't have to just go along sexually."

LT: It sounds good, and I might be tempted to go along with it, except that the men I saw in the Beth Israel urology department and the men I then saw at Montefiore when I moved to that other hospital were not the least bit influenced by this type of rhetoric, and their wives or girlfriends were not the feminist kind of people either. So, while I do agree with you that the rules changed — I think you're right about there being a kind of atmosphere — but I wouldn't say it was because of the women's movement. I think it was more a kind of capitalism, looking for more and more markets — you know, seeing everything as an opportunity for commercialization. Why are there so many urologists in the first place? This is a larger question. Why aren't there more geriatricians? That has to do with economic issues as much as gender issues or sexuality issues.

MO: Right. So, when you create a centre like the Center for Male Sexual Dysfunction, even if men do not attend this centre, there is an atmosphere created.

LT: Absolutely.

MO: Messages were sent that perhaps stress anxiety is being created.

LT: I think that's what happened. There was a lot of news about these centres. There was a lot of coverage of the new medical view of erections, endless stories about, oh, if only we had a drug. Men, wake up here. Ask yourself, what's the matter with you? You may have a problem. Your partner may have a problem. Endless medical go-see-your-doctor messages. And you might say, well that's a good message, because here are these suffering people who never had any encouragement. But I see the other side, which is that we're creating anxiety in people who were just getting along OK or who were having outercourse or other kinds of cuddling and intimacy and pleasure. And were not troubled about it. But now it is absolutely essential to one's self-esteem as an individual and to the couple's self-esteem — you know, we're not in a real relationship, if we're not having sex, people say nowadays. That didn't used to be true.

MO: Tell me, Leonore, some of the stories from the days you spent at this Center for Male Sexual Dysfunction. First of all, what went on there? What happened there?

LT: Well, let's see. A patient would come in and see the urologist first, and it would be a conventional medical interview — you know, how do you do? what's your problem? And then the patient would be assigned to the workup. The workup would consist of spending one or maybe even two nights in the sleep lab with their penis hooked up to an erection-measuring device. Typically, men have erections coincident with their rapid-eye-movement sleep phases, so maybe they have five or six erections during the night, even though they're unaware of these. Men would come in and say, "I'm not having erections. I'm impotent." But the sleep lab might show that they were having erections at night. That meant that the equipment was working OK. And you'd show them this printout. So that would be a part of the workup. Or they might not have erections at night. That was a little harder to interpret, because they might not have slept well. I mean, how many people are going to sleep well in a strange lab with their penis hooked up to something and this technician watching them all night? But that would be part of the workup. Then there'd be a lot of blood work, even though we weren't entirely sure what we were looking for at that time. Then they would have an interview with me, and that would be psychological. I would sit down with these guys, 99.5 per cent of whom had never seen a psychologist before, and certainly not a woman who was going to ask them impertinent questions. So many guys would say to me, "I've never told this to anyone before," that I thought of needlepointing that, you know? Putting it on a pillow in the waiting room so that they'd get ready for the idea that they were going to talk about things they had never talked about before to anyone.

But, yes, everyone started out self-consciously, but I like to think I put them at ease. That was a revolutionary experience, because they would say, "Well, you know why I'm here. I don't have erections" or "I'm impotent." And I would say, as if I was really stupid, "Uh-huh, and how is that a problem for you?" They would look at me as if to say, "I just told you — I don't have erections." "Uh-huh. And how is that a problem for you?" Well, I would keep saying that until they would tell me more about the meaning that this experience had. "Well, it means I can't have sex. I can't make love. I can't go near my wife. It means my wife's going to leave me. It means I don't feel like a man. It means I'm about to kill myself. It means my life is over" or whatever it meant. It usually was pretty intense. Some guys, bless them, to this day would say, "Gee, you know, I never thought about that before." And I would say, "Well, most people haven't. So let's think about it together. Why is it important for you to have erections?" Then they would say, "Well, I like the feeling. I like to be inside my wife. I like to come that way. I like to ejaculate." Or "My wife likes it." Or "She says she likes the other stuff, the fingers, the mouth. She likes this and that. But she says it's a really special feeling when you're inside me. I miss that." So then I would hear something about intimacy, and something about gender, and something about communication, and I would understand more. Sometimes guys would just clam up. You know, "If you don't understand why it's a problem, lady, I can't tell you." That would happen from time to time. And I'd play with them. I'd say, "It's not that I don't understand. It's that every man is different. So just tell me why it's important for you."

MO: But isn't that a huge hurdle that, as a culture, especially when it comes to sexuality — I don't know if it's more intense with men than women, if there's a gender stratification — we want to be normal.

LT: Yes, being normal is a big part of twentieth-century society. The word normal is just a totally medicalized view of being good. In other times and other places, being good consisted of other things — killing deer or praying to God or giving alms to the poor or whatever it was. But we don't talk so much here about being good nowadays. It's all about being normal, and the assumption is that there is a sexual normal. I dispute this. I'm going to go down fighting on this one. I don't think there is such a thing. Of course, there's a statistical average. People say, "Well, doc, I just want to be normal." Okay. Fine. What do you mean by normal? I had one guy answer this. He said, "I just want to go into the bar and be able to sit on the stool with the other guys." Now, you may ask yourself what on God's Earth does that have to do with having erectile dysfunction? But it's this inner sense of masculinity: if I can't get it up when I need to get it up, I'm a worthless man, and I can't go into a bar and hold my head up because they'll know. And even if they don't know, I'll know.

MO: I can't even be in the company of other men, the tribe.

LT: That's right. It's like I give off some kind of aroma of fraudulence. This is terrible. This is spirit killing. This is soul destroying. See, twenty years ago I don't think this guy would have had trouble getting on the bar stool if he'd had erections once in a while. He would have at least felt OK.

MO: Did you see differences? I mean, you told us a really solid narrative about what these men would say and how they made sense of their lack of an erection and what it meant to them. Did you talk to their wives? Were they as stricken by this? What happened?

LT: The wives were much more diverse. Some of them would say, as the man did, "I really miss intercourse. I liked it a lot. I could come that way. I liked the feeling. I felt close." But a surprising number of the women would not say that. They would say, "I don't know what he is so hung up about here. He wakes up in the morning and starts talking about his erectile failure and the same story when he goes to bed at night. That's all I hear out of him. You think he could give me a little massage? You think he could hold me? You think he could learn how to do something other than just stick it in?" So a lot of the women would be angry. He would be going on and on about his pleasure but not about hers.

Many of these women never told their husbands about their disinterest in penetration. I would say, "Have you told him?" And they would say, "Why should I tell him? He's supposed to know." People don't learn about their own bodies, how to communicate, what they want, why they want it. They think they can turn it on in just a second. There are so many "mistakes." It's not so easy to talk about things. Nowadays, communication is technical: "A little more to the left. Oh, that feels really good." It's rarely about the psychology of sexuality, like "When we have a lot of tenderness and foreplay, I really feel like you care about me, and I really feel respected. And that makes me feel so close to you. Then I get really turned on and really hot." I mean, what patient ever produced a paragraph like that? What do you see on something like *Sex in the City*? More about, "So, what do you like? Oh I like blow jobs." Well, that's really informative!

MO: In retrospect, Leonore, do you see a clear path from the 1980s, when men could get surgical rods implanted in their penis or give themselves an injection for an erection, to the pill called Viagra today, the miracle cure, so to speak? Does it now seem like a clear path?

LT: It seems like a clear path, but not without consideration of factors that you didn't mention, like the deregulation of the pharmaceutical industry. There were huge economic changes that happened in the eighties and the early nineties that made it profitable for companies to develop what they call lifestyle drugs. So the industry, because of advantages that they were given by legislative changes, made a pathway. Sex was the poster child for forces that were going on independent of it. You can't boil it all down to a single thing. If I try, I'm going to sound like a jackass, and that would probably undermine all of the swell things I've already said. But you know, we've had huge social changes and out-of-control advertising to sell body products and to create insecurity if you don't have the right kind of body, and to shrink the diversity of how bodies look and function. Then people say to you, "You can be the best you can be." That's Oprah's famous line: be the best you can be. Well, what does that mean? Does that mean I should get breast implants so I can be the best I can be?

MO: And then perhaps there's a certain sector of people who just say, "To heck with it," and turn their backs on it, because it seems to require so much effort.

LT: Yes. I think they do, but they pay a price in self-esteem and in public face. They're ashamed. I know that's true. I talk to a lot of them. The sense of shame at not measuring up to a norm is one of the fundamental social structures, unless they have another rhetorical place to stand, the way I have another place to stand. I stand on feminism. That gives me a rhetoric. It gives me an attitude. It gives me self-confidence. It gives me an explanation so that I can resist the blandishments of *People* magazine.

But a lot of people don't have that. It's so erotic to be with someone else's mind and to feel the comfort, the pleasure, and the acceptance that comes from somebody seeing your naked reality and kissing it all over. But if you've had all of these surgical things done and you've taken three drugs and you're experiencing the side effects and you're wondering how long it's going to last, are you really going to relax and feel your body being worshipped by somebody else?

MO: You may not even feel like it is your body anymore.

LT: Yes. To me, that's making love. There I go, giving away my 1960s orientation. It's about making love, not having sex.

MO: Perhaps it would be enlightening, or at least relaxing, or liberating, to not have as a focus orgasm and the aftermath, but just kind of playing.

LT: Yes.

MO: And maybe even failing to have an orgasm. But not calling it failing, but just not having one.

LT: You know, I'm glad you brought that up, because we haven't talked enough about orgasm. I think that the central focus on orgasm is a colossal mistake. This is one of the ways that a culture betrays the potential of sex, I think. I think orgasm has become such a focus because you can count it. It's a score. It happened. If you have it, you're a success. But I came of age before orgasm mattered to many women. Petting was really popular. Necking and petting, and not orgasm, were the fun. I've talked to other women my age who say it was different for them. So let me not generalize here, but I know it is possible to spend years feeling really sexy, really turned on, enjoying myself thoroughly but never having intercourse, never having an orgasm, because I didn't know about them, and I wasn't missing them because I wasn't told that I wasn't doing the right thing. I feel like some Native American wise woman telling a tale from six thousand years ago.

I think the orgasm, which is, what, a ten-second-long thing, twelve-second-long thing? To work for hours to get the twelve-second-long thing, don't you think that's a little stupid? Couldn't we spend time with whole body pleasure? I don't know how I could feel more strongly about it. I'm jumping up and down in this chair right now, but you can't see me waving my arms wildly. I think that we are creating an epidemic of insecurity about the body, and sex is one of the manifestations. We're all dreadfully insecure and we have to find our way to a new model of how to be with each other in a relationship and in the larger community, and sex is a piece of that story.

MO: Tell me about a campaign that's close to your heart and that you've dedicated a Web site to.

LT: Well, so here I am thinking all of these revolutionary things and working in the urology department in the '80s and early '90s, and I can see that the way urologists and the medical model in general are dealing with sex is, I think, a disaster. So when Viagra comes out in 1998, it's like, oh my God, this is what I've been worrying about all these years. This is the medicalization of sexuality. This is the pursuit of perfection in a very narrow way. And then they started saying, "Where's the Viagra for women?" And I just hit the ceiling. I thought to myself, who wants a Viagra for women? Who said that women should have a Viagra? Who said this would make a better world? How can we have so many sex drugs and no mandatory comprehensive sex education? If people are going to be sexuality consumers, then they need to know something about the subject or else they're going to be just sheep led to the pharmacy counter.

So I started a campaign. I got some people together. We started a Web site. We wrote some books. We wrote a training manual. We've had conferences. We've testified at the Food and Drug Administration when they dealt with their first drug for female sexual dysfunction, a completely new concept that was invented to sound like erectile dysfunction. OK, we've got Viagra, but where's the Viagra for women? Wait a minute, wait a minute. What is the Viagra for woman for? Uh oh, we need a disease. Alright, so men have erectile dysfunction. What do women have? Let's just say female sexual dysfunction and we won't be too specific about what that is. So, when the first drug came out, it was said to be a drug for — listen to this one — Hypoactive Sexual Desire Disorder, HSDD. That means you don't have enough sexual desire. The industry is then going to flood the airwaves and the print media with advertisements so everybody will then think, "I could use a little boost here." Who couldn't use a little boost? And all kinds of unintended negative consequences will flow from this more subtle shift of the meaning of sex and the purpose of sex. Do I feel OK about me? My body? My lust? My libido? My pleasure? Do I feel OK about that or do I need to work on it?

MO: Tell us the name of your Web site.

LT: NewViewCampaign.org. There's going to be drugs. There's going to be lots of drugs. How are we going to deal with them? That's the question. I'm energized by the fact that this is really important to me and that I think I'm making a persuasive case. And we'll see how it all turns out.

Canada and the World

THREE

Breaking the Bargain

DONALD SAVOIE

Donald Savoie is a self-effacing professor of public administration at Université de Moncton, where he holds the Clément-Cormier Chair in Economic Development. His recent books include Governing from the Centre *(1999) and* Breaking the Bargain *(2003). When he is not writing scholarly works, he is advising provincial, territorial, and federal governments here in Canada, the United Nations, the OECD, and the World Bank. He golfs with premiers, prime ministers, and presidents of multinational corporations. Autographed editorial cartoons featuring the faces of famous friends cover the walls in his office. He was born and raised in the Acadian village of Bouctouche, in rural New Brunswick. Paul Kennedy's interview with Donald Savoie was broadcast on* Ideas *on 21 January 2004.*

DONALD SAVOIE

There are days when I think I was quite lucky to come from a small village. We weren't encumbered with anything. We grew up with a sense of freedom that is quite remarkable. When I went to school, there were eight grades in one room. There were only two in my grade and the other one left after grade six, so in grades seven and eight I was the only one. I took great pride in telling my mother I came first in the class.

181

But we weren't encumbered by material things — we didn't have any. We weren't encumbered by what we wore. It was totally irrelevant. We weren't encumbered by the trappings of school or anything. It was simplicity at its greatest. And, on reflection, I think that simplicity equals freedom. We had very little to play with. We had three or four pucks and an outside rink. We had to be creative to use something else, and you can imagine what that something else was. And so there was complete freedom. There was no societal kind of attachment.

So, in that environment, up until grade eight, I'd never felt pressure about anything. I think that gave me a grounding and a freedom that allowed me later on to get complicated and to get encumbered, because I didn't have it when I was younger. And I think that provided the basis for sanity in my work, if I can say that.

PAUL KENNEDY
When did you figure out you would be a person who would analyze the infrastructure of our political society?

DS: Actually, I figured that out a long, long time ago. I was quite young. The question I had was not so much what I wanted to do but whether I had the capacity to do it. But in terms of loving the kinds of things that I do, I figured that out a long, long, long time ago. I was still a kid. I remember that, when I was quite young, I'd devour a newspaper, so that part was easy to figure out. The more difficult part was how to get there. And that's what I had to struggle with.

PK: Take us through one or two or three steps of that. How do you get there? Obviously, education is very important. Talk about some of your teachers.

DS: I was fortunate to have some good teachers. I have to tell you, for my first degree I wasn't particularly good in terms of marks, but I had some great teachers. I'm very fond of my former teachers. Some of them showed me the way. It was really at Oxford that I figured out that I could do it. That's when it clicked. That's when the light bulb came on. And once I figured out that I could do it, then in some ways I lost control.

I really enjoyed it, and I started doing it. You know, when I get into a book, I get lost in it. I can spend two-and-a-half years and think of nothing else. I was very fortunate — more by faith, I suppose — to find a partner who's the most patient. There's somebody in the Bible by the name of Job. Well, my wife is far more patient than him. When I'm in the middle of a book that I really, really enjoy writing, there are many times when it doesn't matter to me if it's Monday morning or Saturday night. And she's put up with me all these years. So my hat's off to her. It's enabled me to concentrate on my work, perhaps a bit too much. But it's very difficult for me when I get into a book to stop. In fact, that's the part I've had to control. Once I figured out that I could do it, I so enjoy it that it's very difficult for me to put the pen down.

PK: Now, we need to know what "doing it" means. "Doing it" means research, but your research is different from almost anybody else's I know. Obviously, it's built on a foundation of a huge statistical understanding. But your understanding also comes from hands-on work with people in government. It's informed by a number of interviews that are vaguely journalistic, I would say. You're talking to power people, you're talking to decision-makers, and you're finding out what makes them tick. All of that is also part of the research. So it's built not only on what we'd call arm's-length academic research, but also on upfront, close-and-personal insights into what actually happens in government.

DS: Well, yes, and I was part of government for a while. But Rob Pritchard, the former president of the University of Toronto, was down in this region a month or so ago, and he said it's quite amazing about Savoie: he writes without fear or favour and yet, after he finishes a book, people still like him. And I thought that was quite funny. I never tried to make anything personal. I've never, in all of my writings, attacked a person. I don't do that. But I do sit down with policy-makers and try to get into their heads and figure out how they see things. And I've been very fortunate, because I've had access. There are days when I don't know why they gave me so much access, but I'll call the minister or deputy minister and waltz in there and have a chat for an hour-and-a-half, and I walk out of there full of ideas.

In fact, I started writing the *Governing from the Centre* book thinking that I was going to write something fairly innocent. So I went to see a minister in the Chrétien government whom I knew, and I told him I was thinking about this book. It was over breakfast. And he said, "You academics, you don't get it." That in itself is a bit of a challenge. He said, "Central agencies, new public management, that doesn't matter. What you really should focus on is that cabinet is a focus group, it's not a decision-making body." I was taken aback — this was a fairly serious minister. And from that moment on, that stuck in the back of my head. So I went to see other ministers, deputy ministers, and sure enough, there was something there. So the new public management and central agencies [idea] was dropped in the garbage can, and I focused on this, and it came out to be quite an important book, if I can say that. But it started from a breakfast meeting.

I find that when you have access, and when you try to see the world from where they see it, and you describe that world in terms of the impact on us, it resonates. So, this access that I've had over the years, I quite cherish it. I think it's terribly important, and I wouldn't want to lose it.

Now, that having been said, I know that some of my writings have annoyed a few people. I know that Chrétien was quite annoyed with *Governing from the Centre*. I told his advisors that I thought it was mainly because he never read the book but only press clippings and the media in Quebec. I recall one headline, something like "Chrétien more like Louis XIV, says Savoie." Well, when I saw that headline, I thought, I can imagine that he'll be less than pleased. But the book was really not about Chrétien, it was about the concentration of power in the prime minister's office — it transcends Chrétien. It started under Trudeau... it's been part of our system for a long time. Trudeau centralized power, and Mulroney and Chrétien — because it suited their style — kept at it. It was not personal, but I think the prime minister took it personally. I know he took personally, and that's unfortunate. That's not what I really write about. Luckily, ninety-nine per cent of the people in Ottawa know that it's nothing personal.

Some deputy ministers tell me that they enjoy the chat because they get an insight as well. So it's been part of my writing style. It's been part of my research. And to just look at the cold numbers and try to make sense out of that — really, in my field, it doesn't work. You have to go and get the colour, get the flavour, and get the real [story of] how things really work. And then you can describe it and come up with something.

PK: But not every political scientist has access to the corridors of power. I mean, you get to be almost a fly on the wall. What's amazing is that the insights come from somebody who can talk to a minister, and the minister will say to him, "The cabinet is a focus group. It's not a decision-making body." That is astounding. To get that kind of insight is very rare.

DS: Had I not known this minister from a previous life, I don't think I would have had that comment from him. So you establish this basic trust, and ministers do open up. One thing I've never done in any of my books, in any of my writing, is quote someone personally unless they say it's okay. In fact, the name of that cabinet minister — he knows who he is, I know who he is, but nobody else does. And I will keep it like that. It's part of the reason I still have access. There are days when I'm tempted, I have to say, but if I do that, then it closes doors, and I don't want that. I still want to go in there, get a sense of what really happens, and describe it. And to have that kind of access, you have to respect the sources. If I had revealed this minister's name, not only would the PM have been annoyed with me, he would also have been annoyed with him. It might have cost him something, so I didn't want to do that.

We Maritimers and Acadians have a deep sense of identity in terms of our roots, where we come from. That's how we are brought up, to be very close to your family, to your roots, and to your community, and you speak on behalf of your community at every turn. People who know me a bit will know that I often talk about Bouctouche because it defines what I'm all about. So, when I went to Oxford and I had to pick a subject for a thesis, regional development made sense to me, partly because the federal government was so heavily involved in our region, partly because the purpose of regional development was to help communities remain viable, partly because federalism means so much in this neck of the woods. And because it resonated with where I came from — my community and so on. That was my first book.

My second book was also on regional development, to try to make sense of all those programs and what worked and what didn't, and so on. And then we moved to Ottawa for family reasons. While there, I was a kind of visiting official at the Treasury Board, and I came across all kinds of fascinating stuff about government and the spending budget and so on, and I got into that. Where I land is where I really get into. So there was a normal kind of progression. It started with where I'm from, and wanting to write about ways to keep our communities whole. That was regional development. That's really where it started.

PK: We were talking earlier about how your writing is informed by hands-on experience. Fairly quickly, your writing, which might have begun as a more abstract thing, became very pragmatically useful. Your writing on regional development in Canada began to have fairly solid, tangible importance. You were influential, politically.

DS: Well, some people have accused me of that. And I have great difficulty writing in the abstract. I think it's partly because of who I am. I think if you're raised as an Acadian, it's very difficult to talk in the abstract, because we've had to deal with so much in our history. We never had the luxury of dealing with abstract ideas. Our existence has been a fight. We've had to survive through all kinds of challenges. So it'd be very difficult for me to write in the abstract. That's point number one.

Point number two: when I first went to Oxford, that's where I learned how to write, essentially. I had this tutor, this Oxford don who was not nearly as patient as my wife. I can tell you that! He was kind of a grumpy...if you have this image of an Oxford don, kind of grumpy, sour. He is quite a well-known scholar, and he really banged me over the head more than once about writing with clarity. Well, he used to say all the time, "Why use a [complex] word if you can find a simpler one?" He drove that home. For the first four or five months I was there, he was very difficult. Very. I remember, we arrived there in September and I met him after a week. He said, "Well, why don't you write a paper?" And I did write a paper — brought it in in early October. He had me over a week later and said, "Oh dear, you do have difficulty writing." And I said, "Yes, but..." You know, in 1969, I finished Université de Moncton, my first university, then I went to the University of New Brunswick — that was the Trudeau era, if you recall. UNB was English speaking, and they started to have pangs of conscience about how they had dealt with Acadians over the years. And I have to tell you, I took advantage of that a bit. I said I had to write this essay in French. And my profs said, "Oh well, we'll allow you to write in French." So I wrote it in French. They had it translated. And I don't know if they quite understood what the hell I was writing, but they gave me a good mark.

So, when I went to Oxford and the don told me that, I said, "Oh, I'm an Acadian." He said, "Oh dear, what on Earth is that?" I said, "My mother tongue is French." And he said, "Well, you know, across town there are some very good universities that teach in French. You should go there." I said, "Well, no, I decided to come to Oxford." "Oh, you have, really." Well, he threw a grammar book on the coffee table and said, "Go home and master this. Until you do, don't waste my time." So that was the pretty grumpy old Oxford don.

So, I remember going home — I was married — and I said, "Linda, this is going to be a tough go. I don't know." But I decided to stick it out. I took about a month. I went to...I think it was Blackwell's, and they had this kit, writing effective English, and I bought it. It was about twenty bucks — back then, it was cheap, of course, in England. I spent two or three weeks mastering this thing.

I really worked at it. I'd get up at seven in the morning and go to ten at night, six days a week, except Sunday. I'd start at noon, because I'd read *The Times* of London. It was a beautiful newspaper. And about November, I went back, gave him an essay, and he didn't say it was good, but it was acceptable. That first four or five months really disciplined me in terms of writing with simplicity and clarity of style that I hope I still have, because he drove it home.

Now, to end this story, after three years, when I finished, he took me out to dinner at High Table at Nuffield College. I reminded him of what had happened three years before. When I told him he had said, "Oh dear, what on Earth is that?" [it turned out] he knew Acadian history as well as anybody I've come across. He knew, but this grumpy old Oxford don said, "What you were looking for was a crutch, and I wasn't about to give it to you." And he was right. So he forced me into it. When I go to England, every two years or so, I drop by to see him. He's still around, still as grumpy as ever, but a delightful scholar who showed me the way. I don't want to stress the point too much, but if I write with clarity, it's because of him. He forced it into me. And those flowery words — he wouldn't tolerate it at all. I owe that to him, and for that I'm grateful.

PK: He was a great teacher. He knew what to tell you at exactly the right time. It's not necessarily an easy message, but he told you that and it worked. You're also a teacher. How important is teaching to you?

DS: That's a very good question. And I have to say, you're absolutely right. He was a very good teacher, in my case. Now, I know he turned off a few others, who gave up. But in my case, he was bang on, and I'm eternally grateful. I have to confess that I could never be as strong as him in terms of my students. I can't do that with my students. There are days I'd like to, but I have never been able to be as tough, as demanding, as cold, as grumpy with my students as he was. But I tell you, it's very difficult.

So, yes, I couldn't agree more. It's the way to teach in many ways. Certainly it was in my case. Unfortunately, I can't do that. In very,

very rare cases in my teaching have I been able to be as tough, as demanding, as cold. It takes, not courage, but something to be as demanding and as cold as he was. After he threw the grammar book on the coffee table, he turned his back on me, because his desk faced the wall. I'll always remember that. He told me that until I mastered this, don't waste his time. And he simply turned his back to me and started writing. So I got up, picked up the grammar book, and left. Now, I really cannot do that. I've thought about it many times, because some of my students really ought to have that kind of medicine. But I've never been able to give it. As I get older and grumpier, maybe. Maybe in a year or two, I'll work on it. But so far I haven't been able to do it.

PK: We talked about what I think was the first primary focus of your work, which was regionalism. If I am correct, I would say the next focus of your work was on the analysis of power in government, on the way the various government departments work. And you actually identified a concentration of power beginning in the prime minister's office. Is that a fair assessment of your next concentration?

DS: Yes, it's quite accurate. The reason I did that was, again, because this minister said cabinet is a focus group and you academics have it all wrong. Cabinet is not the way you guys and gals write about it. It is a different animal. And the real animal is that there's no cabinet. It is a focus group. And the PM will use it if he thinks that he ought to use it and will not use it if he thinks he ought not to use it. So you academics figure that out. That's what he was telling me. And that's what I tried to figure out. Again, I went to see people in Finance, the Privy Council Office, the former minister of finance, Paul Martin — I spent some time with him on this book. And I came to the conclusion that, yes, this government minister is right. It is a focus group.

In fact, when I go to Ottawa now, a number of officials in the Privy Council Office will make reference to the focus group, which I find quite amazing. So I stumbled upon something that I think was terribly important. Important for all of us. Important for all of

Canada. And that is, when you concentrate power so much in the hands of so few, what does it mean for a country as large as this? I think that the implications of this process are quite substantial — it has implications for all of us and all regions. I notice that Paul Martin wants to deal with a democratic deficit, that he has openly said that the prime minister's office has too much power, that who you know in the PMO is how you get things done. Well, the fact that he let the genie out, that he's willing to talk about it, promises that something might be done about it. And if my book had that kind of impact, then great, so much the better. I ruined all chances for a Senate appointment, I might add.

PK: I'm not sure you want to be a senator, do you? I mean, you're having too much fun right now.

DS: I'm having a great deal of fun. But I can imagine that in the Senate you have staff. You could write away and have a...No, I'm quite happy doing what I'm doing now. Seriously.

PK: I want to refer now to your most recent book, and I want to deconstruct the dedication. Five people are mentioned here, and I want you to talk about each of them. The book says, "To those who showed me the way in public administration." The first one is "Professor J.E. Honderich for the light."

DS: Well, let's talk about Ted Honderich. When I submitted my first manuscript to McGill-Queen's University Press, Ted Honderich was the editor. And he was a gentleman. I did something that was quite awkward when I look back on it. I didn't know. I made five or six copies of this manuscript, gave it to McGill-Queen's University Press and to three or four other presses to see what would happen. And Ted Honderich called and told me that's not appropriate. Of course, it's not appropriate, you do not do that. But he did it with such panache and style. You know, here was a young scholar. Here was an established scholar. And he showed me the way. He was so patient and had so much dexterity in taking the manuscript into book form that I am truly grateful and I appreciate it. That's part one.

The second part of Ted Honderich is that his writing is fabulous. He has influenced me. He writes with clarity. He writes about things that I really enjoy. And I've always enjoyed reading his material. So I thought at the top of my list would be Ted Honderich, because he was an established scholar who showed me the way and I truly appreciate that.

The next one is Gordon Robertson and the dedication says, "Gordon Robertson for the wisdom." Five or six years ago, I was in a meeting in Ottawa — senior public servants and so on — and I made this comment, which I didn't think would upset anybody, that Gordon Robertson was the last clerk of the Privy Council that we had. Boy, it got a few people up. They took exception. They said, "No, we've had great clerks since." And I said, "No, you've had some good deputy ministers to the prime minister, but Gordon Robertson had the sense to know the role of the prime minister and the role of cabinet. And in my view, he is the last clerk." He was also a kind of role model when I was a public servant for a few years. I thought that if I could be like Gordon Robertson I would make an important contribution. He has a lot of integrity. He is a public servant of the old school: lots of courage, can speak with power. And that's the kind of public servant I really hold in high esteem. And he published a book as well, with courage, I thought. So Gordon Robertson deserved some mention.

The next one is "Jack Manion for the values." Jack Manion is a mandarin. I worked with him when the federal government established the Canadian Centre for Management Development, which is a training school, if you like, for public servants. He was asked to set it up. I worked as his advisor or assistant. And I thought he had a lot of great values. He could speak the truth. He would risk career advancement to speak the truth. And he never hesitated to tell a minister, "You're wrong, and here's why you're wrong" — even the prime minister on one occasion. I thought, that takes courage and it takes values. Here is an honourable man I would like to take my hat off to.

Gérard Veilleux. When I moved back to Ottawa for family reasons, I went to work as an advisor to Gérard Veilleux for a year. And here was someone with a lot of insights. I remember vividly and I use that still, and I tell that to my students: when you talk about values and ethics in the public service, Gérard Veilleux would say there's only one test. Whatever you do, are you prepared to live with it the next morning? If you read it on the front page of *The Globe and Mail* or *La Presse* and you can live with it, then you've met the test. And it's a very simple test. I mean, if you cheat on your expense account and it comes out in *The Globe and Mail* this morning, can you live with that? No. Well, don't do it, then. Or if you assist a minister in doing something that's not legal and it comes up in *The Globe and Mail*, can you live with that? No? Well, don't do it. It is a very simple test. Gérard Veilleux was quite insightful, and some of the insights in my writing come from him. He would look at things in quite a creative way, so I truly appreciate that.

The last one is Louis Robichaud. He's become an icon. He is the leader of the Acadian society. He is a giant. I think he's five foot four in a physical sense, but he is truly a giant. Every Acadian I know has deep respect and admiration for him. I can say honestly that, without Robichaud, I wouldn't be here. There is no question about that. We talked about the Acadian entrepreneurial spirit and so on — Louis Robichaud gave us all of that and then some. Here is a man who sacrificed everything he had — his career, his life — and gave it to us. You might find that a bit of an overstatement. It is not.

In many ways, you have to be an Acadian to appreciate that, because in 1959, prior to his becoming premier, we were a desperate lot. We had no school. I went to high school here in Moncton. I'm not that old, though I've got grey hair. There was no French high school. So my parents had to dig into their pockets and send me to a private school run by priests, because we weren't allowed to have a school. That was 1959, '60. We were priests, at times, doctors. We got a scholarship to go to Laval, Université de Montréal. Lawyers, we had plenty of those. But we had nothing else. We were construction workers. I often compare our state in 1959 to the state of Native communities now. We were a desperate lot. The unemployment rate was very high. We tore at each other. We weren't a cohesive community. Louis showed us the way. He was a messiah in a way. He gave us everything that we now have, everything in the sense of all the tools that we now have to grow and prosper. He gave it to us. And let me go through the list.

Here at Université de Moncton, where we're standing now, that's him. It's his creation. The *Official Languages Act*, it's him. The program of equal opportunity, it is him. French high schools here in Moncton, it is him. So, everything that we needed to grow as a society, he gave it to us. And so Louis Robichaud deserves that mention and then some.

So, those are the people who showed me the light in many ways, and I insisted on listing them.

PK: I want to confront for a while the basic theme of this most recent book, *Breaking the Bargain*, which is about the balance of power and the way it has been evolving recently in Canadian history. Maybe you should characterize it rather than me.

DS: Well, first, I have to say that on the cover of the book there's a man in back of a stack of papers, and I'm told there's an older Acadian lady in a village north of here who said, "Aw, why did they have to hide Savoie behind that stack of papers?" It is not me. I thought it was quite funny. Well, I have to say I enjoyed this book. I enjoy writing all my books, I really do. This one I quite enjoyed because I think it makes a contribution to understanding where our system of government has gone. It starts with the premise that there was a bargain struck about a hundred and some years ago. It was never written down, it's not part of our Constitution. But there was a bargain struck that outlined the role of Parliament, the role of ministers, and the role of public servants. It was a very simple bargain. Government would be held accountable in Parliament. MPs knew their role. It was to hold government accountable. It was not to govern. And public servants were accountable to ministers, would not be visible, would be non-partisan, would have their own space from which they could speak the truth. That was the essence of the bargain. And ministers could draw on a professional, non-partisan public service and get the best advice possible, and get best program administrators.

Part of the bargain was that ministers would not hire or fire at will. It was the merit principle. There was a public service commission. Ministers would leave proper space for public servants to do their work. All of that came together and there was a bargain. And out of that bargain flowed some good policies and good programs and a capacity on the part of public servants to tell ministers, "No, that's not wise," or, "Yes, it's wise," or, "We think it's wrong, but you're the boss. We will implement it knowing that it's not the right program." That was the essence of the bargain.

I think that bargain's come unglued. There are several reasons. I can list some. I think the media are partly responsible. There's twenty-four hour news. There's access to information to find out who flew where and so on, and we tend to focus on that. The media do not have much interest in sound public policy. They really would rather see who's flown on the Irving jet. So public servants have become gun shy for all kinds of reasons. It's not their test to see the next morning in *The Globe and Mail* if they can [live with what they've done]. They're not allowed the freedom to have their own tests. They're tested by access.

I think the information we get about public servants has made them timid. Why? Well, if a public servant speaks the truth and sends a memo saying, "This is wrong," there's a risk that, three weeks from now, it'll be on the front page of *The Globe and Mail*. And if it makes it there, then that public servant's career is done. Cooked. Finished. Because the bargain protected a public servant. He or she was anonymous. He could speak the truth knowing that that information, that advice would be protected. No more. So we've opened this space up.

Everybody can dance now. There used to be a dance floor that belonged to public servants. It was their space, their dance floor. Everybody waltzes on that dance floor now. Lobbyists: they've become part of the Ottawa system. And nobody's really taken a good serious look at the impact that lobbyists have had. I think they've had a tremendous impact. If a minister gets advice from his public servants on a policy and the minister doesn't like that kind of advice, he now can pick up the phone, talk to a lobbyist who represents a counter-argument, and say, "Send me a two-page memo or come over here and let's have a chat." It arms the minister to counter the advice of public servants. And lobbyists are not without self-interest, deep self-interest. Every time I go to Ottawa, I marvel at the number of think-tanks, groups, networks — whatever the hell they call it these days — mushrooming. And so they now dance on the dance floor of public servants. You look at the dance floor that used to be reserved for public servants — it's now full of strangers.

So the bargain has come unglued. And I think that Ottawa is in deep need of a crash diet on all fronts. Holding a government department to account now in this networking, this maze of think-tanks, lobbyists, and so on — looking at the dance floor, I can't figure out who's who. For Parliament to hold that to account is like grabbing smoke. So Parliament is frustrated, and in that frustration Parliament's trying to govern. Now they want power. They want to be on the dance floor, too. Why not? I mean, they represent Bathurst, New Brunswick, they represent Kamloops. They arrive in Ottawa, they have the full backing of their riding. They say, "Well, there is a dance floor. All kinds of people are on that dance floor, lobbyists and so on; why can't we dance on that floor, too? Why can't we have power?"

So Parliament is searching for a role. It's really finding its role in a way that I find quite worrisome. I was before a parliamentary committee, and I said, "I hate to tell you this, but you're not the government. This is not your role. You are Parliament. If you start governing, if you get your hand in the pot and start governing, who's going to hold who accountable? Who's going to do your job? I know of no other institution that can do the kind of job that you are supposed to do. So don't try to govern." Tough message, I'll tell you. They want to govern. They see the dance floor, everybody on it. They want to be on it. And, they argue, and in some ways they may have a point, they have more legitimate reason to be on that dance floor than everybody else. Ministers make it into cabinet and have tremendous influence, but cabinet's become a focus group, and ministers sense that.

I was reading in the media today that, on bank mergers, the minister of finance supported it, the banks supported it, but it never went to cabinet. They got word from the Vatican: no, it's not going to happen. The Pope spoke: no need for cardinals. I'm told, from people who are in cabinet, that if the Clarity Bill had gone to a vote in cabinet, it would have been shot down. Eighty per cent were against it, I'm told. A number of other issues are like that. So, the Pope rules. Cardinals are frustrated because they don't play the role that they once played.

And in terms of public servants, they don't know where they fit any more. There are all kinds of [reports] that keep spewing out of Ottawa from think-tanks and so on that there's a morale problem. Of course, there's a morale problem. I mean, the notion of space — that's a central message in the book. I'll tell you where I got that. I was in Ottawa doing some interviews for this book, and I stumbled upon a senior public servant who told me he's leaving. I said, "Oh, why are you doing that?" Here's what he said: "Because I don't have space anymore to do my work. Everything I do, there's ten departments. I can't write a paper without involving ten departments, central agencies. There are so many hands out that I don't have a space that I can call my own in which I can do the kind of work that I used to do." That's the light bulb that went on for that book, you know. So, *Breaking the Bargain*, it's all of that. Something has come unglued.

We had a bargain that worked well. In the 1940s and '50s we had a top-notch public service, we really did. We don't have that any more. And I'm not being nostalgic. I think I'm presenting the facts fairly coldly. And it's not that public servants are not competent. Quite the opposite. It's just that we've taken away the space in which they could do their work, and that's where the bargain has come unglued, and I think it's a sad day for us.

PK: Can the bargain be restruck? Can the space be created? Can the situation be improved? I mean, have we gone too far down the road, or how would we fix this situation?

DS: Well, the answer to all of your questions is yes, yes, and yes. I think it can be improved. I think what we now need to do is search for a new bargain. And at some point I want to start working on a book along those lines. Let me give you an example. In terms of access, that legislation, which was introduced in 1983, '84, that gives Canadians access to all kinds of information inside government, let me say a few things about that. One is that there is no evidence that that legislation has made the bonds stronger between Canadians and their government. In fact, over the past twenty years, it's become a bit worse. What's the role of access? I would argue that we should take a good, cold look at that legislation. But there's no market in that. I'd be a lone voice. I don't think any other Canadian would agree with that. In fact, they would say, "Let's make it stronger. Let's have more information." Well, I think we need to ask the fundamental question, is it useful? Is it playing the role that we thought it did. Has it made life very difficult in terms of public servants? I would argue, yes. But we can't go there. I'm not naive to the point that I think we can do away with that. The media would go nuts. Canadians would go nuts. The opposition would go nuttier.

So there are things that we cannot turn back the clock on. The old bargain is gone. I think it worked great. I loved the old bargain. The genius of our system was the old bargain. It was something. It was unwritten, *à la* British tradition, but there was a genius, a glue that made it work. That bargain is gone. We now have to look at a new bargain. I point out in my book that I still favour our system of government. I much prefer the British system to the American system or anything else that we've invented. I would not want wholesale changes.

The solution seems to me to search for a new bargain that redefines the role for parliamentary ministers and public servants. What would that look like? Well, I'd be happy to have a chat with you after I finish my next book.

PK: I don't know if I'm legitimately characterizing your work, but I would say in some sense you're always writing about balance. You're writing about the balance between the margins and the centre in federalism, regionalism, or centralism. You're writing about a balance of power, concentrating in various government departments and eventually the prime minister's office. Or you're writing about a balance in the way things ought to work in terms of a civil service that traditionally was given the space or had the freedom to execute policy, and then a cabinet or a government that formulated that policy, and those lines were very carefully drawn, but there was balance. Would it be fair to characterize your work as by somebody who's interested in that issue?

DS: Absolutely. It's a theme that runs through my thinking, no question about that. In a country as large as this, balance is the only way to go. In fact, I think that where we've gone wrong over the past 135 years is we've lost a sense of balance. If we were living in England or France, balance perhaps may be less important. But in this country it is crucial.

We Maritimers love Canada, we really do. You won't find any more loyal Canadians. We don't like the marital arrangement. We'd like a new contract. But we love this country deeply. It's just the kind of arrangements we've had to live with that we find a bit difficult. I think where we've gone wrong is we've lost a sense of balance, and to recapture the sense of Canada that we had, we have to recapture that sense of balance. And in relations between the regions, balance is the key. It's not balance in the sense of arriving at a consensus so that most people agree — that's not what I mean by balance. By balance, I mean that you don't have a region taken over, you don't have an institution taken over, you don't unbalance a system to give someone too much power. I don't mean balance in terms of public policy objectives. We can have very clear, deliberate policy objectives that might be a bit difficult for some to swallow. I have no difficulty with that. In fact, the politics of public spending went that way. But I mean balance in terms of keeping things in check between regions and within our political administrative institutions. We need that sense of balance to make this country work.

PK: Not only this country, but probably this world. What's interesting about Canadian thinking or Canadian work in this area is that, in searching for balance, we're searching for something that some people would say is a course that the whole world must take, not just Canada. I mean, this is a very interesting society because it's been expending a lot of thought and energy on issues that were primarily Canadian issues, but have now become global. Are we on the cutting edge there? Are we a society for the twenty-first century rather than the twentieth?

DS: Well, that's the conventional wisdom. I have to confess something. I was fortunate enough to get a Fulbright scholarship, and I went to Harvard and Duke for a year — that's where I wrote *Breaking the Bargain*, actually. And I discovered there that I was homesick. I discovered there that what really matters to me is Canada. I discovered at Harvard, at Duke — great universities, tremendous wealth, tremendous faculty, and every night you could go and hear a great speaker and really get into it — that I was homesick. After a month at both places, I longed for this country. I really did. And I discovered that my writing, for better or for worse, from now on would be strictly Canadian. I tried comparative stuff. I wrote Thatcher, Reagan, and Mulroney. And it was fun, and it was published in Pittsburgh. And you're right: you publish in the States, it's surprising how many books you can sell. The market's much, much bigger. But it doesn't do much for me. And when I was in the States, I realized that that didn't do much for me.

But there's a beacon. It takes me back to my roots, to my country, to my village, to my community. And that force is too strong to break. When I was there, it was post-9/11. In fact, we were to arrive at Logan [Airport, Boston] on September 11. Obviously, we didn't make it. So there was a lot of debate that whole year about globalization, international security, and so on, and it was very difficult for me to get my head into that stuff. I really wanted to get my head into *Breaking the Bargain*. Even the lure of all that debate, the role of the UN, the role of the United States, international security, I tried to get into it, but I really couldn't.

I'm not trying to avoid the question you've raised. I think it's a great question. It's just that, as you get older, you get this sense of who you are. I'm not a comparative guy. I'm not an international guy. I'm very much a Canadian. And I've come to the conclusion that to be away from my country for more than a month is very difficult, and I don't intend on doing it much in the years ahead. Something brings me back here. It's a strange thing, but I like to see a Tim Hortons donut shop. I like to see our local newspapers. I like to see *The Globe and Mail*. I like to see *La Presse*. I like to see CBC. I like to see Peter Mansbridge. I like all of that. I don't like to be away from that.

PK: You come back not only to Canada, though, you come back to Moncton. You come back to Acadie.

DS: Yes, and that's another thing I've come to terms with. I think I've come to the conclusion that it's impossible for me to leave. I've been fortunate enough to have had some offers to go elsewhere, but I think the world of academe is opening up, so it's nothing special. I think most people get offers these days. But there have been a number of instances, and there are people who can't quite understand why I would not go to a big university and so on. But I just can't. I cannot. I cannot leave here.

I try to explain to people when I go to Ottawa or Toronto or so on. It is one thing to be a prof of political science in Saskatchewan, raised in Timmins, Ontario, and you go to Saskatchewan and you teach there for ten or fifteen years and then leave Saskatchewan and go to the U of T or Queen's or something. It is a different case if you're an Acadian to leave and to go there. Whether it's Université de Montréal or Queen's or U of T or Carleton or Ottawa U, it is very difficult for all kinds of reasons. Some are self-induced and some are not. But for an Acadian to turn his back on his community, I tell you, you don't do it lightly. We are a very simple people. There's not much pretension about us. We are very straight, simple, community-minded people. So the verdict would be, oh, who does he think he is? Where's he going? Why can't he stay here? And that matters to me. My roots really matter to me. Perhaps because we were put on boats, one-way ticket, and when we finally landed, we said, "Oh, if we can find roots again, we're not moving." And maybe that's part of our history. But it is very, very difficult for an Acadian to leave his community — I would say practically impossible.

Mission Possible

In February 2007, the Conference Board of Canada released a massive report called Mission Possible: Sustainable Prosperity for Canada. *The report, the result of years of study at the Conference Board, recommended some radical new directions for the future of Canada. Anne Golden has been president and chief executive officer of the Conference Board of Canada since 2001. Before that, she ran the United Way of Greater Toronto.* Ideas *host Paul Kennedy's interview with Anne Golden was broadcast on 17 January 2007, shortly after the report was released.*

ANNE GOLDEN

I guess I've always been idealistic, raised in my own home with social justice issues, understanding that you had to be a part of your community, that to separate yourself from your community was wrong. So I always saw, as exemplified in my own home by my parents — my father was very active — that it was both essential and right to be involved in the issues. And so, just growing up, I was involved with community issues, planning issues. As I progressed, I think it was one of the reasons I was attracted to study history — my academic background is history. Most historians really want to understand why something happened, not just what it was. But really, it's all about causation, and it really is implicitly all about the lessons: what can we learn from this?

The older I get, the more I realize that we learn very little, but you go into it with that idealism. And then, all of my experience — twenty years at United Way and, prior to that, working in political venues — was really very much policy oriented: understanding that, unless we get the policy right, the execution doesn't matter. I now, of course, have a great respect for both policy and execution. I often say, vision without implementation is hallucination. So I truly respect the implementation side.

And then I would have to say that I have been privileged to do such worthwhile things with such worthwhile people and to have had the opportunity to pursue and be actively engaged in the issues that really matter to me. You know, the Conference Board is all about building leadership for a better Canada. My goodness, if that just doesn't take you into everything. You know, my twenty years at United Way were all about building a better society, making things better for people. So a lot of things have converged.

PAUL KENNEDY

Another consistency in your career, a trajectory throughout the career, is that you have been somebody who's always been interested in forming a partnership between the business sector, the private sector, and the public sector. And the Conference Board seems to be a perfect personification of that.

AG: That is absolutely true. And one of the things that attracted me to the Conference Board was that it wasn't just about a single sector. We have think-tanks that speak for specific sectors — if you look at the range of think-tanks in Canada, from the Fraser Institute on the Right to Caledon and others on the Left — but the Conference Board does not speak for any single sector. Clearly, it's multi-sectoral, public-private, and not for profit. Another big part of the attraction is that it's evidence based, non-ideological.

Another piece of it, and this does go back to United Way, was the understanding of something that's now fashionable but wasn't then, which is that the economic and the social — "social" meaning "socio-environmental" — are really two sides of the same coin. I can recall, when I used to be involved in raising money for United Way, sometimes getting the answer: "first, we have to look at the net profit, and then, if we have something left over we'll think about the community." As if one had to precede the other. Some enlightened leaders said, "we understand that the social bottom line is absolutely as important as the fiscal bottom line," but generally that was the thinking, particularly as things got tight in the eighties and nineties. But the Conference Board — even though it has a corporate board — always argued that, to achieve what we wanted to as a society, we had to improve our productivity and pay attention to all of the business issues, but the larger purpose was always the public good and society as a whole. I was very attracted to that fundamental understanding.

PK: And that's a theme I'm sure we'll be coming back to again in the course of this conversation. I want to talk though, briefly at least, about your time in Toronto with the United Way. You prepared a report on the homeless people in Toronto which I think was both very important and, perhaps, formative in your own thinking. I want you to talk about that and, I guess, give yourself a report card on your report. What's happened in Toronto since you came down with that report?

AG: You may recall the origins of that report. While [Mel] Lastman was running for mayor [of Toronto], a homeless person died in North York. He said there were no homeless people in North York, and there was a whole political to-do about that. And then he asked if I would take on the issue. And he actually came with me. I remember we went to see Dixon Hall, a shelter that has since been redone, but it was really very graphic and unpleasant. And he said to me, "I know why you've brought me here." But he did want to do something significant, and he insisted we call it the Action Task Force on Homelessness. And that was quite an experience, because then the federal government came in and we made it national.

So I went to all the cities and spoke with all of the groups, and came to understand that homelessness was not just about the people on the streets. It really was much broader. It was about women who were poor. It was about young people who had transgender issues. It was about addictions. It was about so many different issues. And so we produced, I thought, a very comprehensive report. On the report itself, I still give it an A. It's not because of me — I had a task force group, there was a team of us, and we were able to do the kind of research we needed to do. So it was an extremely well-researched, very thorough report, and we had a year to do it. In terms of implementation, whether it's an F or a D, we can debate.

PK: Well, talk about some of the recommendations and where we stand.

AG: A big piece of homelessness is about housing. Let's just take that piece of it. And we demonstrated and documented that a large number of those who we see on the street — which is really the tip of the iceberg with homelessness, because there are also people crowded into substandard housing, et cetera — suffer from addiction, mental illness, and combinations of these issues. We recommended supportive housing. We actually went to the trouble of putting numbers around it: how many thousands of units you would need over what period time, what it would cost, what was the best way to construct it, how it should be funded. So it was a fairly detailed policy document. It wasn't simply strategic or directional. It really gave substance.

And then we talked about affordable housing. What's interesting is that I now participate in sessions on affordable housing from the point of view of the competitiveness of cities. What happens if we can't afford to house our poets and our creative people? What happens to our ability to compete in a globally competitive world? But on the social justice side of the issue, we talked about housing. At that time, an investment of upwards of maybe a billion dollars a year for several years could have dealt with a huge piece of the homeless puzzle. And [to say] it is disappointing would be an understatement, because we could have dealt with it. And we did not.

We put some money into the SCPI [Supporting Communities Partnership Initiative] program, improving shelters and helping with some community programming, and that was good, but we never addressed the housing part of the equation, and I never understood why we didn't. Since then, of course, we've wasted more money on the gun registry, we've spent much more money abroad on foreign battles, et cetera — all of which may be very good causes, or not, but the point is, we had the wherewithal in terms of federal surpluses to have addressed the homeless issue, and we didn't.

PK: You must be very frustrated. I mean, when you put the kind of time and effort and research that you did into a project like that and come up with a report that is universally hailed, but between the vision and reality falls the shadow. How do you deal with that kind of disappointment?

AG: I'm asked that question a lot, and I think part of it is just human nature and, you know, chemical. I'm just not a person who sits on the disappointment side. I look at what came out of it. There were some improvements on the health side for homeless people. We did introduce the SCPI program, and a lot of money went to help the shelter system or the various drop-ins. So there were improvements made. Things were done on the backlog side, and that part was good, but we did not get to address the solution side.

Another improvement was that we created a coordinated information system. At that time, if you were homeless, you had to call each shelter individually. There was no central way to find out [if there was a space], and homeless people didn't have fifty-two quarters with them to make the calls. So we did improve the information system and the coordination of that.

So we have made piecemeal improvements, but there are still homeless people wherever you go in the major cities of this country, and that doesn't need to be. I'm disappointed, of course, but, no, I don't get discouraged.

PK: What's significant and interesting, I think, about that report is that you take an issue, homelessness, and you don't look at just the small immediate details that people would normally look at. You ask bigger questions. You ask more organic questions. I mean you don't leave it as a topic on its own on the side, but try to put it within the context of what's generally going on in a city like Toronto, or any city which has these kinds of people in it.

AG: That's interesting. It's the first time I've been asked in many interviews about this, but you're absolutely right. Again, I do have a need to understand the full context. I believe that, unless you understand the full context, you won't get at root causes, and then your solutions won't really be solutions. They will be temporary fixes, or they will be Band-Aids for specific things that are glaring at us. But they won't be systemic. And I do think that I have a need to understand how things fit together and in as broad a way as possible. To me, it's not satisfying intellectually unless you get the whole picture. I guess I do carry that through in all the projects that I've ever been involved in.

PK: You don't see shortcuts.

AG: I don't see shortcuts. No, I don't.

PK: Let's move on to *Mission Possible*, which is a huge report produced by the Conference Board, subtitled *Sustainable Prosperity in Canada*. It's a three-volume report, and we'll probably spend what we have left in this hour talking about some of the recommendations. How do you feel about this? I guess if you gave an A to your report on homelessness in Toronto, what about *Mission Possible*?

AG: Right now I'm feeling hugely proud and gratified. You can imagine — it's three-and-a-half years, $3.4 million of research, a team of twenty of us at the Conference Board intimately involved. I find that very exciting. You know, some people find other things exciting. To me, this is. Picture people coming in on the weekends, picture people getting excited about fixing up a footnote. Now, I can see that for some this would not be a thrill, but for us it is. I guess we are all policy wonkish. We all care very much. And it started in a very interesting way.

One of the flagship programs of the Conference Board is something we run every year called the Canadian Conference. Only CEOs are invited, about thirty-five people, and we hold it around the third week in January. You have in the room deputy ministers, corporate leaders — again, public-private — so it's a very distinguished group. And the rule is that everything is off the record. Every person gets to speak for eight minutes on something that keeps them up at night — it can't be advertising about their company. And there's absolutely no attribution.

At the 2002 conference, eight people stood up and spoke on the same issue. And what did they talk about? Drift. That Canada was drifting — the world was changing, and no one was getting it. We had economic restructuring, restructuring of global supply chains, the rise of emerging countries like China, India, Russia, and Brazil and others. And we seemed to be like deer caught in the headlights. We were just not reacting quickly enough, smart enough, and we were losing opportunities. And they went on and on. And finally at that point — and I think he won't mind if I mention his name — John Hunkin [then president and CEO of CIBC] said, "Anne, why isn't the Conference Board doing something on this?" And I said, well, the way we work is fee for service, and we don't have the money to embark on something like this. And immediately, several companies said they wanted to sponsor this. So, without too much difficulty, we did raise the money to do the requisite research. We produced twenty-seven independent studies in the course of the three-and-a-half years. We set up advisory groups on each of the issues.

One of the challenges for us was not to figure out what were all the issues in the world. Anybody can sit and draw up a list of forty issues, sixty issues. This is easy to do, I think. You can start with the ones that are in the papers every day: health, education, the environment. You can break them down or you can go, as we did, to the ones that really are fundamental. One of the contributions of this report, apart from the new research, is that it synthesizes the issues. Because if you don't frame the issues in a way that people can absorb and internalize and understand, you're not going to be able to get action on those issues.

And I must tell you, we were a year and a half into this before we figured out how to "cut it," as we put it, or how to frame it. And we came up with a framework that I think people will understand. It's also alliterative: in the short form, it is countries, commodities, and cities. Basically, we took issues like the changing world of international trade, foreign policy issues, regulatory issues, and all of the issues that keep business leaders and policy leaders up at night, and we put them into three categories. Issues that relate to Canada's role in the world and its relationships with other countries, including the United States: that's the countries chapter. And we call that one "Stellar Performance in a Global Economy." The title, *Mission Possible*, by the way, comes from a contest we had among our staff, and I guess that speaks to our optimism.

PK: It is a positive title. *Mission Possible*, not impossible.

AG: We went through a lot of negative titles before we came up with the positive, because a fair bit of this analysis is of where we're not succeeding.

The second category had to do with resources, or commodities. Why? Because, right now, although not every Canadian realizes it, things feel so good because we're being buoyed up by the demand side of our economy — energy, mining, et cetera. And it's not allowing us to see all the warts.

And finally, we decided to look at our cities, because eighty per cent of Canadians now live in cities, and two-thirds of them live in our largest cities. And we really have to focus on what's happening in our cities, where again we have evidence that they're slipping relative to cities elsewhere.

PK: The country chapter is where you first establish that Canada is not doing very well, frankly, in the global economy, that we haven't really responded to huge changes that have been taking place around the world. And, as you said, we're slipping or drifting. Talk about that.

AG: Well, we benchmark a lot, and we're very good at it. For ten years, we've been benchmarking Canadian performance in something we call performance and potential. Again, how are we performing? What is our potential? We take the information we have, then we add our understanding developed through the many different studies we do a year, and we ask what we have learned elsewhere that relates to Canada's performance. We developed a set of about a hundred-plus indicators in six categories, and as we tracked it over the ten years, we noticed we're going really in one direction. So, for example, three years ago, Canada was third in the thirty indicators that make up the economy section. Two years ago, we were sixth. This year, we're twelfth. Now, we're still among the top twelve in terms of our overall economic performance, compared to the other 180 nations in the world or the thirty that we benchmark ourselves against, because we use OECD [Organisation for Economic Co-operation and Development] data as well as StatsCanada data. Sure, you can say we're in the top twelve, we're better than the top half. And yes, if we want to be complacent, we can console ourselves. But we look a lot at the directions.

Take GDP per capita, an important indicator that most people follow as a proxy for performance: we've gone from fifth to tenth place in a very few years. So we see the direction in which we're going. We look at the environment: we're slipping. We look at health: we're slipping.

PK: Why?

AG: Why? Societal: we're slipping largely because of our stats on poverty. Innovation: even where we used to be right up, we're slipping. In each case, the reasons are different. But why? We're not adjusting to the structural changes in the world quickly enough. In big broad terms, first of all, international trade has changed. Global supply chains have changed. That hit me when I was invited out to watch a Ford being built. Have you ever gone to a car plant? It's like a hospital. You're wearing a little helmet and you're going around there, it's very sophisticated. Anyway, as they're putting in the windshield while the chassis is rolling along, it's explained to me that this particular item comes from Poland, this one from Romania, this one from China. And I believe something like two-thirds of a car that we call Canadian now comes from pieces that are brought from elsewhere and assembled in Canada. And that same chassis may cross the border between Canada and the United States two or three times before it emerges as the car that we call the Ford.

Now, we have to understand that we are competing component by component, whether it's a product or a process, whereby companies are seeking the best profit on each item. Now imagine the pressure in the system and how you have to be able to compete, not on just the final product, but on all the pieces and components that go into everything. We're not adjusting to that, and one of the reasons is that we have a regulatory system in Canada that is very, very complicated. And it is not helped by our federal system. So, on any item, there are ten provincial sets of regulations and federal-provincial differences. The chief executives who sit on my board, and particularly those in manufacturing, could give you a lecture on labelling differences and how frustrating that is for a manufacturer to have to compete and the extra costs that go into a product for a Canadian manufacturer because of regulatory requirements that don't really protect us. I mean, we're obviously in favour of the public good. You have to have regulation. But it has to be regulation that really makes sense, that is timely, that is efficient, et cetera.

In terms of our overall trade policy, we're not focused enough. We have a whole section on how we need to focus our trade policy. We have been comforted by being in NAFTA. But NAFTA in many ways has plateaued. Furthermore, we're looking at events that may work against us in NAFTA. A Democratic Congress in the US will probably be more protectionist. We saw during the mad cow situation that it was one thing for our prime minister and the president of the United States to have an agreement on where we should be proceeding with cattle and beef, but it's another thing to deal with the Midwest. So we became comforted by NAFTA; we haven't deepened NAFTA. Now, looking at what's happening in world trade, the Doha Round of trade negotiations fell flat in 2007. We did not make progress on free trade. That affects us in Canada. We appear to be of mixed minds: some of our agriculture sector is very much in favour of supply management, but when it comes to grain, when it comes to beef, we very much want to play on the world stage.

So, again, we have to get our head together. We have to become more strategic in trade, understand what our interests are, and really be very specific. We also have to be looking more at bilateral agreements.

I remember being in Singapore on [my way to] a mission to China, and the head of economic development for the government of Singapore said, "what is with you, Canada? We're negotiating bilaterals all over the place. We can't seem to get you to focus on us." The bottom line is that we don't feel Canada is adjusting swiftly enough, is nimble enough, with a mindset that is entrepreneurial enough, to these structural, economic changes, and global supply changes.

PK: With *Mission Possible*, the Conference Board tackles a number of major themes of crucial importance in contemporary Canada. For example, our problematic relationship with emerging economic superpowers, like China.

AG: By and large as a country, we have not been really aggressive about getting into China or attracting investment from China. I think we have mixed minds when it comes to foreign investment. I was raised in the days of FIRA, the Foreign Investment Review Agency, whose purpose was to watch foreign investment. Foreign investment was a bad thing. Well, it turns out, no, it's not. It turns out that with foreign investment we get better technology. When you look company by company, it's the foreign global companies that actually are more productive and therefore improve our productivity. And so we have a lot to gain, apart from just the money, from a foreign investment.

At the same time, I think most of us have a deep intuitive concern: wait a second, what does that do to the world of business here? Will there be hollowing out if they take over? What happens to the structure? We don't know the full answer. I think we know from StatsCanada that, in fact, we don't lose head office jobs and it doesn't reduce the number of companies in Canada. So, we can say it doesn't hollow out our business world.

What we don't know is, qualitatively, what kind of decisions are made here in branch plants. Do CEOs of branch plants have less discretion? I believe we need to do a lot more study to understand this. Same thing with China: we were all very sensitive to Chinese money coming in and buying up our resources. And one answer is, don't worry, those resources can't go away. We can always control it through regulation. But then, again, I think there's an intuitive concern: can we trust our regulatory system to protect us?

But definitely, the message from our report is that we are losing ground in the world of foreign investment, inbound and outbound. We're not even clear on what we're counting: what is inbound and what is outbound if you have a global company and some of the trade is done intrafirm? Then how do you count?

So, what we're saying is we are losing share. That part of it is not good. And so we have to become smarter, more interested in foreign investment.

And the other thing that we have to do is to think not just in terms of products, but also of services. A country like Australia, much smaller than we are, seems to be much smarter about the emerging world — maybe because they're physically closer to it. But they see themselves as an exporter of services in education. Look at what we do well in terms of health, education. There's a whole world for us to be looking at services as something we can sell abroad. We're never going to be able to compete on the basis of low-wage, bottom-of-the-ladder stuff. We have to look at where we can add value up the ladder. Innovation has to rank high.

So the whole theme of innovation permeates our report right through the country chapter, the resources chapter, and the city chapter.

PK: I want to ask one more question about the first volume, or about one of the issues you deal with there, because I think it's another interesting eye-opener. I have not really thought about the fact that the workforce in this country is aging very rapidly. And you make recommendations about what we can do about that, which could have a net benefit on the economy of the country.

AG: One of the five strategies that we focus on in this first volume is to rethink the workforce. It's a theme that permeates all three volumes. And you've hit a central point. We're aging, clearly. And in certain sectors — for example, in the resource sectors — it's a particular issue. And in the public service, it's a huge issue because people are retiring even before they're sixty because of packages we've put in place. So, one of the things we suggest is, let's rethink incentives and disincentives to work. We're giving people incentives to leave at sixty or sixty-one, on average, when really we should be encouraging them to stay until maybe sixty-five or seventy, and that will help.

Clearly, immigration is a big piece of the answer, but everybody who studies this will tell you it is not the whole answer. Remember that, at the same time, we want to attract the best and the brightest from around the world, so do other countries. And remember also that, while we're trying to attract the best and the brightest from a country like India, India is now getting ready to use its own best and brightest, and people don't have to leave to do well. And so, their engineers — and they're graduating hundreds of thousands of engineers each year — their engineers can find great jobs there, or in China. They don't have to leave, and so we're going to be competing for talent. That's point one.

Then, when we bring immigrants here, we know there are problems around the immigration process itself. There's an unbelievable backlog that's just ridiculous. Most countries have a backlog, but ours is just gigantic, hundreds of thousands. And then we have issues around credentialing. Now, this issue is as old as I am. I remember attending a conference around forty years ago where, instead of calling it credentialing, we called it prior learning assessment. One would think that we would have cut this Gordian knot. And I think we're starting to make progress. But again, from the data side to the implementation side, there are problems all the way along. We don't have good labour market data. We haven't come to solutions on how to inform people while they are in their home country of what they will need. We're not clear on what the standards should be, and what they should have to pass in order to be able to qualify here. We have different competing standards province to province. This is an interprovincial thing. But this is a problem that everybody agrees must be solved. We're just not yet solving it.

Another aspect of this, in terms of rethinking the workforce, is to rethink what we think of as learning. You know, all the benchmarking we do shows that when our kids graduate high school, they read and write as well as the rest of them, although sometimes we are astonished on the grammar side. But leaving that aside, we apparently produce very qualified high-school graduates. But as life goes along, we do not keep up with lifelong learning on the technical side, on the skills side. We do for some, but we really don't promote it the way they do in other countries. There has to be a shift in mindset here.

PK: Before we move on to the second volume, which is about resources, I want to point out another underlying theme that goes through the entire report. And that is, there is a sense of complacency, which is in a way our worst enemy here. As Canadians, we tend to think we're doing just fine, thank you very much. Don't bother us. And we tend to think we rank in the top of the world in various indicators. And yet we don't. One of your worst enemies must be this complacency, I suppose it is, this lack of self-knowledge, this belief that we're doing better than we are.

AG: It is so true. We often say we're a country that just goes for the bronze. And the theme of really striving for global best and striving for excellence is one that is central to every part of this major study. It is true of Canadians that, by and large, we are satisfied with being middle of the pack. And historians can explain that in many different ways. But we do not, as a country, demand the best of ourselves.

We have been saying this for several years. I personally, absolutely, believe it. Every aspect of my own experience has confirmed this. And to me, it is actually a moral issue. It's not just a social issue or an interesting cultural attribute, because unless we really try — and I think this is the passion behind this study — unless we absolutely, try to excel, unless we really are not satisfied with letting ourselves slip, even though we're still good, we will not be able to have the wealth that gives us the choices to create the best society we want for ourselves.

To go back to the homelessness issue, I often heard the excuse — and it was an excuse — that, well, we didn't have enough money. Well, of course we did, but leaving that aside, the feeling was that we didn't have enough money to do all that we wanted to. If you ask people about health care, you'll hear, well, we just don't have the money to ensure the access or the range of services. And what we do as a nation is put down the American system. We say, look how terrible it is in the US. Well, yes, the access issue is terrible in the US, but the quality of service is not terrible in the US. And if you pay for service, you really do get a superior service in many ways — in terms of just simply access to the number of doctors per capita, PET scans per capita, and all of the technology. So, if we want to be able to have the lifestyle we want, the choices we want, we must see it as imperative to do our best, to create the wealth that we can put into human capital so that we can have the innovation that generates the productivity. And that's the abstraction of productivity that is so hard for people to understand, but that allows us to improve ourselves in the world. That's the measure that allows us to close the per capita income gap, which then gives us what we need. And again, that's the absolutely inextricable link between the economic and social sides of the equation.

PK: On now to the resource volume. You said that we're doing quite well, but it's again a false sense of doing well because we're being buoyed up by natural resources that we sell. Again, Canadians have always been hewers of wood and drawers of water, and according to this report, that's what we apparently are becoming even more.

AG: That's right. The interesting thing to me is that this argument that we're slipping seems to be a hard one to make now. National surpluses, surpluses indeed in most governments, including provincial governments — not municipal, where the true fiscal imbalance exists — but surpluses. High demand for our products, certainly in energy and mining, with a less rosy picture in forestry and agri-products. Things feel very good. We have our deficit under control here, and we're paying down our debt. Inflation is under control. Employment is high — that is, unemployment is low. So this is a hard time to convince people that the sky is falling. So it's not falling, but it is slipping. And it's the boiled frog syndrome: we are complacent, and we're not seeing it because we're in the middle of it.

In terms of resources, it's a time for investment. And unless we shake the complacency, we won't be willing to do the investment. But whether it's mining, where we need new mines, whether it's forestry, where we absolutely have to invest in new technology, maybe new, larger sawmills — and, of course, we have to deal with the impacts of that on communities. These are very tough choices to make, but we have to do that if we're going to be able to compete in the global markets.

In terms of energy, my goodness, huge issues there. We have the tar sands, which are very, very important to oil production in the world and to us. But there are huge environmental consequences. And unless we move with major investments on the adaptation side of the energy issue, not just the mitigation side, we are not going to be able to count on this for long. We think we have about a six-to-eight-year window when demand is going to remain high.

So the whole volume on resources is very much about the human resource issues, the people issues, the need to invest in new technology, the need to address some of the trade issues. And it's the time for renewal. It doesn't feel that way because we're riding high, but we have to start thinking renewal and not think so short term.

PK: Who actually has to do the addressing in this case? Who is responsible for responding to the kinds of problems and issues that you identify in the report? Is it government that will be responding. Is it business? Is it a combination of the two?

AG: Yes, yes, and yes. We have seventy-six recommendations that cover all three volumes, and in each case we're specific. We say governments should, or businesses should. But if you're looking at the energy side, for example, in terms of renewal it's very much about governments, federal and provincial. We talk a bit about capital taxes, which are taxes on investment, which we have to remove now at the provincial level to encourage investment on the capital side and the machinery and equipment. Innovation and culture issues are very much within the organizational purview. Changes have to be made on the organizational side. Companies have to get serious about energy renewal, about new types of energy. Another theme through this is that it's not just either/or. In Canada, particularly, all sectors must get involved.

PK: I want to point out, especially while we're talking about resources, that the subtitle of the study is "Sustainable Prosperity for Canada." And once again, "sustainable" is a key word through the entire report. But when we're talking about resources, this is an area where, as you point out in the report, Canada could be a world leader and actually would benefit from being green.

AG: When we first started on the theme of sustainability, we were very much on the productivity side. A lot of the work that was being done was on the productivity side. I think one of the contributions this huge study makes is that it gathers together the best and the latest information on the complex topic of productivity. It then goes beyond that, which no major study yet does, and it injects sustainability into the productivity argument.

For example, we measure ourselves very much around productivity — say, GDP per capita. But, in terms of all of our measurements, we have to start looking at the total cost. And I'm not referring to what is technically called full-cost accounting, but a broader theme where we have to find ways — we don't have them now — of measuring the economic impact of what we do on future generations, which is the sustainability theme. So the kinds of recommendations we make have to do with measurement of what we're doing, so that we really understand what it is we're doing. It has to do with technology to improve the various processes. It has to do with human capital, and making sure we have a supply of human capital going forward in the future, because in the resource sector the workforce is aging actually more quickly than in other sectors.

Sustainability, thinking things through long term, understanding the impact, looking at forestry, not just in terms of pulp and paper and forestry products, but how forestry through sequestration, a particular process, can contribute to the reduction of carbon emissions. Trying to think of things in a circular way.

PK: The third volume of the report is another eye-opener, certainly for me. It paints a picture of Canada's cities. And it first points out one of the obvious things, I suppose. This is now an urban nation, although we probably still tend to think of ourselves as a rural nation. But cities are obviously something that's very important to you. Talk about what you deal with in the report on cities.

AG: Well, cities are so important to me that I asked if I could be the captain of this volume. Sometimes, when you're the president of an organization, you miss the chance to actually get in there and do the writing. So, I've been intimately involved with this particular volume. I have long believed that we've neglected our cities. I've seen it, and it has long troubled me. Ever since I worked at something called the Bureau of Municipal Research years ago, I've had a passion for cities. I love cities. And I feel that, in many ways, they get the short end of the stick.

PK: Certainly financially, and you're very eloquent on this in the report on how underfunded Canada's cities are.

AG: Yes. Thank you. And because I do think people have to understand that that is where the fiscal imbalance lies. That is, mandates have changed. I'm going to try to be concise here, but in the last decade, particularly in [Ontario], we've been through what has been called offloading, or downloading. Mandates have changed, and the fact is that a city like Toronto — and we've actually studied the city of Toronto in detail — does not have enough money to meet its mandate. In one of the studies we did, we showed that, for the next fifteen years, it will be over one billion dollars short in operating funds, just annually. You can't run a city that way, nor can the cities solve the problem themselves through better management and through better use of the resources they have, though they must do that. One of the fun parts of this was to do a little media study, looking at how the media follow elections. And in each case, they seem to ask the candidates one question, which is: will you keep property taxes flat or bring them down? Wrong question, wrong question.

PK: What's the right question?

AG: The right question is: are you willing to raise property taxes so that we can have the services we need and not allow them to deteriorate? Are you willing at least to keep pace with inflation? Are you willing to apply user fees intelligently? Are you willing to look at your debt load again to see if we can afford to carry it, so that we can plan capital investment properly? Are you willing to see changes in a city so that we can accommodate more people sensibly and intelligently, as they have done in Europe? Are we willing to learn the lessons from other great cities in the world? That's at the municipal level.

I want to tell you about one of the interesting pieces of research we did. We looked at GDP per capita in all of the twenty-seven CMAs [census metropolitan areas] in the country and we found that, in nine cases, if you raised the GDP per capita, you raised the GDP per capita in surrounding cities by 1.1 per cent. In other words, there was a tailwind effect, if you like — they actually pushed their regions. Interestingly, the effect stopped at the provincial boundaries, confirming our theory that provincial regulatory barriers really have an effect that is inhibiting Canada from being greater than it is. We often say we're open to the world, but we're closed to ourselves. And creating a single Canadian market is a major theme in this study.

Then we looked at Canada's ten biggest cities and said that if we could lift their GDP, we'd actually lift the GDP of the country, except for the Far North. And so we thought, if we could only get people to understand that being fair with our major cities is actually a win-win for all Canadians. Admittedly, that will take a sea change of opinion. And that is not to say that all funding should go to only these ten cities, or that we shouldn't worry about the issues in other cities. It is to say that when we allocate major funding programs, be it for infrastructure or other purposes, we should not do it on a per capita basis, but analyze both the needs and the potential of that money to have an impact. And so it calls for a strategic investment approach, which is probably the most controversial recommendation in the volume. And yet I have tested it in a number of presentations now, and most people nod and say it does make sense once we explain that this is not an all-or-nothing proposition.

PK: Again, you're going to have an uphill battle convincing, in this case, not just one, but two and even three levels of government. I suspect you'll find easy marks in city halls from coast to coast, but I think you're going to have a little more trouble when you start going to the provincial legislatures and or to Parliament Hill. They're going to talk about these kinds of legislative changes as being almost impossible to imagine.

AG: Oh, without a doubt. And I've already had that experience in the years that I have been talking about cities. And again, I don't get discouraged. I just see this as a question of ongoing education and trying to get people to see it. But we're starting to see a bit of headway in some areas. Certainly here in Ontario, we now have some new governance legislation for the city of Toronto, which wouldn't have been deemed possible. That is, we have the *City of Toronto Act*, which is not the same for every other city. In other words, I'm starting to see a little bit of what I would call differentiation. There was an argument that, whatever you do for Toronto, you have to be able to do for cities across the country, but I'm not hearing that.

We're in a world of differentiation right now, everywhere, on all topics. So we may be able to make some headway, but there's no question, this is going to be an uphill battle. But it is a battle worth engaging in because we have to understand that our cities are competing against cities around the world. We can look at Europe and watch their core cities' approach. We looked at what was going on in the UK, and they are adopting what they're calling a hub cities program — cities that will get strategic investment because of their importance for the region. So, we hope the message will come through.

PK: The report is overwhelmingly positive. It's called *Mission Possible*. Give me some reasons for your positivity. Why are you so optimistic that you can convince people in government, in business, leaders in the community to read the report, to get interested in policy questions, to recognize that we have the wrong picture of our country? That's the first thing you're doing. You're trying to say reality is a little less pleasant than maybe we've been led to believe. But then, what's the source of your optimism? Why do you think you can actually make these changes?

AG: It's a two-part question. First, in terms of getting people to understand that we're slipping, the timing of this is fortuitous. Governments are changing everywhere. And we are completely non-partisan. So, for example, when I listened to Finance Minister Jim Flaherty speak at an event in Niagara, he actually was very much onto this, very much interested in the productivity issue and eager to tackle, for example, the infrastructure issues. Similarly, other organizations are also talking about slippage. And I think we're starting to see an emerging consensus now among the policy interested. But that's how public opinion changes. It cascades down that we're not doing as well as we should. Where there's disagreement is on what the solution should be. And I have to say that, for the Conference Board — because of what our mission is, to build leadership for a better Canada — if we succeed in lifting the level of public debate and getting people engaged in the discussion on our seven strategies and seventy-six recommendations, then whether they agree with every single one of them is less important to us than that we actually get into a real discussion and not a silly discussion. So that part is encouraging.

Now, why do we stay positive? Partly because there's no percentage in being negative. If you go around saying "Henny Penny, the sky is falling," you get a limited audience. It's not helpful to just be negative; after a while, it will wear thin. So I don't see the utility of just being negative.

Secondly, we are, and I am personally, very solution oriented: can we make this better? how can we make this better? It may not be perfect, but politics is the art of the possible. So if you're pragmatic and realistic, moving in the right direction is a good thing. We believe we can influence the debate that will take us in a more positive direction. We may not agree with every single policy decision, and there are things that seem long overdue, but we are positive in our outlook. And the energy is positive.

From Charity to Entitlement

LOUISE ARBOUR

As the United Nations high commissioner for human rights, no Canadian recently has held a more prominent international position than Madame Justice Louise Arbour. Before that, she was one of nine judges on the Supreme Court of Canada. And before that, she was chief prosecutor for two international war crimes tribunals, considering charges of genocide and crimes against humanity in the former Yugoslavia and in Rwanda. Hers has been an amazing career. Ideas *host Paul Kennedy interviewed her about her 2005 LaFontaine-Baldwin Lecture, which she delivered in Quebec City. Her talk, "From Charity to Entitlement," focused on social and economic rights, in which she has had a lifelong interest. This interview was broadcast on 7 April 2005.*

LOUISE ARBOUR

Well, you know, it's much more comfortable to stay at the abstract, more theoretical level. You carve out a sphere that is less demanding of you as a person. I suppose I've always thought of myself as someone who's good at that stuff, the more theoretical stuff, and yet what I like is the human contact. I think I swing constantly between the two, and in the work I do currently, there is such a wonderful mix.

Maybe I could tell you how I got to be interested in looking at this particular history. I think, like most Canadians, I have a slightly romantic idea of where Canada situates itself internationally in terms of its values, commitment to human rights, ideals, and so on. I just assumed that we had always been at the forefront of every single progressive idea — you know, the model of the peacekeepers and, of course, the Pearson Nobel Peace Prize, and so on. And yet, in the work I was doing in Canadian courts, I was always surprised to see what I considered to be considerable reluctance, certainly by litigants and by the courts, to embrace some rights, particularly social and economic rights — the right to welfare, to food, to shelter. Somehow, I felt we were very timid. Then, looking back in history, I found that that timidity was, in fact, probably outright hostility at the outset, at the time of the Universal Declaration of Human Rights, where Canadians figured very prominently in the drafting of that document. Right from there, we were certainly not in a leadership position on these kinds of rights.

PAUL KENNEDY

In fact, we abstained at a crucial point as that legislation was being drafted.

LA: Yes, and this has been described as literally a shameful moment in the history of our contribution to the international scene. We abstained in very bad company, with a handful of countries that were not friends of human rights generally. And what was so surprising is that, even then, Canada was a friend of some more traditional rights — fundamental freedoms, civil liberties, and so on — but obviously was extremely reluctant to embrace social and economic rights. Then, to add insult to injury, it seems that what was said publicly by Lester Pearson, who was then minister of foreign affairs, about why Canada was so reluctant was not actually the truth. There were things said suggesting that Canada had some reservations because of its federalism obligation, that it was reluctant because these matters were within provincial competence. It turned out, according to the historians who looked at the materials at the time, that, in fact, the reluctance came from very conservative elites in Canada, including the Canadian Bar Association, that were pressuring the prime minister and the minister of foreign affairs to back off from embracing these fundamental rights.

PK: It's interesting, because we were working on two fronts. There was the international movement at the UN with the formulation of the Universal Declaration of Human Rights, and on the domestic front, politicians in certain jurisdictions, at least, were working towards a concept of a social safety net and various programs that were fundamental in this social, economic, and cultural rights field.

LA: Yes, what I found most astonishing was that, at a time when we were very actively engaged in constructing the social safety net, which I believe Canadians really embrace, we were expressing great reluctance to transforming these ideals, these values, into rights. And that's why the theme of my lecture was: what's holding us back from moving from charity to entitlement?

PK: This has been a consistent theme. We can go back decades and look at the formulation of the Universal Declaration. But even more recently, Canada has been called on the carpet at various United Nations organizations for our non-compliance with treaties or with documents that we have signed saying that we would uphold certain fundamental rights.

LA: Yes, and particularly so in the field of social and economic rights. It's very unconscionable, I have to say. I should not dismiss the kinds of reactions that you find in official circles when international mechanisms — committees and so on of the United Nations — call a country to task and allege that it's falling short of meeting its obligations. And I'm sure that these kinds of assessments were very poorly received in Ottawa.

Having said that, the other very common response that you get is, well, how dare they, the international community, criticize us? Look at everybody else. But to me, that's not the right test. I don't think Canadians would feel particularly proud of their performance if they felt that they compared well to other countries that don't have half the means we have. So, it's not a question of how much better we're doing than the rest of the world. The real question is, how well are we doing compared to what we can do? How do we situate ourselves on the basis of our resources, our capacity, our values? That's the real question.

PK: Does it put you in any particularly embarrassing position being a Canadian and being the UN high commissioner when Canada is called on the carpet? Does it reflect on your Canadian-ness in the position you're in now, that the country that you come from isn't doing as well as it should?

LA: Well, frankly, if it were an issue on a day-to-day basis, I'd feel pretty good. Let me be very clear on this. Canada is still the darling of the international community. I don't want to suggest for a minute that my nationality is an embarrassment — quite the opposite. You know, the proverbial little Canadian flag on the back of your backpack works right through the United Nations system. But my point is, that's not good enough. In fact, it's very dangerous for us to have what I've always had, this romantic idea that we're the best, we're just so good, and we should be out there teaching others to be just as good. As I say, in the field of economic and social rights, we should pause and maybe learn from others. From courts, for instance, in other countries that have been considerably more aggressive or progressive in searching for the proper legal environment for the pursuit of these rights. Here, I think we've accepted the general proposition that social and economic rights, so to speak, are for the political arena, not for the judicial form. So, I just want to be very clear that we fall short, but on very few things.

PK: Is one of the problems, in fact, that we do have a rose-coloured vision about what we do and what we're like, and that maybe the vision and the reality have fallen apart in recent years, but Canadians generally assume we're doing OK and therefore to draw their attention to it is a very difficult thing to do. They assume everything must be fine.

LA: Well, I think that's exactly true. To a large extent, though, I want to stress that this rose-coloured vision is totally justified. It's difficult sometimes to appreciate in what particular ways Canadians are such good players on the international scene, but I think it's a fact that, in general terms, we're very at ease with a multicultural environment. Even people who, in their own communities, are not exposed to a great deal of diversity of cultures and languages and so on, are well disposed to it. And that helps enormously, I think.

We are certainly not cultural imperialists. We're very interested in others. We are great travellers in every sense of the word, not just in packing our bags. But we're travellers in our mind as well. We're interested. So, in many ways, we fit extremely well in a multilateral environment. The danger, I think, is to overplay that, to think that we're perfect, that we have nothing to answer for, and that we have nothing to learn. That's why I say that, in this whole area of the transformation from a charitable frame of mind to a frame of mind that recognizes the entitlement of others, we have a lot to learn from others who have gone much farther ahead in their thinking than we have.

PK: I get the sense, though, that you think we are learning and that, in fact, there is progress, there is improvement on this front.

LA: There is, and yet, what I discovered was the Canadian attitude, as expressed by its government in 1948 at the time of the Universal Declaration, is to a certain extent exactly the same attitude now in an environment where the international community collectively is searching for a framework to make progress in social and economic rights, beyond international aid and a kind of charitable mode. The Africans, for instance, are adamant that they have a right to development. So there are very challenging issues out there.

And strangely enough, I am concerned that Canada is repeating its own history by playing more or less the same kind of role that it was playing in 1948, which is very puzzling, considering how Canadians have embraced the social safety net and the commitments that we feel we're making to each other to provide basic survival with dignity. That's my concern at the present time — that Canada is not taking the lead, not only in advocating, but in searching for a proper framework for the application of those rights.

PK: Stepping way back and asking a very big question, why is Louise Arbour so passionately interested in rights?

LA: Well, I came to law school, as most people of my generation in Quebec did, very much by accident. In those days, we used to say that law leads to everything as long as you get out of it. So it was then perceived to be the route to journalism, to public affairs generally. And then I got hooked on law and on justice. I suppose what is attractive about law as a discipline is that it has a lot of intellectual rigour. It has frameworks and so on. But at the same time, at least if you look closely enough, it's just loaded with moral imperatives. So it's a very attractive environment in which to work. And I just got hooked on it, I suppose.

PK: But what made you a moralist? If you're interested in the moral aspects of law, how did you become that person?

LA: First of all, I don't think of myself as a moralist. I don't like labels. I think they're not particularly useful. I may have become a humanist, I suppose. When I say it has high moral content, I think what I mean by that is that it's not just rules. You know, when we talk about the rule of law — this, I think, is a very good example — the international community is promoting good governance and the rule of law, and we have to promote in emerging democracies a legal framework so that countries are governed by laws, not by the whim of man. But you have to pause and say, but not any laws. Apartheid South Africa was governed by tons of legislation, all of which was utterly oppressive. So was Nazi Germany. So it's in that sense that there's moral content. It's not just a set of rules. They are rules that express social and political choices, and those have to be the correct ones.

PK: The ones that you seem to have concerned yourself with, though, are not necessarily political rights as much as they are economic rights and social rights. You're concerned with an area of rights legislation that is not the one that is normally accepted as the French Rights of Man — liberty, equality. It's more the social underpinnings of those things that you think can't be separated from each other.

LA: That's right. Well, I think they're all the same thing, frankly. I think of this entire framework of liberty, equality. And then, if you continue, you get to fraternity. It seems to me you could easily argue that fraternity is the foundation of social and economic rights. The Universal Declaration of Human Rights doesn't create distinctions between civil and political rights, and social and economic rights. These distinctions were forced later in the process. But in my own career, I came very late, as most Canadian lawyers, and jurists, and judges did, to this interest in social and economic rights simply because they weren't there. They were not reflected, not in our Constitution, at least not expressly. I've always claimed that they are there, that the right to life, liberty, and security of the person encompasses the whole panoply of social and economic rights, such as the right to health, the right to food, the right to welfare. Others have disagreed with me on this, but these rights were never at the forefront of what we understood to be the legal framework within which we operated.

In my own career, I worked for the most part in criminal law. And inevitably I became interested in law-enforcement issues and checking any potential abuse of power by the state. The environment in which I worked very comfortably for most of my professional life was linked to civil and political rights — freedom from oppression by the state, freedom from arbitrary arrest and detention, and so on. Maybe I'm embracing it with a passion now because I think I came very late to this field of social and economic rights.

PK: Well, I wouldn't want to put too great a consistency on your career either, but when you first came to most people's attention, it was for an inquiry that you led about a riot in a prison in which, once again, the social aspects were involved. You were trying to maintain human dignity in a very difficult situation. So, I think there is a consistency here.

LA: That's right. Now again, this is not something I did as an activist. I mean, this case came to me, in a sense. I was asked to chair this inquiry. But in the one year in which I did the inquiry at the Kingston prison for women, it's quite extraordinary how so many of these ideas that we've been talking about were all coming together. For instance, Corrections is an environment that is overloaded with rules but where the rule of law is absent, the culture of respect for rights is noticeably absent. Yet, an environment that is overly regulated is also an environment where you see the potential for exclusion and the danger of abuse of power. You see it blatantly in a correctional environment. Then, of course, there are women's issues and aboriginal women's issues. It was a microcosm of all kinds of ideas and challenges that I had encountered throughout my career, and all of a sudden we condensed and packaged all of it in one inquiry.

PK: Did it colour what you did after that? Did that experience really put a tone on the kind of work that you did later?

LA: Well, in a sense, it did. First of all, it gave me skills that made it a little more possible, although it was a big jump for me to become the prosecutor of the International Tribunals for the former Yugoslavia and for Rwanda, because I was approached to do that when I was in the middle of this commission of inquiry. I had been an academic prior to that in my life, and then a judge, so my demonstrated skills as a prosecutor were virtually non-existent. But the fact that I was then conducting an inquiry was probably my point of entry into the kind of fact finding and analytical work that you have to do as a prosecutor in international courts, where the prosecutor is also the lead investigator. So, yes, in many, many ways, it was the beginning of different things in my career.

PK: Let's talk for a while about the International Tribunal. When you decided to take that offer, did you ever have second thoughts about it or, much later, having lived through what you lived through, would you have second thoughts about taking a position as chief prosecutor?

LA: Well, I think it's the case for many people that, if you had known what you were getting yourself into, maybe you wouldn't have taken it. I vaguely remember what I thought I was getting myself into and, of course, it was nowhere near what the real job was. I approached it in a very abstract, very academic way, which is the way I approach most things. I thought this was going to be a kind of laboratory of comparative law. Well, not quite — as it turned out, there was no time to be in the laboratory, and not a lot of time to reflect on comparative legal principles, and so on. It was loaded with action. Lots of media work, which I'd never done before and which nobody mentioned I'd have to do. So it ended up being something completely different.

I thought it would bring together the common law tradition and the civil law tradition and become a kind of hybrid intellectual adventure. It ended up being about chasing war criminals in Bosnia, and Serbia, and Croatia, and Rwanda, and the adjacent countries. So, it was a crash course in — let's put it this way — innovative investigative techniques, and tracking initiatives, and so on. Had I known what it would be, I think I would have felt so inadequate for the task. I had no demonstrated talent or skills to do any of that, so I probably would have said you're really coming to the wrong person. In retrospect, I'm really glad I didn't realize that and didn't decline on that basis, because it ended up being amazingly interesting and called for all kinds of skills that you learn on the job, such as making strategic alliances and just making things happen. It was amazing, absolutely amazing.

PK: You mentioned the word innovative, and I think that certainly would characterize the kind of work you were doing there. Sometimes that brought you under a fair bit of international criticism. For example, you didn't publish indictments, you kept indictments secret. Now, this is against much of the common law tradition, the British tradition. This is anathema. And yet it was essential and, in fact, it got certain suspects behind bars and brought to The Hague to be put before the tribunal.

LA: That's right. Well, when I say it was amazingly interesting, this was part of it. I would sit with my colleagues, and you didn't have the comfort of turning to some kind of rule book to tell you what the answer was to fifteen different questions every day. We just had to think it through from first principles, the fundamental one being, what is the right thing to do? And hoping that it would also coincide with the thing that's most likely to work. But you had to articulate it on a principled basis. And we did that on a huge number of issues for which we had no ready-made answers.

I think the second guiding principle was that this was not home. Don't tell me how things are done in Kansas. This is not Kansas. It's not Ottawa, either. This is a totally new environment, to work in criminal law in an international field. Criminal law is essentially the exercise of state power — that's what it is. Well, internationally, there is no state to back you up, which is why, most days, we would say to ourselves, why is this so hard? Why is it so hard to arrest these people? The simple answer is that, in traditional criminal law, the state is on your side when you're the prosecutor. In this environment, however, the state was on the other side, sheltering these people, helping them escape an arrest warrant. So, when people said to me, it's unfair to have secret indictments, I said, well, unfair by what measure, by what environment? What might or might not be fair or unfair in a domestic system where the state has all the powers, and the accused must be equipped, in a sense, to counterbalance these state powers. Here the paradigm is completely shifted.

So, in that sense it was immensely challenging. You had to make something work. It was almost like learning a new language. You couldn't just fall back on the comfort of pulling old rules out of your bag of tricks. You had to think it through, make it effective, but also make it principled, and right, and correct, and not oppressive. You can't cheat, but you have to reinvent an environment to make it happen.

Frankly, I think the most difficult part of the work was that, although I was posted in The Hague, I was the chief prosecutor for both the Yugoslavia and the Rwanda tribunals. So, I had a large office in Kigali, in Rwanda, but the seat of that tribunal was in Arusha, in Tanzania, and I tried to plan to spend every fourth or fifth week in Africa. This became increasingly difficult to maintain when the Kosovo war broke out, because then the demands of the Yugoslavia tribunal, real-time demands, were absolutely irresistible. And it was very hard for me to remain fully engaged on a Balkans issue from Kigali, and the other way around, sometimes simply because communications just didn't work, the equipment didn't work.

So I felt this was a very difficult part of my work to manage, to give equal attention to the two issues that were literally very far apart, and not just in geographic terms: every single issue was completely different. Travelling to Kigali and to Arusha was not just travelling in space; I had to travel in my juridical, my legal, mind as well. For instance, our big arrest partner in the Balkans was NATO. When I first arrived, they still had sixty thousand troops in Bosnia. My predecessor had publicly indicted about seventy-five people, but nothing was happening. Now, if this had been the only model, you would have thought that international criminal law is crippled by its inability to arrest anybody.

Then, you go to Rwanda. All the people we were looking for had left Rwanda, obviously, after the genocide. They perpetrated the genocide and then they ran away when the FPR [Front patriotique Rwandaise], the current government, came down and took over the country. So, the people we wanted were elsewhere and, first of all, we had to find them. We knew that they had left the country. We had pretty good information as to where to find them. Then, we had to develop partnerships with other governments to arrest them. We found a lot of them in the Democratic Republic of Congo. We found some in Cameroon, Zambia, all over Africa. But a huge number were in Kenya. So there, we had to approach the government of Kenya to try to get assistance, not so much in locating them — we found them all by ourselves — but in arresting them. And, of course, there were all kinds of other issues, mass grave exhumations and so on, where the work was very different from one environment to another. My travels were not just a question of going different places and working in different environments. I had to get into a completely different frame of mind working in one environment or the other.

PK: When you look back at the time you spent at The Hague, is there one particular action that you're particularly proud of? Is there something that you can look back at and think, that was well done? You said you were doing it on the fly. Is there something that you'd like to have as a legacy from that period?

LA: Well, I think the thing that was the most important in retrospect was conceiving the idea of secret indictments. That totally unblocked the situation. When I arrived there, about seventy-five people had been indicted, but there were only seven in custody. And they had arrived there almost by accident. I mean, the chances of anybody being arrested were virtually non-existent. So the entire future of the court, of the tribunal as it was conceived, was very much an issue. In fact, the judges were becoming very impatient, and many of them were arguing for trials *in absentia* — just forget it, let's not even try to arrest them, because it can't be done. Of course, if we had moved in that direction, I think it would have become a kind of historical archival body. It wouldn't have been a court of law as we know it, because they would have had virtual impunity. These people would have stayed home forever and would have been tried on paper in The Hague. So, to me, the future of the institution was at stake, and developing a strategy that proved efficient, that worked, was absolutely critical. But it was not obvious. We begged NATO to be more proactive. There was a big media campaign. As I put it, we were in a permanent whining mode — nobody was helping us. So the task was how to get out of that predicament and turn this liability into an asset and develop a strategy and make it work. I think, in retrospect, that the future of the institution turned on developing that strategy, and it worked.

PK: Did you have any qualms about leaving, having done that, having suddenly found very high-profile people in custody and seeing the court actually beginning to move in the direction that you were pushing it? Was there any feeling that maybe you should stay there, or was the invitation to come back to Canada just irresistible?

LA: I always have qualms about leaving. I've never left anything I've done because I was tired of it. I was a law teacher for twelve years until the phone rang, and I was offered a judicial appointment, which took me entirely by surprise. I wasn't looking for another job. I loved teaching. Then I was a trial judge. I adored that. I would still be a very happy Ontario High Court trial judge. But then the call came to go to the Court of Appeal — how can you not go to the Court of Appeal? Particularly in my case — I'd been an academic — and then, who would leave the Ontario Court of Appeal? But going to The Hague was paradise in terms of the companionship, the collegiality of that court, the nature of the work. I adored every minute I spent there and thought I would go back, of course. I had a four-year appointment with the tribunal, and I certainly wasn't looking to leave early. But again, when somebody asks you to take up a seat on the Supreme Court of Canada, how can you not?

In fact, when I was in The Hague with all my international colleagues, they were appalled when I told them that I was going to leave to take up a domestic appointment. The only ones who understood were the American lawyers. They knew that if somebody asks you if you want to sit on the Supreme Court, there's only one answer. And then, when I was on the Supreme Court, the same thing. I very much thought I would be there for the rest of my career. At least, I would have happily reached retirement age. I wasn't looking for anything else. So, the short answer is, I never leave without considerable regret, but obviously I have a pattern of not being able to resist the next challenge.

PK: Well, they're interesting challenges. That list is a phenomenal CV you've drawn up for yourself. The Supreme Court of Canada must have been particularly attractive, though, because what had happened since you were in law school was the Charter of Rights and Freedoms, and the Supreme Court was full square in the middle of very exciting lawmaking, I suppose.

LA: But, you see, I had done a lot of Charter work both as a trial judge and as an appellate court judge. And to my great surprise, when I joined the Supreme Court, I realized, in fact, that it's a lot more fun to do Charter work in the lower courts, for many reasons — certainly in the early days of the Charter, when the litigants and lawyers would come with very novel arguments. So, you could be a lot more creative as a trial judge, even as an appellate court judge, because you knew that, if you really went too far, or if your reasoning was very faulty, there was a safety net. The Supreme Court of Canada can always correct the reasoning. So, the room to be imaginative and so on was much greater in the lower courts, certainly in the early days of the Charter. I suppose now, when the Supreme Court has given so much guidance, the lower courts have to march to these orders more. I always encouraged trial judges and appellate court judges to dare to explore the outer contours of Charter rights, again on the theory that you have to feed the Supreme Court with a whole range of ideas and thoughts.

In the Supreme Court, of course, it's a little more solemn, because this is not the time to be an intellectual cowboy, right? This is where it stops. You've got to be extremely sober about where you're going to position the law. I think law students imagine that it's on the Supreme Court that you have all the freedom to be a maverick and do what you want, but, in fact — certainly in my experience — you have a lot more freedom in the lower courts if you view your role appropriately, or you did, at least in the history of Charter litigation, which is a bit counterintuitive, but I think it's true.

PK: Is there one particular case that you're particularly proud of?

LA:　No. When I look at the whole range of Charter-type litigation that came before me as a judge, it was certainly more challenging for me to do that work when I was more alone — that is, as a trial judge. I was only a trial judge for a couple of years, and you don't get a lot of Charter work. I mean, if you're sitting in motions court and then you do civil jury cases, there's lots of work that just doesn't lend itself to Charter litigation. But anything you do as a trial judge, you do on your own. So, inevitably, you take more ownership, I think, of these issues.

And, of course, for those of us on the bench who had been judges right through the process, I remember almost every case I had as a trial judge, because they were real people in my courtrooms. I remember them. I remember their stories, how they told them. But when I was on the Supreme Court of Canada, people would cite to me decisions that I rendered. And frankly, if my name was not written on the piece of paper, I couldn't remember half of it. I mean, I'd read something thinking, God, I must have been really clever to write this opinion on a fine point of commercial law that I can now barely remember. So, it's the trial work that stays with you, because it also speaks to you emotionally in a very human way, while the appellate work is just so much more abstract.

PK:　It seems to be one of the dilemmas that you functioned with throughout your career as well, the abstract qualities of the law and then the very concrete tangible realities of people's lives. You've been trying to bring those two into some kind of harmony all your life.

LA:　Well, you know, it's much more comfortable to stay at the abstract, more theoretical level. You carve out a sphere that is less demanding of you as a person. And I suppose I've always thought of myself as someone who's good at that stuff, the more theoretical stuff, and yet, what I like is the human contact. So, I think I swing constantly between the two, and in the work I do currently, there is such a wonderful mix of both.

PK: I know you can't take us behind closed doors at the Supreme Court of Canada, and I wouldn't want you to be indiscreet, but you describe it as sober and sedate. I was wondering if there's also perhaps some excitement there when the judges get together, realize that what they're doing is critically important work in interpreting the Charter, which is still very new and quite exciting. Is there a sense that, beyond the sedateness and the sobriety, there's actually some really exciting work going on?

LA: Oh, absolutely, there is. I'll speak again of my own case. The excitement for me was, in part, to try to catch up. I had been away for three years when I came to the Supreme Court, so basically I hadn't read a single Canadian newspaper in three years, I hadn't read case law, so it was intellectually absolutely overwhelming. And it doesn't matter where you come from in the judicial system in Canada to go to the Supreme Court, there will be huge bodies of law that you don't know about. If you come, for instance, from a provincial appellate court, typically you don't do a lot of tax work. You don't do intellectual property. You will have done very little Aboriginal rights law. It's like being in first-year law school all over again, except that every day is exam day. So it's pretty scary. And in that sense, it's amazingly stimulating because, while the Charter work is interesting, there are lots of administrative law issues that come to the Supreme Court. Each one of them has enormous consequences for litigants, for the structure of the law. So, the sense of excitement, I think, comes from every single case. Every time you open a file, even if it's in a field that intuitively you think you're not going to like all that much, you're just drawn by the intellectual content or the difficulty of just figuring it out — figuring out what the question is, never mind what the answer should be. So, there is a lot of that.

It's a ton of work, too. I think it's quite surprising. Again, when you sit on an appellate court, you do a lot of volume, but a lot of it is error correcting. All you have to say is, clearly the trial judge made an error, and here's why. You could write it very briefly. You compare the load you have on an appellate court — the number of cases —

and you look at the Supreme Court, and you think, well, that must be sort of a nice breeze there, you have only a fraction of the cases. But when you get there, you realize each one of them is difficult, and you sit on each one of the cases. And, of course, working on a panel of nine is a very different thing from working on a panel of three, for instance, which is more typical in appellate courts. So, again, the group dynamics are enormously challenging, even in a court such as the current one that is actually very committed to consensus building. It's a very collegial court. I've been away now for almost a year. There are new players on it. But, essentially, I think it's a court that views itself as wanting to speak with clarity, and clarity requires combining the different voices as much as possible so you don't have a plurality of opinions that makes the outcome unintelligible. So, it's an extremely stimulating environment.

PK: You said earlier that you anticipated that you would end your career on the Supreme Court of Canada, and that didn't happen, because another phone call came. What was the attraction of being United Nations high commissioner for human rights?

LA: Well, when the call came, I said no immediately. I thought this just was not even an option. I didn't even say let me think about it. I was so persuaded that I was on the Supreme Court — that I had made, maybe for the first time in my life, a real lifetime commitment. But then, I think the attraction of it was so overwhelming that, the more I thought of it, the more it became clear to me that I should not let go of this opportunity.

First of all, it's human rights law, which, at the end of the day, is where I think I can make a contribution on the basis of what I understand about it and what I like about it. It really calls on me in a very profound way. It also has the perfect mix of intellectual content and action. Also, having worked with the tribunals, I realize how at ease I am in an international environment. I adore the pluralism, the multiculturalism. I work with people of all ages. It just has the perfect balance — people who come from all kinds of different countries who don't think the way I necessarily do, so it's puzzling and interesting to interact with them. It's an ideal environment.

I really believe that this is a turning point for human rights. Certainly, prior to September 11th, we were about to embark on the implementation of social and economic rights. We had done a ton of work in the civil and political rights area for years. It was fair to assume that a lot could be taken for granted; we just had to keep working at it. But the breakthrough had to come in social and economic rights. September 11th froze the environment of social and economic rights because it just took all the oxygen out of it by calling attention again to civil and political rights, law enforcement, counterterrorism initiatives. And we're still in that mode because the events subsequent to September 11th have put such stress on civil and political rights. For instance, the torture convention — widely ratified, very widely accepted, not widely implemented. Let's be very clear, I don't want to suggest for a minute that torture had been eradicated around the world, but at least on a normative basis you didn't hear a lot of questions about whether it was appropriate to have recourse to torture. Now, we have to tread water, just to get back to where we were on issues such as this one. So, all this was happening on the international human rights scene, which I found, frankly, quite irresistible. It seemed like such an important time go and be part of that movement.

And finally, on a more pedestrian level, I figured if I stayed on the Supreme Court another five or ten years, I could always contribute later to international work. But now, the UN is still full of people I know. I have lots of friends still in the system. So, I thought, this will also be so much easier for me. When I went to the tribunals the first time around, I had never been to the seat of the United Nations. I didn't know where things were, who people were. This time, I thought, I'll be able to be so much more effective, because I'll walk in and just pick up from where I left.

PK: Did you have any sense that the history was there as well — that, since Canadians had been around when the Universal Declaration was being formulated, you were, in a sense, just bringing the circle round again? You were another Canadian coming in on a prominent role to do something that we pioneered half a century ago.

LA: In fact, I didn't think in those terms then, but now it's very obvious to me when I think of John Humphreys's work in drafting the Universal Declaration of Human Rights and when I look at Canada's involvement and the role it played then, and what's happening now, I see Mr. Humphreys and me holding hands across the decades to try to carry forward a project to which he made such an important contribution.

PK: Can you reflect on what you've identified as a certain ambivalence in Canadian attitudes? Yes, we're very pro-rights. Yes, we think there should be a social safety net. We think that social and economic and cultural rights are important things, but we're not always willing to put our money where our mouth is.

LA: Well, I'm not a historian, but I could tell you intuitively the kinds of trends or ideas that I see there. The Universal Declaration is linked historically to Roosevelt's Four Freedoms: freedom from fear, which some would say is the root of civil and political rights; freedom from want, which is the root of economic and social rights; freedom of expression and belief; and freedom of religion. And this is always seen as the root of the entire human rights machinery. But, in fact, all of these ideas and ideals actually are rooted much earlier than that in the imperatives that came about from the creation of nation-states and the rise of capitalism. That was, in a sense, the price to pay to make it work. States had to look after their citizens, at least in a bare-bones fashion, to ensure the preservation of a peaceful nation-state and to allow capitalism to pursue profits, but not at any cost. So, in a sense, it's a way of providing a peaceful environment for the viability of the nation-state — a peaceful, secure, and prosperous environment for all those within the nation-state. So, I think these are the real roots of all the ideas that were expressed through the Roosevelt Four Freedoms.

Now, why was Canada somewhat reluctant to be part of that process? Again, this is a very superficial diagnosis, but it seems to me that Canada embraced charity rather than entitlement as a method of delivering these goods. Not that it had any ambivalence about the necessity to provide — I think it's clear throughout our history that we have always made a commitment to look after each other — but, historically, we've made it through our charitable disposition, and we continue to have a preference for what I consider to be a kind of private sector approach, even if it's delivered by the state. And when I say charity, it could be grounded in legislation, but legislation that the next government can modify or overturn completely. It's as though we want to hold on to that as the choice we make every day to be kind to each other. We have to transform these values into validating the humanity of the recipient by acknowledging an entitlement, not just flattering ourselves with our own kindness, which is the root of charity.

PK: It's a right, it's not a goodness.

LA: Absolutely. We didn't make that transition in 1948. I don't think we've made it yet. And we're certainly not promoting it internationally — the transformation from a charitable frame of mind to a rights-based approach to the delivery of social justice.

PK: Now, as high commissioner, you are, I would assume, very aware of the fact that these rights are being acknowledged, even institutionalized around the world, in places that are sometimes quite surprising. I mean, we think of Canada as the perfect place where these things can be enshrined in our Constitution, but there are countries that find it much less easy to do exactly that, and that are making it part of their national legislation.

LA: It's very much part of the current mood of international politics around human rights to advocate these categories, these divisions of rights. For instance, the Western countries are very interested in pressing African governments in the area of civil and political rights — good governance, democratic rights, lack of oppression, the promotion of freedom, and so on. That's what the West wants to export to the South. The South, on the other hand, says, we don't want any of that. We want the right to food, the right to health, the right to education, development. Let's talk about that. But at the end of the day, certainly human rights theory says there are no such divisions. Human rights are, by definition, universal and indivisible. You cannot segregate them. And frankly, counterterrorism initiatives now are very rooted on the civil and political side of rights. I hate to use these categories, because we shouldn't think that way. Yet, a lot of the root causes of terrorism or, if not causes, the root environment — let's put it this way — are linked to severe deprivation, if anything, of the right to education, which can then help you to overcome bigotry or narrow-minded understanding of your own predicament. So, all this is totally interlinked, but it's the politics that uses human rights for other purposes that foster these divisions and try to carve out these two spheres of action.

PK: So is that the biggest challenge facing you as high commissioner, to try to bring the attention of political leaders back to a social, economic, cultural agenda?

LA: Well, I think that when I go to countries like those in Africa, I have to tell them that, although I'm a champion of social and economic rights, that's not good enough. They also have to clean up their house and embrace these ideals of good governance, and rule of law, and democratic rights. And they have to stop arbitrary imprisonment, and arbitrary arrest, and so on. So I have to push them on what they don't want to look at. But, at the same time, when I come here and to a lot of other Western countries, I have to try to persuade them to abandon their reluctance to recognize social and economic rights, to get out of their charitable disposition, and to acknowledge that this is a matter of human dignity, and it should be grounded in legally binding obligations.

PK: How long do you anticipate being high commissioner for human rights?

LA: Well, I have a four-year mandate, renewable once. That's the framework within which I operate. I don't have a very good track record in recent years of even finishing my mandates, but this time I'm telling you I am very determined. I just got there. I have so much to do.

PK: But when the phone rings seven years from now, what job will be offered?

LA: Well, you know the phone never rang with an offer that, from my point of view, was predictable in the first place. I could not even begin to imagine what could possibly be out there for me to do after this. Maybe gardening would have a huge amount of attraction. I don't know.

The Eye, the Word,
and the Ear

FOUR

The Light that Filled the Bed

MARY PRATT

In 2007, Canada Post released a new stamp featuring a colourful painting of three jam bottles by East Coast artist Mary Pratt. Her work displays a nearly photographic realism, focusing on everyday objects connected with raising a family or running a home. Just before the stamp came out, Mary Pratt's official portrait of her friend, former governor general Adrienne Clarkson, was unveiled at Rideau Hall. Although she has been getting a lot of attention lately, she has been painting for most of her seventy-three years. Mary Pratt was born in Fredericton, New Brunswick, where she and her sister enjoyed an idyllic childhood. Her father was a lawyer and prominent local politician; her mother ran the household and tinted photographs on the side. Mary Pratt studied fine arts at Mount Allison University, where she met her future husband, the artist Christopher Pratt. In 1963, they moved to Salmonier, Newfoundland. Mary Pratt spoke to Paul Kennedy in a program broadcast on Ideas *on 21 March 2007.*

MARY PRATT

I was born on the 15th of March, which, of course, is The Ides of March, and I think my parents were very pleased about this. When I was born, my father picked me up in his arms, and Nelson Eddy was singing, "When I Grow Too Old To Dream." I was a very special baby to them. And my father was old. He was forty-three or forty-four when I was born, and I couldn't do anything wrong as far as he was concerned, but as far as my mother was concerned, it was probably a little different. There are little additions in the baby book she kept for me: "I had to spank Mary twice today." But when I got to remember whether I was spanked or not, I never was, so any disciplining was done so early that I don't remember it at all. It was a very, very civilized upbringing, and some people would think it was a sort of upper-crust upbringing. It wasn't. My people had very little money, and we had to make do on a very tight budget, but my father built a house for my mother, which she moved into when she was about twenty-eight, which is still there, one of the loveliest houses in Fredericton, on *the* street in Fredericton. He must have had to dig deep to do that, because, really, he had come from the country, and this was a difficult thing for him to do. Maybe it was just because he wanted to get elected, and he wanted a good address — he was a politician — I'm not sure. But there it was, and it still stands there, and I wish that I were living in it sometimes. It's such a perfect little house.

It was a very visual upbringing. I think that that's one of the things that had an awful lot to do with how I saw. I suppose the first thing I can remember seeing was a stripe of black, a patch of blue, and a patch of pink, and I think it must have been at my Auntie Mary's wedding, because she was married when I was about two, and she was married in my parents' home, which was not that house. It was a great big house on Brunswick Street, with big, high ceilings. It was a Victorian house. It was quite beautiful, but my mother didn't like the high ceilings. But that is the first thing I can remember visually.

The second thing I can remember very clearly is when they brought my sister Barbara home from the hospital, I remember I was playing in a thin, cotton sun suit. It was the 18th of May, which is Loyalist Day in New Brunswick, and I was taking a stick and stirring tar bubbles on the road — they patched all the road holes with tar in Fredericton in those days, and when the bubbles came up in the heat, it was wonderful. And my father came out and lifted me up and said, "We'll go and see the new baby," and we walked up the stairs. And when we got to the top of the stairs, the room was very dark, except for just one line under the blinds. They were those green blinds with circles at the bottom. My eyes had to adjust, and I looked on the bed, where there was a bassinet, with a pink ribbon at one end. I must have seen lots of bassinets up to that point, because I wondered where the lace was. But my mother had lost a baby between me and Barb, and I think she was afraid to frill it up too much, to hope too much for this new baby, so all that was there was this pink ribbon. And I looked at this little face. My sister was a beautiful baby. She was so beautiful that they took her all over the hospital just to show her off. Well, I thought, the pink ribbon isn't right for the pink face. It's not the right colour pink, and that was the first thing I thought when I looked at Barb. It's a shame that there are no frills here, and she's certainly got the pink ribbon wrong. How could my mother do that?

Then I suppose the other colour thing that I remember was when I was about six, I had to present flowers to visiting royalty. They got me a red velvet dress, and I think it was the only pair of patent leather shoes I was ever allowed to have, because they weren't good for your feet. They drew your feet. And I remember they gave me a big, big bunch of red roses and, looking down, I could see that the red roses weren't right with the red dress, and I thought, this princess will think we don't know anything because this red is not right with that red. So, I think I was very colour conscious from a very young age.

Fortunately, my mother painted quite well, and she also tinted photographs. And, in the summertime, when we had nothing else to do, we would be in my father's garden, which was huge and truly beautiful. He was a wonderful gardener. He was a farmer. It was just amazing. There were delphiniums higher than he was and all the whole roundtable of the delphiniums — there were Sir Galahad, the whole lot. And the pink roses would be in front of them — it was really an astonishing garden — and beyond that, the vegetables, every vegetable you could possibly think of.

Anyway, when it got too hot in the summer to let us do the weeding or the cutting of the grass, Mum would set up a table and some kind of a tent, and my sister and I would tint photographs. You had to take little toothpicks and put cotton batting around them, and then you'd get a tiny, tiny bit of oil paint, real Winsor & Newton or Reeves oil paint — my mother only bought the smallest tubes possible. And she would have prepared the paper, which was photographic paper, but a dull finish, not the shiny finish. She would have prepared that with linseed oil and then wiped off the linseed oil, and we would just touch the colour on and then rub it so that all the detail from the grey photograph would come through, but it would be slightly coloured. And I remember her saying to me once, "Well, if you pick up a blade of grass, you'll find that it's green, but if you look at the lawn from here, you'll see that there's pink and blue and all kinds of colours, and if you want the lawn to look as if it has space and distance, you'll have to use these pinks and blues. I don't know why it's there. Maybe it's the air between us and what we're looking at. But whatever it is, you must not paint green from where you're sitting way at the back." And she wasn't giving me a lecture on perspective or anything like that. She would simply say, "Look. Look and see what you can find."

About the same time, I was being read Bible stories. My parents didn't think I was learning very much at Sunday school, so they felt it was their job to teach us some Bible stories. And, of course, the story of Samuel really, really got to me. As a child, I used to kneel up in bed, put my hands like in the famous painting of Samuel in his little white nightie, with his long, dark curls, and I used to say "Speak, Lord, for thy servant is here." And I think that, too, because it was such a mystical, wonderful thing that God or something spoke to Samuel as a child, it made me aware that there were things out there that I needed to listen for, that I needed to look for. I didn't expect ever to be spoken to, but I just hoped sometime it would happen.

When I was about forty, and I was walking down the hall to clean up the bedroom — the children had to do their own, but in Christopher's and my bedroom the bed hadn't been made and so on — and I remember I had a mop and a bucket, and I intended to make the bed. And when I opened the door to the bedroom, the light was just coming in from the river. It was in the fall, so the light from the river was beautiful, just wonderful, and it just washed over this unmade bed, and the pillows, the tumble of the red — I had dyed this pathetic chenille bedcover. I had dyed it red, and it kind of dripped onto the floor. And there was a pink blanket that I had mistakenly put in the dryer, and that was like a felt down over the pink. And then there was one of those sheets that have the blue stripes on them, those flannelette sheets, and that was there, too. And then the pillows, just crumpled and shoved together. And I had this intense reaction to this image. It was — I've said it before and probably nobody believes me — but it was like an erotic punch in the gut. It was as close to being erotic as anything that I could say. And I realized I had to paint this.

And that goes back to something that happened years and years before. I was only about twelve, seeing Susan Hayward dance, and she had this wonderful red dress — red keeps coming into my head. She was dancing, and I thought, wow, I'm going to stay and see this again! Because that would have been the first of the matinées, and then there would be another one for kids. And I sat there and thought, no, it's all right to see it again, but I think I'll get my father to buy that movie, which was ridiculous because people didn't buy movies in those days. It was good enough to get it to Fredericton, leave alone have your father buy it. And how would we ever show it, anyway? And then I thought, no, no, it's not enough to have it; what I have to do is be it. That's what I want. I want to be her. I want to be that person. I want to be it. And that thing — I guess it was kind of a revelation, but it was a thinking down of an experience. I think it just lay forgotten until I saw this bed with all this light, and I felt, no, I've got to have it, I've got to be it, and now I know what I've got to paint. After that, all the doors opened, the windows went up, and I could see things to paint no matter where I looked. The world suddenly spoke to me, and it was like magic.

I never, never belonged to the arts community. I found them tedious. I don't think they were boring, but I decided that they were boring. I didn't really think they were, but I decided, just to save my own skin, that I would consider them boring. They were talking about other people's ideas, not their own. They were talking about other people's paintings, not their own. They were talking about the way other people saw the world, not the way they saw the world. And they had also had the privilege, I think, of seeing great works of art. I hadn't had that privilege. And it wasn't until Lord Beaverbrook opened the gallery in Fredericton that I was suddenly taken with paintings, that they were really what I loved. The Lucian Freud that they had on display at the time, I thought, was one of the most illuminating paintings I had ever seen.

Now, my father and mother had taken my sister and me down the coast of Maine, where we saw Bellows and Feiningers and probably Wyeths, although I don't remember them. So we had been shown what my parents could show us, but they didn't have the money to take us to Europe or even to take us to Montreal. It was hard enough in Fredericton for a lawyer, an honest lawyer, to make a living. I think that was the thing, that we had to be properly clothed and fed, but always a minimum, two skirts, two sweaters, one blouse — that was it — and a party dress, and it was always velvet. No matter how hard we complained that we wanted taffeta, it never was. And we didn't even get patent leather shoes, as I said. We got proper leather shoes that were good for our feet. Everything had a moral part to it, I guess, a moral ingredient. But I remember, one time, a very swish woman that I know quite well and I'm very fond of, said to me, "You know, Mary, clothes are not a moral requirement," and I thought, well, maybe not for you, but somehow they are for me. And I remember my mother saying, "Oh, that lady, she's all dressed up like a Christmas tree." In other words, she was wearing too much jewellery, she cared too much about her clothes, and she didn't care enough about what she said.

But I think my mother despaired of the things I said in later life. One time, when I got a doctorate from Mount Allison, which was my home university, of course, my mother came over for the ceremony and she was sitting beside me. And as the sort of star that was there, I was supposed to be talking to people, and I was doing my best to keep up with conversations. And I felt this little hand on my arm, and she said, "Mary, you're talking too much," and everybody just froze. And I thought, she's probably right, I probably am. But in my life, there's always been this wonderful touch on my hand. One time, when I'd come home from Vancouver, I'd gone straight to see my mother because she wasn't well, and I decided that I would drive her down to a place she particularly liked in Gagetown, where she could have lunch, and we could drive back. And I didn't know I was suffering from jet lag, and I felt this little hand on my arm. She said "Mary?" And I woke up, and I was driving straight into the woods. So this little restraining hand has always been on my hand. I can still feel it. She played an enormous part in my life, but I didn't really know that till my Dad died. I thought he was the hero. But when he died, I rather quickly forgot him in my sudden relief at being able to find my Mum, and fortunately she lived quite a long time after Dad died, because she was eighteen years younger than Dad. So she'd always been a disciplinarian. And, of course, we liked Dad. When we were sick in bed, he'd bring out colouring books and cut-out books and all the great fun things. But my mother was always the one who very quietly said, "You're talking too much, dear." She'd probably say it right now, actually.

I remember one Christmas my grandmother said, "I have a present that I want to take to Miss Wilkinson, and I wonder if you girls could come with me." This would have been on Christmas Eve. My grandmother lived in two rooms, had been left with three daughters and no money when she was in her early fifties. Her husband had been a dentist, but he died very young, so she had always had to live most frugally, and I think she was left something like $3,000, and somehow she made that last until she was eighty. She had a brother-in-law who could invest for her, and I think my father picked up quite a few of the bills. But she was a grand lady, she really was. And everybody in Fredericton thought of her as Mrs. A.T. McMurray. She was a Member of the British Empire for her war work, and she was a grand, wonderful woman. We'd walk along, and Nana would be in her black rabbit fur coat — "lapin," I think they called it. Now, we had this little toboggan made by the Chestnut Canoe Company, and we were walking along, talking about what Christmas carols we liked the best, and we decided "O Little Town of Bethlehem" was the best of it all. And the ice began to crack in the river so that it seemed like a monster cracking, and we went up to my grandmother's place. The Misses Wilkinson owned the place, and so she rang the bell, as though she didn't live there at all. This was a formal visit to take a Christmas present. And the frosted glass was filled with images of cascading grapes and so on that came down from one of these — I don't know — Roman vases or whatever, and there were peacocks in the glass, which I had never noticed just running in to see my grandmother. Because we had to ring the bell, and the Misses Wilkinson had to come to the door, it was a very formal occasion, and I remember my grandmother saying, "Margaret, I have brought this for you" — I think the other one's name was Edith; I'm not sure about that. Of course, it was nothing but a handkerchief, and they had handkerchiefs to give back. It was just this small, simple ceremony on a crisp Christmas Eve, with the ice cracking and my grandmother's fur coat smelling like mothballs and this little toboggan. And every Christmas, that is the image that comes back to me — just genteel, a formal acceptance of formality. I really appreciated that. I knew it then.

Looking back now, we had to stay in the garden my father made for us in those terrible epidemic years of polio. We had to stay there. We could go to somebody else's backyard, and we could go over to the corner store through the backyard, but never on the street. I remember one day in Fredericton, ninety children caught polio. We forget how parents had to look after their children in those days. I sometimes think that they should be looking after them a lot more carefully now, but for some reason or other, all restriction is gone, and the care of raising a child formally has been just thrown away, and I think that's too bad. My father read me *Ivanhoe*. He read me all the classics that he could think of that he thought I would understand, and my mother read us *Tom Sawyer* and all those things in the backyard. I don't think we had a deprived childhood at all.

My grandmother used to have these enormous bridge parties at the house, and there would be maybe four tables of bridge in the living room, and all these ladies were wearing hats, and there wasn't a sound, not a sound. Of course, they all smoked, which got to my father, and we always aired out the curtains and left open the doors after they left. My sister and my mother and I always made the sandwiches for these parties, and every piece of bread had the crusts cut off, and it was all sandwich bread, which was very thin, and every piece of bread was cut into shapes. And then we had tiny little shrimp and little pieces of parsley and I can't remember what all, but we made pictures on these little pieces of bread, and we loved doing it. My sister and I could hardly wait for doing these things. And I think it all added up to a love of the kitchen.

I remember my mother's jelly on the shelf. The kitchen faced west. The rest of the house faced east. And the evening sun and the afternoon sun would come through these rows of jelly jars, and I thought that there could be nothing more beautiful than that. I thought it was so wonderful that I got a whole bunch of bottles and filled them with water and dyed them with my watercolours so that I could look at them in my bedroom. And my mother said, "Mary, I don't mind you doing this, but I'd like you to keep your bedroom door shut because I think if anybody would visit, they might think you were a little peculiar," and they might have, I suppose.

But certainly, the kitchen and my mother's ability to make meringues and sponge cakes — she never made bread, but she did all this wonderful, fancy cooking — never seemed to be a problem to her. She went about it with great ease and with almost-balletic movements. It was lovely to watch. I can see my sister doing the same thing. She's able to make a cake that rises higher than the moon. And these things were never lost on me. I wasn't much good at it. I remember, when I was getting married, my father said to my future husband, "Barb can cook. I'm not so sure about Mary," and he had a right to be saying it, too, because I wasn't as good a cook as my sister. I'm not now either.

In these hot summer days, when we would be allowed to play in the backyard, we would mix up flour-and-water paste, and we had scrapbooks. We had as many scrapbooks as we wanted, not as much drawing paper as we wanted, but as much scrapbook space as we wanted. And we used to cut pictures out of magazines or the newspaper. It depended on which seemed to appeal more, but the magazines were wonderful because they brought the world to us, and really, we used to fight over the images in those magazines, *Saturday Evening Post* and *Life* and even *Sports Illustrated*, I suppose, although she was more interested than I was in that. But we'd fight over the Campbell Soup babies. And there was something called Swan Soap in the United States, which, of course, we couldn't get, but they had these full-page ads for this soap, and there would be a big swan and then all these darling little babies, little cherubs, sitting on its back or doing whatever. We wouldn't have fistfights, but we would grab the magazine as soon as it came in — maybe one of us got home before the other — and that was really the only thing we used to be rivals about: who was going to get the best picture out of the magazine? And I suppose, because of so much advertising in those magazines, especially the Jell-O Pudding advertisement, which was just superb — you'd see this wonderful butterscotch or chocolate pudding coming down off a spoon into a bowl and making these...aaah. I was a very greedy child, and I could just imagine eating this pudding, and there it was in front of me.

I thought that what I really wanted to be was a commercial artist. That's what I eventually decided would be my lot in life. I didn't much like the art society and people who set themselves apart from other people by thinking they knew more about art than ordinary people. I thought that ordinary people knew as much about art as anybody else, and they shouldn't have to be taught, that you should understand these things without having to go to school to understand them or read great tomes to get it all figured out. Certainly, my painting understands that. My painting goes to that every time.

We did have one class in school at Mount Allison where Ted Pulford, who was our design teacher, said, "In London, there are posters all along the Underground, and the Underground trains go very fast. You may never have been in one, but they go very fast, and as the train goes very fast, people looking out the window have to see what these ads are saying immediately. Now, I want you to make me a poster that will do this." He said, "I want you to make it about the place where you live" — for me, Fredericton — "and I want you to use one colour — that's all — and I don't want any printing on it. I just want you to try to say it in one colour so that people seeing it will know what you mean." And that lesson stayed with me. Of course, I did the cathedral, because that would have said Fredericton better than most anything else — the cathedral with the elms around it and so on. We were allowed afterwards to put the printing in, but he wanted to make sure that the image would say it all, and the printing would come after the fact. And, of course, with these images of Guinness stout and these things that you see along the Underground in Britain, you get the message right away! And somebody said to me recently, "You just hand people your images on a silver platter," and I kind of took that as, OK, yes, I do, because I want you to know what I'm talking about. I've got nothing to hide here. I want you to love what I love. I want you to share what I've experienced.

There were lots of teachers and, of course, we had Alex Colville and we had Lawren Harris Jr. He was a much underrated painter, a wonderful painter, and he painted from slides and photography, much as I do, so I learned an awful lot from Lawren, just looking at his work. And from Alex, of course, we learned how to do tempera painting on gesso, and that is a great gift. Fourteen coats of gesso, each polished, and each coat goes on a different way, brushed on differently, the gesso made with egg and with pigment, and everything done carefully and beautifully. Now, it's very difficult to paint with tempera, and I have never really tried, but after having been in Italy this year and seen the great frescoes, all done in much the same way that we were doing tempera paintings on the gesso, I think that there's a huge area in my understanding of paint that has gone unexplored. I only did two or three tempera paintings because it took ages and ages to do them. Every little stroke had the understanding of an egg yolk so that they sort of dried faster on the outside of the stroke, and so you had to paint very quickly, and I never mastered it at all. I'm sorry about that because that would give you a different range of colours.

Now, Mr. Colville no longer paints in that fashion. He uses acrylics, I believe, now. But I can't use acrylics, either. It requires the same kind of understanding of paint, I think, as tempera painting. You have to understand that paint. And oil paint is much easier to understand. It's much more beautiful, if you think that colour is beauty. And you can get wonderful layering effects with oil paint that will come through. It only takes about seven or eight years for your underpainting to show through, and so I, having very little time, I suppose I succumbed to oil painting because I knew it better than any other when I was painting down in Salmonier, and I liked it, and I didn't like tempera painting. But now, having seen these great frescoes, I think, well, maybe you missed something. And Alex was certainly there to teach us, but there were only four girls in the class, and I think that the whole university had despaired of the art department because — what are they getting? — these three silly girls, three or four foolish girls.

I've always liked being a woman. I never wanted to be a man. I never wanted to be a boy. I remember going out with *the* boyfriend in Fredericton. He said, "Your father must have been very disappointed that you were a girl," and it never occurred to me, never occurred to me at all. I didn't have brothers. I didn't understand boys very well because of that. But I never wanted to be a boy, and I never wanted the responsibilities, it seemed to me, that men had. I understood the responsibilities that women had, and I liked them. I loved looking after children. I loved all of that. As far as my career is concerned, I suppose, if I were to get analytical and snarky about it, I could say, "If I were a man, I'd be making much more money." But I'm not sure whether that's true. I certainly can't complain that I've ever been put down because I'm a woman. I think I've benefited by being happy to be a woman. I like being a girl. I enjoy being a girl! I've never felt the tug that the feminists had. And when I first read Betty Friedan, I thought, well, who doesn't know that? What is the problem here? Of course, there was a problem, and there remains a problem. I just prefer to ignore it. I seem to get along OK the way I want to get along. I have never felt put down by men — ever! It may be just that I got used as a child to accepting a certain authority from men and appreciating that. But I've never felt any kind of regret that I was not a man.

I had to be very careful with my time. I had to be strict with my-self. I had to be strict with the children. They were expected to tidy up their own rooms, and they were expected to do their homework without too much help, and, fortunately, they could, because they were bright, and if one could help the other, that was very useful. But I was always there to help if they couldn't get it. And when it came to math and things like that, their father was far better at that than I was, and so the two of us, we had the children together. I think Christopher's studio was more out of bounds than mine, but I'm not sure. Certainly, the children could come and do their lessons in my studio. I had two children who were dyslexic and found it very difficult to read, so they used to come over and read to me while I painted, and I think they both learned a little bit about painting while they were there. I didn't give them lessons but they did learn.

But as soon as the kids were all in school — and I had four children under six, they all came in a bunch, so it was kind of useful from that point of view because, in ten years, they were all in school — my time was really very free. I tried to be in my studio by nine o'clock, which meant that I got up at five in the morning, and Christopher and I ate our breakfast then, and breakfast was really a thing! We had two slices of toast, two hardboiled eggs. I don't know how we ever trundled around, but we seemed to burn it all off. And then I made the children's lunches, and then I woke them up and got them their breakfast, and they were off, and I had the dishes done and so on by the time they were off for school. And they caught the school bus before 8:30, so by the time nine o'clock came, I was off and in my studio. Now, it was a long time before I got a studio. I often worked in the kitchen or any other room where I was interested in painting a particular thing: bedrooms, bathroom — it didn't matter. I've done lots of paintings in bathrooms because that was the only place where there was an air vent where I could get out the poisonous fumes of some of the paint that I was using, so if I was in a condominium or something like that, I often used the bathroom to paint in, propped the paintings up behind the faucets and things like that — astonishing what you can do when you have to.

But I always came over, I remember, at ten o'clock, and Christopher and I had tea, and then I'd go back and work until twelve and get lunch, and then I'd work until 3:30, when the children came home. I always wanted to have something in the oven. Well, when the kids came home, they could smell cinnamon or something good, and I was making my own bread at the time, maybe fourteen loaves a week, because there were so many sandwiches to make and so many people to feed. I guess I did it because I liked doing it. It wasn't an effort. It really wasn't an effort until I started getting arthritis, and then it became an effort, but the kids were gone by then. And so I could apportion out my time according to how much I could work and how long I could work, and that depended on me and the restrictions of having arthritis. I had a daybed in my studio so that I could lie down when I needed to, so that was very convenient.

But looking back now, I don't know how I found the time, but I did. We used to freeze everything that came from the garden and for a while I did the gardening as well. I just loved doing it. It wasn't a chore. It was a pleasure. But I had a lot of time to fill what other women would be spending going to the grocery store. I couldn't drive a car, so I protected myself by not having to take the kids to ballet lessons. There was no ballet in St. Mary's Bay. There were no music lessons. There was only me and the house and Christopher and the garden, and everything the children learned had to come from there, so that there was an onus on us to bring as much to the children as we could. But I don't think either of us ever, ever resented that. The children were a real pleasure. They were adorable as babies. They were smart kids and funny. And sitting around the table at suppertime, everybody would be laughing. Now, I couldn't talk the way they spoke. I didn't have the gift of the gab that my children and my husband had, but hearing them together, I could just sit there and enjoy it. And, yes, I would be the one that would go and serve the food, but they were all getting along so well, it was fine.

I keep painting my life as being idyllic, but, in fact, with a few minor exceptions, it has been. Every day, something really great happens. I know that just sounds so silly, but not for me. Yes, there are times in your life when things turn upside down and all the rest of it, but sometimes you need things to turn upside down. You need a good shakeup. You need your world to be seen from a different angle. You need to see things differently lots of times, and, fortunately for me, I've been able to. I think that just makes you happier to be alive. If you're forced to see things from a different point of view, if you're forced to see another person's point of view, that's not going to hurt you one bit. I think for a painter, anyway. I'm sure for a writer — it must be wonderful for a writer to be shoved around. I think they sometimes look for it, to tell you the truth. But I never looked for it. It just came my way.

Of course, inspiration didn't happen until I saw that bed and the light that filled it. I had no idea what to paint. I didn't know what the world of art was all about. I just couldn't grasp it. I'd look at wonderful paintings, and I'd say, "They were painting for the Church. The Church was demanding this. The Church demands nothing of me." Or "society wants this." You look at the paintings of the Dutch Masters and so on, and this was a new way of looking at the world after the highly religious painters. You had these people who were businessmen, really, in Holland, and the paintings are like that. There are lots of paintings that Rembrandt did that indicate the forces, political forces and so on, in his world, and I thought, I'm on my own. I don't have these restrictions. I don't have these inspirational things going on in my head. I don't think they did, either, to be perfectly honest. I think they did what they were told, and they were considered to be craftsmen, and that was that. But now, people are considered to be artists — big deal! I could never accept that "big deal" attitude about artists. I considered myself a craftsman, I suppose.

But what to paint? I had no idea until I saw that bed. And then, of course, I was very fortunate in that everything seemed to say, "Paint me, paint me," and no matter where I looked, if it was some baked apple sitting in some tinfoil, the glow from the tinfoil just seemed to blast into my face, and I think, God!, and I get the camera. Or else I got Christopher to help me, because he was a much better photographer than I was, and he had a better camera, and so for a few years, he really helped me a lot with the photography, because I didn't really know how. In fact, it was his idea in the beginning to use a slide, and the painting of the supper table was the first one where I used a slide, and I had said to him when supper was over, "I think I want to paint this. It looks perfect to me," and he said,

"Why don't I take a slide for you, and then you can refer to it?" And I said, "I wouldn't paint from slides. I wouldn't do a thing like that. What an idea!" And, of course, I tried to get the drawing down and so on, and the light went, as he said it would. It was in the fall. And the slide came back, and he held it up to me, and he said, "Now, isn't that what you wanted to be looking at?" And I said "Yes, sir," and I grabbed that slide and I used a projector to project it onto a canvas.

I had a light box that Mr. Pratt had in his business. Somebody had come to his business trying to sell some part of equipment — maybe fire engines — and they'd used this light box and left it behind, and Mr. Pratt, knowing how I was struggling with photography, thought it might be useful for me. It was tiny — I could hold it in my lap. But for years, the salmon on Saran Wrap, the baked apples on tinfoil, were all done from this almost-grey image that I could see in this little, tiny light box. And I look at it now — and I've still got bulbs for the thing — and I think, how did I ever see into that? I'd hold it in my lap, and the drawing would be done with a brush as casually as I possibly could. I'd make sure the ellipses were correct, because I had a very difficult time as a young person getting the ellipses right. I didn't understand it and we weren't taught them very well. It's the same top as bottom, and that's not what we were taught, and, of course, I never got it right, because I was trying to remember what we were taught.

But the photograph allowed me to be a voyeur. That sounds silly when you're talking about a ketchup bottle, but a ketchup bottle requires a lot of investigative looking if you're going to get the charm and the wonder of a bottle of ketchup. There is ketchup riding up on the inside of the bottle and on the surface that's nearest to you, and these colours are different. The textures are different. When I first began working from photography, I thought, well, maybe this is the biggest cheat in the world, and maybe I've given up any hope of ever being considered a serious artist, but I don't care, anyway, because I'm not, and I'm just going to do this, because this is letting me do what I want to do.

And when it came to painting the tinfoil and the baked apples and tinfoil or the Saran, I decided that I would paint the textures of twentieth-century North America as well as Chardin had painted the linens and cottons of France in the time when he painted. And I actually did a painting of my daughter in a nightgown, trying to get those textures of cotton as well as he had done. But, basically, I tried to get tinfoil and Saran Wrap, wax paper — all these things that I knew very well myself, because I dealt with them every day — and, of course, I thought they looked beautiful. Tinfoil was quite new, and it was expensive, and we could only buy so much, and we couldn't waste tinfoil. So I tried to deal with that as a cherished thing. And maybe if I did one square inch of tinfoil a day, that was a lot for me to do. It would take me ages and ages to get a painting done because I had to get used to the way colour moves from colour to colour, and maybe a triangle of tinfoil would start at the point with light, a little tiny speck of light. You had to be careful ever to put white on because that'll take over, so you hardly ever used it. And then it would go down to a pale yellow, and then that would move into orange, to red, and then, at the side, there would be a violet. And I remember talking to myself as I painted these things, "All right, this is a triangle. It starts with yellow, goes up to white. Then you've got to bring the yellow through orange to red to purple." And one time, I came over to the house after concentrating really hard on this, and my daughter Anne, who loves to cook, good cook, had got supper ready or lunch or whatever it was, and it was all on the table waiting for me, and all I had to do was sit down, take my napkin, put it on my lap, and start to eat. And as I did this, I put my soup spoon in the bowl, and I said, "There's this amazing colour between red and blue, and it's a very effective colour. It sort of moves you around from one area of colour to the area." And the kids all started to giggle, and Christopher said, "We usually call that purple." I was so concentrating on these movements of colour from one thing to the other that I had forgotten the names of the colours, really. I had forgotten all of the other things that went before and the crayons of my childhood. I was into another realm altogether.

Light and colour certainly go together. You just can't have one without the other. But when I was a child, and we went to church every Sunday, we would look through the stained-glass windows, and my mother said, "There's one thing that an artist will never be able to paint, and that's the light coming through stained glass," and I thought, oh, yes, sure, if you can see it, you can paint it. Your eyes will see. If you look, they'll see. And as a little girl, I would study the light coming through the stained-glass windows in Wilmot Church in Fredericton. I don't know that I listened to very many sermons, but I remember drawing on my hand or on my glove how the light would separate as it went from one colour to the other. So, the idea of colour and light coming through colour had been presented to me very early as something you can't do. You're going to have to paint on top of things. You can't expect to paint the light that comes through. But I'd seen my mother's jelly jars, I had seen the painted water in my own bedroom, and I had thought about it for a long time, and I didn't think that there was any thing you couldn't paint. If you could see it, then your eyes were discerning the differences from one colour to another and from one tone to another and so on, and, yes, if you could see it, you could paint it. I believed that from the time I was very young, because my mother said you couldn't, and when anybody tells you that you can't do something, I think, as a kid, you try to think of all the reasons why that's wrong. You don't like to hear somebody say there's something you can't do. You're sure that you could do anything. It's wonderful. Youth is great.

But doing it, and doing it without glazing — it's all very well to draw something and glaze over it, as we had tinted photographs as children — that's not the same as painting it, as painting every colour. I suppose what I've done is develop a kind of oozing sense of realism, which is, in its way, not great. It will never be great art, and I don't say that in a hangdog kind of way. I say that because I know what great art is. That's Rembrandt. That's the people who were truly great, and they not only understood colour; they understood time, and they understood perspective, not one-point perspective or two-point perspective — not that kind of perspective at all — but the perspective of allowing shadow to intrude from behind the figure that was being painted, allowing the light in a figure to dissolve, all these things which I have not had to do because I've had slides to work from. Now, if I were painting you right now, if I were painting any sitter from the real, I would begin to understand what Rembrandt was all about. Of course, I did paint lots of portraits when I was in school and so on, and I had to come to terms with all of those things, and all the time I was painting without slides, I had to come to terms with that. But I was too immature to understand, and nobody had ever presented it to me like that. But when you go to New York, and you see that portrait of Rembrandt, and he's standing there, this big self-portrait of him as an elderly gentleman, and he's saying, "Don't come any closer to me, this is as close as you'll ever get to what I understand" — and so I stand there and look at it, and I just cry. I can't stand in front of a Rembrandt without tears. Painting does that to me. Really great painting does that to me. I think it's that startling innocence that keeps saying, "Oh, my God, isn't that gorgeous! Isn't that wonderful! I've got to have it. I've got to keep it. I've got to be it." I think it just keeps happening over and over again, and as long as I can see, I assume that it will, because I don't go to the world with eyes that have been trained to look for anything. I don't look for anything. The world presents it to me.

I remember telling students one time that they should scrub their eyes in the morning just to free them of all the grit of what went the day before and just look at the world. First of all, find out the colour of the day. One day, it's green. Another day, it's pink. You look out the window, and the minute that you open your eyes in the morning, you look out and say, "Oh, this is a green day," or, "This is a pink day," or, "This is a yellow day," or whatever. Be that aware that the world will come to you unblemished and not politically biased. Don't be politically biased. There are politicians in the world who are going to look after all of that. You don't need to make a political statement. What you must do is love what you see and tell people that it's worth loving. Let that be all that you need to do, perhaps. I don't think that it's all a great painting does, but it's the best I can do.

A Beautiful Nasty World

LAWRENCE PAUL
YUXWELUPTUN

Lawrence Paul Yuxweluptun is a contemporary Salish artist from British Columbia. On a UNESCO Web site, his work is described as "controversial, historical, surreal, political, enlightening, informative and educational." Yuxweluptun can also be horrifying and is often surprisingly humourous. He has sometimes been compared to Salvador Dalí, but he might be more like Hieronymus Bosch — absolutely idiosyncratic, yet totally himself. Most of his work is pre-purchased on commission by private collectors from around the world. Some people have actually been known to design homes around a recently commissioned Lawrence Paul Yuxweluptun. The upside of this, at least for Yuxweluptun, is that he seldom faces the financially threatening possibility that his work might never sell. The downside is that his work is not nearly so well known or so well appreciated as it deserves to be. He lives and works in Vancouver. This interview was broadcast on Ideas *on 4 April 2007.*

LAWRENCE PAUL YUXWELUPTUN

My dad was trained to become a shaman. Then the law took him away and put him into a school. The law changed, and they allowed Indians to go past grade 12. It was illegal for Indians to get an education. My dad was the second Aboriginal native in British Columbia to get a university degree, and he became a teacher at the residential school in Kamloops. But before that law changed, he went into the priesthood and claimed that he was going to be a priest, and then, when he finished his education, he denounced it and said he wasn't going to be a priest. And then he married my mom, and I was brought into this world. But he was trained in a certain way. And then he went into political rights, to the Union of BC Indian Chiefs, the National Indian Brotherhood. And my mother was in the Native Women's Homemakers Association, and she was working on a newspaper, *The Indian Voice*, an underground paper. And they were looking at cases where, if a non-Native died in the river, they would dredge the river and look for him; if an Indian did, they wouldn't. So, it was basically getting these simple human rights: The simple act of getting a light at a train crossing, where Indians, if they would cross the railroad tracks, a lot of Indians died. For some reason, there are a lot of trains that go through reservations. As a result, a lot of Indians died from them. So these organizations were trying to fight for a lot of different human rights.

Why am I talking about these things? Because my father was trained as a shaman and then he became a politician, and in the end, his journey brought him to that. My dad trained me. I walked everywhere with him and went to all these Native organizations, and I was trained to learn what a politician was, but then I went into the arts. You have to exercise the right of an artist, and the artist is a free will, at any cost, at any price. No matter what, you have to take the risk of your life, wherever you are and whatever you do. In history, artists have done that and have paid with their lives, but some of us don't. But what I found interesting was that, when I was in these rooms with my dad, they changed the law. I was at residential school, and then they changed the law that I had to go to a public school, and that changed the view of what I was dealing with. I was living in a municipality, in Kamloops, and I was going to a public school. The residential school was a segregated construct. I was born out of segregation — they had a squaw room, and Indian women would bring their children into the hospital and only in that room, so even my birth was a segregated construct.

To deconstruct the parameters of what I was to do, I think, is what my journey is about. I look at my experiences, and I think that I work from those. If you're standing in a room, and there's one official in the room, and you're in the back there, and all you see is a bunch of long-haired, black-haired Indians and one white guy sitting at a table, and everybody's screaming at him, there was nothing there that was going to change this world because no amount of Indian chiefs were going to get anything done, with the limited rights that they had under the *Indian Act*, to change the mind of that person sitting there at that meeting. And I've seen it. I've looked at it. It is a waste of a life. I watched my dad do it, and he paid with his life. He had a bad heart from it, and he eventually died from wear and tear of just that brutal colonial fight and battle, and I didn't want any part of that. I think I wanted to take a different approach and talk to the outside world. I would say that you don't have to go to the Amazon forest to talk to an Aboriginal person about his forest being cut down. If you actually turn around, I'll be that Indian standing there, waving at you, standing in this clearcut, going, "Yeah, I'm right here. You're doing it over here as well." So it's really disgusting that Canada can stand up and say that it fights for human rights, because it can't look after all the oppressed Aboriginal people here. They're not free, all of these Aboriginal people in this country.

Sometimes, in my work, I go to that place, once in a while, to "before contact," what it was like to truly know the meaning of freedom. It's only a dream. But people did have that experience of having to govern themselves in a real, true manner without the white man's gun in their face.

PAUL KENNEDY

How did you learn about that? Who told you about life before the white man came?

LPY: If you look at totem poles, if you look at objects, they tell you how free they were, and I think that's what I was looking at. I spent a lot of time looking at Northwest Coast work and reading some of the poles and the styles and the designs, and an oral history is passed down. You can read the white man's version of the history, but it's not true. These mountains had names. All of these places. I think that's part of the history that we have, as Aboriginal people.

And, sure, I have an idea of the meaning of freedom, but that day is not for me to have. I may have that dream. I may have a reason. I think that Native people have different reasons. Like I told all my friends, I said, "I think. Therefore, I am." Or I changed around, and I said, "I think. Therefore, I am. And you are an idiot" — and my version was, "All my relations. Therefore, I will have wisdom." Its philosophy is you have to care for everything. Everything is sacred, and traditionally I was a mask dancer. We're shamans, and we look after and bless everything in this way: traditional. So they care for everything, and so we have different responsibilities to the world and to our people, and we're answerable to our people. I was a blackface dancer, and I was taught in the ways of the Salish world, that everything is sacred.

So how do you teach a world of philosophy that goes against the grain of everything? How will you communicate to the outside world? How do you tell people that in 1938 there were only thirty-seven thousand Aboriginal people left after smallpox? They were at the brink of extinction. How do you tell people that different tribes were given blankets, and they came canoeing down here, and Aboriginal people had guns and told them that if they came onto shore, they would shoot them? No, I didn't want smallpox. Our people didn't want smallpox. Am I supposed to be thankful for smallpox, too? Thank you very much, by the way. I really enjoyed the smallpox epidemics that you gave us. This is mighty colonial of you. And where is that national monument for Indians that died from tuberculosis, from all the diseases? This country won't allow Aboriginal people to mourn their dead, and we're just supposed to forget. That's a very difficult thing to do sometimes.

You can't claim something that really doesn't belong to you, and it's theirs. It's like, if you walk in the bear's path, the paw marks are five hundred, six hundred years old, and you're walking in his footsteps, and you're not talking any longer about traditional Aboriginal land. It's a grizzly bear's land. It's his free space to freely walk. They shouldn't hunt grizzly bears, either. I've never shot one. I've seen them come, close encounters, but if you shoot it, you eat it, so that's a part of it. But I respect those bears and animals that I've seen. I go hunting in the Okanagan, and I have one of these status card things — my mother was Okanagan, my father was from the island. So, in terms of traditional hunting rights, as a person, my being is that I am from two different nations. Under the white man's law, under my status card, if I look at my number, I get game wardens claiming that I have no right to hunt, and I say, "You can't extinguish my rights instantly under the *Indian Act*," and I fight it, and hopefully I'll shoot a moose, and they're going to be there, and they'll arrest me. But I go up every year. I've got moose in my freezer right now that's from the Okanagan, that I shot, and if they consider it illegal, then they can come and arrest me, but I did it, and I will continue to exercise inherent rights. "Use it or lose it." It's like whale hunting. I've never extinguished my right to whale hunt — never did. I never brought the whales to the brink of extinction. Neither did our Aboriginal people. See, you can't blame the Indian this time. We didn't do it. I don't need Greenpeace to tell me when, where, how, and why. Why would I want another white man to tell me what is green? I know what is brown. I know what is "Brownpeace," and I think we really have to clarify this position that they do not speak on my behalf.

I never did like Rodin when I was a student, but when I went to Paris and you're standing in front of his work, then you have a different view of things. That will probably happen for what my work is. A lot of people do not like what I say, but when you go stand in front of it, it's really beautiful, but it's pretty creepy about what the world is like sometimes. So it's beautifully nasty.

I think the biggest problem I have right now is how I'm going to paint global warming, and I've been pondering it. It's easier to say than do, but that concept is still on my mind. How do you paint American foreign policy that seems to want to ethnically cleanse any person of colour on this planet? How do you paint that concept? How do you paint the nuclear bomb that the United States of America has that can blow up the planet three hundred times or more? So these are new things that I'm always going to be challenged to confront culturally. Not that I'm responsible for those things. It's just that I'm concerned about them. Or even, how do you paint Canadian policy, poking their noses around places they shouldn't? We don't have the population, so we don't have the economic base to actually have an army. We don't have subs because we don't need submarines. They have tanks, and the only reason they have tanks in Canada is that they've been used on Indians.

I'm working in sculpture right now. So I'm always changing. I've done different styles. I've done performance art, painting, etchings, drawings, photography. I did a piece once — I showed it in Barcelona once as a photography piece. It was a panoramic.

It's nice that Canada can claim to have the biggest clear-cut on the planet, that you can see it from outer space. Standing in clear-cuts is a real issue. I have real issues about forestry management in this province. How much can you cut down? How much can it really take? Claiming sustainable forest — it's not true. This is propaganda by the provincial governments and the multinationalists. I've walked this earth. I've walked into clear-cuts, and these are dead zones, and that can really affect a person psychologically when you're standing in a clear-cut. You end up suffering from post-colonizational stress disorder syndrome. You don't want to be around human beings. You can become anti-establishment from looking at all the destruction. These are some of the reasons why Indians are suicidal, because they feel everything is destruction. It goes against the ideology of their whole reason, and that has an effect on people. That's what the nature of humanism can bring you to. So I look at that, and I will record everything in history, and if a suicidal Indian is one of them, it's a part of it.

If an Indian is going to go and hunt and fish, I like to make paintings about Natives hunting and fishing because I think they're exercising their right. Canadians are trying to oppress Aboriginal rights, and they're trying to say that, well, if you take away all of our rights, you will be equal to them. And so that's the dilemma of the *Indian Act*, that they have this old colonial construct, which is the same old "hiding behind the skirt of their Queen" — the game wardens and the colonials. It's pretty shameful that they have to drag out some queen and claim that they're doing it for "God, country, and

Queen" and the protectionism. It's not. It's about, "we really don't like you. We want to starve you. We don't want you to have rights. We don't want you to do anything." Wishfully, they just think they want to kill us all. They have to let these things go. They have to say, "If an Indian wants to go hunt a moose, let him go hunt a moose." Non-Natives go out hunting moose in their time, and they feed their families. Non-Natives go out hunting bears and kill bears, and they don't always eat them. They leave the carcasses there, and they just shoot the bear for the sport of it. Hunting rights are still a dilemma. You can make a national park, but if an Indian's going to march onto a national park and shoot something and walk away from it, piss off, Canadians. He's going to feed his family. You've already starved the damn bastards and stuck them on reservations and that, and you've taken all of their hunting grounds away, and then tell him that he's hunting on a national park — get fucking real. That's the disgusting thing about Canadians, that they oppress, and they're the oppressor. I think Canadians should get over themselves. I am going to exercise my right, and I am free, and I don't live on a reservation, and that's my choice. But if I want to exercise my right, the colour of my skin gives me the right to hunt. It's not a God-given right. I was here first. You were here second. You came over on boats. Let us remember these things. You were second, not first, second. When you're first in line, when we were here first, we have these privileges. We will hunt. We will fish. Natives should never extinguish inherent rights. Never should. Never will. It's a birthright. It's an inherent right. And that's a great battle to fight for.

And art brings me to that. What I like to do is look at what materials to use. You have an idea and concept. You want to create the piece. I theorize about things for a long time. I've been theorizing about land claims as a piece. I wanted to make little bags and put soil in them and have it as traditional, authentic Native Indian land for sale. I figured I would get more money for the pound rather than trying to sell it all at once. I figure that Natives should not sell their land to British Columbia. I think they should sell it by the pound. It would be a better deal. Just be like a farmer. You create things for the idea. Would I get arrested for selling my own Indian land?

My own people would probably be annoyed at it, but then they're trying to sell it anyways. So, I'm playing with the concepts of art to create something. I think that's what I've always done. I have a lot of sketchbooks over the years. I've got about fifteen different sketchbooks, and I keep my preliminaries and keep doing them and keep developing things, and so, as a result, from time to time, I get a good painting done. The National Gallery has one. I went to go see it.

It's actually a real experience that I went to see the shaman, and he asked me what was wrong, and then I was telling him what was wrong with the world, and then he said, "I can fix your spirit, but what you're trying to fix is a lot bigger than just you." It's like, what are the symptoms of post-colonial stress disorder syndrome? There's no "post" in that. If you look at destruction, you're going to have the feelings of anxieties and that, so he wanted to fix that. Well, that's what I went to see a shaman for, to spiritually make me feel better, which he did, and as a result, I made this painting that made me feel better. So, it's no longer about my emancipation and my problems that I may have at the time. It's about the world. That's why I paint. It's the world coming to visit me because I said it, "It's a dirty job, and somebody has to do it sometimes." So, I'm just lucky that I've been able to hit the world in a way that everybody can relate to it. To me, I like to look at my work as a process of looking at things.

You look at residential schools. I remember when I was a kid, and I went to a funeral at a residential school in Kamloops. The child was not returned home to his parents. The child was buried right there at the residential school, and I remember seeing the whole school and all our classmates and our friends and that, and I actually remember the girl, because she was around my age, too. She was a couple of years older and that. But she died because she wasn't looked after, because she got a tick in her hair, and then it went into her body and killed her. That's only one Indian that died at residential school. There's hundreds and hundreds of Indians, thousands of Indians that died in residential schools. Those things were torture chambers in many cases. The history of residential schools reads like an internment camp. They were treated very, very badly. They were starved. My father, as a result, when he was seventeen, he got a gum disease, so their solution was, well, we starved him, now we'll just pull out all his teeth. So they put him in a chair and strapped his hands and his head, and they didn't give him any anesthetic, and they pulled out all his teeth, and he was seventeen. His eyes were shut for three months. That's what residential school was like for Indian children. How do you compensate him for what happened to him? I talked to a lot of other people, and they talked about stories where they would line up. They would be in a lineup, and they'd only have so much anesthetic and that, and then the rest of it was, they'd tell the kids that they're just putting it in, but they'd use water. They would proceed to do any dental work on children. More than anything to me, to remember the residential era, there's no public place for Aboriginal people to have a national monument for residential school children in this country, and I think that's what's really sad — that there's no national monument for Aboriginal people in many ways to deal with the death of the Indians.

If you look at World War One, World War Two, it only starts when it's a colonial construct, but when you take into consideration the conquest of America, what world war was that? So, sometimes I think this world doesn't know how to count. I think in terms of World War One, it really did start when Columbus came over or even when the Vikings came over, when they tried and failed. But in terms of the human number, the price of human lives, hundreds of millions — estimates from one-hundred-and-fifty million to two hundred to two-hundred-and-fifty million Aboriginal peoples in the Americas — that's a big price that Native people have already paid with blood to this planet.

PK: Last time I was on the West Coast, I drove with Lawrence from Vancouver up to Squamish to visit the eagles. Every winter, bald eagles assemble at Squamish to feed on the salmon. On any given day, there can be almost a thousand of them, flying in from as far north as Alaska and as far south as northern Mexico. When we got to Squamish, there didn't seem to be all that many bald eagles, but Lawrence suggested that we could go to a secret spot on the river inside a Salish Indian reserve. There, we found dozens and dozens of eagles. It was an awesome experience. Lawrence smiled from ear to ear when I observed that our other option that day had been to visit the Museum of Anthropology at UBC.

LPY: The anthropology museum, it's a museum of death and destruction. It's not a place where you can go worship your own culture. It's a sad, depressing thing that happens to your people, looking at their art and what happened — all those things. I've walked along the coast, and I remember coming onto a Native burial site of our own people, and I said a few prayers and that, and I was really happy. They may have put me on this reservation, but that person was not going to be taken and his bones grabbed by them and taken somewhere and put on display. Or the unfortunate ones that were completely exterminated, and then their bodies were put on display.

Somebody has to say these things. Somebody has to record them. I was finding the dilemma of traditionalism was not dealing with what was going on. How do you record a pedophile priest in a traditional form, as a sculpture, as a totem pole, in terms of history? It's not very pretty. It can look pretty scary with an Indian child and a priest having his way with these kids. That's our history. That's what happens when you lose.

I remember watching an Indian shooting heroin. I was invited — I was drinking a beer at the bar, and these Indians asked me over and they proceeded to shoot some heroin. They asked me if I wanted some, and I said, "No." I said, "Can I watch?" They said, "What do you mean 'watch'?" I said, "I'm having my beer. I just want to watch." They said, "Yeah, OK." So I watched this piece and these two guys heating these needles and spoon and a little candle and that and getting themselves all fixed up and that. No mask, no song, no art. What I was confronted with was a problem. Here is history in front of me, and how am I culturally going to deal with this? Because a lot of other Natives are experiencing this same thing played out in history somewhere else at the same time over and over and over and over again. And what really made it interesting to me was, you have to change. I have to change the idea of the rules of engagement of art in traditional mannerism. The manifestos of traditional design had to be changed.

It's like I did "Haida Hotdog." When a Haida is eating a hotdog, when does the hotdog become Haida? When it's in his hand? When it's in his mouth? Or after he's had a bowel movement? And that's the dilemma of the cultural metaphor for a lot of things. It's like the baloney sandwich. I know that an Indian has eaten a baloney sandwich, as you look at it in its form and its colour and its palette and its smell, and it's not the most beautiful smell if it's kind of a little bit overripe, and that's poverty. And so I drew out this baloney sandwich with Northwest Coast designs, and that's modernizing what I was confronted with. It becomes expressionism, traditional, neo-Native expressionism, or it becomes Salish, shamanistic, surreal visionism. A lot of people compare the work with surrealism, but if you look at the history of surrealism, where did they go to get surrealism from, the manifestos of surrealism? They came to look at the primitives that were actually doing surrealist work. Northwest Coast work is very surreal. It's a very intellectual surreal. What I've done is just intellectualized it even more in its direction in paintings like "Red Man Watching White Man Trying to Fix Big Hole in The Sky." It's about me looking at the world or an Indian looking at the world and with scientists, these scientists with the coats and that, and they're standing on a totem pole to the sky with a screwdriver in hand, trying to fix the big hole in the sky, and it's a very humorous. It's a nasty slag on, can Humpty Dumpty and all his men fix the big hole in the sky? And so there's a timeline of events that's going on right now with the big hole in the sky, and the planet has to pay the price for it, and it's not getting fixed, and it's still broken, and we're going to pay dearly for that. But I made the painting. And the history is there, and a hundred years from now, somebody's going to say, "It was those Indians," and somebody's going to turn around and say, "No. We have an artist that actually made a painting, and you can't blame the Indian this time," and that's what it is about. I take control of history. I am writing history. I am making history. I am creating. Art is history. It is the manifesto of art — it's an absolute position of the pure reality in its essence, and I think that, in its intellectual realm, you can't take that away from me.

PK: Tell me about your name. What does Yuxweluptun mean?

LPY: Yuxweluptun is Salish. It came from a man who had gone out into the wilderness and talked to the world, in this area that we live in now, talked to different animals and brought back six masks, and so his name means "man of the masks, man who possesses many masks." It's a very honourable name, a very prestigious name to have for what he did. So I was given his name, and now I've gone out into the world, and so, when I pass on, the next person that carries that name will have to surpass what he did and what I did. So there's always going to be a Yuxweluptun, but it's a matter of who can carry it, who's big enough to carry that name, and I just so happened to make that name a little bit bigger. And I think a lot of Native members in our family will want to have that name, my name, because I've made it very honourable.

I don't understand "Lawrence Paul," never did, and it came out of my parents' era of the residential school and public school and registration, the European contact thing, and so I got stuck with that. But Yuxweluptun is my real name. I'm on the Internet. It says "Lawrence Paul Yuxweluptun." I sign my artwork "Yuxweluptun," so I think that I've outgrown the colonial concept of "Lawrence." Some people call me "Lawrence." Some people just call me "Yux" or "Yuk." My brother calls me "Yuk," but it's "Yuxweluptun." He shortened it just to be nasty but that was OK. I thought that was pretty cute. But I like "man of the masks." I've given great honour to that name and respect as a mask dancer, as a shaman. That's the name that I carry, and so the family is really proud that I've done the name pretty good. So that's my name.

PK: Talk about mask dancing and about the longhouse, and what it means to you, what's important there.

LPY: The mask dancers are for ceremonies and namings, pictures, showing pictures, and funerals, and brushing coffins, to blessing the ground, to cleansing, to purifying space, people. So they're shamans. It is about being in those sacred places. The Salish world is completely intact, but it's a cultural space within the Indian world, and the continuation of traditional mask dancing is alive and well, so our culture is alive and well.

I've made paintings about spirit dancers, but I've symbolized the usage of the mask dancers. But I've never documented pictures of mask dancers because some things are meant to be left alone. It's like bringing a picture camera into a sweathouse. It's just not done. Same thing with the longhouse. *National Geographic* has offered millions of dollars for them to try to come into longhouses, and we've refused to allow them. They've gone into Africa and gone all over the place and put their camera into those cultures, but here it's just not allowed. No cameras, no recording instruments are allowed there. It's a funny thing. It's kind of strange because I was in a longhouse once, and then I heard a telephone, a cellphone ring, so you have this double standard: somebody painted up in blackface paint and that, sitting there talking on his cellphone in a longhouse. I asked someone, how did electricity come into a longhouse? And they said, after the war, in about the 1940s, they brought in electricity. By the time I got there, there was always electricity in the longhouse, these bulbs in a longhouse up on the ceiling and that. Kind of odd to not know your history of electricity. How does electricity become my history? How do you explain that to anybody? How do you carve a light bulb in a longhouse?

I was asked if I would teach, but I'm not ready to be an instructor. I think an instructor, that's a different position. I'm still in the creative process. I'm still creating. I'm not finished with creating pieces of work. We're sitting in my studio right now, and there's a fourteen-by-sixteen-foot painting in my studio that I'm working on, and I'd like to go bigger, I'd like to go higher. I think that's the world of art. I work on private commissions and public commissions. More of the public will probably come to terms that I have more in private collections than what the public has actually seen, and that's where

I've been. I've been out of the public because the private sector seems to enjoy my work and buys my work, and that's where I am. I am in public collections, but I don't mass-produce. I just make them when I'm damn good and ready. I don't go really fast, I take my time and make them. I enjoy the work. I'm a free person, and I answer to the maker of art, and that's myself. When I pass on, then I'll answer to my Great Spirit, but until then, I'm a free and nasty person that, on a good day, can make a great piece of work. I'm in a position where some people really hate my work and hate what I say, and other people... I get a lot of people that have seen my work, and I really enjoy the comments about what I do.

I am the protector of this land. I am the person that is saying something about this land. I am saying something about this land that is our traditional territory. All of this land is my territory. I am living that experience, and so, when I stand at a river, I see water. I've looked everywhere, but I didn't see the "Fraser River" written on the water. Until I do — until some smartass goes and says that he'll float some image that will say "Fraser River" down the river and that I would see it on this particular day, that they could claim it — to me, those waterways and those fishes that travel through there, is an inherent right of salmon, and it's their sacred grounds to swim in and swim up. We have to respect those things. That's what I look at.

A lot of people have seen my shows, and they're wishing that they were privy to deciphering the symbolism of my work, and there's not really that much to decipher. All it was doing was taking the symbolism and deconstructing and reconstructing design, and so, as a deconstruction, I was able to formalize a new way of expressing an old construct and transform it to where it is today, and I think that is what I've been doing. The difference is that it really does allow you to create in a different way, and so that's what you're seeing. A tree — the symbolism is what it is, but it's transformed into a metaphor of a tree. It's a spirit of a tree. It's a respect of a tree, a tree that's five hundred years old. When I go out hunting, if I want to hug a tree, I will hug a tree. If a tree wants to give me shade, and standing there when it's raining and that, I've enjoyed many moments with trees that have given me a great feeling and honour. It's a great honour to stand underneath those things, and it's about me exercising...I am Brownpeace. I'm not Greenpeace. And my work is about my Brownpeace. I don't need Greenpeace, and my work is about our people's philosophy of environmentalism — only take what you need — and that's good enough.

Freedom and
All that Jazz

Nat Hentoff is one of America's most prolific journalists. A music critic, civil libertarian, and free speech advocate, he has written more than twenty books of non-fiction and six novels. His scope includes jazz, politics, biography, education, freedom of expression, capital punishment, and the US Bill of Rights. He wrote a biography of John Cardinal O'Connor, the controversial archbishop of the Roman Catholic Diocese of New York. Hentoff's columns have appeared in such magazines as the Village Voice, Down Beat, Jazz Times, *the* Wall Street Journal, *and* Jewish World Review. *Paul Kennedy's interview with Nat Hentoff was broadcast on* Ideas *on 2 September 2003.*

NAT HENTOFF

I'll start with how I introduced myself to the late John Cardinal O'Connor, the cardinal of New York, who became a friend of mine, to my great surprise, growing up in anti-Semitic Boston, where the local cardinal said nothing whatever about anti-Semitism. But John O'Connor was an entirely different person. Before he came to New York, he had gotten a terrible greeting in the press because he's pro-life in a very vehement sense, so I thought I'd tell him where I was coming from. I said, "I am a Jewish, atheist, civil libertarian, pro-lifer." He took out a pen and asked me to repeat that. I think he thought he had discovered another sect. So, that's part of what I'm about. Since I'm an atheist, if anybody asks me my religion, I'd say the Bill of Rights and the Fourteenth Amendment and most of the rest of the Constitution. It's at the core of everything. One of the things about being a reporter is you get to know people you wouldn't otherwise have a chance to even talk to, and I became quite friendly with Justice William Brennan, who, along with William O. Douglas, was the most ardent supporter of freedom of speech, religion — whatever — and non-religion as well. And I once asked him a corny question: "What's your favourite amendment in the Bill of Rights?" And he said, "It has to be the First, because how else can you protest and do anything to counter abuses of all the other amendments?" When you have, for example, an attorney general who says that, if you dissent from his policies in this war against terrorism you are giving comfort to the enemy, that is an attack on the First Amendment.

PAUL KENNEDY

Tell me about how you first learned to love jazz. What was your first exposure?

NH: First of all, the music that I first heard that really moved me was klezmer music. That's a Jewish form of largely improvised music, started in Europe back in, I guess, the nineteenth century, when musicians would travel around, Jewish musicians. And when they weren't the subject of pogroms, they would pick up the culture of the various cities or towns they were in, and it's a very merry, lively music. When I was about five or six years old, there was a synagogue down the street that also had weddings, and they'd have klezmer bands for the wedding, and I'd go running down the street, followed by my mother to catch me, to hear that band. In the synagogue, where I had to go because my father would otherwise have been displeased, I was especially moved by the cantors, the *chazzans*. That, too, is largely improvisatory, and they were able to explore in their singing the essence of being an outside culture. In fact, they'd often argue with God in the course of it. Then, when I was eleven years old in Boston, walking down the main street, the record stores then had public address systems, and I heard music coming out of one of them. It made me shout with just clear pleasure, which was not what a proper Boston boy would have done in those days. I rushed in. "What is that?" It was Artie Shaw's "Nightmare." And that started it. I was already working. This was the Depression, so whatever I could save, I would go into stores. Then, you could buy Billie Holiday, Count Basie, Bessie Smith records, three for a dollar, and that's how I started, and I've been hooked ever since.

I've been influenced by a lot of people in my life, Duke Ellington being among them, William O. Douglas, whom I hardly knew except for what he did. But if any one person shaped what I was to become, it was Frances Sweeney. She was the daughter of a saloonkeeper in Boston. She ran a news...well, you can't call it a newspaper. It was a six-page, four-page sheet. It was dedicated to exposing political corruption in Boston, which was not a hard thing to do. You could just open the window, and people would give you some information. But she was also fiercely opposed to anti-Semitism, which was rife in Boston at the time, and she enlisted some of us kids — I was fifteen, sixteen or so — to become reporters for her at no pay, and one of the things I did, for example, was undercover work. There was a group of rather well-to-do suburbanites, whites, who believed they were the true Children of God, the Chosen People, and they were very anti-Semitic. Anyway, what I learned from Fran, first of all, was the sheer wonder of independence. She wouldn't take any ads for her newspaper because she didn't want to be beholden to any advertisers. She had the courage, which was enormous for her because she was a devout Catholic, to defy the cardinal and criticize the Church for its silence on anti-Semitism. And then one day, she came in and gave us a paper test, so we wrote down our answers, and a week later she came in, slammed the papers on the desk, and said, "You are among the most bigoted fools I have ever seen." Because it turned out we were — we didn't realize it then — we had stereotypical, bigoted views of Catholics, blacks, everything but Jews, I guess, and that was influential.

Fran had a weak heart and her doctor told her to stop all of this, and, of course, she wouldn't. And one evening, she was walking down Beacon Street, which is a highfalutin' street in Boston, collapsed, lay in the gutter for a while in the rain, was conscious, and she could hear people coming by, saying, "Look at what liquor does to these young women," and she later died, without regaining her speech. But I sure can hear her all these years later. I owe a great deal to Fran Sweeney.

PK: In some ways, she was, in spirit, not unlike I.F. Stone, who was another person who much influenced you.

NH: Izzy Stone, who has been falsely accused of having been a communist accomplice, was a reporter, a very independent reporter. He had a magazine, again a sort of a small newspaper, called *I.F. Stone's Weekly*, which influenced a lot of reporters in the mainstream publication, like *The New York Times*. Izzy taught me a lot about reporting. For one thing, he never went to press conferences, and I don't either. He said, quite accurately, "I used to go. All you do is hear them telling their lies." What he did show me was, you find somebody in the heart of the bureaucracy — whether it's city, state, federal — reporters never go to see. Usually, there needs to be some attention paid to you, and you can get some very good stories there. I covered education here in New York, and invariably, when I want to get the real facts on dropouts, on other things going on in the schools that the reporters by and large don't get to, I find one of these people in the bureaucracy, and they're very happy to give me the information. The thing about Izzy that most characterized him was what Tom Wicker, a long-time reporter and columnist for *The New York Times* once said: "Izzy never lost his sense of rage." That keeps me going. I get up in the morning, first thing I do is read the comics to stay sane, but then I read the papers, and something in it always makes me furious. Then, at last, I can write.

I can't think of retiring. I would just blow up if that happened, which reminds me of my favourite retirement story. I once saw Duke Ellington come off the road. He used to take these two or three hundred one-nighters a year, with trips like from Toronto to Houston, Texas, overnight, and he looked terrible. He was in his late sixties.

Those bags under his eyes were huge. And I presumptuously said, "You know, you don't have to do this. You could retire on your ASCAP royalties" — that's what you get for writing standards, and he had a lot of standards. And he looked at me, and the only time he ever snapped at me, he said, "Retire! To what?" But I think it's especially true of those of us in the news business. I have a real luxury after all the years of being a reporter. I get paid for opinions. But if you can't say what you feel, reading the papers in the morning, it's a terrible way to go out.

I don't know what I was thinking of, but I wanted to major in Greek in college — God knows why. We had to take Greek and Latin and all that stuff, none of which I remember at all. And one of my teachers warned me. He said, "You want to go to Boston College? You want to go to any of those places where the classics are taught in the original language? They're gonna have Jewish quotas." He was right. So I finally found that I could go to one place that also was very inexpensive, and that was Northeastern, which was a working-class school. Among my classmates were social workers, cops — it was very interesting to get to know a cop socially — and kids of immigrant parents, and kids of parents who weren't immigrants but who couldn't afford any other place. And there, I decided I was going to be a journalist. I applied to the school paper, *The Northeastern News*, with, to show you how naive I was, a piece of handwritten copy, and the editor looked at me and said, "Next time you come, it has to be on a typewriter." By the way, I've been typing ever since with two fingers.

Anyway, I became the feature editor and then the editor-in-chief, and we decided we were going to be muckrakers. We found by accident, in the printing plant that put us out, some of the anti-Semitic literature going around, and we traced where it came from. We went to the local Jewish defence organizations. They didn't want any piece of that — they figured the more attention you pay to this, the worse it's going to be for the Jews. So what got us in trouble with the Northeast administration was, we were very critical of many things in the school, and I started a series on the Board of Trustees. Were they on that board because they knew or cared about education, or just because they had money and that did it? The president, Carl S. Ell, sent his hatchet man down and said, "You stop that. You just write about the lunchroom or the football team, but not too curiously, or you have to leave." Well, we all, but one, left. There's always a scab somewhere. He became the editor. And that was a great lesson. I had never thought about the First Amendment. Of course, it didn't apply to Northeastern. It was a private, not a public, school. But I got very interested in the First Amendment and from there inevitably in the rest of the Constitution.

Later on — I've always been interested in Stalinism, whether it's called by that or not — I called to find out whether they had some back issue I had edited for something I was writing on, and one of the guys on the newspaper then looked in the library, and all the issues that I was editor on had disappeared, and I found that very interesting. So when they called me back to give me an honorary degree of law, I pointed that out in my acceptance speech. Izzy [Stone] was criticized all the time. He never got any honours, never got a Pulitzer, but, as he once said, "I have so much fun at this, I should be arrested." I agree with that.

PK: Take me to the Satellite Café.

NH: Because of my obsession with jazz from the time I was eleven… Boston then was a town with a number of really good jazz clubs. People would come in from out of town, like Sidney Bechet, Frankie Newton. And I was shaving early so I could pretend to be of sufficient age to sneak into these places. And then I was very lucky; I got to be a radio announcer on radio station WMEX in Boston while I was nineteen, and there was a fair amount of unsold time, so I convinced the boss to let me have the jazz program, and we then also went and did remotes from the various jazz clubs, including the Savoy. I was already practically living in the Savoy when I wasn't at the station. The Savoy was in the black part of town. They had some of the best jazz musicians in the world come in for fairly lengthy stays. I got to know them and interviewed a number of them for the radio station, and some of them were very kind to a kid. Some of Ellington's band members were mentors of mine, as was Ellington himself. By the way, they were world travellers because of the nature of their work, so I learned a lot about what they saw in countries overseas. Ellington once told me, "I don't have to read Walter Lippman, though I look at him once in a while, because I've been where he's talking about." But to see these men — there were very few women in the business then, except for singers — but to see them really taking chances every night... Jazz is risk taking — sure, you have scores, but what you really are, how you feel, what your experiences tell you to improvise at the moment... And they were really so sophisticated because they were world travellers, and I must say, of all the adults I knew, they were the ones I most looked up to. That's not saying I liked them all. Some of them were unfortunate and had a temperamental background, but some of them were just extraordinary. I learned a lot from them. And I've said since, as a reporter, I've interviewed Supreme Court justices and all manner of politicians and defence lawyers and prosecutors and Lord knows what, but if I had a choice, I'd rather spend time with jazz musicians than any other group of people I know.

While I was still in radio, doing the jazz program, among many other things, including wrestling matches — that's how I learned how to ad lib — I was a stringer; that is, a part-time, very part-time, reporter for *Down Beat*, which was *the* jazz magazine. And because I was so vociferous and bellicose, they gave me a column, and that got a lot of people very annoyed. Anyway, there was an opening in the New York office of *Down Beat*, and Norman Grahams, whom I later became a lifelong friend of, who has done more for jazz than anybody who's not a musician, recommended me to fill that spot. So I moved to New York. A jazz fan's fantasy life came true. Every night, I was in one or more of the clubs. I could interview and talk to people all the time. And finally, in the late '50s, the early '60s, the fantasy became beyond anything I'd ever dreamed of. I was asked to be an A&R man — that is, to run record sessions. I could choose whomever I wanted, and over, I guess, a year-and-a-half at Camden Records, we put out a lot of recordings that are still around in Japan, sometimes in other countries. In England, I know they are.

Sometimes a student will say, "What do you think you'll be most remembered by?" The answer is, not anything I've written. But, in 1957, Robert Herridge — who was the most creative television director, writer, I think, in the history of the business, which is why you never see his name in any of the encyclopedias of television — decided he wanted to do what he called a jazz program that was, in his words, "as pure as *Partisan Review*." That was a very intellectual magazine of the time. So he asked Whitney Balliett, who later became *The New Yorker* jazz critic, and me to put together a show. He said, "I don't care about the names. I don't want Benny Goodman, Gene Krupa, but people you want to have on." And we got Count Basie, Thelonius Monk, Coleman Hawkins, Lester Young, Billie Holiday — on and on, everybody we wanted. And the result was an hour in what was then prime-time Sunday. The Revlon people, I think, were sponsoring it. And it was interesting. Herridge, who was as independent as any jazzman…We were doing a lighting check one day, and the page from the sponsor's booth came to Herridge, gave him a note, and he looked at the note and tore it up. And I said to him after, "What was that about?" "Oh, they say that, because Billie Holiday has been in prison for narcotics, we don't want her coming into America's homes on Sunday afternoon. So I told him, 'OK. In that case, I'll leave, Balliett will leave, Hentoff will leave, and the musicians will leave'," and that was the end of that.

PK: Was that the show where you also had an argument with Ms. Holiday over her costume?

NH: I knew Billie, and she came in for the sound check or the lighting check, and she said, "Hey! I just bought a gown for $500." I said, "Billie, I guess I wasn't clear. This is not *The Ed Sullivan Show*. This is the set. What you're in now is the set. The guys are going to come in the way they do in a rehearsal or a recording session. The cameras are going to be allowed to take any kind of shot they want. So if you dress up in something like that, you're going to stand out." And she swore at me. There are videos of *The Sound of Jazz* generally around. The one clip that most stations have used here and abroad was a segment with Billie surrounded by a small group of players. Roy Eldridge was one of them, and Lester Young, who had been very close to Billie, then had some kind of falling out. And Lester was not in good health. In fact, he couldn't take part in other parts of the show, but I told him on this one, "Look, just keep sitting, and you can play whatever you want to." Well, in the middle of that segment, Lester got up and played the purest blues I have ever heard, and the camera guys, who didn't have to worry about the producer saying, "Do this, do that," they caught Billie and Lester in a conversation without words, just their eyes meeting. In the control room, the producer had tears in his eyes. So did I. So did everybody there. And the fact that we were able to get that on tape forever is why, when somebody says, "What's your most important accomplishment?" it's *The Sound of Jazz*. After the show was over — this was live television — Billie came over and kissed me, and that was the biggest prize I could have gotten. There was no one in the history of the music, I think, who could make the words sound so autobiographical. She'd had a hard life. It got harder because her choice of men was usually so terrible. But even at the end, when she had some bad nights and her voice would crack, as Benny Green, who was a wonderful writer on jazz, a former musician — he wrote for English papers — pointed out, by that time, she knew even more about what the lyrics were saying, incorporating that into her own memories of desires. So the late Billie Holiday was even more compelling, if you were able to listen to it, than anything she had recorded before. But the whole work is just remarkable. She wound up in a hospital bed, locked to the bed because the cops found some heroin or something, and that's how she died, with very little money left. I don't know how much she was aware of the fact that — this sounds corny — what her life was about and her music, of course, would never die.

Charlie Parker said it best — of course, Parker was many people in one, so maybe it applied even more to him — he said, "Whatever you play comes out of your own experience. That comes into your horn." And Jo Jones, the master drummer, would say the same thing. To play the music, and I think to listen to it, too, you approach it in terms of your own experiences, your own memories, your own disappointments, your own moments of exultation and satisfaction, and it all comes out in what Whitney Balliett once described as the "essence of jazz, the sound of surprise." Musicians will have frameworks — I mean, good musicians, the ones that last — that they use to sculpt a solo, but the essence of it is how they feel at that moment or what happened to them that afternoon or what's conjured up in the audience. Gene Ramey, the bassist, said, "Charlie Parker incorporated everything into his music. We'd be on the road, and the way the wind blew at a certain point or what the weather was like or, in a club, the way a woman walks across the back of the hall — all that became part of his music." That's why, when it works, it's so immediate.

A wonderful player died recently: Ruby Braff, a cornet player. He based his whole conception, although he had his own voice, strongly on Louis Armstrong, Lester Young, Billie Holiday, and the headline in *The Times* was something like, "A musician who played old-time music." That would have driven Ellington to distraction. The essence of that music defies timelines, categorization. Bix Beiderbecke once said, "The thing I like about jazz, kid, is you don't know what's going to happen next, do you? And that's what it's all about, and that's why who you are, who you've been, who you are now, who you want to be all comes out in the course of an evening."

PK: How did you lose the job at *Down Beat*?

NH: After a while, it occurred to me — it should have come a lot sooner — that, here we were at *Down Beat*, main office in Chicago, other offices in Los Angeles, New York, correspondents all over the place. We did not have one black employee, let alone an editor or a reporter, and here we were making money out of what was essentially — not exclusively, obviously — black music. So I decided I was going to hire someone black. And a woman came in — we had an opening for essentially a receptionist. She was black, or so I thought, and I hired her. And the front office in Chicago found out, and because I had broken protocol and indeed put a black person on the payroll, I was fired. Years later, when I wrote about that, she wrote me and said, "I was always glad to get the job, but I'm Egyptian." According to identity politics theories these days, she would probably be black.

So then I was totally without any kind of steady income, and I was married. There was a child on the way. Norman Grahams helped me out. I did a lot of liner notes for him, but you can't live for long on liner notes. And there was a newspaper in New York called *The Village Voice*, which had started in 1956. It started out as a neighbourhood newspaper, but it was very open to almost any kind of political, artistic — whatever. I guess you could call it a bohemian newspaper past its time. And I was asked to write a column for them. Now, I'd been subsisting on freelance work, but I was typed as, among editors and regular newspapers or magazines, as a writer on jazz, and it was very hard to get assignments on other things I was interested in, like education, like the Constitution, like journalism. So I said I would do the column if I didn't have to write about jazz, and, in return, I was paid nothing. Hardly anybody was at the time. There were three people in the front office. But I began to write about education, civil liberties, civil rights, then the Vietnam War, et cetera. And one of the things about the news business is, if you write about something long enough, people who don't know any better think you're an expert, so I began to be able to write about this in other places as well. And finally I asked for $10 a week and was refused, but decided to stay anyway.

Eventually, we got a union in, and that's a story unto itself. This was some years later. Rupert Murdoch bought *The Village Voice*. He didn't really want *The Voice*. He wanted a magazine in New York called *New York Magazine*, but it was a package. Well, we knew from news reports that Mr. Murdoch was not very kindly towards unions. So those of us who had been trying to organize the paper for some time, we couldn't do it because the staff was young, practically everybody was against the war in Vietnam, and the AFL-CIO, the leading labour organization, had been, with one exception on the main council, for the war. They didn't want anything to do with the unions. But when Murdoch bought the paper, I tell you, the next day there was a long line of people going down to Astor Place, where there was catch-all local, District 65, and we joined the union. And Rupert finally sold the paper at a handsome profit, and he told *The New York Times* he never interfered with the paper. I couldn't stand it. But I knew that the reason people bought it was because it was anti-establishment, it was independent, so I didn't want to destroy that image — smart man.

The one thing I miss about the paper: during the time when its founder, Dan Wolf, was here, Dan Wolf would not hire professional reporters, even when he could pay them a meagre sum of money. He wanted people, he said, untouched by the circumlocutions and the circum-limits of the profession, and, as a result, a lot of people who came out of here became very well-known reporters. But what we had under Dan Wolf was something called "The Press of Freedom." Anybody could write for that column, whether he or she was known or not. And we also had, under that kind of freedom, a lot of criticism of each other.

My favourite *Voice* story is when I was asked to speak to the Nieman Fellows at Harvard University. They had Nieman Fellowships, and they get journalists from around the country to study whatever they want at Harvard. This was at the time of a ruinous school strike in New York. The union was beset and besetting a black group in Ocean Hills-Brownsville who wanted to run their own schools, and *The Voice*, week after week, had criticism and criticism of the criticisms by the staff members, by union people, by black people, and this Harvard professor said to me, "I don't understand your paper. I don't know what its editorial policy is. It's all mixed up." I said, "You've just described the paper." Very few papers are like that.

PK: Another job you had could arguably be called the "best job in journalism," and that was being a staff writer for *The New Yorker*. Talk about William Shawn and *The New Yorker*.

NH: I was surprised to have gotten there. When I was working in radio for almost ten years, we had some time, and I would read *The New Yorker* every week, and that to me was the apex of journalism: Joe Mitchell, Rachel Carson, Richard Revere — who was a brilliant political writer, and the guy who didn't start the idea of press criticism, but was one of the best — A.J. Liebling. And I was covering the Newport Jazz Festival, the first one, and Lillian Ross of *The New Yorker* happened to be there, and I guess she liked what I did, because she recommended me to William Shawn, who was the legendary editor of *The New Yorker*. And I came there first as a freelancer and eventually on staff.

Shawn was an extraordinary editor. He once tried to reach me on a Sunday. He found me in Connecticut. He wanted to change one word and wanted to make sure it was OK. On the other hand, one of the things that he did that was maddening, not only to me, he wanted every issue to have a kind of balance that he liked. I was a long-piece writer, what they called a profile reporter-at-large, and if you were lucky it might get in three months, six months, eight months later, or never at all. You got paid for it, you got paid handsomely. But it was very frustrating. But to be in *The New Yorker*, to have the freedom... One of the profiles I did was of John Cardinal O'Connor, and there were no deadlines. I spent over a year. I figured I had to learn a lot about the history of the Catholic Church. I spent many hours with O'Connor, with other priests et cetera. And when you were ready, you turned it in. We always went through the same routine. I would pick up the phone. He'd call and he'd say, "Oh, Mr. Hentoff, that worked out very well. We must run it very soon," and then I knew I'd have to wait, maybe until the end of time. But the experience of having that kind of freedom and getting the kind of editing, whether it was from him or anybody else, and, annoying as it was, the fact checking... The one time they missed, though, I did, I think, the first national magazine piece on Bob Dylan, and he was like Woody Guthrie — he could tell some tall tales. And he mentioned that, as a boy, he had run away from home, and he was on the road with Big Joe Williams, not Joe Williams of Basie, but the legendary blues singer. He never did that, but it passed the checkers and made me look like a fool.

PK: You wrote the liner notes to *Freewheelin' Bob Dylan*, probably the first thing I ever read that you wrote.

NH: What happened was that John Hammond, who was one of the few people who were not musicians who changed the course of jazz... Hammond came out of a rich family, but decided he wasn't going to do what rich kids usually do. He became very much interested in music. He could afford, however, a high-powered radio in those times, so on his journeys around the country, he picked up the Count Basie Band in Kansas City, brought them to New York. In Harlem, he discovered, as it were, Billie Holiday singing in a joint. He integrated jazz, and these guys would play after-hours, black, white or whatever, but the first well-known band that had black and white was Benny Goodman, who happened to be John's brother-in-law, and John had got Benny Goodman to hire Teddy Wilson and Lionel Hampton. He had an ear, and he found Bob Dylan, and one day he called me up. This was after Dylan's first record for Columbia. He said, "Look, I know you've got a lot of records. Will you take the Dylan out of that pile and listen to it?" And at that point — I didn't become much of a fan of the later Dylan — I saw what he was talking about. So, I got to write the liner notes, and there was a phrase in it that I found again many years later that showed me, in retrospect, this guy was pretty astute. We were talking about the blues. He was talking about the blues, and he said, "The mark of the true blues singer was his ability to go outside the pain, the memories of what he was singing and writing about, and look at it from that perspective," and, of course, that's true, and that's what those people were doing. They were standing outside, feeling it, but, like any artist would do, being able to describe it in ways that'll mean something to somebody else besides the person who's feeling it.

PK: Tell me how you got to know Malcolm X.

NH: I used to read, and I still do, the black press. I started that even before I was a teenager. I was just curious. And then I was looking for jazz, but the black press then didn't run much about jazz because middle-class blacks thought jazz came out of bordellos and stuff, and so it wasn't the image they wanted. But I learned a lot about Jim Crow and prejudice et cetera, and I learned about the Nation of

Islam and somebody named Malcolm X. I decided I wanted to see Malcolm X, so I called the local mosque here in New York, and they said you can meet him at a Nation of Islam luncheonette in Harlem. And I came in that day, and it was as if I had not been there. Nobody paid any attention at all, and somebody started putting a nickel in the jukebox there, playing a recording called "A White Man's Heaven Is a Black Man's Hell," kept repeating it, and I loved the tenor voice. It was almost like a *chazzan*, a cantor. And on the machine, it said it was Louis — it wasn't Farrakhan then — but I later found out it was Louis Farrakhan, who later became the head of the Nation of Islam. But, anyway, I finally decided, the hell with this, and I was going to walk out, and at the corner table, a man was sitting there and said, "Who are you looking for?" I said "Malcolm X." He said "Sit down." And for the next two hours, I heard a lecture and wrote about it. By the way, there was an angry letter from one of the heads of the NAACP, National Association for the Advancement of Coloured People: why are we giving so much attention to this offshoot? They won't last.

But then I would see Malcolm once in a while at panel discussions on the era — whatever — and we liked each other, to our mutual surprise. He had a very sharp sense of humour, which didn't come out with his public persona, and he was also very gracious at times. I got to know Dr. Kenneth Clark, with whom Malcolm debated. Kenneth Clark was a very influential black psychology professor who did research for the *Brown v. Board of Education* decision by the Supreme Court, which said that segregated public schools were inherently unconstitutional. Clark's son, however, began to gravitate toward the Nation of Islam, and Kenneth was worried about that, and I mentioned that to Malcolm. He said, "Tell Kenneth I'm not going to take away his son."

The last time I saw Malcolm X was at a radio station here in New York. He had just finished an interview. I was coming in for one. And we were joking about a writer we both knew who was an expert at getting advances for books that never got completed, but then it was the only time I'd ever seen Malcolm frightened. His home had just been firebombed, maybe a couple of weeks before, with his small children and wife in it. Nobody was injured, but the message was clear. And he told me he had, just the weekend before, checked into a hotel in New York, because he was writing a piece and he wanted not to be disturbed by anything. And as soon as he got into the room, the phone rang, and he picked it up, and the voice said, "Malcolm, we know you're there." So, as he was leaving, he said, "Whatever happens to me, it's not going to be Elijah," meaning Elijah Muhammad, the head of the Nation of Islam, with whom Malcolm had broken, because Elijah was fooling around with the secretaries and otherwise doing the opposite of the morality he was trying to inculcate into his followers.

I think I figured out what that meant. I'm not a conspiracy theorist; otherwise, I wouldn't be a decent reporter, if I am. But I did know that, all the time Malcolm was travelling through Africa and speaking at the UN, he was being followed by one or more members of the CIA, the Central Intelligence Agency, which at the time was a country unto itself. They had no limitations on their authority. And if you looked at Malcolm's FBI files — and Lord knows what was in the CIA files — he was considered very dangerous because he was very articulate and he was building a large following, even though, toward the end, he was also building an integrated following, because he had decided that whites could well work with blacks.

But, anyway, I don't know what happened. I do know — this is fact — that Louis Farrakhan was in the Newark mosque from which the assassins came the morning of the assassination. I'm not sure that that wasn't a contract assassination — maybe, maybe from the CIA. It's interesting: one of the assassins died in prison, another got a fairly light sentence. And I talked to the lawyer for one of them, who's a very famous lawyer, a very decent lawyer, and I said I wondered about that assassination. He said, "I wonder about it, too, but I can't tell you anything because lawyer-client confidentiality continues after death," so I'll be frustrated until I die as to who actually killed Malcolm.

It was a great loss because he was changing. He had gone to Mecca for the *hajj*. He had gotten very sick, and on the way back, white Muslims had brought him back to health, cared for him. And as he wrote in *The Autobiography of Malcolm X*, here were these blue-eyed, blond people who cared. So, toward the end of his life, he was speaking at a college in upstate New York, and a black student got up and started talking about, "The Jews control this...and the whites control that...," and Malcolm exploded. He said, "That's the kind of bigotry that's been pounding us all our lives. You've got to get over that." With his brains — and he was a very bright guy — and his, to use the cliché word, charisma, he could have been a very important leader, not only of blacks, because we don't have much of that now.

Ralph Ellison has a wonderful book called *Living with Music*. It is the best book on jazz ever written. And he describes what it was like growing up in Oklahoma, a segregated city, but being able to hear people like Jimmy Rushing, Charlie Christian, who came from there or worked there, and he said, "For a black kid, to hear these orchestras, to see these orchestras come into town, particularly Ellington's, these urbane, beautifully dressed men, playing this extraordinarily sophisticated music, was more than a model. It was an example of what life could be like."

Ellington, all his life, was like that. I got to know him when I was a kid, but even then, in his public interviews, he was always on. "We love you madly" and that sort of thing. So I finally figured out... I had an interview scheduled one day, but I was sick, so we did it by phone, and then after, all our interviews were by phone, because he was not performing for anybody, and that's when I got some very good copy from Duke. He taught me, which I think a lot of jazz critics these days ought to realize, not to categorize music. He said, "I don't want people analyzing my music. I want them to become part of it." "For example," he said, "when we play dances, which hardly happens anymore with jazz, and somebody would sigh on the floor while Johnny Hodges was playing a ballad," he said, "that became part of our music." And he couldn't stand terms like "modern jazz." He said, "I heard cats in the '20s doing what they call 'modern' now." He also didn't like the term "jazz." And in the '20s, he went to Fletcher Henderson, who had probably the most famous black orchestra at the time, and he said, "Look, why don't we stop the confusion and simply call what we play 'black music,'" but Fletcher wouldn't go along with that. But then Duke said, "Guys came along, black, white, or whatever, who could play anything." There was a wonderful evening at the Lincoln Centre when his alumni would talk about Duke, and when he wrote for the band, he didn't write first trumpet, third trombone; he wrote for each individual. This was an orchestra, but he wrote for each member, including their strengths, and he knew their weaknesses. And one of the men that night said he had just come on the band and there was a passage with no notes in it, and he said to Duke, "What am I supposed to do?" And he said, "Listen, sweetie, just listen," and that's a good recipe for anybody involved in jazz.

There is something about live music of any kind that, when it is really alive, fully alive, can never be equalled by any kind of editing on tape or whatever else they're going to use for recordings. When I was maybe fifteen, at Symphony Hall in Boston, I heard Sergei Koussevitzky conduct the Boston Symphony in Beethoven's Ninth Symphony, and I've never forgotten it. Shortly thereafter, I heard Ellington at Symphony Hall doing "Black, Brown, and Beige," which was his history of blacks in America. It was live. The wonder of *The Sound of Jazz*, the television show that I was lucky enough to be associated with — was that it was live television. I hate to think what would have happened if it was not live, and they screwed around with it on tape to make it better. Glenn Gould was a genius, and his temperament was such that he wanted everything to be perfect, but life ain't perfect, and jazz is life. That's why, when it's live, it's what the music is all about.

PK: Do you have any regrets?

NH: When I was a kid, I was then playing clarinet. I played some alto. And my dream was that I would some day be sitting in the Ellington reed section, alongside Johnny Hodges and Ben Webster — talk about far-flung dreams. But then, when I was thirteen, I was practising the clarinet by an open window on a summer day, and I heard this shout from below, "Hey, kid, you want to go to a session?"

I figured I could read anything, so I went to this session, and the kid who corralled me got up, put his trumpet to his lips, and I knew then I would never be, not only in Ellington's section, but in nobody's section. That was Rudy Brown. He had it then. So, that's one regret. Insofar as I can be creative in that sense, I do write novels. I love writing fiction. I often don't have the time because people like John Ashcroft, our attorney general, keep getting in the way of the Bill of Rights, and I feel I have some obligations to say something about that.

Other than that, no. I thought I was going to be a professor. After I went to Harvard Graduate School for a while, and I was in the Widener Library, this huge library, doing research on a paper on James Fenimore Cooper and the Indians — I later found out he didn't know many Indians — but that night, Sidney Bechet was at the Savoy, and I'm sitting there. Why am I here when I could be listening to Sidney Bechet? And I loved the library. I loved Harvard Graduate School. And then, becoming a journalist, for somebody like me, it's the best possible world because if you're continuously curious, then you can find out what you want by talking to the people whose work you're curious about. And that, combined with the ability to meet and get to know the people whom I most admire, who are jazz musicians, I can't think of anything else I would rather have done. So, in that sense — what is it Thoreau said? "A lot of people lead lives of quiet desperation." I don't know if that's true, but I know a lot of people look forward to retiring because then they can do what they want to do. And I've been very lucky because every day I do what I want to do.

Futures

FIVE

We Do Invention Here

Stewart Brand is a man of many hats. Most famous in many circles as a futurist, he has worked with multinational corporations such as AT&T and Xerox to develop models of the way the world might develop. A pioneer of Internet technology, Brand was the author of an influential 1988 book called The Media Lab: Inventing the Future at MIT. *Before that, he was the founder of a countercultural bible called the* Whole Earth Catalog. *Earlier still, Brand was a card-carrying member of Ken Kesey's Merry Pranksters, much celebrated in Tom Wolfe's journalistic masterpiece,* The Electric Kool-Aid Acid Test. *He is also author of an architectural book called* How Buildings Learn, *pioneer of a magazine called* Coevolution Quarterly, *starting partner in an organization called Global Business Network, and Webmaster of an influential chat room called* The Well. *Paul Kennedy's interview with Stewart Brand was broadcast on* Ideas *on 9 April 2003.*

STEWART BRAND

I've been hi-tech all along as near as I can tell. *Whole Earth Catalog*, which started in 1968, was sixty-four pages. That original first edition, if you go back and look at it — and, in fact, it was reprinted recently for a thirtieth anniversary or something — is full of hi-tech. It's got computer stuff in it. It's got how to learn BASIC, how to build your own computer, how to sneak into the basement of computer centres and get cycles during the night. Not in the very first one, but shortly, probably by 1969, I think I did the only review of Nicholas Negroponte's book called *The Architecture Machine*, which was in some ways unreadable but absolutely revolutionary. And I'm sure it's what got me later an appointment as a visiting scientist on *The Media Lab*. Nicholas later became a superb writer, I think, because of e-mail. But it really was tech from the beginning. And I'm glad of that, because tech, especially computer tech, was one of the few things that the '60s and '70s generation really got right. I think we were experimental and interesting and wrong about a lot of stuff, from Buckminster Fuller domes on. But personal computers were started by that bunch that I was somewhat in the thick of in the mid-peninsula in California and around Palo Alto and so on. That bunch set out to revolutionize and democratize communication and computational technology, and absolutely succeeded on schedule, on budget, and changed the world and continued to — all of those pioneers are basically still working and have gone through yet more revolutions with the Internet and so on.

PAUL KENNEDY
Do you remember your first contact with a computer?

SB: Well, I was fortunate. My first contact with the computer was the very first computer game, called *Space War*, which was being played after I got out of the army in '62 or '63, I was for some reason being shown the computation centre at Stanford University. And there, in the middle of the day, were a bunch of young programmers hunched over a graphical interface playing a very crude game called *Space War*, which was the only computer game for ten years until *Pong* came along. And what was impressive about it was not the look of the game, which was pretty crude, but the involvement of the players. They were absolutely out of their bodies, locked in mortal combat within the screen, and clearly living a rich life, an exciting life inside the computer. And, you know, the only thing like that

I'd seen up 'til then was psychedelic drugs and this clearly was way better.

PK: Psychedelic drugs — you brought them up. Let's talk about Ken Kesey and the Merry Pranksters. There must be some stories there.

SB: Well, actually it was American Indians that got me to wind up connecting with Ken Kesey and the Merry Pranksters, because he wrote a book, *One Flew Over the Cuckoo's Nest*, in which the hero was, probably, a Warm Springs Indian — anyway, an Indian from Oregon — Chief Broom, and, at the time I read the book, I had just spent some time on the Warm Springs Reservation photographing, and I began to see that there is a deeply profoundly different America that I knew nothing about that was extremely interesting. And I was impressed that Kesey got it right with actually even less contact than I did. But I sent him photographs that I'd taken of the Indians, and just through a friend I got his address and got a message back from him to come on down to Perry Lane, where he was at that point, near Stanford University. I showed up at the door, and somebody opened the door, took a toke on a joint, and handed it to me, which is not what you did with marijuana in those days. You know, it was always smoked in the bathroom so you could flush it down the toilet, and you never trusted strangers and all this kind of thing, so sort of instant Prankster.

Kesey was very disappointed in the movie that was made of *One Flew Over the Cuckoo's Nest* and had nothing to do with it, and always claimed he never saw it. Because what he wanted the movie to do was to tell the story from inside Chief Broom's semi-schizophrenic, semi-insane reality. And what's brilliant about that book is, as Kesey said, that it's a kind of a standard Jesus-Christ-saves-the-insane-asylum story, but because it's told from inside Broom's mind, you see it basically through his hallucinatory vision of things. And through the basic good mental health of Mick Murphy, Broom becomes sane. The Indian gets out of his craziness, and as soon as he does, escapes from the asylum. And that version of telling it, Kesey felt, could be done especially well with film. He'd studied TV and film at the University of Oregon, so he felt that the story was betrayed by being such a conventional movie, even though it won Academy Awards and so on.

PK: What was Kesey like? I mean obviously he was a serious artist and a very creative man. We get pictures of him painted by other people, notably Tom Wolfe, that make him look more like a crazed-out dope fiend. Which was the real Ken Kesey?

SB: Wolfe's story was almost all second-hand. He was there for what was called the acid test graduation, and that's why I turn up more prominently than I should in *The Electric Kool-Aid Acid Test* book. Most of the rest was him brilliantly teasing the story out of people who had been in the bus going across the country and so on. He wasn't right about details, but he was right about essences. And the essence of Kesey that he got right is that this is an intensely charismatic character whom you could never pin down, you could be very close to, and yet he would always come from outer space somehow and surprise you. And a person who can do that is absolutely riveting. Indeed, from Kesey I learned a lesson that I've spread around a little bit, which is that, in my humble opinion, charisma is theft. Kesey had the ability to turn it off. I've met other charismatic characters, like Huey Newton with the Black Panthers, who were not able to turn it off. And the ability to turn it off is important because it gives everybody a respite and a chance to get back inside their own story. What a charismatic character does is draw people to him — some few cases, her —and basically becomes the author of their story and sucks you into their story. You become a character in their story.

So, Kesey was, in so many ways, the author of the Merry Pranksters tale. You know, we were all giving each other names, and that becomes part of this work of fiction that we were living in. The problem is, when the story ends the charismatic goes away or you become disappointed in them and go away on your own. Often, people have to take a couple of years to refind their own story. So, I'm a great approver of charisma, and I was sort of taught how to do it as an infantry officer because it's part of leadership, but both for the sake of the charismatic and other people, you need to be able to turn it off. You know, just go to the phone booth and become Clark Kent again. And especially for the sake of the people who are being subjected to your charisma, you need to be able to turn it off so they get a vacation and also realize that you're an ordinary human being.

PK: Even in those days, you characterized yourself as probably the most conservative of the Merry Pranksters, didn't you? You weren't quite in the centre of the party all the time.

SB: No, I was a peripheral Prankster, on the bus some of the time and not all of the time. Took only some of the drugs, not all of the drugs, which would have been difficult, and I was one of the few Pranksters who never had a Prankster name. In fact, I was always Stewart Brand —first name, last name, you know — but there was also the implication with that that I was the designated driver or someone who could help organize the event and actually make it happen, which I did with the Trips Festival, or the person who could get introduced to the governor, which I did later with Kesey and Jerry Brown. At the time, I was a little stunned by not having a Prankster name, but I think, in a way, it was a form of both disrespect and respect.

PK: Are there Prankster reunions? There's not many left, I suppose, but have you got together in the years since and reminisced about what you were doing and maybe try to look backwards through history to see whether there was a little bit of you back there then.

SB: The Pranksters are admirably non-sentimental. I was impressed, when we buried Kesey last year, that they had his carcass — it was sort of stuffed right out in front of everybody at the burial — and people went up to put things in his pockets and to inspect his face to see how good the embalming job was, a completely unsanctimonious approach to our dead friend and the whole ceremony. On the other hand, there was also an honouring of the process, especially of the family. It was a very Oregon type of experience, low-keyed but deeply felt. And likewise the Pranksters in general have stayed in touch with each other. They get together. The Grateful Dead, you know, continue to be strongly identified with that whole thing and they're back now as The Dead, still playing very good music. So it goes on, but there's more continuity than I would like, in some ways, I think. One of the mottos was "once a Prankster, always a Prankster," and that is both freeing, because you can always fall back on pranking, and not freeing, because maybe not as many people moved on as completely as they should have.

PK: Let's talk about an idea or a concept which I think can be deemed almost exclusively to you, and which has to be one of the most epoch-making ideas of my lifetime, and that is the iconic significance of looking at a complete photograph of the planet Earth. When did you come up with the idea that that was something that was important that we could do, and how did it spin out that you understood the implications of it?

SB: What came together in the spring of 1966 was, I'd finished a big public event called The Trips Festival, in which Ken Kesey and many others starred, and I think Tom Wolfe was right that Haight-Ashbury and the whole hippy movement kind of took off that Saturday night. I was coming off of that. I'd been spending a lot of time paying close attention to Buckminster Fuller, both in his books and in person, actually. He'd been teaching at San Jose State College. And I took a mild dose of LSD one afternoon and went up on the third-storey rooftop of an apartment I lived in North Beach, in San Francisco. It was a real ho-hum, nothing-better-to-do, get-high kind of day, which I didn't do that often, frankly. And I noticed that the buildings of downtown San Francisco were not parallel. They were not going up perfectly perpendicular. They were perpendicular, but because of the curve of the surface of the Earth seen from my altitude of two hundred micrograms and three storeys, they diverged slightly. And for some reason, that then sent me thinking, OK, here I am three storeys high. What would it be like at three miles high, how about three hundred miles high, how about way out there where you can see the whole disc of the Earth at once? When an acid trip was going well, you could fixate on something and sort of go layer after layer after layer into it, and that's what went on. And I persuaded myself that seeing a photograph of the Earth from space would change everything, and I spent the rest of the afternoon, the rest of that trip, basically wrapped in my blanket shivering on the roof trying to figure out how to make a photograph happen.

I'd been following the space program, because my mother had always been extremely interested in it, growing up in Illinois, so I took it as a good thing, where many of my contemporaries did not. I knew that we'd been in space for ten years and still had not taken what I thought by this time would be an epochal photograph. So, I was going to leverage the Russian government or the US government to make the photograph, compose a button, and I would sell the button — that was my fantasy. So I spent the rest of the day figuring out what the button should say, and realized the best thing to do is leverage paranoia, so the terminology on the button was, why haven't we seen a photograph of the whole Earth yet? You know, as if they owed us this photograph — I sort of put in an assumption that actually wasn't there. But it was mysterious that we'd been out there for ten years, we could have done it in '57 or '58 and it still hadn't happened.

In any case, I sold the buttons at the University of California, at Stanford, at Harvard, at MIT — various places — and some of the people bought them for twenty-five cents a piece. I was out there in a sandwich board and a white jumpsuit and a top hat with a crystal heart and a feather. It got in the newspapers, and that spread it around a little bit. And some people took buttons back to NASA. I also sent one button to Marshall McLuhan and one to Buckminster Fuller, whom I'd later talk to about it, and I also sent them to the various relevant senators and congressmen and to their secretaries, and to appropriate Politburo people in the Soviet Union. And, lo and behold, indeed we started to see in 1968 and '69 first-rate sketchy photographs of the Earth from space, and then the beautiful ones the Apollo astronauts took as they looped around the moon. I think the most impressive one was what they called "Earthrise." It was the moon in the foreground and the Earth rising behind it. And for the first time we not only saw our place from a distance, but we saw the difference between a dead planet and a live planet, and they're dramatically different and the live one is extremely beautiful and it's where we live. So, the next year, 1970, the ecology movement took off with what they called Earth Day, and we've never looked back.

PK: Can you try to unpin the iconic significance of that? What do people see, how do they read a photograph of the planet on which they live?

SB: It's well to remember what the governing global icon was leading up to the late '60s. Pretty much from 1945 it had been the mushroom cloud. This was the great threat shadowing everything, and it didn't get better, it got worse, basically, through the Cold War as more important people thought this could happen, we could really have an Armageddon, a truly disastrous exchange of military weapons. As I grew up, my first dream, I remember, was being the oldest survivor in Rockford, Illinois, after it had been destroyed by an atomic bomb. So that was the frame of reference. And then to have another global image of iconic quality, which was not a destructive one but was in some ways as symmetrical and beautiful and equally real. I mean, the bomb was real, the mushroom cloud was a real threat, and here is a photograph that said a lot of things. It said, here we are, here we are stuck together, here we are in something which is conspicuously alive, and here we are outside ourselves looking back. It was the announcement that humanity had gotten to the point of being able to get off-planet. So, I think it was important that the best of those early pictures came from humans holding cameras in their hands.

PK: Tell us how you got involved in Global Business Network

SB: How I got involved was the following sequence of events A close reader of *Whole Earth Catalog* and *Coevolution Quarterly* was a futurist, then at the Stanford Research Institute, named Peter

Schwartz. Schwartz was good enough at that that he was hired by Royal Dutch Shell to come and basically lead their scenario planning, the group planning in the Shell Centre in London. And he stayed in touch with us. He wrote some things for *Coevolution* under a pseudonym that were exceptionally insightful on global affairs and so on. And then I took a sabbatical from *Whole Earth* in '84, went to Africa, and started to think about systems in a big, broad way. I had been studying systems for many years at that point, starting with Norbert Wiener way back. And I came back through London. Peter said come by and visit him, and I told him I was interested in systems, and he said, well, his boss was interested in organizational learning. So, eventually, Shell got together with AT&T and Volvo, and they hired me to do a series of conferences on organizational learning. And to that I brought people I'd met by then, like Danny Hillis, whom I'd met through the media lab at MIT, and Catherine Bateson, and Seymour Papert, and Marvin Minsky — an interesting group of strange thinkers — and it was a great series of conferences. The deal was that fairly senior people from these three massive organizations would come and hang out with pretty bright intellectuals in a free-floating way and have these conversations.

Well, it went very well, and about that time, Peter Schwartz was being asked to stay forever and become a Shell man after five years or he could leave and go back to California. He loved California and decided to go back, and wanted to start a company built around scenario planning, which is what Shell had really perfected using Herman Kahn's original invention from the 1960s, and that was Global Business Network, which was an outgrowth of the learning conferences that I'd done. And it exists today. That was started in '87. What we do is basically strategic planning for usually very large organizations that have to think pretty far ahead to function. And scenario planning has a great book that Peter wrote called *The Art of the Long View*. A quarter of my time still is on salary with GBN, helping various organizations think long term.

PK: Now, that was a revolutionary concept again, to think beyond tomorrow, and this is something that big business jumped into fairly quickly. But your real love is not big business but small business, isn't it? And how are those interrelated? Does small business have greater or lesser insights into those kinds of changes than big business?

SB: Typically, a small organization is making a bet that the world is a certain way and is going to go a certain way, unlike a large organization, which has to hedge all of its bets that the world might go various ways, because it wants to survive. A brand-new smaller organization really isn't concerned so much with survival, it's concerned with trying something. And so it just goes dead ahead on its idea of the world, and the world comes to fit or it doesn't. And if it doesn't, you shrug and go try something else. With a very large organization, shrugging is not an option, and that's why scenario planning is so important to them.

The Internet — there was a point at which it was being run by the Pentagon and it was called Arpanet. They wanted to sell the commercial aspect basically to a private entity, and they offered it to AT&T, the telephone giant. And AT&T, to its eternal shame, in one of its sequences of profound mistakes, said, no, no, no, nothing to do with us. That's not our model of the universe, it's way too distributed. We like a centralized, controlled communications system. That's what you really need if you want dial tone in the world. And so they said no. And basically it went commercial, but in a very distributed way and, indeed, became a tremendous environment for no end of not only commercial start-ups, but mostly pre-commercial start-ups. This is what I was referring to in the line in *The Media Lab* which has become sort of etched in stone, "information wants to be free." That was just reflecting that, then, in the era of personal computers — because I wrote it back in '84 — it was so easy to copy and casually distribute information that it was essentially free, and then, with the Internet, it absolutely blasted out into the world in an extremely free mode. Now the other view is that information wants to be expensive, because in an information age the right information at the right time is absolutely priceless. And the debate between those two approaches has gone on to this day, and I think that's because there is a very powerful paradox operating there and it's one of the reasons this is such a fecund area.

PK: You mentioned *The Media Lab*, and we should spend some time, there as you did. It's a pretty amazing place and you got to spend some time there at a very crucial time, too.

SB: Well, I was invited to the Media Lab at MIT in '87 when they'd just moved into their dreadful new building by I.M. Pei. And so they were kind of feeling their way at that point. What are we now? We're all in one building. A lot of money has been bet on this operation and we need lots more, and they were out shaking the bushes with corporations. And Nicholas Negroponte, the founder and director, along with Jerry Wiesner, had devised a brilliant technique of drawing money in, especially from corporations, which was that, instead of a corporation putting in $200,000, which was the minimum at the time, and then just getting some particular program that they were paying for, for $200,000 they got in the door and they could see everything in the building that was going on, including things sponsored by lots of other people, including their competitors. And Nicholas was able to sell this by saying, "You're going to see everything that's in the building, but you have to allow everybody else to look at everything that is in the building, including yours. And, look, we don't do development, we do invention here. You're going to do the developing — that's the part you want to keep secret. Don't worry about it." And they'd swallow hard and come up with the money, and the model worked very well. And, indeed, the idea there is that they were basically inventing out in front of the expectation that technology was going to keep self-accelerating to more and more power for less and less money. So, they would spend a bunch of money five or ten years ahead of what would eventually be very cheap, and be able to model something now with big computers that soon you would be able to do with something on your wrist, and thereby invent out in front of the technology in a very humanistic frame, which was also something that the Media Lab brought to the game. And, indeed, they did, and, of course, it attracted new students as well as sponsors, and it was a hot place to be.

PK: When that happens, it's almost like a historical moment when a critical mass is reached, the right heads end up in the right place at the right time and ironically can talk to one another and actually cooperate to make something happen.

SB: Yes, the physical co-presence was important. It's probably getting less important as time goes by because there's so many ways to connect through the Internet to do collaborative things. But certainly, at that time, in the late '80s, it was essential. And also, you'd gotten to the point where it was worth having. I mean, there was a while, when the hackers took off back in the early '60s, when the pioneer programmers very quickly knew more than their professors about how to play with the technology. But by the late '80s that had flipped back, and often you needed serious computer science and/or materials science or whatever it took to be able to make inventions way ahead of the curve, which was what Media Lab was attempting to push. So, having it in a good technological academic environment there worked out pretty well for the students, for the sponsors, and certainly for the university.

PK: One of the things that you've done to make actual presence in the same place not necessarily necessary is create something called the WEEL, the Whole Earth Electronic Link.

SB: Well, the WEEL — you have to spell electronics sideways to make it really work — was a response to an invitation from a man named Larry Brilliant, who was running a company in Ann Arbor at that time which was an early computer-connectedness company that lasted about two years and tanked horribly. But during the brief time they had money, they wanted to put some into some kind of public service, like on-line conference systems, and so they offered us some software which was just good enough and leased a minicomputer for us to run it on, and said, you know, go forth and do a Whole Earth something-or-other that's on-line world. So I and others created this thing called the WEEL, which was an on-line community and is still an on-line community this many years later. It's now owned by a dot-com called Salon, which is in great trouble financially. It may or may not survive. But I'm sure the WEEL will, because the people who live on the WEEL — that's where they live, that's their village. Several thousand of them, ten thousand, I suppose, and they've been there for, lo, these many years and they're not about to move.

So, one of the things we discovered is that an on-line community is tremendously revolutionary in some ways and tremendously conservative in others. But, in any case, it does serve as a great good place, you know, like a pub or a beauty salon or something, where you can just go and hang out and tell stories, and find out who needs some help and actually help them, and find dates and get married, and consult with people about raising your children, and, you know, the whole world starts to come through that kind of thing. But it was just somebody offering us a tool and we sort of applied the Whole Earth thing to it and came up with something that worked.

PK: Someone, though, who had a foot in both worlds, the cyberworld and this world, I'm really interested in the similarities and the differences. I mean, are the laws the same in each place? Plainly not — I mean, truth cannot be truth sometimes in an on-line community. You're allowed or sometimes you're almost encouraged to stretch the truth, to elaborate on it. How are the two related? When you're wearing your cyberhat, how are you different from when you've got your ten-league boots on?

SB: People experiment with their identities a lot on-line, which I greatly approve of, and so you see it in these massive multi-player games. You see it in people adopting various personas in places like the WEEL or more often in what were called MUDs, multi-user domains. But, on the WEEL, we insisted that people have real identities for the following reason. When you can be anonymous or quasi-anonymous, very typically people become very insulting on-line, so people say stuff that, if they said it in person, they would get their block knocked off, and they sort of revel in the freedom of being able to insult freely. The WEEL started as a regional system in the Bay Area of California, and I wanted everybody to have a real presence there, so there was always a feeling that, if you said something truly obnoxious, somebody was going to show up at the door and knock your block off. And to just back that off a little bit so there's no anonymity on the WEEL.

We've got another version of that going now with the on-line thing from the Long Now Foundation called longbets.org, a place where people make predictions and bet about them and so on. The deal is there, not only do you have to be a real person, but you use your real name, your true name, as it's called in the jargon. There's discussions and voting and all those sorts of things about each of these predictions. The people who are making the predictions are putting their name on the line that they believe something or other is going to happen, and they're right or they're wrong. Accountable predictions is what the site is about. So we want to be sure that people who are arguing about that in discussions or voting about each of these bets on-line also are taking the same risk and the same accountability that the bettors and the predictors are. So on-line identity, in a sense, has gotten even stronger there — you've really got to be who you are.

PK: It sure makes for more interesting discussions.

SB: It makes for more responsible discussions. In so much of the on-line world you can pretend to be somebody or try on a personality, try on a frame of mind, pretend to be of the opposite sex, things like this. And that's great. That's cover, so I figure this is a spot to be who you really are, say what you really think, and stand by it.

Well, these things always come in sequences. I did the book called *How Buildings Learn* out of a sense of rage. I was at MIT, and across the street from each other were two buildings, one was the Media Lab building designed by I.M. Pei, which was beautiful and severely dysfunctional. I mean the Media Lab worked fine anyway; they could have worked in a barn because of the excitement of the people and the projects. But across the street was a genuine barn, a thing called Building 20, which is a truly funky building built during the war to develop radar which eventually won the war, and it was the building where anything could go on because it was so uncomfortable. It was so cheap that all the new disciplines came out of there, because students would get interested in something having to do with chemistry and something having to do with physics and something having to do with biology, and they couldn't do what they wanted in any of those departments, so they'd be given a corner of Building 20 and they'd just go do it. And Building 20 was one of the two most-loved buildings on campus. Absolutely adored. Desperately ugly building. And, you know, hot in the summer and cold in the winter, but the attraction was freedom, the attraction was, when you're in there and you wanted to knock a hole in the wall, you didn't ask anybody, you just knocked a hole in the wall and ran wires through or joined two small spaces or whatever you wanted to do. And I realized, what's wrong with this picture? Because the I.M. Pei building was getting all the glory and all the photographs and a hundred times greater budget, I'm sure, than Building 20, and yet Building 20 was the loved building and it was indeed the productive building in terms of how its design actually served the kind of experimentation going on. So that set in motion both the continuation of that question and the continuation of the earlier question I had of how organizations learn. I thought that buildings might be a physical trace of how organizations learn over time.

The other thing I loved about it is, I had just done the *Media Lab* book, which was screaming to be not too far behind the actual technology and things you could read about in the daily newspapers and the weekly tech magazines, and I knew there were a lot of other hi-tech books in progress and they were all in a big rush — they were all on huge deadlines trying not to be old news by the time they were in print. It was great to have a book I could take six years to research knowing absolutely confidently that nobody else was going to be looking at what happens to buildings over time, and so I could take the time and go to lots of libraries, collect hundreds of photographs, interview all over the place, learn enough about that profession, which was not my profession. To do a book that I hoped would be able to stand on a shelf with Jane Jacobs's *The Death and Life of Great American Cities* or with Christopher Alexander's *A Pattern Language*, and, lo and behold, that seems to have come to pass.

Well, I live on a tugboat which was built in 1912 in Oregon, and it was a dead tugboat when we got it for $8,000, and some amount of investment later it's a living tugboat again and we take it out every month or so. It does have a library on it. I have another library at my office, another library at the Long Now Foundation office, another library in a container, and there used to be two libraries in the container, two containers so they're scattered all over. I keep books.

PK: You don't give them away.

SB: So far. Well, *Whole Earth Catalog* gave them away, because we got thousands coming through as review copies, but the ones I like, I keep.

PK: How do you stay constantly a decade or two, or a half century, or whatever ahead of things? I mean, you have basically managed to be just ahead of the wave all the time. How does that happen? What's the recipe?

SB: Part of it, I suppose, is reading the current news and being careful to be bored. Part of it is being kind of in the prediction business and professional futurist in a way with Global Business Network. For some reason, when I was doing the *Whole Earth Catalog*, when I was asked to come and speak, I would be described as a futurist, which always puzzled me because at that point I wasn't. But it does have to do with looking at things that are moving out there in the bushes and you just see the tips of their ears but they look pretty interesting, and often you can sense that something is building. But it's because it's interesting. You go to it not necessarily because it's building. And more often, the sign that something is up is that somebody interesting is up to something, and you sort of learn to find out who those folks are and go and hang out with them, and whatever they're doing tends to be the next thing.

I remember, one time we were doing some work — this was Global Business Network — some scenarios for Xerox, and Xerox was trying to rethink their future beyond copiers, in a sense to a much larger area of information handling. This was at a time when the Internet was not yet an object of popular expectation, it was just sort of out there as something that geeks did. And what I knew from personal computers and everything else is that whatever geeks did was going to come for everybody pretty soon anyway. And they were doing it. And so part of my contribution to that particular scenario-planning session with Xerox was kind of a wild-card scenario, which was, what if the Internet takes over everything and changes everything, and what reasons do we have to believe that would be the case? I mean, you just start naming some of the pioneers who are in the thick of it and where they are doing stuff, and the world tends to change. And that did come to pass. I don't know that Xerox was ahead of that curve at all, but at least they weren't as surprised by it as others.

The stuff I've been doing since 1996 is for the Long Now Foundation, and that's three-quarters of my time. It's unpaid time, but it's superb time. And this is an activity to try to reframe the time space in which people think. The one way we phrase it is, we're trying to make long-term thinking automatic and common instead of difficult and rare. And so we've set in motion various kinds of projects to help. One is a completely iconic one of building a ten-thousand-year clock that is meant to keep good time, so that when you visit it inside a mountain in eastern Nevada — and it will probably take a day to experience the clock — hopefully, you come away with a sense that this thing is going to be in here ticking away, no matter what happens, for the next few thousands of years, at least ten thousand. And that might reframe thinking much the way the photograph of the Earth from space reframed people's thinking.

One of the things I've learned is that, while business incubators didn't work very well as businesses, the dot-org non-profit can be a very effective incubator where you spin out ideas, and because they don't have to prove themselves commercially right away, you can take the time to try to make them work and get them right. So, the Long Now Foundation is doing longbets.org, this on-line site where people can post predictions that they will defend and keep until they come true or don't, and then there'll be full discussion of why they came true or didn't in all of that. Another thing we do is called the Rosetta Project, rosettaproject.org, which has now got fourteen hundred languages all in one place on-line, and if we get the funding to get all the languages in the world, six thousand languages or so will be in one place on-line. It's become a kind of collaboration engine where linguists and translators and native speakers go to constantly improve the representation of their language and this site in the context of all the other languages. There's word-list search capabilities, so you can compare words from a wide range of different languages to each other directly, and so the people who are studying the evolution of human languages are using that as a tool, and so on. That's the thing which has taken off, much to our surprise.

Another area we're doing is, because most of the information that civilization creates now is going digital and most digital information disappears because of obsolescence every ten years or so, there's a fairly serious problem coming along of how you go back and find what happened. Danny Hillis has said that the period we're in now might be referred to by future historians as the Dark Age, not because it's a grim time but because whatever happened during this time will be so lost that they won't be able to reconstruct what happened except what came out of it. So the Long Now Foundation is setting in motion what we call a long server, and we're working with Global Business Network and with the Library of Congress, which has gotten surprisingly enough very serious money from Congress to set up a digital preservation architecture that might actually begin to solve this problem of everything digital being lost every decade or so, and has flipped me from being a real pessimist about that to being quite optimistic that, within five years, we should have a globally usable architecture for being sure that things that are digital are, in fact, easy to preserve rather than very difficult and expensive to preserve.

Another spinoff of this incubator is a project called the All Species Foundation, which is an idea that Kevin Kelly came up with at a dinner we had with a bunch of billionaires three years ago. And the question came up that it's so hard to do philanthropy when you're a billionaire, when you're young and you're busy, and to do it right really takes full time and nobody has that, and so wouldn't it be swell if there were just some place you could put a billion dollars, and they said giddily they would do great good. And Kevin Kelly said, "Well, I've got a project. How about identifying all the species on Earth? You could probably do that for a billion dollars in about ten years." There were some chuckles and we went on, but then Kevin and my wife Ryan Phelan and I started asking some scientists: is there anything here?

And what we learned is that, in the two hundred years since Linnaeus — I was trained as a biologist, so I was a little attuned to this — we had only identified maybe 1.3, maybe 1.6 million species out there. Nobody even knows how many have been discovered because the discoveries have never all been put together in one place, unlike, say, stars and celestial objects, which are all in one catalogue and numbered and named. So that's already interestingly problematic. But then, when you raise the question of how many species are out there, including all the microbes, the parasites, and the nematodes, and the mites, and the things that aren't charismatic, the lowest estimate was ten million, so that would say we have at most sixteen per cent identified so far. The moderately high estimates are 100 million, which means we have less than two per cent identified so far. And, as Kevin Kelly said, if we went to another living planet, the first thing we would do would be inventory all the life forms on it, and here we are on a living planet and we have no idea what all the life forms are here. Not even in ourselves. There's never been an inventory of any large organism, though there's going to be.

One of the things we helped set in motion is the inventory of the wood rat; we expect to find maybe three or four hundred species inside the wood rat. This will transform biology, certainly. It'll make biology move more in the direction of becoming a predictive science finally, and there'll be no end of discoveries of new materials, and proteins, and metabolisms, and understandings of how nature really works. And we as living creatures are particularly interested in getting our living science going better, but we are losing species all the time, so there's a certain amount of urgency from that side.

One of the things I was taught in officer training at Fort Benning, Georgia, was that there were four kinds of officers in the world: the industrious, the lazy, the stupid, and the brilliant, and you've got the four combinations — you know, lazy and brilliant, and lazy and stupid, and so on. So then the question is, what's the best kind of officer and what's the worst kind of officer of these four combinations? And the worst kind is industrious and stupid, because it just busily gets you into all kinds of trouble. And the best is brilliant and lazy. We're talking about officers here, not non-commissioned officers. And the idea of brilliant and lazy is that this is somebody who's going to figure out a way to get the thing done with the minimum effort, not only on his or her part but on everybody's part, and also be a much more inspirational model and a supervisory model, rather than just, you know, "you're not doing it right, I'll do it." Well, this is not what an officer is supposed to do. So I've been very careful to be lazy all my life.

Immortality Guaranteed

RAY KURZWEIL

Inventor and futurist Ray Kurzweil believes in a concept he calls "the singularity." He projects that, at some point in the not-too-distant future, computers will equal and even surpass human mental and intellectual capabilities. When that happens, we will have achieved the singularity. And by downloading our minds into a computer hard drive, we will be capable of a form of eternal life. As a very young man, Kurzweil figured out how to translate printed text into spoken word using, of course, computers, which were still fairly primitive at the time. One of his first customers was Stevie Wonder, who suggested that Kurzweil turn his attention to music and try to find a way to make electronic instruments sound authentic, or acoustic. The result was the Kurzweil Piano, which is the size of a portable keyboard with the sound of a Bösendorfer Concert Grand. Ray Kurzweil has been described as the rightful heir to Thomas Edison, and has been inducted into the Inventor's Hall of Fame. Paul Kennedy's interview with Ray Kurzweil was broadcast on 22 January 2008.

RAY KURZWEIL

I really had the idea that I would be an inventor when I was five years old, and I can really remember the feeling I had, and I think it's an actual memory as opposed to a memory of having had a memory. I had an Erector Set and I was putting things together, and I had this feeling that if you could put things together in just the right way, you could create magical effects, something that would transcend the ordinary pieces that you were starting with, and that you could change the world. I just had this sort of intuition about it. I was actually building a rocket to the moon that didn't quite work. I built all sorts of virtual reality systems, mechanical systems. I remember building this puppet theatre where I had this command station with mechanical linkages, and I could move characters on or off the stage and move the sun in and out, and clouds and background scenery, and I could command in a God-like way this virtual world from my command station. And that actually worked — I demonstrated that at school.

But I had this idea that there's a transcendence you can achieve with invention. And that is actually the goal of an inventor. Not just to have a cool demo, something put on a table like a little magic show, but actually to have your invention used by people and have it change their lives in some way. That's the goal. And when that works, that is a kind of transcendent feeling. So that's the challenge.

PAUL KENNEDY

I don't want to put words in your mouth, and I certainly don't want to tie up ends that might be loose and try to make it all look neat, but if you read the sort of list of things that you've done, and it begins with inventor and now ends with futurist, I wonder if they're not really the same thing — that an inventor, by putting an invention into the world, is imagining a future, usually a better one, and hoping that it will improve things.

RK: Well, that's actually a good insight because my interest in futurism comes directly out of my interest in being an inventor, because I realized over thirty years ago that the key to being successful as an inventor was being able to project the future and understand technology trends. And that timing was crucial to being successful: most inventors fail not because they can't get their gadgets to work, but because the timing is wrong. Not all the enabling factors that are needed in the world will be in place at the right time.

Realizing that, I became an ardent student of technology trends for the practical purpose of timing my own technology projects. And being an engineer, I gathered a lot of data, and I discovered, actually to my surprise, how predictable certain aspects of the future are. The common wisdom is you can't predict the future, and that's true if you look at specific projects and specific companies. But if you look at overall measurements of information technology — things like the number of bits being moved around in telecommunications through wireless channels, or the price performance of computing, or the amount of data we're collecting on the brain, or the amount of genomic data that's been gathered around the world — these things follow exquisitely predictable, smooth, exponential curves. For example, the price performance of computing is a beautifully smooth, doubly exponential curve going back 110 years.

And when I plot this out, it makes this very smooth curve, and you see no evidence of human history — two world wars, the Cold War, and the Great Depression in the United States, et cetera. There's something inexorable about these progressions. People say, well, how could that be? How could you get these predictable phenomena when each project is unpredictable? Well, look at thermodynamics. A gas — and this is actually nineteenth-century science — is modelled as a bunch of particles where each one is following what's called a random walk, so you can't tell where this molecule of air will be ten seconds from now. And that's true of each one of the molecules. Yet, this very complex system of unpredictable particles has very predictable properties according to the laws of thermodynamics. And they're considered scientific laws to a very high degree of precision.

So, if you have a complex, dynamic system where each thing, each element, is unpredictable, the overall impact can nonetheless be very predictable. I've actually used this to tie into my own technology projects. I have a group of ten people now that gathers data in methodical fashion in different areas, and when we do a technology project, we write down what the underlying technologies will be in January 2007, July 2007, January 2008, and build that into our plans. Most people don't do that — most people assume that the trajectory of these technologies is linear, whereas, in fact, it's exponential, and it's an important point we should talk more about, because exponential growth is not intuitive but very explosive. If I count to 30 linearly, I could go 1, 2, 3, and get up to 30, but if I count exponentially, 2, 4, 8, 16, I get up to a billion. And that's actually the nature of the trajectory of information technology.

I got into this because of the necessity of timing my inventions. However, it does have a fallout, and that is that we can now use these models to look not just two or three years ahead for a technology project, but twenty years ahead or thirty, and see what the world would be like in future and see some of the remarkable impact that these different technologies will have. I've actually been making forward-looking projections for several decades. In the early 1980s, for example, I projected the emergence of the World Wide Web in the nineties, because I saw the precursor, the Arpanet, doubling every year — it went from 10,000 nodes to 20,000 to 40,000. Well, that wasn't on anybody's radar map. People didn't notice it when it was 20,000 nodes. But doubling every year is multiplying by 1,000 in ten years, so this would be 20 million in the 1990s, going to 40 million, to 80 million, to 160 million, and would be a worldwide phenomena, ultimately tying together hundreds of millions of people. So I projected that, and people thought that was ridiculous when you had this very cumbersome, slow, unreliable network in the eighties, but in fact it happened very, very smoothly. So I've continued to make these kinds of projections.

PK: I want to talk a bit about what might be a eureka moment. When did you realize you could see those kinds of patterns? Obviously, they're very useful, but when did it come to you that this was something that you understood?

RK: Well, it was, I think, a gradual insight, because I was exploring this issue, trying to predict the future to be an inventor. And I think that if you're an inventor you do have to predict the future, because you're really preparing your invention for a future world. The world changes quickly enough now that, by the time you finish your project, it's going to be a very different world. Think back even five years ago: most people didn't use search engines. That sounds like ancient history today. Three years ago, people weren't using blogs, social networks, podcasts. These were all new concepts. The pace of change is really is accelerating.

But it was really in the eighties that I began to formalize these ideas. I wrote my first book. I had hundreds of predictions in that book about the 1990s and this first decade of the twenty-first century, which I've tracked very accurately. And it's not just applicable to electronics and computers, but also to things that you wouldn't think are information technologies, like health and medicine, or even energy.

PK: Your first book was *The Age of Intelligent Machines*. As you say, there were a number of predictions in there that proved to be almost immediately accurate. You were predicting the collapse of the Soviet Union — the book was published in 1989 or '90, I think — and almost immediately it happened.

RK: Right. Well, I wrote it in the mid-eighties and it came out in 1989. I talked about how the Soviet Union had this dilemma. They had been banning copiers and anything that would disseminate information, but there was this emerging technology of work stations, and fax machines, and e-mail using teletype machines, and they would either provide their professionals with these tools, which would destroy totalitarian control, or they would deprive them of the tools and that would destroy their economy, and I actually felt they would do a little bit of both. And both would do them in. And that is what we saw. I mean, there was the coup against Gorbachev in '91. It was this clandestine network of e-mail over teletype machines and fax machines that kept everybody in the know. So the old paradigm of grabbing the centralized TV and radio station and keeping everybody in the dark with one source of information didn't work anymore — just swept away totalitarian control. And the Soviet Union collapsed.

In fact, we saw this wave of democracies in the 1990s. There's a lot of publicity now about a few countries that are holdouts, but think back to the eighties when there were much fewer countries that were democracies. And that definitely has been fuelled by the Internet. And now, even countries like China and Iran are being democratized, transformed by the unstoppable power of communication in a decentralized manner.

It's democratizing on another level, too, which is that the tools of creativity are now democratized. Go back twenty years and you had to be a big Hollywood studio to make a movie, or you had to command a multi-million-dollar recording studio to create an album, or have millions of dollars of computing equipment to create computer technology. Today, a kid in her drama room can create a high-definition, full-length motion picture or command the equivalent of millions of dollars of recording equipment. A couple of kids at Stanford with their $1,000 laptops created a little piece of software that revolutionized web search and started a company worth $150 billion. You really have this transformative power in everybody's hands. So, the tools of creation have been democratized.

I saw chess supercomputers doubling in power every year, so I predicted the crossover [would happen] in 1998. That seemed ridiculous in the eighties, when an average chess player could defeat the best chess machines. Kasparov did this in '93, and when he was asked, he said, "Oh, that's ridiculous. I've played the best chess machines in the world and there's no way they'll ever touch me. They're very predictable...brittle. They're not really intelligent." And, of course, they passed him, in '97. And [the book] has pretty rich descriptions of the different worlds of communications, and the social, educational, military, and health impacts of these technologies.

PK: What's interesting is that the change as you describe it is exponential, rather than arithmetical. And this is not at first an easy concept to wrap a head around. We tend, as you say, to assume arithmetic progression, but these things are explosive and they're increasing in velocity every second.

RK: That's probably the most important point I try to make in my lectures and writings. Our intuition is that things progress linearly, and I think that's actually hard-wired. We have an ability to predict the future and it's a linear one. We see some creature heading toward us and we make a linear projection of where we'll be so that we can avoid encountering it. That was a built-in defence mechanism that evolution gave us, and it worked just fine for that process. If you talk about technology progression, it's not linear, but we use that linear intuition to anticipate the future. A good example I like to give is when I was at the Future of Life conference a few years ago that *Time* magazine organized. This was the fiftieth anniversary of the discovery of the structure of DNA, so all the speakers were asked to answer the question: in the last fifty years, we've seen lots of progress; what will the next fifty years bring? And every speaker there used the last fifty years as a model for the next fifty years. But that's wrong.

If you talk about just the basic rate of technical progress — what I call the paradigm shift rate — according to my models, it's doubling every decade. So, in the next fifty years, we'll see thirty-two times more progress, more change, than in the last fifty years — that makes a huge difference. So, all of the predictions from these other speakers were very conservative. Jim Watson himself said, "In fifty years we'll have drugs that enable you to eat as much as you want and remain slim." And I said, "Jim, we've done that already in animals by blocking the fat insulin receptor gene." There's a new technology that just emerged that [acts as] interference that can turn genes off. The fat insulin receptor gene basically says, "Hold on to every calorie, because the next hunting season may not work out so well." Remember, our bodies evolved thousands of years ago. Conditions were different then. It made sense to hold on to every calorie because you didn't know where your next meal was coming from; there were no refrigerators, so you'd store them in your fat cells. That now underlies an epidemic of obesity. And when [the receptor gene] was turned off in animal experiments, these animals ate ravenously and remained slim, and they got the health benefits of being slim. They lived twenty per cent longer. They didn't get heart disease or diabetes. And several pharmaceutical companies are rushing to bring this concept to the human market. And I said, "Well, see they're well within a decade, even including regulatory approval processes. Not five decades."

So, similarly, all the projections were radically conservative because of the failure to take this exponential progression into account. If you talk about information technology, it's doubling now about every year, and even that rate has increased. I mentioned the smooth exponential progression of computing technology, but it took three years to double the price performance of computing in 1900, two years in 1950, twelve months in 2000, and now it's already down to eleven months. But even if you just take one level of exponential growth doubling every year, that's multiplying by a thousand in ten years, a billion in three decades — actually, twenty-five years, to be exact.

A while back, when I went to MIT, they had a computer, took up a huge building, cost $11 million dollars, and it was shared by thousands of students. The computer in your $50 cellphone is a thousand times more powerful than all the computation that all of MIT had when I was a student. And as powerful and influential as information technology is today, it will be a billion times more powerful in twenty-five years.

And the size of devices will shrink. We've seen that. We went from building-sized computer to computers that fit in your pocket. I have my whole photo and movie collection on a flash drive that's the size of my fingernail. And they're going to continue to shrink so that, in twenty-five years, these technologies will be a billion times more powerful, a hundred thousand times smaller. And we draw some very dramatic scenarios of what that will make feasible.

The other point that's worth making is that it's not just limited to electronics and computers. Every industry is going to transform from a pre-information era to a post-information era. One that's doing that right now, undergoing this very dramatic transformation, is medicine. Now, medicine didn't used to be in information technology — we didn't have the genome until just four years ago. That, by the way, was an exponential process, too. The genome project was announced in 1990. Skeptics said, "there's no way you're going to do this." We just had our best Ph.D. students and the most advanced equipment around the world. We collected one ten-thousandths of the genome in 1989. And halfway through the project, the skeptics were still going strong, saying, "I told you this wasn't going to work. Here you are, seven-and-a-half years into a fifteen-year project and you've finished one per cent of the project." But that actually was right on schedule, because that's how an exponential works. If you double one per cent seven times, which is what happened, you get to a hundred per cent, and the project was finished on time.

But prior to 2003, we didn't have the genome completed. So we didn't have the software code underlying biology. Now, biology is a set of information processes. Our genes are software programs. They're linear sequences of data. They evolved thousands of years ago. They're outdated software. But it is a set of information process-es. Prior to the collection of the genome, medicine was hit or miss. We'd find something — it seems to lower blood pressure, we don't know why. And invariably these crude tools had lots of side effects. Most of the drugs on the market today were done that way. In fact, drug development was called drug discovery. We've automated that to some extent. We methodically go through many compounds to find something that would work. But we can now model in math-ematical terms the information processes underlying the progression of disease and aging. Equally important, we have tools to reprogram these information processes just like we reprogram our computers. Our interference can turn genes off. New forms of gene therapy can add new genes. We can turn enzymes on and off. We're really get-ting the tools, in a precise way, in a targeted way, to reprogram these information processes, which is what biology truly represents, away from disease and aging. And now that health, medicine, biology has become an information technology, it's subject to what I call the law of accelerating returns, doubling its power every year. So this will be a thousand times more powerful in ten years, and that'll be very transformative.

Now, we've been making progress. I mean, human life expectancy was in the twenties a thousand years ago. It was thirty-seven in 1800. Mozart and Schubert died in their thirties — that was typical. It was forty-eight in 1900. It's now pushing eighty. We've been adding three months every year. But that progression is from this hit-or-miss process. Now that [medicine's] an information technology, and once we get to the steeper part of that curve in about ten or fifteen years, we will be adding more than three months. In fact, we'll be adding more than twelve months every twelve months. And that's really a tipping point. Now, that's a guarantee of immortality. It will mean that, instead of the sands of time running out, they'll be running in as time goes by. According to my models, in fifteen years we'll be adding more than a year every year, not just to infant life expectancy, but to your remaining life expectancy. And that will be a very dramatic change because of our increasing ability to reprogram biology away from all these causes of disease and aging and really understanding how biology works.

It will also transform energy. You might think that energy is not an information technology, and that's correct. Today, it's principally fossil fuels, and fossil fuels are not an information technology. It's an old, nineteenth-century industrial technology. There's a lot of concern about climate change. Actually, I think there are other problems with fossil fuels even greater than climate change. There are hundreds of chemical and pollutants that come from every stage of using fossil fuels, extraction shipments, utilization, not to mention the geopolitical effects. We would like to get away from fossil fuels. Well, there are emerging technologies that are information technologies — for example, nano-engineered solar panels. Now, nanotechnology isn't an information technology. It's being able to manipulate matter and energy at the molecular level and reorganize it to create useful physical products. There's already a first generation of nano-engineered solar panels that are much more efficient than we've seen. But this will actually go into high gear: because it's an information technology, it will double its power every year. We're actually only a few years away from a tipping point there where solar energy will be less expensive than fossil fuels.

Now, you might say, "Well, how far can we get with that? We don't really have enough sunlight to replace fossil fuels, do we?" Actually, we are awash in sunlight. We have ten thousand times more than we need to completely eliminate fossil fuels. In other words, if we captured one part in ten thousand of the sunlight that falls on the Earth, we could meet one hundred per cent of our energy needs. And I believe we will be able to do that well within twenty years. In fact, we're doubling the amount of solar energy every two years. That means multiplying by a thousand in twenty years. Solar energy already meets several parts per thousand of our energy needs. But it's a fraction of a per cent, so people scoff at it and say it's insignificant. A fraction of a per cent's not a big deal, but it's growing exponentially and will continue to because it's becoming an information technology: basically, nanotechnology-based solar panels and nano-engineered fuel cells to store the energy because of the intermittency of sunlight. I believe that within twenty years we will meet all of our energy needs without any use of fossil fuels using extremely inexpensive nano-engineered solar energy. So that's another application.

And we're going to transform every aspect of our lives. Information technology is relieving poverty. The World Bank reported that, in the last ten years, poverty's been cut in half in Asia due to information technology, and it's also been cut around the world, including Africa, by somewhat lesser amounts. But over the next ten years, according to the World Bank, poverty will be cut ninety per cent in Asia and by substantial amounts in other parts of the world. We see decentralized electronic communications entering Africa, for example — widespread use of cellphones, the introduction of the Internet. And these are revolutionizing education. MIT, where I went to school, is giving away all of its courses for free. And you've got thousands of schools around the world taking free MIT courses on the Internet, and you've got kids organizing in an African village and taking an MIT course for free. Access to the Internet is not yet ubiquitous, but it's growing.

The key thing is that information technology has a great inherent capacity to keep the exponential growth going. As one approach runs out of steam, we find another one. Now, you might say there must be some ultimate limit, regardless of the approach, to the exponential growth of information technology. Yes, there are ultimate limits based on what we know about physics and computation, but they're not very limiting. For example, one cubic inch of nanotube circuitry would be ultimately a hundred million times more powerful than the human brain, given the most conservative estimates of how much computation would be required to simulate the human brain. So that's a limit, but it's not very limiting. And even that is not the ultimate. We can even go beyond that in theory.

If we go to three-dimensional circuits, we'll be able to continue to grow information technology well into the twenty-first century, well past a point where non-biological intelligence greatly exceeds biological intelligence.

PK: You are perhaps the most optimistic person I've ever met. What you write is about change, always positively. You see these things as beneficial developments for humankind. Some of the things you've said here just now, though, upset some people. When you're talking about applying these kinds of models to biology and in the health sciences, people begin to wonder about what your task actually is here. It's ironic, in a sense, because you're so optimistic and it all seems to be for human good. But people seem to wonder whether you're not engaged in an activity that is not necessarily ethically straight on the board.

RK: Well, you bring up actually two issues. One is whether I'm optimistic, and the other is the ethics of changing who we are, biologically, or even going to the non-biological realm and merging with machines.

On the first one, you might think I'm optimistic because I talk about how we're overcoming disease and poverty and the energy crisis with technology. And we have made tremendous progress. People might wax romantically about how wonderful it was when we were all natural a few hundred years ago. But I think Thomas Hobbes described human life more accurately when he described it as poverty filled, disaster prone, diseased filled, filled with extremely hard labour, and so on. I mean, human life was very, very difficult two or three hundred years ago. We had no understanding of disease, no sanitation, and so on.

But I'm also a principal exponent of the downsides of these technologies. Technology is a double-edged sword. I do think the benefits outweigh the peril, but I've actually talked quite extensively about the peril. In my 1999 book, *The Age of Spiritual Machines*, I talked a lot about the downsides of all three major revolutions: genetics, nanotechnology, and robotics. Bill Joy, who's an eloquent spokesperson about the downsides, wrote this cover story in *Wired* magazine right before 9/11, "Why the Future Doesn't Need Us." He talked in dire terms about bio-engineered viruses and self-replicating nanotechnology run amok, or the killer AI [artificial intelligence] that's out to get us. It created a firestorm because he was an arch-technologist, the founder of Sun Microsystems, developer of Java, and so on, talking about the downsides of technology. A little bit reminiscent of when arch-capitalist George Soros talked about the downsides of capitalism. But this actually created a bigger firestorm. The *New York Times* reported ten thousand articles commenting on Bill Joy's article, more than any other in history. But Bill Joy's article stems directly from my book. In his opening paragraph, he says he got these concerns from reading my book. I talked about them in my book, and he did his own further research and concentrated on the downsides. There have been a lot of panels since, with myself as the optimist, Bill Joy as the pessimist, but he actually got his pessimistic or concerned ideas from the conversation we had and from my writings.

Now, some people look at these downsides — we actually face one right now, which is the possibility that the same technologies that could, say, cure cancer and heart disease could also be applied by a bioterrorist to take a benign virus — say, a flu virus or a cold virus — and engineer it, change it, to be more communicable or more deadly or more stealthy. That technology exists, and there's a real danger to that. And I've had a major campaign to deal with that. But some people say, "These dangers are so great, let's not go there. Yes, there are some benefits, but it's not worth the risks. So let's relinquish biotechnology, nanotechnology, and so on."

I think that's a bad idea for three reasons. First, it would deprive us of these profound benefits. Try telling the millions of people suffering from cancer, "We're really on the verge of some major breakthroughs, but we're going to cancel all that because we're concerned about the downsides." Second, it would require a totalitarian system to implement that. I mean, the belief in technological progress is so deeply rooted in our world civilization today that it would require a world totalitarian government to ban it. That was the basic plot concept in *Brave New World*. Third, it wouldn't work. Just as in *Brave New World*, it would just drive these technologies underground where they'd be actually more dangerous because there'd be even less control. And we would deprive the responsible scientists from easy access to the tools to create the defences. And that's really the right answer, which is to develop rapid response systems to deal with abuse.

That's exactly what we've done in software viruses. We have a rapid response system. We have an immune system on the Web. A new virus emerges, brand new, it's very destructive. It's captured, reverse engineered, an antidote is coded. The antidote is spread virally out on the Web, and within hours you have a response. You could say, "Well, that doesn't work perfectly." No, but it works well enough that nobody has taken down even a portion of the Internet for even one second over the last ten years. That's actually a pretty remarkable record of reliability.

We can't cross that off our worry list, but we do have a technological immune system. We have to do the same thing for these other dangers. And we do have the tools to do that. RNA interference, for example, turns genes off, as I mentioned. It can also turn off viruses, because viruses are genes. There are new vaccine technologies that could be geared up very quickly that are safe because they respond to the antigens on the surface of viruses. So, we could set up a rapid response system, and that is underway. It's really a race: we need to have that in time. But that's really the answer: to have ethical standards for scientists so that we build these technologies in safe ways, and so that we have a way of defending ourselves against intentional abuse now that we know that there are terrorists who will find some rationale for being destructive. We can't just assume no one would ever do that.

You alluded to another issue, which is that people are concerned about reprogramming biology or merging our biological selves with non-biological technology. The latter actually seems to be less controversial. I mean, there are people walking around with computers in their brains, calculator implants. Parkinson's patients have computers in their brains. You don't see anyone demonstrating against putting a computer in the brain of a Parkinson's patient. You do see demonstrators against certain biological technologies. People seem to be more sensitive about that.

But I will say that, in my mind, we should not be defining our humanity based on our limitations. Rather, what's unique about our species is we seek to go beyond our limitations to overcome problems. If that weren't the case, very few people listening to this broadcast would be alive today because human life expectancy was twenty. That's what was natural. You want to be natural? It's natural to die in your twenties. That was in the interest of the human species: when you were twenty-five, you were done raising your kids because they were twelve and they were ready to go out on their own, and you were just going to use up the precious food and resources of the tribe.

So we've been pushing beyond those limitations — that's not a new story. And the tools that are doing this are getting more and more powerful, particularly now that we can do this in the information realm. Despite the controversy on an intellectual level, when something new comes out, when there's a better treatment for cancer or for any disease, nobody thinks, "Is it ethical to do this?" It's just adopted with great enthusiasm and without any hesitation.

The same thing is done in terms of introducing non-biological systems. There are all kinds of devices with computers in them getting stuck inside human bodies temporarily or permanently, and as these devices get smaller and smaller and more and more intelligent, that'll go into high gear. I believe that in twenty years we'll be putting millions or billions of blood-cell-sized devices into our bloodstream, going through the body and keeping it healthy at the molecular cellular level. If that sounds ridiculously futuristic, I point out that it's already being done with a first generation of experiments in animals. There are dozens of experiments. There are major conferences on what's called bioMEMS — biological microelectro-mechanical systems. Scientists cured type 1 diabetes in rats with a blood-cell-sized device that lets insulin out in a controlled fashion. At MIT they have a blood-cell-sized device that can go through the bloodstream, scout out and find cancer cells, latch on to them, and destroy them. So these are very impressive experiments today. You go out twenty years, when these technologies will be millions of times more capable and thousands of times smaller, and they will be mainstream and readily adopted.

You know, if you could take a pill that has these nano-engineered entities that can prevent cancer or cure your cancer, people aren't going to worry about the philosophical debate. And that's really how these technologies unfold. It's not that we're going to take this big leap. Do you want to put millions of nanobots in your body and change who you are? That's not how it happens. It happens one little step at a time. Hundreds, thousands of little steps, each one fairly conservative, each one benign, each one tested out. And through these thousands of steps, we go from here to there. Look at how different the world is today than it was hundreds of years ago, and we're going to see as much change in the next twenty years as we saw in the last thousand years because of this acceleration. That's how this technology evolves.

PK: We're moving inevitably towards a topic that we should spend quite a bit of time on as well. You've got a book title that features it prominently: the singularity. Much of what you've been saying about biology and information technology coming together is brought together in that concept. Tell us what the singularity is.

RK: Well, the singularity is not one sound bite, because a number of different concepts go into it. A very important one is this issue of acceleration and exponential growth, which we have been talking about. And the most important aspect of the singularity is achieving human intelligence in a machine and then merging with that technology. So, if you ask if we can actually make machines that have the full range of intelligence of humans, the first point I'd make is that we have hundreds of examples of narrow AI in the world today. Every time you send an e-mail or connect a cellphone call, intelligent algorithms route the information. Intelligent algorithms help us design products, design drugs, manufacture products in robotic factories, control and adjust time/inventory levels, make billions of dollars of financial decisions, detect credit card fraud, fly and land airplanes, guide intelligent weapon systems, automatically diagnose electrocardiograms, blood-cell images. I could list a hundred more things. These are software programs doing intelligently what humans used to do at human levels or beyond. They're narrow applications, but the narrowness is gradually getting less narrow.

Now, if you go out to...the date I have is 2029, very inexpensive computers will be equal to or greater than the computational power of the human brain. So, we'll have the hardware. As for the more complex issues — will we have the software, the methods, the algorithms, the content of human intelligence — for that I look at the human brain itself. It's not hidden from us. In fact, we are making exponential gains in understanding it, reverse engineering the human brain. And every aspect of that is scaling up exponentially. We're doubling the special resolution, the brain scanning, every year. We're doubling the amount of data we're collecting every year, and we're turning these data into working models and simulations of brain regions. Regions of the auditory cortex, the visual cortex, the cerebellum have already been simulated and tested. There's a simulation underway at IBM of at least a significant portion of the cerebral cortex, where we do our abstract reasoning. I make the case in chapter four of *The Singularity Is Near* that we'll have all the models and simulations of the human brain within twenty years, and this will provide us the algorithms and methods of human intelligence. We'll have machines that are not just narrow AI, but that actually have the full range of human intelligence in terms of our supple, subtle qualities, ability to handle human language, and so on.

The next point is that this is not an alien invasion of intelligent machines. We're going to merge with these intelligent entities. I mentioned nanobots earlier. We'll have billions of nanorobots going through our bloodstream, keeping us healthy from inside, but also going inside our brains through the capillaries, providing capabilities like full-immersion virtual reality from within the nervous system. So, if you want to go into virtual reality, the nanobots shut down the signals coming from your real senses, replace them with the signals that your brain would be receiving if you were in the virtual environment, then it feels like you're in a virtual environment. You go there with other people. It'll feel like you're in that environment. Some will be full-immersion, highly realistic recreations of Earthly environments. Some will be fantastic new, artistic creations that'll be a new art form. You don't have to have the same body that you have in real reality. In virtual reality, you can be someone else.

But most importantly, it's going to expand our human intelligence quite directly by interacting with our biological neurons. These nanobots will be on the Internet or have direct brain-to-brain communication. In some ways we're already doing that, even if most of the computers in the world are not yet in our brains. A few of them are — in fact, the latest generation of neural implants for Parkinson's patients allows you to download new software to the computer in your brain from outside the patient. And you can also get communications from the computer to outside the patient. So there's already two-way communication with computers in our brains. But even with the computers in our hands, we can access human knowledge with search engines — that's an expansion of human intelligence right there. But they're going to move into our clothing, and ultimately into our bodies and brains.

So, in the 2030s, you're going to be talking to a brain that is partly biological and partly non-biological. The biological portion of our intelligence will be fixed. Right now I estimate we have ten to the twenty-sixth power calculations per second among all the human brains in the world. And fifty years from now, that'll be still be ten to the twenty-sixth power. I mean, our biological intelligence isn't going anywhere. But non-biological intelligence is subject to the law of accelerating returns, this multiplying by a thousand every decade. And so, when you get to the 2040s, the non-biological portion of our civilization's intelligence will be, by my calculations, actually a billion times greater than the biological portion.

Now, that's a pretty profound transformation. So we use a meta-phor borrowed from physics to describe that: a singularity in human history. In physics, the singularity is a point of matter and energy that's theoretically infinite, so the matter and energy around it are so warped that you can't see beyond the event horizon of a black hole. Similarly, metaphorically, we can't easily see beyond this event horizon coming in human history because it's so transformative. So we call it a singularity. But one of the implications is that the pace of change will be so fast we won't be able to follow it unless we enhance our intelligence with this non-biological intelligence, which I think most people will do. You might say that some people won't want to do that. Again, it's not going to be one leap. Do you want to change your mind and make it a billion times more intelligent? Here, take this pill. It's not going to happen like that. It's going to be thousands of little steps, each one conservative by itself. And there'll be early adopters and late adopters. Very few people will completely opt out of this idea. Nonetheless, it's going to transform our human civil-ization. And it is on the continuous line of what we've been doing, which is extending our reach. That's the unique aspect of human civilization. But the observation is that this is going to greatly accel-erate because of the exponential growth of information.

The difference between what I'm doing and science fiction is that science fiction writers can use their imagination to write stor-ies about what will happen when certain future capabilities come to pass, but they're not really responsible necessarily for getting their timing right. In general, they don't have mathematical models that tell them what'll be feasible at different points in time, so a lot of the timing in science fiction stories is not realistic or not accurate in various ways. And a lot of science fiction suffers from describing one change — for example, the movie *AI* has human-level cyborgs in the future, but nothing else has changed — the cars are the same, the coffee maker's the same. There's no virtual reality. It's actually a challenge to the science fiction genre to describe some of these future times when so many things are different. It's hard to develop a nar-rative when you have to explain that so many different assumptions are different about human life.

PK: That must be a problem for you, too, though. I mean, you must have trouble being understood by people who don't understand exponential change, for one thing. Also, you're describing a world that must be as far away from their imagination as that of a science fiction writer who would have to change coffee makers and fridge magnets or whatever.

RK: Well, if I have enough time I can describe these ideas, and also convince people of just how remarkably smooth and predictable these exponential trends are. In my speeches, I show thirty or forty graphs in different areas, and we have hundreds of these showing just some remarkable exponential growth. The number of transistors you can buy for a dollar. In 1968, you could buy one for a dollar, but you could buy 300 million today. But it's not just that dramatic comparison. If you look at each year of the data, look at the graph, it's almost a perfectly straight line. You would think it would be very erratic given the unpredictability of human history. But, no, it's very, very predictable. And people become convinced that, yes, exponential growth is remarkable.

Young people, even though they haven't seen all this history, have seen so much change that they readily pick up on this. You only have to follow the news broadly in all these different areas to see how rapidly change is happening. Then think, not just beyond the next turn of the screw, but about what's going to happen in the next generation of these technologies. It's only one or two years away. Think about ten or twenty years from now, after many generations of new technologies, of how different life will be.

PK: It's interesting that you describe young people as being more adaptable, more cognizant, or more ready to look at change as a good thing. I wonder if that's also not a key to a kind of fountain of youth. I know you're very interested not only in the biological merging with information technology, but also with other aspects of changing our physical presence in order to make it something that would last longer. Are you becoming young because your mind is flexible enough to bend around some of these topics, and is that in any way related to some of your other interests and activities in life?

RK: Well, another area I've been interested in is health. My father died [when I was] twenty-two — that was the first thing that got me interested in health. I developed type 2 diabetes at thirty-five. The conventional treatment made it worse, so I actually approached that as a engineer and developed my own way to overcome my diabetes. I realized that we can overcome our genetic dispositions. Now I'm pushing sixty, but I've actually slowed down the aging process. When I was forty, I came out at thirty-eight on biological aging tests where you measure different blood levels and reaction time, memory, tactile sensitivity, and so on. Now, at fifty-nine, I come out at about forty. So, according to these tests, I've only aged two years in the last nineteen years. And I'm very aggressive about it. I take lots of supplements to reprogram my biochemistry.

We know how to stop and reverse things like arthrosclerosis, which is a disease and aging process. A number of different processes are going on — aging is not one thing — and there's already a lot you can do to slow them down. People say, "Ray, do you really think that taking all these supplements is going to enable you to live hundreds of years?" And the answer is no, not by itself. The goal of that program, which we call bridge one, is just to get us to bridge two, which we believe is only fifteen years away. So, fifteen years from now I'll still be in good shape and young, and I hope many of my baby boomer peers will be as well, so that we can benefit from bridge two, which is the full flowering of this biotechnology revolution. We will have very powerful tools to turn off genes that promote disease and aging, add new genes that promote health, and reprogram biology away from disease and aging.

And that is just a step to bridge three, the nanotechnology revolution, maybe twenty years from now, when we'll be able to merge our biological bodies with non-biological intelligence, like nanobots going through our bodies augmenting our immune system. That will really provide indefinite longevity. So we want to be in good shape. People think if they exercise, it'll add 2.6 years to their life, but is it really worth doing that? The issue is, do you want to be the first person in line who doesn't get to the second bridge? That should be motivation enough to take care of yourself today so you can get to the second bridge and the third bridge in good health.

PK:　How long do you expect to live?

RK:　I would like to keep living. You know, people say they want to live to a hundred or a hundred and twenty, but does that mean that when they're a hundred and nineteen they're going to want to die the next day? The fact is that my goal is to feel thirty by the time I'm eighty — I feel I'm forty now that I'm pushing sixty — and really enjoy this future period. Now, people say, "But Ray, if you live hundreds of years, isn't it going to be very boring?" And the answer is yes, it would be very boring if we had radical life extension without radical life expansion. But the same technologies that are going to keep us alive are also going to expand our horizons. We're going to literally expand our minds by merging with intelligent machines. We're going to be able to appreciate and create knowledge at an ever greater level. And by knowledge I mean art, and music, and science, and engineering. So it won't be boring. Radical life extension will go along with radical life expansion, and I want to see that. I think this issue of life or death should be in our own hands, not in the metaphorical hands of fate. We should be masters of our own destiny, and I think we'll have the means of doing that.

Research without Walls

Dr. Joseph Martin is the former dean of the prestigious Harvard Medical School. He is widely regarded as a key figure in the groundbreaking research that paved the way for the latest developments in the treatment of such neurodegenerative disorders as Alzheimer's and Huntington's disease. On his way to the dean's office at Harvard, he held similar positions at the University of California, San Francisco, and at McGill University. In fact, his career began in Canada, where he was also born, on a small dairy farm in Alberta. In 2006, Dr. Martin was the first winner of the Henry G. Friesen Prize in Health Research. Paul Kennedy's interview with Dr. Joseph Martin was broadcast on Ideas *on 4 September 2007.*

PAUL KENNEDY

Why do you suppose they chose you for the first annual Henry Friesen Prize?

JOSEPH MARTIN

Well, I wondered about that when I got the call to tell me that I had been awarded the prize in his honour. I think it is appropriate that the prize be given to a Canadian. I think it's appropriate to give it to someone who has had an impact in the field of human health and

347

research, and [to recognize] the importance of biomedical research to improve the human condition. And certainly that's been the work that I have undertaken in many institutions over the last forty years. I was surprised that it would come to me, but very pleased.

PK: I suppose it's a long way from a farm in Alberta to becoming the dean of the Harvard Medical School and the first annual Henry G. Friesen Prize winner. Let's go back to Alberta. Take me to the — what do they call it? — "the Best in the West by a Damsite." Tell me about growing up in Alberta.

JM: Well, that town is Bassano. The history there is important because the dam that was placed across the Bow River established the Eastern Irrigation District, which is a fertile plain of prairie soil, and the availability of water made it one of the most productive agriculture areas anywhere in Canada. My grandparents were Pennsylvania Dutch, and found the opportunities of homesteading to Western Canada, just after World War One, to be an attractive opportunity for them. So my parents were children when they moved to Alberta. They were American citizens. I was born in Alberta. My father was a dairy farmer. He had moved from doing mixed farming to having a small herd of dairy cattle.

So my earliest memories are of a farm, rising early in the morning to deliver milk to the local village, which was actually Dutch. That's near Brooks, Alberta. I aspired to be a doctor from my earliest memories. I think it was driven in part by my acquaintance with missionary doctors who came to talk about their work in India and Africa, and I wanted to do that. I wanted to do something that I thought would contribute to the world's health. So I made plans to try and get to be a doctor. My mother and my father both were very supportive. Neither of them had gone to college, so this for them was a new adventure. And I was able to make it into pre-med at the University of Alberta, [even though I came] from a small high school in southern Alberta that had twenty graduates in its grade 12 class. I was able to scrape by into pre-med and then did well enough to get into medical school. So I feel very lucky to have been given the support I had from my parents and, I guess, to be endowed with sufficient intelligence to be able to accomplish that.

PK: Missionaries coming through must have been quite inspirational in Alberta at that time, which would not have been as close to the centre of the universe as it might now seem. But, why neurology, which is your speciality?

JM: In medical school, I think my first inspiration was when we studied the anatomy of the brain, when I realized that who we are, how we feel, how we speak, and how we move are all driven by critical functions in the brain. My education in that area in medical school wasn't as deep as I would have appreciated or wanted. So I wanted to specialize. Now, I would comment that my career choices, where I moved from family medicine or missionary medicine to specialization, were driven by some extraordinary faculty at the University of Alberta who said the future of medicine was going to be in research and I ought to think about doing that. And so I took an interest in neurology, which I had developed during medical school, to explore areas where I could be trained and educated in that field. That took me to the United States, to Cleveland, where I trained from 1964 to 1967.

PK: Your first actual academic job was at McGill, though. You came back to Canada, and McGill was a very special place, especially in neurology, especially at that time. Can you take us back there?

JM: Well, it's a fascinating bit of memory for me. When I finished neurology training in Cleveland, I set out to do graduate work. Having completed medical school, five years of residency, and now certified by the Royal College of Physicians and Surgeons as a neurologist, I decided that I wanted to do more fundamental work. And I got a Canadian Medical Research Council Centennial Fellowship, which was awarded in 1967. And that Centennial Fellowship provided extraordinary support to me, my wife, and our four children to allow us to survive during the period of training.

With the Centennial Fellowship came the obvious commitment to return to Canada, and I began to explore places where I could continue the kind of work that I had begun in my graduate years. In those days, there was no better place than McGill, the Montreal Neurological Institute, in neurology and in endocrinology, which was a field that overlapped with my neurological interests. I was recruited to the Montreal General Hospital by two wonderful colleagues, Carl Gureski and Charlie Hollenberg. Charlie subsequently came to Toronto, where he had an extraordinary career in medicine. But the attraction to McGill was what I would say is critical for young people coming into academic medicine: protected time to do what your creative instincts allow you to do. I was given limited clinical responsibilities. I was grateful again to the Medical Research Council, which awarded me a scholarship, paid my salary. And I was able to spend those early formative years in research thinking and doing and having the time to explore the areas of my intellectual curiosity. I can't emphasize how important it is to give young people protected time to do the things that they're curious about doing.

PK: What's interesting, though, is that you've not only been interested in research, which has been foremost, I would say, in your mind, but you have also maintained a constant practical involvement in hospitals, in medicine, in what doctors are doing from day to day. And you don't see the two as being necessarily divorced. That began at McGill?

JM: Yes. I've always considered myself to be a good doctor. I like patients. I enjoy clinical medicine. I have found the connection with patients to be the most sustaining and important aspect of anyone's intellectual inquiry in a university or medical school setting. I've always taken that part of the life that I've been privileged to lead as a critical component of who I am and what I wish to accomplish. I've always worked in clinical departments. I've never been in the basic science departments alone. And I've always had a small but sustained practice of clinical work that has really kept me close to the ground in terms of what the real issues in neurology are. There's no better way to appreciate a family's set of problems that influence the work you might want to do in research than to talk with them, know them, learn about their clinical problems.

PK: In what other ways did the experience at McGill paint the picture that would be the rest of your career? You rose through the ranks there — you eventually became the head of the department. You saw that department, one of the most exciting places to be in that field at the time, from all angles, from the bottom to the top. Did that colour or enlighten or show you how to act in later life?

JM: It was a moment in the history of neurology in Canada and at McGill that contributed powerfully to an intellectual environment. There was, as in so many cases, a degree of competition within the university itself that led to some of the most important things that happened. I was at the Montreal General Hospital. The Montreal Neurological Institute (MNI) was across town. We championed our own family. We grew, in some form, in competition with the larger, more well-established group. Wilder Penfield had established the MNI back in 1929, I believe. So, as I was given the privilege to do the research that I had undertaken, I found myself in a position to bridge that family. I was invited to join the MNI as the head of neurology, then subsequently appointed the chair of the department of neurology and neurosurgery. So, a time of growth and maturation of the larger neurologic community at McGill actually gave me an opportunity to build some bridges, to move from one institution to the other.

And all of that, I think, showed me my interest in administrative areas and in trying to pursue the kinds of collaborative interactive functions and activities that would produce more results than individual entities working on their own. So, it was a very important time for me to appreciate that I enjoyed administrative activities and that I like working to help other people accomplish the things that they were setting out to do.

PK: Given that, when the call came from Harvard, was it an easy call
to take or a difficult call? What did it feel like to be leaving Canada
to go to another centre of the universe? Were there misgivings about
it at all? Was it something that you were waiting for?

JM: Well, Paul, there was a push and a pull. This is some history I
haven't ever really talked about publicly, but not everyone at McGill
was happy that a neurologist — not a neurosurgeon, for the first time
in the history of the MNI — had been asked to head the department.
That opposition was palpable. So when the invitation came from
Harvard and Massachusetts General Hospital, it made me more
interested to look at it than would have been the case if I had been
sure that the future at McGill was going to be comfortable. Now,
that's sort of academic gossip, but in fact it was part of the reason
that I found the opportunity at Harvard to be particularly attractive
at that time.

The invitation to visit Harvard came as a total surprise. I had no
reason to believe that they were likely to approach someone like me
for the position of chief of neurology at the Massachusetts General
Hospital — MGH, as it's called. Ironically, when I was looking for a
place to train in neurology, MGH was one of the places on my list,
but my application from the University of Alberta to Harvard and
to MGH received no kindness on their part. In fact, they wouldn't
answer my letter until one of my favourite faculty people at the University of Alberta, who knew a colleague at Mass General, said send
the boy an application, which they did, but they turned me down.
So I went to Cleveland, as I mentioned.

So, to be invited to come to the institution that I had at one point
thought of training in but didn't get invited to do so was an interesting vignette. It was, in many ways, the plum position in American
neurology at that time, with tremendous resources and a tremendous
patient population, and access to the most remarkable students, fellows, to carry out the emerging molecular biological approaches to
disease. For me, it was the most important decision... well, I would
say going to McGill was the most important decision in terms of

an academic start, but going to Harvard at that point provided the entrance into a whole new world of research that got me interested in Huntington's disease, and Alzheimer's disease, and so on. But it was a surprise. I didn't anticipate such a thing.

PK: Since you've mentioned them, we should spend some time talking about Huntington's and Alzheimer's neurodegenerative disorders, which are your speciality in terms of research. What got you interested in those initially, and why are they as important to you as they obviously are?

JM: Well, I am a great believer in serendipity. A year after I arrived in Boston, the widow of Woody Guthrie, who had Huntington's disease, and a number of other important people lobbied the US Congress to put Huntington's disease as an area of interest in the public view and to point out that this was a biological problem that could be approached with modern science methods. So the National Institutes of Health came out with a request for proposals to do research in Huntington's disease. We were able to put together a team in the Boston area; it was an intra-institutional team. The patients with Huntington's disease were mostly at Boston University Medical Center. The emerging field of human genetics and of looking at DNA for markers that would allow one to search for genes for these disorders was being developed at MIT, the Massachusetts Institute of Technology.

So, what I did was to put together the whole Boston community — we called it Huntington's Disease Center without Walls. And I was able to attract young Canadian Jim Gazella, who was finishing his Ph.D. at MIT in one of these laboratories that was working on methods for DNA analysis. He took the risk at the end of his graduate program to join me at the Mass General Hospital and to carry forward the molecular genetic efforts that led eventually to the discovery of the Huntington's gene. Jim was a brilliant scientist — still is — and he now heads a large group in genetics at the Mass General Hospital. His willingness to take the risk of crossing over the Charles River from MIT to Mass General was really, I think, a symbol of how science was going to be applied to human conditions and human diseases in a way that wasn't appreciated before.

We got the grant, which was one of two awarded to the US — the other went to Johns Hopkins. And three years later, we were working with patients and their families. One family that had developed the disease was from the Lake Maracaibo region in Venezuela and had been studied for years by Nancy Wexler, who is a very famous human geneticist in the US and whose mother had died from Huntington's disease. A second family, studied in Indiana, allowed us to identify a DNA marker, the first time that a neurologic disease of this kind had had its gene localized to one of the chromosomes through polymorphism, as it's called, which allows one to take DNA itself, analyze it, and find differences that then follow and mark the course of the disease genetically from generation to generation.

That discovery was published in *Nature*, and it became a kind of model for how to approach other disorders through so-called linkage analysis, [where you] follow the gene in a family, do the DNA study, do the polymorphism markers of the DNA, and show the connection between those changes and the family presence of the disease. That process has now been used widely for hundreds of genes over the past twenty-five years.

PK: The process, though, probably wouldn't have been discovered if you hadn't put together people working in a hospital with Huntington's patients with people literally across the river who were working theoretically on the research, the genetic components that are involved in this. You had to bring together high-level thinking and frontline work to make that kind of discovery, and that's something that you've done consistently throughout your career.

JM: Well, that was a very important example of how breaking the boundaries of traditional academic connections will allow for adventures in science that wouldn't have been possible without it. The strength that we had at the Mass General Hospital was that we were experts in brain pathology, so we were able to look very carefully at details in ways that had never been done before, at how the brain changed as Huntington's disease progressed from early onset to later stages. That was a strong component at the Mass General. But without the other two pieces — the patients that we needed to work with and the molecular diagnostic — we couldn't have done it. It was a stroke of some serendipity that I had the opportunity to find the right people and ask them if they wanted to join — convince them we should a least put in the application. Then we got funded — the very important principle here is that, if you have resources to carry work forward, people will come together and try to be effective in ways that won't work with promises but that actual resources and funds will permit to happen.

Neurology went through several epochs of discovery from the first descriptions in the 1800s of the lesions in strokes, and multiple sclerosis, amyotrophic lateral sclerosis (ALS) — which is called Lou Gehrig's disease — and Parkinson's disease. These conditions were described clinically, then the brain was examined and the pathology of them unfolded. That's about where we were until 1980, '85, when it became clear that there were ways, through genetics, to identify the genes that underlie the disorders, and then to find the proteins that those genes encode for and begin to understand why those proteins do bad things.

These neurodegenerative disorders are all characterized by abnormal, often premature cell death in the brain. Nerve cells, the fundamental units of how everything is accomplished in the brain, these electrical-discharging structures that determine thought, as well as movement, and sight, and hearing, and feeling, fall apart in these disorders and die. And the symptoms that emerge are the result of whatever part of the brain happens to be affected. For example, in most cases of Lou Gehrig's disease, paralysis of the muscles of the arms, legs, face, and even swallowing is the primary finding; the mental state remains perfectly preserved, usually. So, in that condition, motor neurons are affected.

In Parkinson's disease, the disorder is associated with stiffness, rigidity, and tremor. And the disorder there was linked in that period to a deficiency of dopamine, which can be replaced with L-dopa as a treatment. But what happened, as the genetics emerged, was that the proteins that were collected in the brain in abnormal ways were discovered. And that led to the opportunity to do experiments in animals, where the same transgenic, replacing genes in animals with the disorder genes in humans, provided models for exploration of treatments and approaches to understanding the basic underlying cause of the disorder.

So, it was really the recognition of the DNA changes — that genetic mutations could cause these complicated syndromes, and therefore you could trace it back to individual proteins that those genes encoded for — that then allowed one to think about what happens, and why it goes wrong, and how you can intervene to slow it down or eventually even fix it.

PK: Those sound like revolutionary changes. How far along the road do you think we've come, and how far do we have to go still in finding cures to any or all of these problems?

JM: Well, just think for a moment about Alzheimer's disease, which is the commonest of all these disorders. You know, it's estimated that in the US there are about five million patients who suffer from Alzheimer's disease. It's associated with an aging population — we know it comes on in increased frequency as we grow older.

The condition was described a hundred years ago by Alzheimer, a German psychiatrist who looked at the brain of a woman who died at age fifty-one and saw plaques and tangles. Plaques are deposits of a protein, and tangles are early signs of nerve cells dying, with an accumulation of a clumped bit of material within the cytoplasm of the cell before it dies. Those plaques and tangles now have been defined biochemically. We know that the plaque is due to the deposition of a protein called beta-amyloid, and we know that the tangles are composed of a protein called tau, which is collected together in an aggregated form to cause the tangles inside the cells. Having identified those two proteins, it's now possible to think about ways to modify their function or change what they accomplish. And in that regard, there are, I would say, two or three strategies that look very promising.

In the case of beta-amyloid, which is toxic to nerve cells, it's possible to reduce its formation in the brain by modifying the enzymes that are involved in the synthesis. And that's been successful in animal models, where the genes of Alzheimer's have been put into a mouse, and you can show dramatic changes in the accumulation of this toxic protein in the mouse brain. That has led to early efforts to develop drugs. Many pharmaceutical companies are looking at inhibitors of that enzyme, which is called gamma-secretase, in order to try and see if it can be used safely and effectively in humans.

There are some caveats here. The pathway that's involved in the formation of beta-amyloid is also involved in other important cellular functions. So, to find a selective gamma-secretase inhibitor that will block amyloid but not cause other untoward effects is a challenge that we face. Nevertheless, those trials are going forward in several early stages and are going to be watched closely.

Perhaps even more fascinating is that we know that beta-amyloid circulates in the blood, so it must get out of the brain, and presumably there is some transport of it across the blood brain barrier. And if you take a piece of the beta-amyloid protein and inject it into mice, antibodies to it can be produced that are capable of pulling out of the brain some of the abnormal deposits of amyloid — and that's been done in people. The problem has been that there have been unexpected and unfortunate side effects from the vaccination for Alzheimer's disease that have caused damage to the brain in some patients.

So, there are new efforts now to try and find modified forms of antibodies that are induced in this way, including taking the test-tube production of antibodies to beta-amyloid and injecting it into people to see if that will work to pull the amyloid out of the deposits in the brain. This looks quite promising, and we're all excited in the past year by the development of two new techniques to image the presence of amyloid in the brain using positron emission tomography, which is a technique where a small isotope is injected into the brain so that you can look at metabolism in the brain. Two different groups now, one in Pittsburgh and one at UCLA, have identified compounds that label the amyloid and allow you to analyze the activity of the radioactive material — it deposits on the amyloid and causes it to light up. This gives us a biomarker or a way to follow the amyloid deposits and to see if we can remove them with the kinds of therapies that I've just mentioned.

So, I think we're on the edge of a really an extraordinary set of tools — a toolbox, if you like — to look at this disorder and find ways that potentially will have a major effect.

PK: Given that, I'm interested in asking you whether you have a problem in trying to convince funders to back your research when there's research in many medical areas — cancer, diabetes — all of which can claim to be crucial, life saving. Do you have a battle trying to get the attention of the people who would be funding the kind of work you do?

JM: I would start by saying that the most important support is for fundamental biomedical research. It is the accidental discovery of something you never thought connected to a clinical problem, which often becomes the clue to the next step you want to take. So, whatever we do in responding to the requests that individual families, or associations, or disease-connected entities make to place their efforts at the forefront, we should never forget that it's really the discovery of DNA structure, the double helix, and the discovery of the fundamental mechanism of immunology that allow us to think about a vaccination for Alzheimer's.

The first thing we have to be absolutely sure about is that we don't compromise the creativity of the young, brilliant minds who are doing the most fundamental work. Now, having said that, the application potential has never been greater, so balancing the support that we want to encourage at that basic level with the so-called translational opportunities to work toward solving human problems in disease means that there are pressures on us to try to ensure that it's adequately funded as well. Of course, I'm of the mind that we never provide enough funding for these activities. In the United States, we are in a period of a very flat trajectory on the National Institutes of Health budget. I've heard this week that the budget in Canada for biomedical research has been a disappointment to many of the scientists in Canada who feel that their future opportunities are going to be diminished by choices that are being made here.

PK: In that context though, I was actually a bit surprised to hear you talk about the role of pharmaceutical companies in working on the basic science — not just creating pills or vaccines, but actually figuring out what they have to do in order to help things. And from somebody who has spent most of his life in the ivory tower, I find it interesting that you are pointing to the private sector. Can you talk about that partnership, or that relationship, and how it works?

JM: Well, the drugs that have changed the course of human illness have been discovered by pharmaceutical companies, and we need to give credit to that process. If I were to say what are the major discoveries of the past twenty years, they would be treatments for blood pressure, treatments for high cholesterol. In the case of HIV-AIDS, they are treatments with new drugs that allow people to live with that illness for essentially their entire lives. So the pharmaceutical industry has a great track record of developing these agents. And they have depended in major ways upon the fundamental research in the US of the National Institutes of Health in supporting individual investigators to take the step from the basic discoveries to drug development.

Now, the disappointment recently has been the gap between what basic research can do and taking a discovery to promising clinical returns. Where the pharmaceutical industry's willing to place its risks has created a gap of resources and funding that potentially could be very damaging in the long run. It came about, in part, because, for about twenty years, in the 1980s and 1990s, many pharmaceutical companies put a lot of money into academic basic research through contracts or through agreements to support various components of research, and many of those failed to produce the results that the pharmaceutical industry, as a for-profit sector, had hoped to accomplish. So, we've moved away from that rather promising set of collaborations, and we need to rethink more practical ways in which those two communities can work together again. And that's a challenge that all of us have to work on together. But I think it's critical if we're going to provide the resources that will take the basic discoveries to the bedside in a way that will allow scientists to feel that they're accomplishing something and the pharmaceutical and biotech industries to feel that their investments are paying off. So, it's a real academic, industrial collaboration that needs some fresh views on how to do it.

PK: It comes back again to something I would say is a basic impulse in the way you work, and that is breaking down walls. You create a centre without walls that brings together various academic institutions. In your tenure as dean at Harvard, you have tried to make interdisciplinary connections as much as possible — I understand you're also overseeing the construction of Harvard's biggest academic building — to bring that kind of cross-disciplinary group of people together. You break down walls all the time, so breaking them down between the pharmaceutical companies and ivory tower academics is one way of doing it, too.

JM: Yes, I think there can be an important role for convening those communities in ways that will help address the concerns on both sides. I would take the example of cancer, which was one of the major collaborative efforts that we undertook at Harvard. We have five major institutions that deliver cancer care, and yet, although they may compete for patients to take care of their problems with cancer, we now have assembled all of them into a single centre for the purposes of research and clinical trials in new potential therapies. The Dana Farber Harvard Cancer Center, which has about eight hundred investigators involved in cancer at various levels of inquiry, has allowed us to put together a new way of investigating potential treatments that wouldn't have happened otherwise. It's dependent in large measure, again, upon the National Institutes of Health for

support, and they've been very appreciative of our bringing our
efforts together under one umbrella and have provided more funding
for us as a result.

PK: You recently announced that you'll be stepping down as dean.
Are there misgivings there? Are you sad to be leaving? Is there something wonderful on the horizon? Can you talk about that decision?

JM: I have no regrets about that decision for a couple of reasons.
First, I would say that I still have personal intellectual inquiries
I want to pursue, particularly in the field of neurodegenerative
disorders, and thinking of how to help our community work together
at Harvard in a better way. I'll remain on the faculty there, in the
department of neurobiology, which is my home base.

  Secondly, I think regime change is important. I believe strongly,
and I guess my own career has illustrated this, that we do our best
work in the first five to ten years of an engagement, and the turnover
— new ideas, new innovation, new creativity — is part of moving
to the next stage. I look forward to hearing about who my succes-
sor will be, and if I can help in some way, of course I'd like to do
that. But I have absolutely no regrets, personally, about turning this
over and now going back to where my intellectual activities actually
began.

PK: Can you talk about some of the personal projects you're excited
about working on?

JM: We have a centre that was modelled on the Dana Farber Harvard
Cancer Center that deals with the neurodegenerative disorders. It's
called the Harvard Center for Neurogeneration and Repair. Now,
repair means trying to fix things that are broken. In that regard,
stem cells become part of the topic — that's another whole issue.
But I have been involved with this group for the last five years. It's a
separate virtual centre, not a physical institute. It's not a building, but
a way of bringing people together to think about big ideas, supporting
graduate students who are going into the field, providing funding

for early clinical trials, trying to bridge this gap that I've referred to between basic discovery and where a pharmaceutical company might pick up the subject. We've created one of the first academic drug-discovery units that is actually screening compounds looking for promising leads in Alzheimer's, Parkinson's disease, and ALS. For me, intellectually, that's a home that I will enjoy participating in more than I've been able to. You know, that's maybe thirty per cent of a job — it's not a full job.

We're also establishing a new laboratory for the study of aging, and have had some very interesting results in one of our departments around agents that can slow down the process of aging. One of the compounds in red wine that everybody notices is called resveratrol, which was discovered to be an agent that, given in doses that people can't take yet, causes a slowing down of aging in mice. And that group has been working with industry to develop new approaches to thinking about therapies for, not curing aging — we're all going to die — but slowing it down. So, that laboratory is another area. Some of the people there have trained with me before, and I'm delighted to be closer in association with them.

I'm also personally involved with several companies on the board of directors, because I believe that's one way to learn how business works and how to work with business. I have enjoyed being on a couple of public company boards, and want to continue to do that as well.

PK: This is perhaps off topic, in that it's not necessarily something that is at the centre of your work or your research, but, as somebody who grew up in Canada, was trained in Canada, worked at McGill, then went to Harvard, also worked in California, came back to Harvard, always at the upper levels of the medical world, would you care to comment on the differences between our two countries, both on the research level, because funding is very different in the United States than it is in Canada, and on the practical medical level? I mean, Canadians think of Medicare as a national identifier, and the United States works under a completely different system. I'm interested in your thoughts on those two different worlds.

JM: Well, I would begin by saying that there is some extraordinarily important science going on in Canada in many fields. Institutions in Canada have led the way in human genetics, the discovery of genes for cystic fibrosis, for example. Major discoveries in cancer have been made here. And in the neurosciences, what began mostly at McGill has expanded to the University of Montreal, which has a very strong neuroscience community. And this is also true in some of the Western provinces, in Alberta and British Columbia. I think it's important to recognize that there are world-class people doing research in Canada who deserve the same kind of support and level of appreciation that we have enjoyed perhaps to greater degree in the US. If one looks at how well Canada is doing economically, at its ability to balance the budget and to create opportunities like I've witnessed in Alberta... In that case, twenty-five years ago, the provincial government established a fund for the Alberta Foundation for Medical Research, which has a total asset value of now over a billion dollars, which has transformed the two universities there in Calgary and Edmonton and created for them the opportunity that wouldn't have happened if the province, with its extraordinary resources, hadn't stepped up. So, the intellect is here, the development of a broader base of science is happening, and I believe Canadians ought to try and make it even better, and find ways to support it at levels that it hasn't enjoyed in the past.

PK: That's research. How about health care?

JM: We both have major problems in health care. They're different problems, but they're both serious problems. I remember vividly when I went to Montreal in 1970 at the time that Medicare came into effect. Every patient had a card that they could bring to the doctor. You didn't have to worry about whether they had insurance or not — you knew you could see them, do what you needed to do, and thirty days later you got a cheque from the provincial government for the services you'd rendered around a fee structure that everybody understood. Now, that was pretty ideal, and it worked very well for a while. The issues that Canada faces now clearly are the sustainability of the costs of health care and the difficulties that patients here experience, particularly in waiting for elective procedures, which has become such a national, political issue here.

In the US, our system has problems with the moral issue of the right to have access to health care. We have forty-six million people in the United States now who have no health care. We have another thirty or forty million who have inadequate health care or who have periods of time from job to job when they have no health care. Those figures and facts don't fully describe the calamities that occur in individual lives with catastrophic medical problems when there is no insurance, and when the families go bankrupt and lose everything because they can't provide financially for the care that I think every citizen deserves.

So, it's really a measure of social values. I think Canada has responsibly taken the issue of health care as a right and a social responsibility, and in the US it's been transformed into a market economy around health care, which has put too many resources into the administrative structures required to manage multiple ways of delivering care. I think both countries need new solutions and new directions. And it'll be interesting to follow. I don't personally have an idea of how best to do that, but I certainly think the conversations that are ongoing now in both our countries will be important in moving toward a solution that's better than what we have now.

PK: So, if there is a kid growing up on a farm in rural Alberta, and he or she is looking for something to do with their lives, you would advise them perhaps to go into medicine and maybe into neurology?

JM: One of the most important parts of my job as dean, both at California and now at Harvard, has been my close association with the students. I really believe that they are the future. And I tell students regularly, either those applying to medical school and wanting to know about the future in medicine or those starting off early in their education in medicine, that there isn't any other field that carries so much potential for interests and activities that can range all the way from Nobel Prize-winning, basic biomedical

research to global health to the challenges that we face around the
world, the conditions that we've lived with for a long time and
still haven't solved — malaria, tuberculosis — and to health care
economics and government influence. A medicine base provides the
opportunity to do any of that, and it allows switching from one
area to another in that field of opportunities. So, I think it's the best
profession in the world, by far.

Hooked on Water

DAVID SCHINDLER

David Schindler, Killam Memorial Professor of Ecology at the University of Alberta, has been called one of the foremost water scientists in the world. Somebody once said that if there was a Nobel Prize for ecology, he would win it. Well, there is no Nobel Prize for ecology, but David Schindler has received the first Stockholm Water Prize and the Volvo International Environment Prize, the only Canadian to win either one. He has also won international awards in limnology and the 2001 Gerhard Herzberg Canada Gold Medal for Science and Engineering. Dr. Schindler has also been labelled by the Hudson Institute as a professional public hand wringer for his frequent warnings about potential environmental dangers. Through his four decades as a scientist, he has maintained a clear vision of the importance of understanding the complexities of water, and the responsibility of a scientist in public debate. His interview was broadcast on Ideas *on 22 October 2003.*

PAUL KENNEDY

It's a sunny morning in early summer. We're walking through high grass on a patch of land about a hundred kilometres west of Edmonton, near the village of Wildwood. Just to the right, a stretch of the Lobstick River glints as it meanders through thickets of poplars. Those dense stands of trees are very unusual around here. For many

366

kilometres in all directions, the poplars have been bulldozed and cleared to make way for farmland. This particular land is unusual in another way. It's the home of David Schindler.

So, tell me what I would be seeing if I were you. I'm on a piece of property that you know very well, in which water matters a great deal, obviously.

DAVID SCHINDLER

Well, this land was all spruce forest with a bit of poplar in it, originally. The site of our house is actually the site of an old sawmill. And the first thing that happened when people started moving into this country was they went through and high-graded all of the white spruce, and when that was gone they started on the poplars. Now they're clearing the poplar and also turning what they clear into farmland. People have been complaining about the quality of water, not only here but pretty much right across central Alberta. What they don't realize is that just stripping the land of forest will usually cause an increase in the nutrient runoff to water by two- to fivefold.

And it's pretty rich water to begin with, so the end product is poorer water quality. Just upstream, about two miles that way, we have Chip Lake, which is a collapsed walleye fishery, one of the many across central Alberta. And I don't think it'll be recoverable. This river flows through farmland for twenty or thirty miles above Chip Lake, and now it takes the runoff from all that cleared land. Usually, when it's cleared, people pasture cattle, so there's manure that goes in.

The other thing that happens is that, once the poplars are bull-dozed, there's nothing for the beaver. So we've changed the whole dynamics of the river. The few stretches like ours that still have forest tend to be overutilized by beaver. Pretty well every one of the riffles you see on the river is the remains of an old beaver dam.

This is also an unusual stretch of forest. While the large white spruce were mostly cut before we owned it, we have forty acres of forest that we've just left alone in the thirteen years that we've been here. We're going to be one of the few places along the Lobstick River that still has natural riparian vegetation.

The other thing farmers do is fill in the wetlands, because they're inconvenient, and strip vegetation right to the bank to graze a few more cattle and let them have access right to the stream bank. Upstream, there are some really messy places where the cattle have broken the banks down and erosion is carrying silt into the river to be deposited downstream.

So, all of that affects the water quality. And, of course, the next thing that usually happens when all the wetlands are filled in and all the beaver dams are gone is that people's wells start going dry. And they can't figure out why. You know, the science to show that has been around for forty years, and we're not using it.

PK: Nobody's been listening.

DS: No. Well, I've begun to think more and more that we don't do a very good job at using our science. We have a scientific community that puts its findings in journals that very few people read. They're specialist journals. The language is pretty jargony, and a few of their colleagues read them for their amusement. But somehow we need a better way of getting that information to people who actually make the decisions that affect our water catchments. I think we'd better move. The bugs are catching up with us.

PK: Important work. How do you make them pay attention?

DS: I don't know. I think part of it is culture. I've probably played as much sports as anyone, and how anyone can insist on fifteen minutes every hour of prattle on sports and there's nothing on science, just absolutely nothing on things like water, pesticides, climate warming, which are absolutely vital to the critical decisions that we need to make about our life-support systems. People are going to need a generation or two to make the change. I think the media could help us a lot, and I think the media would if more journalists understood a bit more science. Sports are easy to understand, so they're very comfortable prattling on about them.

One of my favourite authors is Wendell Berry. He has a saying, the gist of which is that people ought to be limited to hand tools and the damage they could do. That would certainly be welcome here. I think the average farmer, when he gets a bit bored, wants to keep his bulldozer skills up, so he goes out and bulldozes another quarter-section of trees.

PK: What do your neighbours think of you?

DS: I've got a fair number of friends in the area. The people right to the north who own the big chunk of land are really good land stewards. They have immediately gone in and fenced their cattle away from the water, and pump the water up into tanks for them to drink. Both the father and his two sons have taken environmental courses to understand what sort of damage agricultural practices can do, and what they can do to prevent them. I'd say it's a real mixed bag. There are very few really bad operators. There's a fair number of people who don't realize what they're doing, and would probably change their ways if they recognized how they are harming the land. And they're the key people, I think, to get.

I've got to set up this light meter this afternoon. I'm supposed to take that to Lac La Biche to teach some of my students how to operate it. It just came in. In my day, you turned them on and there was a needle that moved back and forth, and you wrote down the number. Now you've got to learn to operate a computer to do the same thing. And there's two manuals. I got through one of them last night, and the second one I decided to do with the instrument sitting in front of me.

PK: So it does...what?

DS: This is for underwater light. We always used to do our readings on clear, bright days, because when a cloud passes over the sun, your meter needle drops. And we want to get relative readings with depth, which allow us to calculate how fast light becomes extinct with depth. This one will integrate for several minutes, so it takes care of that swinging needle problem, accounting for passing clouds. But the other thing that's nice about this instrument is that we used to have to take readings in several directions, whereas this meter integrates light from all directions. It's a so-called spherical collection. So, underwater, it'll collect light coming from down below that's bouncing off the bottom in shallow water as well from above and reflecting from wave action and so on. So it integrates a lot of things.

PK: The data you could collect then must have been a tiny fraction of what's now available to you.

DS: That's true, but one part that hasn't changed is it all has to go through your brain. We do a lot more data collection and a lot more science. I'm not sure we do any more *good* science. The creative part of science is not something you can get out of instruments. Sometimes I think the instruments are detrimental. We spend too much time trying to figure out something like this computer, and if your brain were actually trying to solve a problem creatively you'd probably be farther ahead. It's so easy to get bound up in your computer and think that ecology comes out of computers. It's just not the case, no matter how much data you might be able to collect.

PK: Dr. Schindler has a global reputation for his innovative and influential research on eutrophication of lakes, on acid rain, and on climate change. Eutrophification is the overfertilization of lakes from human sources, such as detergents and agricultural fertilizers, resulting in rapid and abundant aquatic plant growth and dramatic changes in the lakes animal population. Dr. Schindler pioneered the use of whole-lake experiments to determine that elimination of phosphorous was pivotal in controlling eutrophication. These whole-ecosystem experiments were conducted at the Experimental Lakes Area, near Kenora, Ontario. His research has brought him world renown, and he speaks with politicians, and kings, and prime ministers. But he always comes back to his rambling house overlooking a seemingly pristine stretch of the Lobstick River where it veers north just before spilling into the canyon of the Pembina.

The river flowing quietly below his house is a constant reminder of the intricacies and the fragilities of water systems. Water levels have dipped so much recently that he says he sometimes sees ducks walking across the Lobstick instead of swimming.

David Schindler has had a steady fascination with water. I asked him where that started.

DS: I don't think I can think back far enough to when I became interested in water. My grandmother was very fixed on lakes, and my earliest memories are of going to the lakes in northern Minnesota on weekends and swimming, and a little later fishing. And by the time I was ten years old, I was already addicted. I have always been hooked on water. I didn't realize there were any careers in it, though, until I was a third-year university student. At that point, I was an unhappy engineer who found engineering to be a pretty dreary subject. I was going to university in Minneapolis, but I got a summer job working for what was called a limnologist, a profession that I'd never heard of. And I found it was the freshwater equivalent of oceanography. And that summer, working for him and borrowing books from him and reading them just made a total convert out of me.

The first book I read was one that I think to this day is one of the most important books of all time. It was Charles Elton's *The Ecology of Invasions by Animals and Plants.* It was written two years before Rachel Carson's *Silent Spring*, and it's much better written, but, for some reason, that book didn't catch on. And yet I look back forty years, and the alien species that have invaded this continent and other continents have had far more impact than pesticides or chemicals, big as the chemical impacts have been. And that, of course, was the subject of Elton's book. But the book literally made my hair stand on end. I got a Rhodes Scholarship to go and study with Elton — I did my Ph.D. in the UK.

I went back to Minnesota, and what we've been seeing this morning around here was already happening to Minnesota at that time. The forests and the lakes were really under industrial assault. I decided that I'd had enough of the States and moved first to Trent University and then later to northwestern Ontario when I got invited to head the Experimental Lakes Project. When I moved to Experimental Lakes, the logging in that area was still done with horses. There were only a few patches of forest cut, and, of course, that changed very rapidly. So, I've kept moving ahead of industry, like some refugee on the run from an army, but always studying water.

Water is interesting in a lot of ways, even if you're interested in what's happening in the watershed above it. I tend to think of rivers as the sewers for the landscape, and yet that's where people have to draw their drinking water. That's where we go to catch fish. So, if you want to drink from the sewers and rely on those sewers for food, you'd better be pretty careful about what you do to the areas that are being sewered.

I stayed at Experimental Lakes for twenty-two years. It was a very satisfying place to be. I had top-notch colleagues, was able to attack and solve some of the big freshwater problems that Canada and the world faced. But due to the government cutbacks of the eighties and nineties, Experimental Lakes started to fall on hard times. So, in 1989, I accepted an invitation to join the University of Alberta. And my wife, who's also an ecologist, and I moved here, and we've been very happy.

PK: Let's pause for awhile with Experimental Lakes, which is an interesting concept. How does one use a lake almost as a test tube?

DS: The idea is actually not mine. The director of the Freshwater Institute, who hired me, was Dr. Wally Johnson. When he was a student, he had worked for a professor at the University of Wisconsin who made whole-lake additions of lime to try to make acidic lakes neutral enough to grow fish. So Johnson was fascinated by the idea of whole-lake experiments. When he moved to Canada, he found that a lot of the people who were making policy were reluctant to base expensive policy on just small test tubes. So it was his idea that if they had full-ecosystem scale results to rely on, they would probably be much more confident.

At the time, the big problem in the St. Lawrence-Great Lakes, the lakes of Muskoka-Haliburton, and many other lakes of the world was overfertilization with nutrients. There was a lot of test-tube-scale scientific evidence that indicated that one element was responsible for the epidemic development of algal growth in lakes: phosphorous. But, as has always been the case, industries that produced high-phosphorous products didn't like to hear that. Most notably in this case, the detergent industry was producing cleaning detergents that were fifty per cent phosphorous by weight. So they launched a big Madison Avenue campaign. If anyone has followed the debate over Kyoto, it's very, very similar — you could almost white out words and insert eutrophication for climate warming. But the detergent industries were able to put out enough propaganda to confuse non-science people who were making policy, like politicians and bureaucrats.

So, with that impasse, we decided that this was an ideal test for our first experiments: we would add phosphorous to lakes that didn't have algal blooms and see what happened. These lakes were all very small — from five to fifty hectares would be the whole range. We collected background data, then, in some cases, we'd add fertilizer. We were able to show within three or four years that industry's claims that controlling eutrophication would require controlling several nutrients were false, and that we could indeed pin the blame for eutrophication in most cases on one element alone.

Luckily, phosphorus was an element that was easy to control. In those days, we had only to get rid of two sources to get most of the phosphorus. One was phosphate-based detergents and the other was human sewage effluent. Most places, like the St. Lawrence-Great Lakes, required phosphorous removal at municipal treatment plants. And Canada also banned high-phosphate detergents. And, of course, it's been one of the most successful applications of science ever.

However, eutrophication has come back to haunt us. While we've controlled human excrement and human phosphate detergents, the clearing of land and the pasturing of cattle, the fertilization of agricultural land, and increasing human populations have brought the same problem back to haunt us once again. Some of us had foreseen this in the seventies, but the politicians were determined that the money spent for eutrophication research could be better spent elsewhere, so we were forced to look for new problems. But the eutrophication experiments were the Experimental Lakes' first success.

PK: What does it feel like when you've discovered something like phosphates being the enemy? Is it a white charger — you suddenly realize that you're on to something that general society doesn't have any idea about right now, and yet this is something that is critically important and you know the importance of it? Do you feel like you're a crusader, that you have to do something to bring this to the attention of the general public to try to, I don't know, save the planet?

DS: I think those feelings come with time. I was occupied full time with setting up the camp and doing the experiments for the first few years. So the first person to use the results and see the effects on policy — in this case, largely in Canada — was Jack Vallentyne, my boss. But, about 1972, Jack decided to move on to other things, and he just told me one day, you have to do this stuff — interact with policy-makers — now. At that point, most of the action was in the US, so I started going to state hearings, where typically the detergent companies would appear with a travelling circus of a couple of dozen people, experts on various things from the cleaning properties of detergents to environmental things, making all sorts of false claims that phosphorous was not the culprit. And I had the evidence that it was. It was a very powerful and influential position to be in. And I guess I got to see how hungry people were for real information, and how you didn't need to present the information in a highly technical way — that, in some cases, a few pictures would tell the story.

The case that's probably best known among our experiments is one we did in an hourglass-shaped lake, where we got the idea of curtaining the lake in half using the sort of sea-curtain that had just been developed for containing oil slicks in the ocean. We separated the two basins by stringing that across the middle and sealing it with rocks on the bottom. We added nitrogen and carbon to both sides of the lake, but to one side we added phosphorous as well. The claim at the time by detergent companies was that we could never control eutrophication by controlling phosphorous alone, because it was recycled too rapidly. Well, we showed in that experiment that the basin that produced a big algal bloom was the one that received phosphorous. It turned bright green. The other basin didn't change at all. You could see the results of this experiment from an air photo. I found that all I had to do was to go to a hearing and show that photo. This basin is with no phosphorous, but it has the other key elements in sewage. And this basin is what happens if you add phosphorous. I really didn't need any more evidence than that to convince judges, or hearing panels, or legislators.

And to this very day, that picture is popular. I probably still get twenty-five or thirty release requests each year from people who want to use it in their textbooks. Over the years, it's been reprinted several hundred times, perhaps more times than any other picture of a lake. So that experience showed me right off that it was worth looking for things like pictures showing simple changes that were easily understandable to a lay audience, changes to the things that they valued in a lake ecosystem, and you could explain the changes in those things to them. You could have a large impact.

PK: After the success of Dr. Schindler's whole-lake experiments and confirming phosphorous as a leading source of eutrophication, he turned his attention to one of the major environmental issues of the last few decades: acid rain. He says that the big contribution of the Experimental Lakes research showed that even mild lake acidification caused food chains in lakes to break down as fish and their foods started to die off quickly. The research made headlines in the *New York Times* and ultimately forced governments on two continents to enact crucial environmental legislation to protect fish and water by controlling emissions. David Schindler also says the research had another unanticipated result. It was thought that if the lakes were acidified there was no point in trying to stop emissions because the lakes would never recover. There was some natural buffering action in the lakes, like Tums has on an acid stomach. But it was believed that the buffering action only came from limestone and similar rocks in the drainage basins of the lakes. But the Experimental Lakes research showed that microbial action could also help recover the lake, maybe not fully, but at least to the point where fish might grow again. He says that second finding gave people more courage to control acid emissions, and that the research overall led to a more predictable result: another showdown with industry.

DS: It's fair to say that we faced even stronger resistance from industry, particularly in the US. Power plants, in particular, that relied on burning coal in the Ohio Valley and much of the eastern seaboard didn't want to hear that their sulphur emissions were causing problems. Similarly, the coal-burning facilities in the UK did not like to hear that they were causing acid rain problems in Scandinavia. So, in this case, I think our experiments were able to offer some key incisive discoveries that wouldn't have been made elsewhere, or at least not as rapidly. They certainly weren't the whole story with respect to acid rain. But, I'd say a combination of our work and that of others was able to show that these industries were not correct.

I think one of my most memorable times was when I was asked by the Royal Society in the UK to attend a meeting to review the results of what they called the Surface Water Acidification Programme, to study the impact of acidifying emissions from the UK on the resources of Scandinavia. Talks were given by Scandinavian and UK scientists over a period of several days. The final dinner, which was in the Royal Society residence, was attended by Margaret Thatcher herself. And for some reason, probably because they thought we would be less cowed than a UK scientist, they seated Margaret Thatcher next to Eville Gorham and myself. Eville was a Canadian scientist who'd spent most of his career in the US, and I was the opposite. Through supper, she grilled us about the results of this meeting. There were also the environment ministers from Norway and Sweden sitting right next to her. She would argue with us. She was no dummy: she had first class honours in chemistry from Oxford. But at the end of the evening, she stood up and announced that she was convinced by the results and that the UK would be changing the way it generated power. Pretty impressive performance by a politician, I'd say.

PK: Not something that you've seen paralleled on this side of the Atlantic. I mean, you've had easier access to politicians elsewhere than you have to politicians in Canada.

DS: Canada's always struck me as a bit odd. I spent twenty-two years with Fisheries and Oceans, and I seldom ever saw a deputy minister, very occasionally an assistant deputy minister. Yet, I'd go to the US and meet with senators, the secretary of the interior, the head of the EPA. I'd go to Sweden and meet with the minister of environment or with the king and queen to discuss environmental problems. It's almost like we have no science in our culture in this country. And I don't think very much has changed over the years.

PK: When you set out to be an ecologist, a scientist, a limnologist, did you have any idea that it would involve the kind of political commitment or the kind of actions that you have been involved with, which have put you into a different world from that of the laboratory or even the experimental lake? You've become a somewhat controversial person, locking horns with people who make decisions beyond the laboratory.

DS: No, I didn't have that at all. Actually, if I were left to my own devices, I would probably be a very introverted person, as my wife would tell you. I find that doing these political actions requires a lot of me. Sometimes I don't think I have much more to give. But I think of the taxes that my family paid to maintain institutions of higher learning and the taxes that everyone pays that go to the privileged few to spend on research. I feel that we owe it to those people to reveal what we find and how it ought to affect their decisions. I don't think I'd want to see a system where scientists make the decisions. I think in most cases they'd be pretty poor at it. But the public pays a lot for environmental science, and what we know should be on the table when decisions that affect future generations need to be made.

I also come from a family that's always been very outspoken. I think my father and his father before him had a very good sense of when they were getting ...bullshit, to put it crudely, and they had a very highly developed "bullshitometer." They were also very hungry for information that should affect their decisions on managing their land or other things that they were interested in.

PK: Let's talk a bit about ecology. As you described the work you did on acid rain, on phosphates, what was important was asking questions that were beyond a narrow scientific spectrum, but looking at a bigger picture. Is that what an ecologist is, somebody who looks at the whole picture?

DS: Well, ecology ranges over a whole spectrum. The focus, of course, is interactions of organisms and their environment in nature. But some people focus on individual populations and even sub-population, physiological-ecology-sorts-of-things. My focus has always been at the other end, at the ecosystem end: how organisms interacted [with each other] and with their environment. I think a lot of that came from reading things that really turned me on. I mentioned Elton's readings. That was clearly his end of the spectrum. But I also found, growing up in an area where I had access to the outdoors and being influenced by people like Elton, who was as much a natural historian as he was a scientist, that it was important just to make keen observations when I was outdoors. Some of my best ideas have come not from knowing the technical side of science, but from just simple observations in nature.

I also found that a lot of what I learned in textbooks was out-and-out wrong, that often the only "person" who knew what was going on was Mother Nature, who had an infinite bag of dirty tricks to throw your way. One example: I had a cabin, which was across the lake from the Experimental Lakes field camp so that I could get some peace, not have to listen to a generator; I could canoe to work or walk a trail around the lake. One day, I was walking around the lake, thinking about lake-acidification problems. I crossed a small creek, and it occurred to me that this creek was draining the watershed of the lake that's supposed to supply all the buffering to neutralize acid rain, and yet this creek was much more acidic than the lake into which it flows. When I got to the office, I fished out data and looked over all of our streams in the area and found that was the general case. These stream systems were not supplying buffering capacity to lakes, as everyone was teaching. If anything, they should have been acidifying the lakes. So this led us on a search for what was causing these lakes to generate their own internal buffering capacity. It was almost like an unfolding mystery story where we first looked at chemical, then geological, then microbial mechanisms.

I had a couple of students working with me from Lamont-Doherty [Earth Observatory] who were absolutely crack geochemists. They are senior professionals in their own right in the US these days. But the people who made the difference were the microbiologists. After we found that the answer wasn't a strictly chemical one or geological one, I had some students and younger colleagues, who were excellent microbiologists, [investigate]. They found that the microbial reduction of sulphate to sulphide, which could then combine with iron and precipitate into the lake mud, removing the strong acids from the lake, was the key to the recovery of lakes.

I like that example because it's pretty typical in an ecosystem. It's almost like solving a mystery story, where you get leads and you follow them and find they're a cul-de-sac, and you turn another way and look for more clues. Sometimes you use chemical tools and sometimes biological tools or microbiological tools. In this case, finding the answer and how things really work took the better part of a decade, but we got there. I find that kind of approach to science is a very exciting thing to do, especially when I can see that the answer, when we find it, has some real impact.

PK: David Schindler's research always seems to have an impact. Now he's focusing on climate change. Using long-term reference data collected in the Experimental Lakes Area, he's shown that climate warming and drought have severe and previously unrecognized effects on the physics, chemistry, and biology of lakes.

DS: While we were doing the Experimental Lakes' experiments, we were also studying the natural systems of the area, because we needed to tell what changes were caused by natural phenomena rather than the things we were adding to lakes. It became very obvious that there were some natural changes happening both to lakes and their watersheds that were the result of a relentless period of climate warming. Over the twenty-two years that I stayed at Experimental Lakes, the average air temperature went up by about 1.7 degrees Celsius. It was also a period of considerable drought. As a result of this "double whammy" from increased evaporation caused by warmer temperatures and decreased precipitation, streams that flowed all year when I first moved to Experimental Lakes were dry for all but about a month after the end of the spring freshet due to snow melt. We found that the result was changes in the chemistry of lakes and in the organisms of lakes, which could reproduce faster. Also, though, we had declining cold water habitat — that's critical for organisms like lake trout and some of their key food organisms.

That experience made it very obvious to me that climate warming, via its effects on fresh water, was going to be one of the critical factors that we would face first, not the science of climate warming, but the impact of climate warming. So it got me interested [in further work on the problem]. Since moving west, I'd say I've become even more interested because Alberta has such a water-scarce climate to begin with. For example, some of the analysis that I and some of my colleagues have done recently has shown that the glaciers are melting at a very, very high rate. We found that the climate of the prairies has warmed very considerably. In Alberta, some of the northern sites have warmed by four to five degrees centigrade. Not due to urban heat islands — I'm talking about places like Fort Chipewyan. And here in Edmonton, Edmonton International [Airport's] temperature records indicate an increase of about two and a half degrees.

We've also found that there are other human actions that are aggravating the sorts of droughts that we've had on the prairies. One of my former students is now a professor at University of Regina, Peter Leavitt. He and his colleagues have found that you can trace three or four major prairie droughts per century in most centuries back to before the birth of Christ. This was done by analyzing the fossils deposited in lake mud that can be dated using carbon-14 or lead-210 dating. So, ironically, they and the tree-ring people have shown that the century that we have come to think of as normal, the twentieth, because that's when the prairies were occupied by white people, is probably the wettest century in the last two thousand years and perhaps more. They found that, in centuries past, at least one drought per century was usually ten to twenty years long. When they compared their indices with twentieth-century records, even what we think was a disastrous drought, the Dirty Thirties, was a very minor drought by comparison with past centuries. We will probably discover in the next hundred years that John Palliser was right when he reported that the prairies were uninhabitable, that they were not suitable for agriculture and so forth. I think in this century we're going to see a major drought, even if we don't have one of the long major droughts that we've seen for nineteen of the twenty past centuries. We're doing things now on the prairies that are going to aggravate drought. Even in the Dirty Thirties we didn't have three to four million people on the western prairies, with their fifteen million head of livestock that also need water, with the destruction of wetlands and the zones along rivers that protect them from insults, errors made in land management. And we didn't have any industry in the thirties, which we have now. And the climate is on average two to three degrees warmer on the western prairies than it was in the Dirty Thirties. All of these things are going to put us into a water squeeze that we cannot imagine.

PK: That's scary. That's almost like a death sentence, no?

DS: Well, a couple of things are fairly interesting. We were talking earlier about the rapid melting of the glaciers. That glacial melt is what keeps the major rivers of the prairies flowing in mid-summer. Typically, the snowpack in the Rockies and in the rest of the watershed melts in six or seven weeks in the spring and we get a high-water stage [on our rivers]. But by the middle of June to early July, depending on where you are, that annual snowmelt is gone, and then the glacier melt comes into play during the warm part of the summer.

I don't think it's any accident that the only places that there are big cities on the prairies are along major rivers. That's where there was timber to build houses and to heat houses. Until a few decades ago, rivers were also major transportation arteries. Those rivers are going to be mere streams by the end of this century. You can see from the data that this condition is well on its way already. Probably the most conspicuous example is the South Saskatchewan, which in summer was flowing at five times the volume in the early twentieth century than it is on average today. And the trend is still downward, and with increasing human use and climate warming, it will be downward more still. The average river in Alberta that we've analyzed from historical records is flowing at somewhere between sixty and seventy per cent of historical flows in summer. So they've all taken some hits. But a few cases are worse, including the Saskatchewan system, the most important river system of the prairies. It has really taken a major hit from climate warming and human use.

PK: What do you do as an ecologist, as a scientist, and as a concerned human being when you see evidence such as you quoted earlier? That is, that scientists can say the drought we're experiencing now is just a tiny fraction of what has been experienced in the past. These are natural trends. "We have to stand back," say these scientists, "and see the big picture." And sometimes that science is used by people who are saying, "Don't worry about what we're doing right now. It's a tiny factor. The human race has little impact on planet Earth, and we really should just relax, enjoy what we've got, and continue to extract what we need from this planet." I mean, science can be used as a double-edged sword, I suppose. It can support certain arguments and oppose other arguments, but there is a correct answer. There is a capital-T Truth here, and you can see it being used in both directions.

DS: I'd say that the biggest danger of science in that way is selective use of science. The most conspicuous example of the last decade or so has been this book of Bjørn Lomborg's, *The Skeptical Environmentalist*, which treats a very, very selective choice of problems. I think there are a couple of things [that confuse the issues]. Some people confuse environmental scientists with environmentalists. I have a lot of environmentalist sympathies, too. There are some things that I would choose to do or not to do simply because I don't like the way they look at the end, not because of any scientifically documentable environmental damage. But there are other things that you can see via scientific methods that are having major impacts on the landscape. We've got some success stories. We've been sitting here talking about acid rain to some degree and eutrophication. Lomborg talks only about success stories. And on the other side, he has chosen to talk about mistakes that were based on phoney claims, not by environmental scientists, but by environmentalists with no science for backup. And I think it illustrates very clearly that environmental scientists have to be careful. I don't think you, as a scientist, should hold back your feelings as an environmentalist, but I think you need to be really careful to tell where science ends and your other feelings begin.

Some scientists believe that they shouldn't reveal those feelings, that they should stop where the data end. And I think that's absurd, but the example I always tell my students is: imagine you're stranded in an outpost and your plumbing quits. It's a very unique plumbing system that nobody knows, and you can make one phone call for help. And you've got three friends. They're a politician, and a priest, and a plumber. Which one are you going to call for advice? Even though he can't diagnose the problem, he can advise you based on his intuition. Similarly, I submit that it's the people who spend their time studying ecosystems who are going to have the best intuition about unknown impacts of new environmental threats What's important is to identify it as gut feeling, as opposed to science.

You develop a good intuition for ecosystems by working with them all the time, in the same way that you develop good intuition about motors if you're an automobile mechanic or plumbing if you're a plumber. So people should realize that professional insights are not without value. We need to make moderate decisions, decisions that exercise the precautionary principle, where we consider what the worst case might be. We also need to think about maintaining natural resources and ecosystem services for our children and grandchildren. I guess that's my big worry now. I see us leaving a world full of mistakes behind for the next generation, and I don't think that people sitting here in the next century are going to be anywhere near as prosperous as we are. It makes me feel very guilty. I think we could be doing a better job of leaving a few of our resources behind for them.

SIX

Three Great Ideas

PETER WATSON

Peter Watson is a British journalist and popular historian of ideas, a researcher at the McDonald Institute for Archaeological Research at Cambridge University, and a great believer in science, secularism, and the scientific method. He is the author of Ideas: A History from Fire to Freud, *which chronicles the advance of ideas from ancient times until the contemporary period. This interview was broadcast on* Ideas *on 15 May 2007.*

PETER WATSON

"What is an idea?" That is the most frightening question, I think. Ideas are obviously abstract things that occur in the mind, in the brain, but they're expressed in all sorts of different ways. And my idea was to write a history as close to a narrative history as possible. We left out a lot of material, practical things that are in other histories — like politics, wars, battles, treaties, surrenders, and so forth — and really just explore how we had interacted in the past with our environment to produce new ways of thinking which would lead to new ways of living. So, I think "new ways of thinking" is perhaps the most succinct way I can put it.

PAUL KENNEDY

Now, how do you distinguish an idea from, say, a series of interesting facts or a theory or a concept? In the first chapter, you talk about instinctive collections rather than ideas, so foraging, for example, is something that is a pre-idea.

PW: Well, I think all ideas become expressed, for instance, I was criticized a little in Britain for describing the guillotine in the French Revolution as an idea. But the reviewer missed the fact that the guillotine was introduced as an equal form of punishment. At the time of the French Revolution, there were two hundred and fifty types of capital punishment in France. And so Dr. Guillotine produced this method which would apply to everybody. It was a kind of grisly form of equality, but it does illustrate that all ideas exist inside one's head but then they are expressed in words or in actions or in material things.

If you look at history overall as either a history of ideas or a history of human experiences, then I think maybe you get a different take. And I would say that there are perhaps five or four crucial periods. There is the change from foraging to agriculture, which more or less immediately leads to civilization. There's a change in man's living circumstances which produces a whole raft of new ideas. That's — what should we say? — between 5000 and 3000 BC. There's a second change between 1500 and 500 BC, when there's a general change from polytheism and spirit gods to monotheisms, which is a profound change in the way we think about ourselves, the way we think about the past, the way we think about the universe, and so forth. There was a further change around the twelfth century with the rise of accuracy and the rise of individualism, the imagination of the secular society, and the discovery of the experimental approach, which eventually gave rise to science. And there was another change, obviously, beginning around 1750 with the growth of industrial society and mass society, which is the society in which we live. And so it seemed to me that these are ways of looking at our past that are not normally employed by regular histories, and that's what I set out to do.

PK: It's interesting that you defined five great terminal or critical stages in history when major change took place. You also in the book describe the fact that many people, historians looking at ideas, like to think in threes. And you're not exempt from that yourself. You like an idea of three different concepts which have been the crucial central facts of civilization.

PW: Yes. I think in my case the rule of three is an old journalistic one — having been a journalist for many years, you know, something's not happening until it's happening three times. An anthropological colleague of mine at Cambridge wonders whether there's not something basic about three, because a lot of our experience is divided into three, sort of an inner surface, outer, past, present, future, up here, down. You can divide many parts of our experience into three. And it is true that many people in the past, looking at intellectual history or looking for ways we have changed in our thinking about the world, have come up with three varieties.

PK: Your three are the soul, and then the idea of Europe or the West, I would say, and then the idea of experimentation, of that kind of science which takes things and manipulates them in order to find an intellectual result.

PW: Yes. I think these three are not only important, but they describe how we've got to where we are and what our predicament is now. The soul is a relatively new idea, historically speaking, certainly insofar as we imagine something immaterial existing after death. You see in early classical Greek literature references that the gods cannot keep death off even those whom they love, but then we find in around the fifth century, I think, ancient Greeks being buried with a small obal, a small coin. The purpose of this was to pay Charon the ferryman as he took them over the River Styx to the other world. But I think that the existence of the soul — that there is something within us which is not fully realized and which doesn't die in death but goes on — has been really very, very powerful. And in many ways, though it may sound a bit curious to say so, even more important than the concept of God, because concepts of God vary, whereas, by and large, concepts of the soul do not vary. I even think that, at the present time, we have our own secularized modern concept of the soul, which we call the unconscious. This was brought in not just by Freud, which everybody knows, but it was a great stream in late eighteenth- and nineteenth-century German thought that there is part of us that springs up and shows itself in art and religion and in almost everything that we do, and we're not fully aware of the reasons for it. And I think that's been a very, very powerful theme throughout history.

If I can then move on to the experiment, then this, as well as being just a methodology, is also now a rival form of authority to religion and the Church and so forth — that we don't really believe anything now unless an experiment has been done to prove it one way or the other. That was obviously a very important development, generally held to have been made by the English priest Grosseteste, bishop of Lincoln and chancellor of Oxford University in the Middle Ages. This idea that we should check things, try to repeat occurrences, obviously gradually grew to be a very, very important element in the advent of the West and Europe. And that's why I call Europe as an idea the second of these three ideas, because it was in Europe where universities were developing, where the power of the church was waning, where various thinkers began to imagine a life outside the Church, that the experiment, in a sense, got its chance. So the openness and, at the same time, the learnedness of Europe in the Middle Ages made it the place where the experiment in modern life developed. Of course, that is a big issue now, because the openness of Europe is held to account for its advances and is contrasted strongly with the Islamic world in particular.

PK: And that, in a nutshell, in about two-and-a-half minutes, is approximately seven hundred and some odd pages in the book, so that's a great summary there. Can we talk about just one idea that jumped out at me that I really wanted to hear you speak on, and that is the idea which you say is probably the worst idea of all time. We'll get to some of the better ones later. But the worst idea of all time was ethical monotheism. Why?

PW: Well, this is the change that takes place all over the Old World, let us say, sometime between — what? — 1500, 1400 BC and Jesus. It is the idea that, instead of having lots of little gods who behaved like extraordinary human beings with curious paths at some stage and less curious paths at others, there is one God, and this one God is a more or less abstract entity. And because this God exists in this way, there comes into being a belief that we have to behave well in order to secure a position in another life, in a later life, whatever name we give it. This idea did not really exist in this form beforehand, and we can discuss, if you like, the reasons why it came in. But the reasons why I believe it to have been a very bad idea is that it closed people's minds. And, yes, it accounted in many ways — in the form of the Crusades for instance, and in the form of the wars of religion, the Thirty Years' War in Europe — for many deaths, but it chiefly held up thinking from — what shall we say? — 400 AD or perhaps a little earlier until 1200. And it's still holding up advance in the Islamic world, where they turn in and they still operate according to the law of a book written in the seventh century, which has changed very little. And so ethical monotheism, by its very concept, says that there's a one all-powerful God which we must obey, and that's it. No argument. Mohammed said he was the final prophet, there will be no more revelations, and all you need to know is contained in the Bible, the Old Testament or the New Testament, or the Upanishads if you're a Hindu, or the Koran if you're a Muslim. I think this idea is essentially ludicrous, but it has been undoubtedly very, very powerful, and has closed our world down, basically held up progress of the human race by one or two thousand years in different parts of the world.

PK: And, in fact, in some ways, polytheism is more rational in that it allows more explanations than monotheism would.

PW: Yes, absolutely. Polytheism allows new ideas to come forth and to be incorporated into the body of doctrine that already exists. It's a much more tolerant approach to life. It does not force unpalatable things down people's throats to the same extent that monotheism does. And there are plenty of people around the world, small civilizations, small cultures, who have always embraced polytheism or no-theism. But we pay attention to the three great theisms. I try to say in my book that there are alternatives, and that we should do our best to pay attention to them and get over this dreadful idea of ethical monotheism.

PK: And beyond that, you're also not closed to ideas about the soul. In fact, it is the first great idea. So, although you might dislike organized religion, you're not opposed to thinking that could be called religious.

PW: Well, yes and no. I mean, I think that, living in Britain at the moment, which is a pretty godless place, you see that the faith schools do better than others. And you have to agree that — I mean, I'm fascinated by this paradox, if you like, that I have no faith, I think ethical monotheism is a ridiculous idea, yet religious history, Church history, is probably the most interesting form of history that there is. You could set out quite a long list of good things for which the Church has been responsible, and we, in a place like Britain — and you, too, in Canada — would not be where we are without the help of the Christian Church, and many of its achievements in marriage, in morality and so forth, in art and architecture and music have been wonderful. I know that people decry the state of the Anglican Church, but it seems to me that a church which gives you such wonderful architecture and great music, some wonderful literature, but doesn't believe in God very strongly, is exactly what you want.

PK: Not to mention the fact that a number of the people who figure prominently in the book were Churchmen — Aquinas, Augustine — these are important contributors to the intellectual tradition.

PW: Church was the place where the learned people were for a time. So it didn't wholly hold things back. There were great thinkers. Of course, a lot of them, even someone like St. Augustine, got themselves into extraordinary knots trying to explain the inexplicable. But that was an earlier world, and Augustine wrote in a very beautiful way, so we can relate to that. But, in the end we got over it, and we found our way through it, and where we are now is where I think Isaiah Berlin had it right: we're living in a sort of halfway house or, to change the message, we're trying to get the best of both worlds. I mean, most people believe in both the experiment and the soul, and so they look both in and out at the same time. And as Berlin put it, we shift uneasily from foot to foot, depending on where we are that day in our lives.

PK: When you're talking about the soul, you mention as well that it contributes to the idea of inwardness, which eventually leads to a form of individuality and to a kind of questioning that led ultimately to science.

PW: Well, yes and no. The Greeks, as always, were there first, and you can characterize the history of ideas if you so wish as Platonism versus Aristotelianism... Plato looked inward and thought that he saw an ideal world with a higher form of reality, and this was the way to the truth and to happiness. Aristotle, on the other hand, looked out, sent his researchers around the Mediterranean to look at the way things were done, and tried to use research to come up with the best way of arranging one's affairs. And I think this has continued throughout history to be the general way that thought has been divided. You could also divide history into great turnings in. We mentioned ethical monotheism — that was a great turning in. You have Luther — that was another great turning in. There was a great turning in after the Black Death, a great rise in church building and faith and so forth. And even Freud represented a turning in — we live in a therapeutic society at the moment, where people are perpetually looking inwards into their alternative behaviour. Kant was in some ways both a turning in and a turning out, but he thought that one had to look inwards for one's moral sense, that there was something inside which produced moral ideas and which didn't come either from God or from experience. So, yes, this has been a big tradition in thought. It's a big tradition in non-Western thought, in Buddhism and Confucianism.

In my view, though, I don't think at the end of the day we have much agreement about what is inside us and what it means. Here's an interesting exercise: could you put together a cumulative history of art in the way you can put together the cumulative history of science? Science builds on what went before, but does art? The answer, I think, is yes and no — it's not a straight line, and the end result is that, even if you'd read all the novels in the world, would you end up wiser? Is there a collective message that they have, or do they all have lots of little individual messages? And that's the truth of life — that there is no agreement.

PK: I know I'm oversimplifying, but I hope I'm not misrepresenting you if I say that, in the book, Aristotle is your hero and Plato is the anti-hero.

PW: Yes. I don't think that's an oversimplification. I think that the Aristotelian approach leads to more agreement in life and eventually led to the comforts and excitements that science has provided. You and I are talking to each other separated by thousands of miles — this is a mundane point now. But we are talking to each other because of science. We couldn't have done this but for that. No amount of Platonic or Thomistic thinking would have produced the radio.

PK: Quite true. At one point in the book, you say that the person who moulded or fashioned the first axe ultimately started a road that led us to the moon, and I think that kind of technological progress is a line that runs through the book.

PW: Yes. I mean, I think that is true, although no one can predict where that line leads. It's interesting — and this is a profound point, I think — a lot of scientific breakthroughs are made by accident.

There's a very good book by Harvard scholar Gerald Holton called *The Scientific Imagination*, in which he compares thinking in the sciences with thinking in the arts. And one of the points he makes is that a lot of breakthroughs in science are made by accident and they're small breakthroughs. The point about the significance of small breakthroughs is that they can easily be checked, so you can prevent people fairly quickly from going off in the wrong direction, whereas in the great age of speculative philosophy, for instance, people would have big ideas and say, well, life is down to this or down to that, and construct huge systems. And these systems were so huge that nobody could check them. You either believed them or you didn't. And fifty years later, it's too late, it just didn't work.

PK: Can we move on to your second great idea, and that is the idea of Europe or the idea of the West. Recently, a lot has been written about why the West suddenly went ahead in the years after, say, 800, 900 AD, and other civilizations, other cultures, like China, India, which were far advanced over the West at the beginning of that period of time, fell behind. Can you explain that briefly? You've actually almost exhaustively gone through various theories of why this happened. Could you do that, and then tell us which one you prefer?

PW: Well, there are some theories which say that the Eastern civilizations dropped behind primarily because of the Black Death, which affected their populations, affected transport and trade, and ideas have always followed trade. A place like Britain was furthest from the Black Death, and although we were very badly affected, we were nowhere near as badly affected as civilizations further east. On a more positive note, one theory has put it down to religion — that you get a change in the Christian Church around about the millennium, 1000 AD, where the Church, until that point, had been much more militant and triumphalistic, then turned in on itself because nothing much had happened in the millennium — the great disappointment, if you like, because there hadn't been the Second Coming, and the nature of faith changed. It turned inward. That has something to be said for it, but I think it has to be put alongside what you might call the first Industrial Revolution — the invention of, for instance, the water wheel and the arrival of the stirrup from China, technological things like that which created cities in Europe in a form and number that hadn't been seen before. It enabled a change from the two-field system to the three-field and four-field system so there's more crop rotation, which produced more crops, allowing surplus so that there was more trade, but also allowing the rise in population. You got also a change from the monastic system, where churches that were the centres of learning in the countryside now moved into the new cities.

And you got the growth of schools, which were generally in the environments and the cloisters of the great cathedrals, which were themselves an example, of course, of the new religiosity that was emerging. Then those schools developed into universities. And it's in the universities that you get a lot of religious thought, but you also get a lot of competition for the new pupils and great developments in the competition between various universities, and the rediscovery of Aristotle's texts, and this showed that there were great societies, great writers, great thinkers that existed before Jesus. This, of course, had a big impact on the development of the idea of a secular society, eventually culminating in the rise of the notion of the experiment.

The new technologies also allowed for a far more accurate world. The clock was invented, which changed the nature of work. Spectacles were invented in almost the same decade as an aid to reading, and several other developments like those in mathematics and bookkeeping and so forth. And — this is my favourite explanation — a lot of these very practical things came together in Europe — in particular, double-entry bookkeeping for instance, and some of the maritime inventions and mathematical inventions having to do with navigation, which allowed the great age of exploration to be technically possible. Double-entry bookkeeping allowed advances in banking, which allowed expeditions to be financed. So the great age of exploration started in Europe rather than elsewhere, and that all came together between, let us say, 1050 and 1350, and it accounts for the great acceleration of Europe.

PK: What's interesting about that is it precedes what people normally think of as the crucial turning points. That would be the Renaissance, the Reformation and the Scientific Revolution. This is prior to those fundamental changes.

PW: Absolutely! You put it well. I think the Italian Renaissance and the Scientific Revolution are symptoms of what went on earlier. This is one of the points that professional historians have long accepted, but where the general public lags behind, possibly because the paintings of the Italian Renaissance are so glorious that we'd like to spend our lives surrounded by these wonderful images. But, no, they're relatively late in the day so far as these changes that I'm talking about are concerned.

PK: Can we move on now to what is probably your favourite topic: the world that can be known, Aristotle's world, where there are laws that can be discovered, that can be experimented with, that can be understood. I guess this is the beginning of science as we think of it. You say this started with the Greeks, with Aristotle.

PW: Well, yes. It starts with the idea, so far as we know, that the world can be known, that it's not just the placing by the gods of mysterious occurrences. What is now called Ionian Positivism — that is to say, a science which grew up in the Ionian area of Greece — simply starts from the observation that, if you look around you in a systematic, calm, and judicious way, there are observations that you can make and inferences that can be based on those observations. For instance, people can spot the systematic variations of the sun and the moon and the stars in the sky and make various predictions based on those, and that gives one, not a measure of control, but at least a sense that one's not living in an arbitrary universe, that there are rules and sets of order around that can be known. This is really the birth of science and of philosophy — of course, in those days, there was no difference between them.

PK: And how is that distinct from the sort of drive towards abstraction which is personified by Plato?

PW: Well, I think that there are two senses of abstraction. For instance, all numbers are abstract, all mathematical concepts are abstract, but they're based on observations outside, whereas Plato primarily — not invariably — looked inside himself to see what we might conclude about human nature. Now, a brilliant man, which Plato was, can make certain observations but he can't know everybody. He can't know how everybody varies from him and others. In his idea of idealism, there is a hidden realm of reality. He defines this realm as one that we cannot fully know, and in this you already have a break, a divide of systems of a sort. Whereas Aristotle was just content to look around him. He made an interesting observation, for instance, that fire burns in the same way in all different places, whereas people govern themselves with different laws in his world around the Mediterranean, and so he observed — it's a very simple but a very profound and important observation — that some aspects of life, some phenomena, operate according to natural laws, and other phenomena, like politics and the laws by which we live in an urban society, vary according to the ideas that we have and the size and composition of our society. So there's a big difference between human laws, or laws governing human conduct, and laws governing nature. And these are massively important things, and although observations must have occurred to other people at other times, they were set down and codified in Greece in the most amazing way.

PK: Now, it wasn't in Greece that the Scientific Revolution that we know of actually took place. It took place much later and for different reasons. Can you describe where and when and why?

PW: Well, the Scientific Revolution that we generally refer to begins, I suppose, with the astronomical observations of Copernicus and Galileo and ultimately of Newton, and what was then the terrifying discovery that the sun didn't go around the earth but it was the other way around, that the earth, even more worryingly, was just one small

speck in a vast universe, and that the heavens, which in the Christian
Church had always been held to be immutable, unchanging, actually
did change, and this, of course, changed everything. It changed
our understanding, both Christian understanding of the earth as
somewhere special and of man as something special, as set apart from
nature. It was these laws of astronomy — which gradually become
more widely understood with the invention of the telescope and
Galileo's discovery of the moons of Jupiter circling it just as our moon
circles us and as the earth circles the sun, culminating in Newton's
laws of planetary motion and gravity — that shook the foundations
of the Christian world and caused a massive re-evaluation of who we
are and, therefore, why we are and so forth. But that was based on
systematic observation, and technical improvements like the telescope
brought into view vast areas of the skies that we hadn't seen before.
What were thought to be just smudges in the sky turned out to be
vast galaxies of stars. At the same time, people discovered through
the microscope a whole hidden world of animals — very, very small
organisms in water that proposed or at least floated the idea for
some people that there was spontaneous generation or that these
were forms of life midway between stones and humans, or stones and
animals, or plants and animals, and this provoked a fantastic growth
of scientific inquiry.

So, from the fifteenth and sixteenth centuries on, discoveries
began to proliferate and proliferate, and that's what we mean by the
Scientific Revolution. So, at this time, you've got what is also probably one of the greatest changes in intellectual history, and that is the
rise of science and the growth of doubt, the advent of religious doubt
going, for many people, hand in hand throughout the seventeenth
and eighteenth centuries. The period that interests me in particular at
the moment is between, if you like, Newton's *Principia Mathematica*
in 1688, when this sets the seal on the astronomical discoveries and
gives doubt a real nudge, and 1859, with Darwin's publication of *On
the Origin Species by [Means of] Natural Selection*, because, in that
period, in a sense, the idea of God has been severely downgraded
but there is nothing to replace it. There is no biological conception
of man. That doesn't really arise until the theory of evolution. So it

seems to me that this would have been a very, very curious and perhaps even slightly alarming time to be alive, when the old rules have been taken away and there are no new rules to replace them.

PK: And how did people of ideas respond to that void?

PW: Well, you get great searches for truth in new ways. For instance, the truth was sought in history. This is the first time that people started to pay attention to history and to study how things changed over history. Because, if you can see how things have changed in the past so as to bring us to where we are now, then maybe you could predict where we're going in the future. So up comes the idea of progress. You get the rise of biology at this time. The word biology was not coined until 1802. It's a relatively new world, so you get the rise of ideas of perfection. There's a lot the romantics were trying to do to improve themselves at the time. They didn't quite know where they were going, but they were trying to make more of themselves than they had been. So you get these three or four different ways of trying to move forward without really knowing what you're going forward to.

PK: Now, you put a closure date on that period of Darwin and the theory of evolution. Would you say that, since Darwin, we've continued to move ahead? Are we in an age of great scientific innovation now?

PW: Well I think that Darwin shows — his algorithm, his system shows — that you can't know where you're going ahead, that it's essentially accidental, so he removed, in a sense, any kind of futuristic thinking. I think that's a liberation, but at the moment I happen to believe that we're not living in a very interesting time or a very innovative time, but I don't think that has much to do with Darwin.

PK: It has to do with...?

PW: Well, I think that most new inventions and new thoughts come with new forms of energy. And solar energy, which is perhaps the latest form of energy that we can tap, has not really come on stream yet. When that is able to be harvested efficiently, then there will be a whole host of new technologies and new thinking. But it seems to me that, if we were to go back a hundred years, 1907 was a much more interesting time, much more was happening than in 2007. Picasso was making his great paintings, Einstein was making his great breakthrough, there were great medical breakthroughs, there were great technical breakthroughs in lighting and electricity. And now, we're living mainly in an age of consolidation. Radio, television, computers, airliners were all invented before the Second World War. Yes, we've got a great deal of mobility, and everybody has access to something that only very few people had access to before. At the moment, you could say that the World Wide Web and stem-cell research are the two really new things that we have, but I don't think that much else is radically new. I'm not saying there aren't little breakthroughs, but our experience of life is not so different from fifty years ago as our experience of life in 1907 would have been from 1857, for instance.

PK: Nonetheless, you do have the view that science is your favourite subject. It is the intellectual pursuit that you prefer. If it is as powerful as it obviously is, and has been throughout history, why hasn't it eliminated your big bugaboo, ethical monotheism? Why is religion so persistent right through to the twenty-first century and, indeed, why are fundamentalist religions more powerful than other, more tolerant religions?

PW: I think religion is powerful because there's so much suffering in the world, and whilst science can offer great help in that regard, the population of the Earth has been exploding and continues to explode in certain regions, and this results in great poverty and huge suffering. I don't think that science directly addresses this need, and what you're getting in the West, in particular, is a sort of sedimentation effect, whereby the rich are getting richer and the poor are getting poorer, and the rich nations are getting richer and the poor nations are not. And this separating out directly accounts, I think, for fundamentalism that rises when people don't see any hope. It happened with Christianity in ancient Rome, and led to the martyrs and the suicide bombers of early Christianity, which people are apt to forget. The fundamentalist thing that's happening is the late flowering. I mean, we're getting fundamentalist Islam because Islam has demonstrably failed its people. All Islamic countries are poorer with the exception of one or two dictatorships that are lucky through oil. All Islamic countries are backward, and these societies will collapse at some point at the latter end of this century. So I don't think that Islam is quite the threat, the long-term threat. Obviously, it would be irresponsible to say there aren't short-term threats. But I think that, in the realm of history, Islam is over. It sounds a silly thing to say at the moment, I know, but we're talking long term here, not in the next three weeks or whatever. This is a political issue with which we have to grapple if global warming doesn't get us first.

PK: It almost seems that we are cornered and we're being attacked from all sides.

PW: I think that's true. I mean, if you go back and back and back in history, the Earth had no atmosphere. It only got an atmosphere of oxygen because, over several billion years, the world was taken over by bacteria that excreted oxygen to the point where we had an atmosphere. Now we've got so many people on Earth that we're consuming our oxygen at such a rate that we're beginning to resemble the bacteria of billions of billions of years ago and having a direct effect on the planet. Let's face it, science has been predicting this for thirty years, and it's only now that the politicians and the general public have awakened to this dilemma at a time when, according to some people, it may be too late.

PK: Give me your assessment of two important thinkers who are said to have advanced the cause of reason that led to the growth of science and rationality — namely, sixteenth-century English philosopher Francis Bacon and seventeenth-century philosopher Baruch Spinoza, who lived in the Netherlands.

PW: I think Bacon took a rather simplistic scientific view of the world. He was a pretty regular guy. I mean, I don't really rate him as that important. You seem to rate him as more important than I do.

PK: Well, I thought just because he was somebody who did try to systematize and was interested in the history of ideas.

PW: Yes, I think he was, but I don't think he had anything particularly original to say. I think his value lay more in the fact that he drew attention to this aspect of the world than to anything he said that was particularly new. In the same that, say, Voltaire drew attention to the sociology of the day, the history of the day, and took the thinking away from the Church. I don't think Voltaire had a particularly interesting mind scientifically. He fulfilled a function of a gadfly bringing our attention to where it should be directed. He was performing a function a little like Al Gore has been recently. I mean, he hasn't had anything original to say about global warming, but by his position and by his presentation he's undoubtedly had an impact on public opinion. And I think that's how I would characterize Bacon and, say, Voltaire.

PK: But the other one I wanted you to talk about, and this is somebody you did think we needed to reappraise, and that is Spinoza.

PW: Well, Spinoza and Vico, it seems to me, are two of the least-well-known important philosophers of the last two or three hundred years, who really taught us, or taught other philosophers who were perhaps better known, that we should look at humanity as scientists. They took the view that what we can most know is what we have produced and that, therefore, the history of civilization is very important, that how history developed tells the story. The story is history. And, therefore, that we should not believe speculative philosophers who have intuitions. I mean, the Christian Church, in particular, has always had this doctrine that an intuition is a thought that a special person has received direct from God. This is what revelation is, and so these thoughts have a special status in our lives. This is what religious people in the past certainly always understood, whereas Spinoza and Vico did not agree to this. They thought that we had to look at how we had behaved in the past, what we had produced, and deduced from that how to lead our lives and what to believe in. All I was trying to do in my book was to say that Spinoza and Vico were the originators of this idea and are more important than they're generally given credit for.

PK: In fact, though, they're the originators of a tradition that you're not necessarily in favour of, and that is a search for an inner unconscious, which again leads directly to Sigmund Freud.

PW: Well, I don't think it leads directly. I think that they obviously had some influence because when they lived, they had some notion of the soul. The soul hung on and on and on, and it was very difficult for people not to think in terms of the soul in their day. But I think that they are more crucial for what they said over and above that than the fact that they couldn't quite jettison the idea of the soul.

PK: I want to give you a chance, before we finish, to have a go at Sigmund Freud. Why are you so opposed to his way of looking at the world?

PW: I think that he closed our minds, that he provided a lot of false hope to people, and that happiness is more likely to come from getting out of your study or your flat and going out and meeting people and doing things and reading books and so forth, rather than visiting overpaid, poorly trained psychotherapists. We used to have a phrase when I was at university, "those who can, do; those who can't, teach; and those who can't teach go into therapy as therapists." I'll give you an example. In 1900, by curious coincidence, three great breakthroughs were announced: the discovery of the gene, the discovery of the quantum, and the discovery of the unconscious. Now, the three people who announced all this could not know what would happen in the twentieth century. But what in fact happened was that physics and genetics came together — we can see around the world now that physics leads us to the understanding of the molecular structure behind DNA and so forth, to an understanding of the way people vary around the world and how the world was populated and how people differ. In other words, physics and genetics are different aspects of the same reality.

However, the unconscious has not come anywhere near any other sciences over the last hundred years. It has retreated up its own backwater, and nobody really believes anymore that we have this unconscious that Freud said is like a sort of hydraulic system and that, if you don't let it out, it will come out in all sorts of odd ways, and that it's all down to sex, of course. I mean, he didn't cure anybody. We now know, since many of his papers have been found and compared to other papers, that he made up a lot of his case histories, that he told untruths about the ways that they'd been cured, or if they had apparently been cured, his patients then went back into other mental hospitals. I find it absurd that people believe all this quite so much. Now, a lot of people I know claim to have been helped by this, but I don't think that they were ill in the first place. I think psychotherapy is designed to help people cope with failure, not with illness, and maybe there's a need for that, but we have to be clear about what it is. I do think a lot of people in life fail. Maybe they fail more now in modern life because there's more attention being paid everywhere, undoubtedly, although it's not changing fundamentally, life is speeding up and maybe we were cruel to each other when people failed in the past. But I do think that psychotherapy has more to do with failure than with what we traditionally call illness. Maybe we should change the notion of illness, of course, but that's not down to me.

PK: Right. Well, I've kept you talking for exactly an hour now. It's all been fascinating. I don't know if you've said everything you want to say, but I'll give you a chance to stand on a soap box and talk to Canada now.

PW: No, I don't have any soap-box things to say. I think that, just to go on from what I was saying, at a time when everybody in the world is chasing money, chase education. Nobody can take that away from you. And the more you have, the more you enjoy that. Remember that famous actress who said, "I've been rich, I've been poor. Rich is better." Well, I can say, I've been ignorant — because we've all been ignorant, we've all been children — and I've been educated. And make no mistake, education is better. Much better.

Acknowledgements

The following broadcast transcripts are published with the permission of the Canadian Broadcasting Corporation and by permission of the following authors and their agents:

What Is an Idea? The Estate of Lister Sinclair; *Radical Imperfection*, The Wylie Agency (UK) Ltd. (for John Gray); *Political Theology*, Mark Lilla; *Novelty and Coherence*, Jerome Kagan; *The "Vulgarity" Correspondent*, Theodore Dalrymple; *Cognitive Dissonance*, Elliot Aronson; *Phallocentrism*, Leonore Tiefer; *Breaking the Bargain*, Donald Savoie; *Mission Possible*, Anne Golden; *From Charity to Entitlement*, Louise Arbour; *The Light that Filled the Bed*, Mary Pratt; *A Beautifully Nasty World*, Lawrence Paul Yuxweluptun; *Freedom and All that Jazz*, Nat Hentoff; *We Do Invention Here*, Stewart Brand; *Immortality Guaranteed*, Ray Kurzweil; *Research without Walls*, Joseph Martin; *Hooked on Water*, David Schindler; *Three Great Ideas*, Peter Watson.